War Memory
and the Making of Modern
Malaysia and Singapore

War Memory
and the Making of Modern
Malaysia and Singapore

Kevin Blackburn and Karl Hack

NUS PRESS
SINGAPORE

© 2012 Kevin Blackburn and Karl Hack

Published by:

NUS Press
National University of Singapore
AS3-01-02, 3 Arts Link
Singapore 117569

Fax: (65) 6774-0652
E-mail: nusbooks@nus.edu.sg
Website: http://www.nus.edu.sg/nuspress

ISBN 978-9971-69-599-6 (Paper)

National Library Board, Singapore Cataloguing-in-Publication Data

Blackburn, Kevin, 1965–
  War memory and the making of modern Malaysia and Singapore / Kevin
Blackburn and Karl Hack. – Singapore: NUS Press, c2012.
  p. cm.
  Includes bibliographical references and index
  ISBN: 978-9971-69-599-6 (pbk.)

  1. World War, 1939–1945 – Social aspects – Malaysia. 2. World War,
1939–1945 – Social aspects – Singapore. 3. Collective memory – Malaysia.
4. Collective memory – Singapore. 5. Malaya – History – Japanese occupation,
1942–1945. 6. Singapore – History – Japanese occupation, 1942–1945.
I. Hack, Karl. II. Title.

D744.7
940.53595 — dc22   OCN755871946

Cover image: On the sidelines of a ceremony, joss sticks are burnt and offerings
are made at Singapore's Civilian War Memorial. This ceremony happens every
15 February, to remember the fall of Singapore and the war dead of the Japanese
Occupation.

Typeset by: Scientifik Graphics
Printed by: C.O.S. Printers

CONTENTS

PLATES & MAPS

Plates

Maps[i]

[i]   Courtesy of Kevin Blackburn and Karl Hack
[ii] Courtesy of K.R. Das
[iii] Courtesy of the Australian War Memorial
[iv] Coutesy of the *Malaya Tribune*
[v]   Courtesy of the National Archives of Singapore
[vi] Courtesy of Singapore Press Holdings
[vii] Coutesy of the Imperial War Museum
[viii] Coutesy of Patta Tolputt
[ix] Courtesy of Hayashi Hirofumi and Senda Jiro
[x]   Courtesy of *Star* online, Malaysia
[xi] Coutesy of *Nanyang Miscellany*, 1947
[xii] Unknown photographer
[xiii] Courtesy of Shaw Brothers
[xiv] Courtesy of Grand Brilliance
[xv] Courtesy of Filem Negara Malaysia
[xvi] Courtesy of Sentosa Development Corporation
[xvii] Courtesy of MediaCorp

NOTE ON SPELLINGS

Malay

The new romanisations of Malay are used wherever possible, although older romanisations may be occasionally used to reflect the character of the time.

Chinese and Dialects

We try to give preference to the modern Hanyu Pinyin system for transliteration of Chinese characters where possible. In practice, just giving the Hanyu Pinyin form would sometimes mean even many of our Southeast Asian readers might not recognise some personal names. So for personal names, we will follow the way they appear in their dialect. Where common usage in Malaya/Malaysia and Singapore means that the Wade Giles form of transliteration may be the only one many of our readers (even in Asia) would recognise, we give that form first. But in that case, we provide the Hanyu Pinyin in parenthesis or footnote. Wherever we think it might help, we try to give the alternative form as well.

Japanese

Names of individuals are written in the traditional Japanese order with the family name first, except in cases where the name is usually written in the Western fashion of family name last.

PREFACE

WE WOULD LIKE TO THANK SOME OF THE many people who helped to make this book possible, not least the successive intakes of students at the National Institute of Education, Nanyang Technological University, and the numerous people who allowed us the privilege of interviewing them over the years.

First and foremost, we owe a debt to our own students since the 1990s who helped educate us about their own history through the thousands of oral history interviews they conducted while we were teaching them. We only have space to name a few: Haslin Mohd Zain, Zarinah Bte Ali, Nuryani Bte Suneh and Arzme Rahman assisted in translating Malay testimony; Edmund Lim, Daniel Chew, Terrence Tan, Wan Meng Hao, and Liam Hsiao Wen helped in translating at Chinese war veterans' gatherings and memorials in Chinese cemeteries; and M. Anitha, Poongodi Chinnah, and Usha Rani Janarth made Tamil accessible to us.

We would also like to thank the National Institute of Education's librarians, Tim Yap of the National University of Singapore Library, Ch'ng Kim See, Head Librarian of the Institute of Southeast Asian Studies, and Noryati Abdul Samad and Gracie Lee of the National Library Reference Collection in Singapore. Tan Kheng Meng of the Singapore Chinese press has always been keenly interested in the research and helped us track down material in Chinese. Jeff Leng helped in the reproduction of maps and illustrations. For the National Archives of Singapore, we are indebted to the kindness of Chio Shu Yu.

Joseph Fernando, Loh Wei Leng, Abu Talib Ahmad, and Arujunan Narayanan all gave sound advice on how to access the National Archives of Malaysia. Peter Londey at the Australian War Memorial also made invaluable suggestions, while Glenda Lynch helped us access the War Memorial's collection, the collection at the National Library of Australia, and the National Archives of Australia.

C.C. Chin helped to open the world of ex-comrades to us, and on the other side of the fence, Leon Comber helped us to understand the world of the policeman and the *mata mata* (Special, Branch, from the Malay for eyes) and all they connect to. Lee Kip Lee was very helpful with contacts. Over the years, discussions with Wang Gungwu about what we were working on helped better shape our ideas.

We acknowledge the financial support of the National Institute of Education, which provided two research grants, and the funds to seed both a Japanese Occupation Conference and a public forum for veterans in 2005.

Paul Kratoska as both a researcher on the Japanese Occupation and our publisher helped make this a better book. Over the years, Anthony Reid (now Emeritus Professor at Australian National University) has been supportive. Mr Kwa Chong Guan, Head of External Programmes at the Rajaratnam School of International Studies, has also been a vital source of support, encouragement and information.

Dr Hack would also like to thank the History Department and Asia Research Institute at the National University of Singapore for helping him to sustain his Asian research since he left Singapore in 2006. Without their repeated invitations to workshops, combined with regular access to the Singapore-Malaysia Collection at the National University of Singapore library, he could not have sustained his contribution to writing this book. He would also like to acknowledge the support of the Open University, for providing funds for travel between the United Kingdom and Southeast Asia, and for allowing study leave to complete this book.

In the United Kingdom, Rod Suddaby of the Imperial War Museum was generous with his time. The work of Roger Nixon at The National Archives was also invaluable.

Finally, the 2005 conference and accompanying workshop with the wartime generation, both key events behind this book, were made possible by the collaboration of staff at the Singapore History Museum (now the National Museum of Singapore). Director Lee Chor Lin gave generously of the museum's space and her and her staff's time, and senior curator Iskander Mydin provided warm and incisive comment.

To these people we say "thank you", and hope that this book offers a small down payment on our debt of gratitude.

Kevin Blackburn and Karl Hack
Singapore and Oxford
January 2012

INDIVIDUALS

CHAPTER 1

Introduction

THIS BOOK ADDRESSES DEBATES ON WAR, memory and heritage, but for us it is more than a mere study of things done and dusted. The themes it tackles have formed a part of the fabric of our lives for nearly two decades. We have encouraged successive cohorts of students at Singapore's National Institute of Education to interview their parents and grandparents, and have immersed ourselves in heritage projects: climbing down rusting ladders into old gun tunnels; interviewing the Secretary-General of the Malayan Communist Party in Canberra; listening to memories of the Burma-Thailand Railway while sharing tapioca; and taking in the silence in the Chapel of Changi Prison in its last days before demolition. We have attended ceremonies for anti-Japanese guerrillas at Nilai, with Indian National Army veterans in Kuala Lumpur, for Australian and British soldiers at Kranji, and at Singapore's Civilian War Memorial.

This personal involvement, and participation in commemorative events, befits our topic. For our theme is not just the past per se, but also the ripples on the pond: the after-effects of the battle for Malaya (8 December 1941 to 15 February 1942) and of the Japanese Occupation that followed (February 1942 to September 1945). We examine the relationship between event and memory, and in so doing we look for what is emphasised, suppressed, and reshaped by individuals, communities and states.

Our focus on these three levels — individual, community, and state — has in turn emerged naturally from our teaching, research, and publications. As present (Kevin Blackburn) and past (Karl Hack) historians at Singapore's National Institute of Education (NIE), we have been a part of Singapore's machinery for educating students about the war. This has given us intimate experience of, and interest in, state attempts

3

to shape war memory. We have also been participants in the development of Singapore's war heritage. In 2001, we led a consultancy which culminated, on 15 February 2002, in the opening of the "Johore Battery" heritage site at Changi. The original Johore Battery had comprised three of Singapore's biggest, 15-inch, coastal defence guns, two of which turned round to fire at Japanese troops early in 1942.[1]

The research for that project provided the seed material for our first joint publication: *Did Singapore Have to Fall?* (2004). Writing that confirmed for us how differently Australians, British, Chinese, Indians, Eurasians, and Malays experienced the Fall and Occupation. We saw how their varied community and national preoccupations even fuelled different answers to the questions of whether Singapore had to fall, and of why it did. Hence, Churchill suggested that the island's fall was an unfortunate, unintended, but ultimately necessary by-product of sending almost all spare aircraft and tanks to save Russia and the Middle East. By contrast, some Asians berated Britain's failure to better harness the bitter anti-Japanese sentiments of local Chinese.[2] In terms of explanation as well as experience, it seemed that there was not one "Fall" and Occupation, but many.[3]

Our attempts to understand these different national and community perspectives included interviewing individuals from each of them. But as we did so, and as our students conducted interviews with the wartime generation, it also became obvious just how far the memories of some individuals jarred with the wider "collective memory" of the communities they identified with.

We realised that these individual experiences and memories needed to be studied in their own right. Hence, after *Did Singapore Have to Fall?* had been published, we sought out more individuals, not as "representatives" of wider groups or themes, but for their unique stories. We organised, for September 2005, a public forum with the "Wartime Generation" at the Singapore History Museum, in order to bring as wide a variety of such personal stories as possible to public notice. We continued gathering accounts afterwards, until we had enough to form the bedrock for this book. These stories underpin most of the following chapters, including those on community and state narratives about the war. For it is only possible to fully understand the process of selection and suppression of memory that goes into making such community and state stories, if you first start with the individual. You cannot confidently make judgements about how far community or "collective" memories are "representative" or distorting, unless you have a large enough sample of personal stories. So we have tried to recover individual voices by as many means as we can think of — newspaper reports, archives, observation and participant-observation of ceremonies, and oral history — and to place these portraits onto bigger canvasses.

In doing this, we have included the stories and voices of people who feel that their views have been neglected. It is important, both for therapeutic and historical reasons, that people who feel their memories have been marginalised are re-integrated into the public memory of their communities, and into the wider, overall story.

In sum, individual memory threads through all of what follows, reflecting our belief that, in terms of experience, there was not one "Occupation", but multiple experiences of it; not one "collective memory" for each community, but rather contestation of memory and a cacophony of echoes within each community. Hence, this and the following chapter emphasise the need to see events, first and foremost, through the eyes of individuals. This has involved flitting to and fro between the personal and the political, and between historical fact and the concepts — collective memory, myths, and ideas such as the therapeutic nature of commemoration — which help us to understand the former.

This approach allows us to create a tension and dialogue throughout the book, between the attempts of communities and states to create a "collective memory", and the more divergent recollections of individuals. This relationship has many layers: for instance, in the tension between the individual's desire to mark the uniqueness of their own experience and yet to belong to a wider group; and between the need to imbue the past with meaning, and yet also to retain some "authenticity" or trueness to actual events.

This holding in tension of national, community and individual narrations ultimately allows us to re-examine how the Malaysian and Singaporean states have sought to shape war memory. It has been argued, for instance, that there was a 50-year "Memory Suppression" of the Occupation by the Malayan (and from 1963, Malaysian) state, as a response to the "contesting narratives of war" championed by different groups. Hence, many Chinese Malayans saw the wartime Malayan People's Anti-Japanese Army (MPAJA) as nationalist, anti-Japanese heroes. By contrast, many Malays blamed this group for sparking Sino-Malay ethnic clashes in 1945–1946; and its communist leadership for starting an anti-government insurgency in 1948. This left the dominant United Malays National Organisation (UMNO), which has ruled

Malaysia since independence in 1957, determined not to recognise MPAJA ex-comrades as "nationalist" war heroes. It seemed as if such war memory was more likely to erode than to build national unity in Malaya.[4]

According to Diana Wong, the result up to the 1990s was that "the war has not been memorialised [by the state] ... its memory has been deliberately silenced",[5] leaving individual and collective memories to lead a "rhizomous"* existence: lurking outside the scope of national newspapers and textbooks, in family and community institutions.[6] This situation supposedly continued until the 1992 50th anniversary of the Fall of Singapore. By then, most of the wartime generation had passed away, and "the collective silencing of war memory was broken". Singapore then led the way towards a more overt harnessing of war memory, by emphasising how all races had started to draw together in the war, due to their suffering together.[7]

Wong's analysis of the politics of memory, and of state attempts to induce "forgetting" or amnesia, captures the way both Malaysia and Singapore did attempt to marginalise some accounts. Her thesis on a long silence — a kind of enforced collective amnesia — has been supported by historians such as Cheah Boon Kheng.[8] As late as 2005, Asad-ul Iqbal Latif went so far as to entitle a piece of his "Singapore's Missing War". This claimed that, for Singapore, "World War II has gone missing in action".[9] Our research has also been informed by the idea that the Malaysian and Singapore states sought to suppress or at least dampen some memories.

There was, however, never a blanket suppression of memory at the national level. From the 1940s to the 1970s, both Malaya and Singapore supported a limited memorialisation of the war, based in each case on a highly selective choice of what to remember, and what not to remember, at the national level.

Hence, the Malayan state did initially try to marginalise the war memories of particular groups of Chinese and Malays, and from the 1960s, tried to shift the main focus of war memory onto the Malayan Emergency. Chapters 6 to 8 below show how the memory of Malay and Indian victims of the war, notably those who died building the Burma-Thailand Railway, were largely ignored. Chapters 4 and 9 demonstrate how the Malayan (and then Malaysian) state marginalised memories of

---

* A rhizome is a horizontal stem or runner of a plant, usually below ground.

Chinese wartime guerrillas of the MPAJA. In the early postwar years, it also tried to marginalise the memory of radical Malay nationalists, from the *Kesatuan Melayu Muda* and its successors, whose leaders had collaborated with the Japanese. Likewise, it played down the experiences of the many Malays who had joined Japanese-run militias, such as the *Giyugun* and *Giyutai*. Indeed, the stigma of wartime collaboration was for long sufficient to encourage "biodata blackout syndrome", whereby some key public figures suppressed mention of wartime membership of these groups.[10]

But the Malayan state simultaneously celebrated the actions of Malays who had resisted the Japanese. Malays who had fought in the Malay Regiment, as volunteers, and as guerrillas in association with Britain's clandestine Force 136, were lauded as heroes in the early post-war decades. The Malay Regiment in particular was held up — in ceremonies on *Hari Pahlawan* (Warriors Day, celebrated from 1958) and "Malay Regiment Heroic Day" (each 14 February),[11] and in the acclaimed film *Sergeant Hassan* (released 1958) — as the embodiment of Malay martial prowess, and of the good Malay's preference for unity of the *bangsa* (Malay community or nation). The state's selective commemoration was used as a buttress to Malay unity, as an example of desired Malay characteristics, and to reinforce the centrality of Malay identity to the broader, multicommunal nationalism of the postcolonial state.

What the Malayan state favoured was thus not silence, but rather the exercise of highly selective memory. We go on to show, in Chapter 9 on "Memory and Nation-Building in Malaysia", that what the Malaysian state chose to select for national consumption also evolved over time. From Mahathir becoming Prime Minister in 1981 to the early 21st century, two particularly important changes took place.

First, parts of Malay memory that formerly had been marginalised — those of wartime nationalists whose leaders had collaborated with Japan — were reintegrated into heroic narratives of Malay resistance and nationalism. Now Malays who had collaborated and Malays who had resisted the Japanese were *both* presented (for instance in new school textbooks) as contributing to the wartime growth of Malay nationalism. This reflected the rise within UMNO of former leftist nationalists.

Second, even the wartime group which the postcolonial Malayan state had least toleration for — the MPAJA guerrillas — was ultimately able to take advantage of the space the Malaysian state left for plural commemoration. There had (as Wong's idea of "rhizomous" private memories suggests) always been an element of "plural commemoration". Malayan Chinese, for instance, remembered civilian victims of Japanese massacres in their own, separate languages and "deathscapes" after the war, as described in Chapter 5. The Malayan state had always left room for communities to openly commemorate the war in their own ways, even when it chose not to incorporate those at the national level. Such commemoration was not so much rhizomous (suggesting semi-hidden, horizontal underground plant stems or runners) as stoloniferous (stolons generally being runners that plants spread visibly, above ground). In other words, plural commemoration, while not mirrored at national level, was widespread, visible, marked by public monuments and ceremonies, and might be supported by community leaders.

Memorialisation of the MPAJA, however, had been largely excluded from this model of plural commemoration. It was suppressed (or self-censored) between 1948 and 1989, because after 1948, the Malayan Communist Party which had led the wartime guerrillas resorted to armed resistance. The Malayan Emergency (officially lasting from 1948 to 1960) would have marked anyone openly commemorating ex-guerrillas as a possible communist, and so as a target for detention. Not surprisingly, most such commemoration went into the jungle with the communists.

With the MPAJA, and to a lesser extent Dalforce (wartime Chinese volunteers) tainted with communism, Chinese community leaders had looked for more acceptable wartime heroes. Chapter 4 traces how they had settled on Force 136 member Lim Bo Seng. As a business leader and supporter of Nationalist China — and so safely anti-communist — Lim had been built up first as the main Malayan Chinese war hero, and later as a Singaporean war hero too. Meanwhile, the new Malaysian National Monument opened in 1966, the *Tugu Negara*, had openly identified the communist insurgents of 1948–1960 as the enemies of democracy and the state. As late as the 1980s, therefore, the memory of the MPAJA was still largely marginalised in both Malaysia and Singapore.

By 1989, however, the Cold War was juddering to a close. In December of that year, Malaysia and Thailand signed a peace agreement with the remaining communist insurgents on the Malaysian-Thai Border.[†] This allowed ex-fighters to return to Malaysia. Greater public

---

[†] Singapore was not a party to this agreement, and continued to allow ex-fighters to return only by individual agreement.

discussion of wartime, communist-led, anti-Japanese fighters followed, and their role began to be openly commemorated in Malaysia, notably at two new monuments opened at the Chinese memorial garden at Nilai, in Negeri Sembilan (officially unveiled in 2003 and 2007).

This became a matter of sometimes heated debate in Malaysia, with veterans' organisations and letters to UMNO-influenced parts of the press angrily denouncing this as commemoration of communists. There appeared little chance that the state itself would embrace commemoration of the MPAJA in the foreseeable future. But in the spirit of plural commemoration, the open championing of the MPAJA's memory by Chinese memory activists, and in some newspapers and online publications, was not prevented.[12]

The state in Singapore, meanwhile, took a contrasting approach to managing the disparate, and potentially disruptive, war memories of individuals and communities. As with Malaya, this state effort to control war memory was well underway by the 1960s. Where Malaya chose to emphasise the memory mainly of Malay groups at national level, Singapore sought to impose a unified, and unifying, national story. This was the narrative of how disparate emigrants were forged into an embryonic nation by common wartime suffering.

The state's unifying efforts arose in response to a Chinese desire to erect a memorial to the — overwhelmingly Chinese — victims of the Japanese massacre on the island of February 1942: the "*sook ching*". The state deflected this Chinese project into a national one. When a Civilian War Memorial was officially opened in February 1967, it was to all races which had, in the state's narrative, suffered together, been disappointed in British protection together, and so emerged from the war as an embryonic, multiracial, nation-in-waiting. Thereafter, a ceremony was held at the monument every 15 February, the date Singapore had fallen in 1942.

By this point, Singapore had also secured, as a Japanese gesture to Chinese demands for war compensation, $50 million, equally split between a loan and a grant.[‡13] With the two main issues of war memory now resolved, the People's Action Party (PAP), which had ruled Singapore since self-government in 1959, prioritized Japanese investment in the 1970s, and there was little new war memory activity.

---

‡ The Japanese agreed to the grant and loan in October 1966, following a long campaign for them to meet the "blood debt" left by their 1942 massacres of Chinese in Malaya and Singapore.

As we show in Chapter 10, however, this lull did not last long. In the 1980s, history made a comeback in Singapore schools, with new textbooks highlighting wartime suffering. The press and government also responded periodically to Japanese moves to present its wartime record in a better light to its own students — the "textbook controversy" — and to other perceived Japanese insensitivities about the war.

The early to mid-1990s then saw significant adaptions to the way the Singapore state presented the war. From the key 50th anniversaries of the beginning (1992) and end (1995) of the war, the Singapore state tried to bring a greater variety of community and individual narratives under the umbrella of its unifying state narrative.[14] Efforts included the construction of a large plaque to mark the original memorial to the Indian National Army (1995), and later the opening of a Museum (Reflections at Bukit Chandu, opened 2002) on the Malay Regiment's role in Singapore's defence. This adoption of community stories into the state's overall, unifying narrative allowed it to influence how they were narrated. This reflected its unifying, as opposed to a "plural" approach to commemoration.

There was a more dramatic shift in the late 1990s, as the Singapore state elevated the war to an even greater level of significance. As illustrated in Chapter 10, it now gave war memory an important, if not central, place in National Education for students, and in efforts to sustain the sense of threat to the island (and so of the need for state-instilled discipline), which had pervaded the 1960s to 1980s. The first-generation PAP leadership, aware that they and their memories could not live forever, now tried to institutionalise what they saw as the crucial lessons they had imbued from war and Occupation; to render their personal "memory" as state-sanctioned "history".

The Singapore state thus progressively upgraded the significance of 15 February. In 1992, it was designated Heritage Day, to preserve the idea that the war first saw the island's diverse races bonding to defend the island, in the suffering of Occupation, and in determination to win freedom from the domination of any outsiders, whether European (British) or Asian (Japanese).[15] By 15 February 1998, the day had been redesignated as "Total Defence Day". In the years that followed, schools marked the day, and it was associated with messages about the fragility of society, the need for unity, and the necessity of National Service. Chapter 10 details the extraordinary degree to which war memory was promoted in Singapore in the following years.

Malaysia and Singapore thus responded in very different ways to the increasing number and variety of war memories which — by the 1990s — were now being published, and discussed in the press and online. Though some of this increasing memory production simply reflected the wartime generation's desire to write down their experiences before it was too late, something else was happening as well. Some groups, such as Singapore's Eurasians, sought not just to publicise their unique community stories about the war, but also to have these acknowledged at national level, and integrated into newspaper reports, textbooks, heritage sites, and generally into an overall national story. Memory activists continued to put pressure on the two states, on behalf of wartime groups such as the MPAJA, to better reflect their specific community memories in national accounts. In addition, the multiplication of internet and printed publication outlets was eroding the two states' ability to dominate the agenda on war memory, however slowly.

These ongoing tensions between different levels of memory are embedded in the structure of this book.

This first section, on individuals, comprises this chapter and Chapter 2. Chapter 2 will look at how individual experiences and memories of the war were shaped. It will do so by focussing primarily on five individuals, so that we can outline their stories from prewar, through wartime, right up to their 21st-century memories.

The second section, on "Communities", will divide people by community, with chapters for the British and their authorities in colonial Singapore (Chapter 3), Chinese (Chapters 4 and 5), Indians (Chapter 6), and Malays (Chapters 7 and 8).

The final section, on "Nations and States", will then deal with attempts by the Malaysian (Chapter 9) and Singapore (Chapter 10) states to harness war memory for postcolonial nation-building. These complement Chapter 3 (European memories) insofar as the latter looks at the colonial state's attempt to shape war memory.

Hence the general thrust of the book is to progress from what happened to individuals, through what communities sought to commemorate, to how states have attempted to utilise and reshape memories. We try throughout to give a large part of the space to individuals' memories and words, allowing the story, and the analysis, to flow from these.

We should, before you embark on the rest of this book, make two significant disclaimers. The first is that this is not a history of wartime events — of the Fall of Singapore and the Japanese Occupation — for their own sake. We do provide an outline of these in Chapter 2, but little more. We do discuss events in each chapter as well, but for the instrumental purpose of better understanding the memory of the war. This book thus does cover a lot of the history of the war, but its main focus throughout remains the memory of the Fall and Occupation, and attempts to uncover that memory and its meaning through the voices of different people, communities, and levels of society. If you want more traditional and detailed histories of the wartime events, there are any number of good books you can turn to.

For a concise analysis of why Singapore fell, we immodestly recommend our *Did Singapore Have to Fall? Churchill and the Impregnable Fortress* (London: Routledge, 2004, paperback in 2005). That finishes with a chapter on "After the Battle", which summarises commemoration from Japanese ceremonies and monuments in the Occupation onwards. If it is a history of the Occupation of 1941–1945 that you require, a good starting place is Lee Geok Boi's *The Syonun Years: Singapore under Japanese Rule, 1942–1945* (Singapore: National Archives of Singapore, 2005), or for more detail, Paul Kratoska's *The Japanese Occupation of Malaya, 1941–1945* (St Leonards: Allen & Unwin, 1998). If you want to be directed to books and articles on specific events, you cannot better the annotated bibliography in Constance Mary Turnbull's *A History of Modern Singapore, 1819–2005* (Singapore: NUS Press, 2009), pp. 417–23. Turnbull's chapters on the fall and occupation remain excellent short summaries of events.

Our second disclaimer concerns Japan. We have not covered Japanese memories in detail. This is a book about the memory of the people the Japanese attacked (including British and Australians), and conquered and ruled over. Hence, we discuss Japanese memory only in so far as it has made its presence directly felt in postwar Malaya and Singapore. The Japanese were banned from returning until 1952, and have been low key in commemorating their wartime experiences since then. Despite this, their war memories do appear in our text from time to time. In Chapter 4, we discuss the Japanese retrieval of the remains of the war criminals hanged in Singapore. We also discuss how Japan's relations with Malaya and Singapore in the 1950s and 1960s were affected by the issue of wartime Japanese atrocities, including the local desire for Japan to pay some compensation to atone for them. In Chapter 10, meanwhile, we cover the response in Singapore to the publishing of nationalistic textbooks in Japan, and to visits by prominent Japanese to the Yasukuni Shrine in Tokyo, in order to honour their own war dead.

If you wish to learn more about how these controvesies were driven by the development of war memory in Japan itself, we recommend Philip Seaton's *Japan's Contested War Memories* (London: Routledge, 2007). Seaton argues that there have been "memory rifts" in Japan from the 1970s, which have made its wartime past highly contested. John Breen's edited collection, *Yasukuni: The War Dead and the Struggle for Japan's Past* (Singapore: Horizon Books, 2007) also argues that there have been multiple perspectives, this time on the significance of high profile visits to the Yasukuni Shrine.[16] For the Japanese history textbooks controversy, Yoshiko Nozaki's *War Memory, Nationalism and Education in Postwar Japan, 1945–2007* (London: Routledge, 2008) is excellent. Finally, Franziska Seraphim's *War Memory and Social Politics in Japan, 1945–2005* (Cambridge, Massachusetts: Harvard University Press, 2006) is a useful introduction to the role of interest groups, such as the Association of War-Bereaved Families.

The growing volume and complexity of work specifically on Japanese war memory makes the case for books such as ours — which do the same for countries Japan occupied — all the more compelling. What follows, then, is our contribution to the memory of the Fall and Occupation in Singapore and Malaysia, and more indirectly to our understanding of the wartime historical events themselves. We begin that contribution by taking one snapshot of individual memories, mostly provided by the September 2005 forum in Singapore which brought together a wide range of the "wartime generation" to mark 60 years since the end of the Japanese Occupation.

CHAPTER 2

Personal Narratives of British Defeat and Japanese Occupation

IN THIS CHAPTER, THE MAIN FOCUS IS on five members of the wartime generation. The five include an Australian (Don Lee), and two Indian National Army veterans (Mr Kalyan Ram Das and Mrs Rasammah Bhupalan). There is also a Chinese volunteer who served in Dalforce (Choi Siew Hong), and Mohd Anis bin Tairan. The latter was a ten-year-old Malay boy in 1942, who subsequently joined a school for the Japanese *Heiho* (auxiliary force). Between them, they provide examples of Western, Indian, Chinese and Malay experience.

All five spoke at a Forum with the Wartime Generation, held at the Singapore History Museum* in September 2005, and were also interviewed individually. Some of them have written and published accounts of their experiences, and one (Mrs Bhupalan, subsequently taking the title "Datuk") is the subject of a book published by Malaysia's *Arkib Negara* (National Archives).[1]

This rich vein of material means that we can construct a fairly coherent account of their wartime experiences. By focussing on just a few case studies, we can in addition follow each individual from their youth, through the Occupation, to their 21st-century memories. This individual life story approach will allow us to demonstrate the way in which personal war memories were constituted and reshaped by a complex cocktail of their respective pasts (including myths they subscribed to about previous conflicts), their personalities, their unique wartime experiences, and the postwar communities and countries they lived in.

---

* This has since relaunched as today's National Museum of Singapore.

14

Plate 2.1   Three war veterans at the September 2005 "Forum with the Wartime Generation": Kalyan Ram Das (left); Don Lee (centre); and Choi Siew Hong (right). Together with Mrs Bhupalan and Mohd Anis bin Tairan, their stories shape this chapter.

Taken together, our five main characters also encompass a broad range of wartime experiences, including the fighting; captivity as POWs and as labourers on the Burma-Thailand Railway; the Japanese massacres of 1942; civilian collaboration; and the war's impact on Malay nationalism. Working around the personal stories, we will be able to outline the most important wartime events and experiences that future chapters will keep referring back to.

None of our five, however, could claim to have participated in the anti-Japanese resistance in Malaya's jungles. In order to give a flavour of that, we will briefly introduce Ong Boon Hua, who under the alias "Chin Peng" led Malaya's postwar communists. Even more briefly, Private Miyake Genjiro flits on and offstage to give a Japanese eye view of the massacres of Chinese of February to March 1942; and Eurasians Eric Paglar and Victor Grosse make fleeting appearances.

The main focus, however, will remain firmly on our five principal characters. As we shall see, these had very varied experiences not just of the war, but also of war memory afterwards, ranging from feeling marginalised by the nations and communities they lived in, to having their stories feted as exemplars of national character.

We start with Don Lee, who at 93 was the oldest of the wartime generation to address the Forum at the Singapore History Museum in 2005.[2] He was also the most confident that his personal story fitted into an honoured, national tradition: one which motivated his entry into the war, shaped his experience of it, and then his memory of it afterwards.

This sense of participating in a wider national story had been passed down through his family. His father had fought alongside the British in the Boer War of 1899 to 1902, and owned a farm in the Manjimup District, near Perth. Don Lee was born in Western Australia in 1912, and always wanted to follow his father's example, and own a farm of his own. He worked as a jackeroo (stockman) on a sheep station, and hunted kangaroos on the rugged landscape around the ranch, selling their skins to boost his meagre savings. Then the Great Depression struck. With work now hard to find, he became a "roustabout" (general worker), then a wool classifier, travelling the length and breadth of sheep country with a team of shearers.

The Depression had put an end to dreams of pursuing one family tradition, that of being a farm owner. War now gave him an opportunity to follow another: that of being a rugged volunteer soldier who fights alongside the British. He had already joined Australia's part-time Citizens Military Force in 1937. When war broke out in 1939, he was commissioned as a Lieutenant and joined the 2/4th Machine Gun Battalion of the Australian Imperial Force (AIF). Don joined with a sense of pride in Australia's military, based on the Anzac legend. He self-consciously sought to locate himself as part of an ongoing collective memory about the Anzacs.

Anzac stood for Australia and New Zealand Army Corps, and referred to the young men from Britain's antipodean colonies who had fought in the First World War. The Anzac legend was an Australian myth (a public story, however true or untrue, which ascribes values to events) which asserted that these soldiers had been superior to the British.[3] Australians supposedly eschewed the rigid hierarchy of the British. Instead they emphasised "mateship" between all ranks, and exhibited resourcefulness and a rough-cut suitability for warfare inspired by the values of the Australian frontier: its outback. The campaign the Anzacs most famously fought in, at Gallipoli in Turkey (1915–1916), produced futile stalemate, followed by withdrawal. But that merely allowed Australians to counterpoint British failure in planning with Anzac steadiness in battle.[4] In short, the Anzacs were made to stand for qualities Australians wished to hold up as national characteristics, and in contrast to the British "mother" country.[5]

The reality behind the Anzac myth is hotly debated, and the majority of Australians actually lived in towns and cities by the First World War.[6] But for Don, the Anzac legend was a reality, and he was precisely the sort of person the Anzac legend conjured up. 27 years old in 1939, he had experience of the bush. He had worked as a "jackaroo"; his father had served in the Boer War, and had subsequently followed the progress of the First World War Anzacs. When he and his brothers joined the regular army in 1939, they hoped to uphold the Anzac tradition.

In January 1942, Don was brought to Singapore as a Lieutenant in the AIF's 2/4th Machine Gun Battalion. He was positioned in the island's north, responsible for keeping six machine guns trained over a 180-degree arc of the Johor Strait. At the right hand side of this arc was the Causeway which joined Singapore to the Malayan mainland opposite, and in which the British had blown a gap. He and his men were told to rain machine gun fire on any Japanese who dared to cross the calm, narrow stretch of water that separated Singapore from Malaya.

Other Australians were already adding new chapters to the Anzac legend. In central Johor (the last Malayan state before Singapore), Australian gunners cut up several Japanese tanks near Gemas in mid-January 1942. The Australians there took nearly 10 per cent casualties before retreat. That was in turn necessitated by events on the west coast of Johor. There Australian units had been stationed, with Indian troops, behind the Muar River. The Australians were sent reeling as the raw British Indian Army troops of 45 Brigade were outflanked and crumbled. Finding the Japanese blocking the road to safety just beyond Bakri on 20 January, Lt.-Colonel Charles Anderson ordered one unit into battle singing "Waltzing Matilda". In the words of the official Australian historian:

> ... they sang:
> Once a jolly swagman camped by a billabong
> Under the shade of a coolibah tree ...
> 'Waltzing Matilda', never sung by Australians with more enthusiasm than when they meet in surroundings strange to them, had become a battle song.

Only a handful made it back to Singapore. The Anzac myth was further enshrined in popular memory, and is still celebrated publicly on Anzac Day, every 25 April. Indeed, if anything, it has probably become even more popularly supported — particularly in schools — over the past couple of decades.

The reality for Don in Singapore was less heroic. The Japanese crossed the Johor Strait from the north and west, from creeks and beaches on the Malayan coast, on the night of 8–9 February 1942. Their force was smaller than that of the defenders, but they achieved surprise and so local superiority. Don soon had to retreat as the Japanese infiltrated between scattered shore defences along the Johor Strait. He eventually became a POW. After 15 February, he joined the 50,000 British and Australian soldiers who streamed across the island to the Changi area in the east. There they sub-divided amongst the military barracks available, which the Japanese fenced into one vast POW area. The Australians occupied Selerang Barracks, the British Roberts Barracks. For both, the defining experience of captivity would come in 1943, when POWs were despatched to help build the Burma-Thailand Railway.

Speaking in 2005, Don's testimony increased in emotional force as he recalled the decreasing rations and increasing brutality of 1943, as the Japanese accelerated the pace of work on that railway. This "Speedo" phase (May to October 1943) culminated in his men having to cart the bodies of Asian railway labourers — victims of cholera — to a ravine eight at a time. There they were "tossed away like garbage". After the war, Don made "pilgrimages" back to Singapore and the railway. The tradition of celebrating Anzac soldiers' distinctive Australian qualities — which extended to displaying "mateship" in captivity — provided an encouraging environment for Don to tell his story. Australia has memorials not just to those who died in battle, but — at Ballarat since 2004 — to all Australians who have been held captive.[7] While in Britain, Far Eastern POWs for long felt the taint of defeat, this was not the case for Australians.[8]

When Don visited the Burma-Thailand Railway in 2004, he addressed Australian tourists at the Australian-run "Hellfire Pass Museum", near where he had worked on the pass of that name. In common with a number of fellow Australian POWs, Don also wrote a memoir, *A Yarn or Two*, which was published in 1994. His fictional account of life on the railway, *The Silvered Shovel*, was also picked up by an international publisher, Vantage of New York.[9] Don, living in a Perth retirement village with his wife, felt assured in 2005 that his and his comrades' experiences were part of Australian public memory: part of national memory.

At the forum, he argued that even his comrades who perished on the railway — 2,802 out of 13,004 Australians who worked on it — were heroes as well as victims.[10] Heroism was about displaying the right, Anzac, attitude. Don asked, "What does dying for your country mean? I saw men who were just decomposing. Is it fair to say that they did not die for their country?" He recalled a man "slumped against a tree decomposing", able to joke cheerfully that, "I only have a week to go, you know". Two men greeting each other as "mates" in the face of death.

Don Lee's story demonstrates how an individual can find meaning in suffering when it can be placed in a collective story about the past. Despite playing little effective part in the fighting, and being part of a defeated, imperial army, Don could be confident that other Australians would interpret his experiences — including his time as a POW — in the light of a glorious, or at least glorified, Anzac tradition. Indeed, his story illustrates the way that memory and event can act in a loop. He joined the regular forces specifically with the aim of continuing an Anzac tradition, and then interpreted his experiences in the light of that tradition. Memory was not just something that resulted from his experiences, but also something that helped to cause them, shape them, and imbue them with meaning.

Our next veteran, Kalyan Ram Das (K.R. Das), could not have the same confidence that his experiences would slip into the national story of his adopted country.[11] He felt that the memory of the Indian National Army (INA) for which he had fought had become increasingly marginalised within Malaysia.[12]

K.R. Das was born in Mysore in southwestern India in 1918, and was 87 years old when he addressed the audience at the Singapore History Museum in 2005. His wartime memories took him right back to his time as a schoolboy in India:

> For this Indian, the blood in me is out of a bottle I drank as a child from the wells of remote Indian villages ... As a child of eight or so, I heard Mahatma Gandhi addressing a mammoth crowd at the beach in Calicut. I had heard Pandit Jawaharlal Nehru and Subhas Chandra Bose, Ansari and K.F. Nariman addressing huge crowds in Bombay, usually at Bori Bunder grounds.

He recalled the British suppression of a non-violent demonstration in Calicut in 1931: "I have seen with my own eyes bullies charging people, beating them with *lathis*, a thick cane two feet long".[13]

Das identified with the Indian nationalists and protesters. But he compromised his ideals by signing up for the British Indian Army: "Poverty and difficulty in getting a decent permanent job in Bombay made me go to the Army Recruiting Centre there to enlist ... as a mercenary in the British Army".[14] The army paid well for his fluency in English and Indian languages. He was sent to join the 13th Pioneer Labour Battalion, a non-combatant unit meant to supply labour for frontline units, and which was attached to the 45th Indian Brigade. This was the same Brigade mentioned above as stationed behind the Muar River, before the Japanese sent it into headlong retreat alongside Australian forces.

Das, like Don Lee's Western Australian machine gunners, arrived late in the campaign, when British Empire forces had received defeats in north and central Malaya. The story behind these failures can be summed up briefly. "Singapore Fortress" had been built between 1923–1938, comprising fine barracks, airfields, docks, and coastal artillery right up to 15-inch guns taken off World War One battleships. These turned Singapore into an unsinkable battleship. Should Japan attack, the island would hold out for a "Period-before-Relief" while a British fleet sailed from the west. Japan's nearest bases were thousands of miles away, and Malaya's road system was poor, especially on its east coast. There was little need to hold much of the Malayan peninsula.

From 1938–1941, this strategy had to be torn up, as war in Europe saw the British stand alone against the German and Italian navies from mid-1940. By mid-1941, the Japanese had taken bases in French Indochina, just 400–500 miles from northern Malaya and southern Thailand, and an extensive road system had been built on Malaya's west coast. By now, the British fully foresaw that any attack would start with the Japanese seizing in advance air bases in northeast Malaya and neighbouring Thailand, before tearing down the west coast of Malaya to Singapore. They also understood that a relieving fleet, if it ever came, could take months to assemble.

So the British devised a new forward defence strategy, around "Operation Matador". This was intended to keep Japanese aircraft and artillery as far from the Singapore base as possible, delaying them for weeks if not months. As battle loomed, the British would rush across the Malayan-Thai border, and dig in on the southeastern Thai beaches.

That would block access to Malaya's northwest with its good roads.[15] If forced back, they would make a fighting retreat down the peninsula. Over 100,000 troops, half of them Indian, the rest almost evenly divided between British and Australians, were pumped into these colonies. It was hoped that this would bluff the Japanese into not attacking Britain's "dollar arsenal", where the sap of Malayan rubber trees was turned into Britain's top dollar earner. Failing that, the troops would delay the Japanese until the United States could blunt the Japanese advance. By early December 1941, Churchill had American assurances — as concrete as the United States ever gave — that they would respond to any further Japanese aggression in the east. Churchill now assumed that any Japanese attack on Malaya was near certain to be blunted by American action elsewhere.

What went wrong, and left Das and others to become POWs? First, the attack on Pearl Harbor temporarily neutered United States naval power in the Pacific. Second, Churchill endorsed Operation Matador, but insisted all tanks and almost all modern aircraft go to active theatres. Hundreds went to the Middle East, and from June 1941, to the Soviet Union too. So there were around 160 aircraft to Japan's 600 plus when Japan attacked Malaya. There were also zero defending tanks initially, to face light Japanese machines. In these circumstances, the Thai beaches could never have been held, and in the event the British confirmed the imminence of Japanese attack too late to even attempt to take them. Third, many of the reinforcements were raw: half-trained and insufficiently acclimatised. Fourth, the concept of a fighting retreat — especially with poor air cover — condemned the defenders to never committing enough men to win individual battles. By contrast, the Japanese adapted German blitzkrieg tactics into their *Kirimoni Sakusen* (running charge), and made continual outflanking movements.

The Japanese were able to land unopposed on southeastern Thai beaches on the morning of 8 December, and against some British opposition in northeast Malaya. Then they tore down the west coast of the peninsula. In North Malaya at Jitra (11–13 December) and in central Malaya at the Slim River (7 January 1941), Japanese tanks blasted holes in British positions. In between these defeats, British-led forces did hold the Japanese at Kampar (90 miles north of Kuala Lumpur), from 29 December to 4 January. Wedging themselves between rising hills to one side, and open fields of fire to the other, the British and Indian defenders repulsed attempts at outflanking. But "fighting retreat" meant that other troops, dispersed across the country, were not brought up to support the Kampar position. Consequently, the Japanese were able to sweep wide around and behind Kampar, forcing retreat. After Kampar, it was a matter of when the Japanese would reach Singapore, not if. Retreating British troops now dubbed the mauled Royal Air Force "The Penguin Club", "because they had wings but didn't fly".[16]

Das' formation, the 45th Indian Brigade of the 17th Indian Division, was originally supposed to sail from Bombay to Burma in late December 1941. But with Indian forces mauled in Malaya, Das found himself diverted to Singapore.[17] His unit arrived on 3 January 1942. The brigade trained briefly, before taking up positions in the southernmost of Malaya's states: Johor. They were deployed south of the Muar River, alongside Australians.[18] In sum, Das' formation arrived when the fighting retreat was going horribly wrong — drip, dripping away resources and sapping morale — and when the British were making their last stand in southern Malaya.

For Das, however, the nakedness of British strategy and brilliance of the Japanese "driving charge" were far from his mind. What was bothering him was his superiors. He was billeted at an oil palm estate near the Johor town of Cha'ah. He recalled with disgust that "It was here that I first learnt how Indians were treated by their British masters".[19] 1,600 Indian soldiers were billeted at the bottom of the hill, their commanders on the top in large bungalows. When the Indians awoke, they had to wait hours in tropical humidity for a drink. This was so their four British officers could finish their morning breakfast and showers, before the use of the water at the bottom of the hill would reduce the water pressure. His commanding officer, Major McNicoll, also sent Das out to scout for gin. When Das returned, McNicholl waved his gun in Das' face, ranting that he had stolen a crate of alcohol. Indian soldiers, meanwhile, were given "a type of biscuit called 'sakarpara' which today even a dog won't bite", while "every weekend, the quartermaster would receive a supply of beer and liquor for the officers. Every night they were 'high' on booze".[20]

Das' personal success did nothing to stem his simmering resentment. He was promoted from *havildar* (just above sergeant) to Warrant Officer. This was not a common rank in the British Indian Army, but rather of the British Army. He was promoted because he was the only one in his 1,600-man unit who could speak fluent Urdu, the language of the British Indian Army commands, as well as good English. The British officers knew no Urdu; the Indian soldiers no English. Thus

Das was like gold dust, despite not being able to write the Arabic-based script in which Urdu was written. As he put it, "In the kingdom of the blind, a one-eyed man is king". Hence, the linguistically agile Das — he could speak some Malayalam, Tamil, and Urdu as well as English — held a trump card.[21]

Das escaped the fate of most of Indian soldiers of the ill-trained 45th Indian Brigade. This was the Brigade which was cut off when retreating from the Muar River with the Australian 2/29th and 2/19th battalions from 19 January 1942. The Japanese crossed the river by stealth and threatened to outflank, sending the defenders scurrying backwards. The brigade was encircled by the Japanese at Bakri and all but annihilated. Only 550 Indians and 400 Australians made it back to their own lines. As we saw above, the Australians, true to the Anzac tradition, wrote up their role in this fiasco as heroic defeat. By contrast, Lieutenant General A.E. Percival, General Officer Commanding, Malaya, concluded that, "The 45th Indian Infantry Brigade had ceased to exist. Those killed included the Brigade Commander" and "every battalion commander". He noted how:

> This brigade had never been fit for employment in a theatre of war. It was not that there was anything wrong with the raw material but simply that it was raw.[22]

Das recalls that "Members of the [45th Indian Infantry Brigade] had very little training for battle. Except in the use of Lee Enfield .303 rifles and orderly march past they received no instruction". Even worse, they were issued new weapons shortly before battle, with virtually no time to train with them.[23]

Das and his men experienced daily bombing attacks on their retreat. He took shrapnel wounds to his leg, but made it to Singapore. As a logistics battalion, his comrades then spent the battle for Singapore (8–15 February 1942) "crammed into the Guthrie godown somewhere near South Bridge Road".[24] For Das, then, defeat was about the way an imperial officer class was more interested in using and abusing privilege than in preparing for war.[25] We should, of course, be wary of over-generalising. His formation had been undertrained and badly beaten up, in contrast to the better seasoned Indian troops who had performed so well at Kampar over the New Year.

After the Fall of Singapore on 15 February, Das and other Indian POWs were concentrated at Singapore's Farrer Park. There, on 17 February 1942, Captain Mohan Singh urged the 45,000 Indian POWs in Singapore to take up arms and march with the Japanese to liberate India, in an Indian National Army (INA). For Das, however:

> many Indians thought that it was an opportune time to fight the British ... [but] there was no general confidence in the leadership of Mohan Singh, of whom hardly anyone had heard. The I.N.A. movement, therefore, lay dormant[26] ... Mohan Singh was not a real leader, but he was a good man. Mohan Singh had support in the Army, but no support among the Indian public ... South Indians make up most of the Indians in Malaya ... Tamils would say, 'He is not a Tamil, why support him? He is not a Nehru, so why support him?'[27]

Das went into captivity, with the majority of his Indian brothers-in-arms, in his case at Bidadari in Singapore. The camp conditions were poor, and "as a result, dysentery broke out on an epidemic scale, and large numbers of Indian soldiers died. Many escaped or were sent elsewhere from the camp, whose strength was depleted to almost half when it was shifted to Nee Soon [in northwest Singapore] ..."[28]

The Japanese regarded big Singapore camps, such as Changi for British and Australians and Bidadari for Indians, as holding areas, from which to disburse POWs to labour or to the INA. The Japanese in charge scarcely seemed to care whether the Indians stayed in the camp or went out and did not return, so Das left.

Das then picked up some Japanese with the aid of a Japanese dictionary, and joined a Japanese medical unit (*Imushitzu*) as an assistant cook. There he experienced cruelty and kindness. When a Japanese soldier asked him to climb a coconut tree, and he did not know how, he was beaten and slapped. Yet when his Japanese unit found out that he was learning their language, its 140 members gathered around, "They were all very happy ... completely they changed because I speak Japanese".[29] Das became good friends with one Japanese soldier, Kikuchi Sekine from Hiroshima. In this, his experience echoes what would later become stock images of occupation, of generalised harshness leavened by the occasional "good Japanese" who helps a particular person, family or employee.

While in *Imushitzu*, Das also mixed with members of Mohan Singh's INA, "Every Saturday afternoon, being off duty, I used to visit a pub in Dhoby Ghaut where I.N.A. officers, civilians and Indian prisoners of war used to gather in fellowship meetings. It was there I met Prem Saghal, Shah Nawaz Khan [prominent INA members who were tried after the war] and others for the first time".[30] When the

Plate 2.2   K.R. Das and his Japanese friend, Kikuchi Sekine, in Singapore, 1942

Japanese 25th Army departed Singapore for Sumatra in March 1943, Das was left alone, and resorted to trading Japanese cigarettes on the black market. So by 1943, Das had been nationalist-tinged youth, disgruntled British Indian Army Warrant Officer, POW, assistant cook for a Japanese medical unit, and black marketeer.

Then, in July 1943, something happened that would transform Das' war. Subhas Chandra Bose arrived in Singapore. S.C. Bose was an electrifying speaker, and an ex-President of the Indian National Congress (1938–1939) who had split from the party in 1939, and now believed that violence would have to be used to win India's freedom. The very fact that he had made it to Singapore at all might have suggested that fortune favoured him. He had escaped house arrest in Calcutta in January 1941, slipped across the border to Afghanistan, and from there made his way to Nazi Germany via Moscow. He then travelled to Sumatra by submarine, and from Sumatra flew to Tokyo. By the time he arrived in Singapore, the Indian Independence League there had already voted him their leader.

On 4 July 1943, Bose was due to speak at the Cathay Cinema Building, then Singapore's tallest. Das "... was mildly surprised to see large numbers of workmen putting up scaffolding, bunting, Indian national flags, all in a festive mood".[31] He saw Bose accept the Presidency of the Indian Independence League and allegiance of the INA. Two days later, he saw the march past of thousands of INA soldiers at Singapore's Municipal Hall, with Bose and visiting Japanese Premier Hideki Tojo taking their salute. Das recalls that at last there seemed to be a chance to restore pride:

> Indians were never respected by anybody because we were slaves, we were mercenaries. We would go and fight and make others slaves. We conquered our own people, joined with the Europeans and made Indians slaves. Our Indian mercenaries conquered Burma, conquered Malaysia, conquered Sri Lanka, conquered so many places. So when we find an opportunity to fight and be free we will be respected by other people.[32]

Das joined the INA in September 1943. His experience as a Warrant Officer and knack with languages again ensured progress. The recruiting officer recommended Das for the INA Officer Training School at Newton Circus in Singapore. There he also taught fellow officer cadets, mainly Tamils, map-reading using Urdu commands. Once they had mastered the basics, he would lead them into the forest at Bukit Timah, and tell them to find their own way out.

After two months, Das was commissioned as a 2nd Lieutenant and sent to the Kuala Lumpur Bharat Youth Training Centre. For the rest of the war, he "trained over 2,000 men in the use of small arms".[33] The basic military training that Das gave was based on his own British Indian Army training, but with a nationalist twist:

First month: To teach the recruits the importance of discipline in the army and their role as liberators of Mother India.

Second month: Unquestioned obedience to superiors and thorough knowledge in the use of .303 rifles and machine guns, and how to take cover when suddenly attacked.

Third month: The use of Bren guns, knowledge of first aid and test of proficiency with live bullets …

Fourth month: Intensive repeated practice to turn battle field movement into automatic reflex actions.

Fifth month: Training continued. On the recommendations of company commanders, some recruits would be promoted as 'Lance Naiks' [Lance Corporals], others posted to various regular units needing them, where they received specialised training … [34]

Towards the end of the war, a new group arrived at the Bharat Youth Training Camp. One of the INA's paramilitary organisations was *Azad Hind Dal* [Free India Party]. It grew food for the INA. The men were enraged when they discovered that their own officers were pilfering food and selling it on the black market. At Seremban in June 1945, they threatened to shoot their officers.

The mutineers were disarmed, and sent to the Bharat Youth Training Camp. Because they were all Malayalees from Singapore, Das translated Bose's rebuke to them into Malayalam. Bose let them off leniently, detailing them to work under Das at an agricultural settlement in the Kuala Selangor district, about 65 miles (100 kilometres) north of Kuala Lumpur. Malaya and Singapore were food deficit areas that traditionally relied on exporting commodities such as tin and rubber, and importing rice and luxuries. With the Japanese merchant navy rapidly diminishing by 1944–1945, the Japanese were anxious to increase food production.

Das finished the war with the new agricultural unit. The India-born Das decided to stay in Malaya: "I came from an extremely poor country. I found Malaya an extremely good country where I can easily get along". [35] His facility with languages was ideal for polyglot Malaya. He found work in accountancy and finance with overseas companies operating there. For Das, the war had transformed not just his own personal fortunes, but Indian consciousness in Malaya in general:

He [Bose] turned the servile Indian labourer in the plantations of Malaya into a proud, self-respecting man. Prior to the war, the Indian labourer had to dismount from his bicycle when the European estate manager's car approached him on road. He had to take off his turban on such occasions. He was not supposed to wear clean clothes unless he was attending a wedding or a funeral or some religious function.

When the planters returned after the war, they found a different Indian. Many were the instances when European planters were hit and kicked for assaulting Indian workers. Indian workers organized themselves into powerful labour unions and negotiated with the employers on an equal level. They secured better wages, bonus, provident fund, social security plans and better living quarters.

The origin of these can be traced back to the I.N.A. days when under Netaji's leadership every Indian held his head high ...[36]

In the 1950s, Das became part of this rising Indian nationalism in Malaya when he became active in the Malayan Indian Congress (MIC). For him, "There would be no MIC without the INA".[37] He was involved in MIC negotiations with the other political parties representing the Malays (United Malays National Organisation, UMNO) and the Chinese (Malayan Chinese Association, MCA) in order to achieve a coalition to which the British would hand over power. He recalls that, "I was a member of the Federal Alliance Council [Alliance National Council, its coordinating body] ..."[38] This hammered out the "*Merdeka Compact*" or agreement on power sharing between the parties representing different communities, which was then embodied in the constitution of Malaya. But Das became disillusioned with the MIC when V.T. Sambanthan won control and turned it into a mainly Tamil entity. The MIC also showed decreasing interest in the INA over time.[39]

Das turned away from the MIC to concentrate on business, and to look for other ways of keeping the memory of the INA alive. From the 1980s, he became active in the Netaji Service Centre, which represented local INA veterans, and which gave out scholarships in Bose's honour. From his perspective, the Netaji Service Centre was fighting a battle to stop the gradual decline of the memory of the INA — and of its impact on Indians and on Malayan nation-building — both in the Indian community and in Malaysia more generally.

Another of the speakers at the 2005 Forum with the Wartime generation spoke even more passionately about the INA and its energising effect on the Indian communities of Southeast Asia. That speaker was Mrs Rasammah Bhupalan (in the war, still known as Rasammah Navarednam), a Christian Indian who had grown up in Ipoh. She was just 16 years old in July 1943, when the Bengali nationalist S.C. Bose arrived in Singapore.

This was the point at which K.R. Das had stumbled across Bose and joined the INA. Bose's aim was to transform the locally recruited, Japanese-sponsored INA into an effective force for the liberation of his homeland. First raised in 1942 from Indian POWs in Malaya and Singapore, the INA had at this stage stalled due to mutual distrust between Japanese and its Indian leaders. The Japanese now wanted to revitalise it, so that it could help their drive from Burma into India.

Bose soon went to speak in Rasammah's hometown of Ipoh. Already fired up by reading works by Jawaharlal Nehru, she decided to join the INA's all-female unit: the Rani of Jhansi Regiment.[†] She was trained in Singapore, and then sent to Burma with the first contingent of the regiment, whose marching song often rang out in Tamil, the language of the majority of Malaya's Indians:

> Fear not! Fear not!
> We march on Netaji's orders,
> Forward march! Forward march!
> Rani of Jhansi's women,
> March to liberate
> Our beloved India;
> Kill Americans and British
> Wherever you see them,
> Fear not! Fear Not![40]

Heady stuff for the rank and file, many of whom were the children of immigrants who, unlike Das, had never seen India, or whose work had not long before consisted of rising at dawn to tap rubber trees: lives Mrs Bhupalan characterised as "drudgery", and the virtual "slavery" of an "underclass" of coolies.

The anger which fired the young Rasammah continued to burn in Mrs Bhupalan, whether at the treatment of rubber tappers or about the British shooting of unarmed Indian protesters in Amritsar in 1919. Mrs Bhupalan emphasised that the Regiment were real soldiers: an integral part of the military forces of Bose's Singapore-based government of *Azad Hind* (Free India, formed October 1943). In her view, this was no puppet government, but a nationalist regime-in-waiting, to which the Japanese transferred control of the "liberated" Andaman and

---

[†] She joined with her sister Ponnammah after the regiment's leader, Dr Lakshmi Swaminadham, overcame their mother's objections.

Nicobar Islands.[41] While Das trained batches of male recruits in Singapore, the women trained in night marches and bayonet charges.[‡] In 1944, they clamoured to fight — if necessary die — for "a sacred cause": India's freedom. Her voice betrayed lasting disappointment that:

> We would not be sent to the front until we reached the border of Bengal. Bengal which was the real dynamite, a whole force of freedom fighters, and it was just the right time if they could see women soldiers — Indian sisters — dying on the frontline. Then it would be a meaningful rebellion that would come into India, like a volcanic eruption.

Too soon, however, British Indian forces defeated the Japanese and INA attack in the battle for Kohima and Imphal (April to June 1944). The attackers were sent reeling back from the Indian border. The women soldiers were obliged to retreat along the Burma-Thailand Railway to Bangkok, without ever having reached the frontline.

Officers such as Rasammah Navarednam — and the doctor who headed the unit, Captain Lakshmi Swaminadhan — had wider horizons than the young women recruited from Malaya's estates. What is more, though inspirational, her story echoed the collective memory of the Malaysian and Singapore Indian communities. In this, the INA's brief existence is seen as a seminal moment of Indian (rather than Malayan) nationalist passion, and as part of the bigger story of India's independence movement. Her role as a female fighter gave a particular idealism to Mrs Bhupalan's memories. The Rani of Jhansi Regiment excites the imagination even more than the male component of the INA. The men's story, often involving transfer from the British Indian Army to the Japanese-sponsored INA, is more ambivalent. By contrast, the arming of daughters from "sheltered homes" offered purer vistas of nationalism. As did the unit's titular invocation of the heroism of the historical Rani Lakshmi Bai of Jhansi. The Rani was one of the stalwarts of the Indian rebellion of 1857–1858 who — according to Indian accounts — died in battle.[42] It is clear that, for some at least, involvement in the Rani of Jhansi regiment was a life-changing experience.

Mrs Bhupalan continued her role as fighter as a postwar advocate for the rights of all women in Malaya. She persuaded the first Prime

---

[‡] Bose was eager to show that the women were real soldiers. Initially a minority trained as nurses, though more assumed this role as INA casualties increased.

Minister of an independent Malaya, Tunku Abdul Rahman, to legislate to give women equal pay when leader of Women Teachers' Union of the Federation of Malaya, and served as a leader of the National Council of Women's Organisations. She continued to pursue her ideals in areas which had significance for all Malaysia's ethnic groups. For her, INA involvement had been a stepping stone to continuing leadership roles after the war.

Das and Bhupalan epitomise one Indian story about the war, in which the INA is made an important part of wider Indian nationalism. But we should not forget that many did not join the INA.[43] About 16,000 of approximately 55,000 Indian POWs were armed by the Japanese in 1942. The Japanese only agreed to arm larger numbers, including many local civilians, after Bose's arrival in mid-1943. In 1942, a minimum of 5,000 POWs in Singapore refused to put themselves forward when the INA was mooted, while the 10,000 held in Malaya were not asked. In addition, thousands of Indian civilians were recruited to labour on the Burma-Thailand Railway, where they suffered appalling death rates (see pp. 198–203).

It is those who refused to join the INA, were never asked and so remained POWs, and the Indian civilians who were recruited as labourers on the Burma-Thailand Railway, who are the true "forgotten" amongst Indians. Amongst the POWs, refusers' reasons may have varied from a sense of "*izzat*" (honour) in loyalty to their unit and profession, through distaste at the idea of working with the Japanese, to positive experiences of service under particular British officers.[44]

As powerful as the INA myth was, it could not therefore represent the experiences of everyone. It also spoke to a time of anti-colonial Indian nationalism, which seemed less relevant after Indian independence, and as Malaya developed its own postcolonial identity after 1957. Worse still, the postcolonial states did not accord the INA significant attention. In Malaysia, there was scarcely any mention of the INA in school texts and in history books and the press: it is after all specifically a story of Indian, not Malaysian, nationalism.

In Singapore, meanwhile, museums such as the Changi Chapel and Museum focus primarily on white POWs, not the British Indian Army soldiers who were held captive. In Singapore, local television programmes such as 1990s TV serial *The Price of Peace* focussed mainly on the Chinese experience of suffering, not the agony of the Indian labourers of the Burma-Thailand Railway. In addition, Indian soldiers under British command blew up the INA memorial on Singapore's

Padang, or central green, upon their return in September 1945. It was 1995 before a plaque was erected on the spot where this memorial had once stood.

This wider context may go some way towards explaining why Das felt that fellow Indians had become less and less interested in INA wartime experiences over time. Their children and grandchildren were reluctant to accompany them to veterans' reunions. When, on the 50th anniversary of the fall of Singapore in 1992, Indian veterans put together a book of personal reflections, they had trouble even giving this away to libraries in Malaysia and Singapore.[45] Delighted to have a receptive audience across generations at the 2005 forum, Das took the opportunity to give copies away, in particular to historians.

Our next veteran, Choi Siew Hong, also felt that his wartime experiences had limited national resonance in Malaysia, though he too fought for a group that became famous. This was Dalforce, otherwise known as the Overseas Anti-Japanese Volunteer Army.

Choi Siew Hong was born in Kuantan, on the east coast of Malaya, in 1921, and so was aged 84 when he addressed the Forum at the Singapore History Museum in 2005.[46] He came from a comfortably off Malayan Chinese family in Kuantan, but saw poverty as a child. When the price of Malayan rubber collapsed in 1932:

> unemployed Chinese rubber tappers would come into town to beg
> for food. They were in a horrible way. My father agreed to help one
> rubber tapper by sharing the proceeds of our small rubber acreage
> in return for the tapper's work. However, the price of rubber was so
> low that the tapper could barely earn enough to feed himself. We
> had to learn to do without, but we were better off than the poor
> from the villages. My father had to sell his coffee shop in town,
> but kept his beef selling business, which allowed us to get by. The
> Great Depression taught me to study hard to get a secure good job.
> I worked hard to get into Raffles College at Singapore in 1939 so
> that I could go into teaching and the civil service.[47]

Haunted by his childhood memories of the Depression, he specialised in economics, in the hope of understanding the causes of the appalling poverty that he had seen. His examinations were about to commence when, on 8 December 1941, bombs started falling on Singapore. Classes ended, the College became a military hospital, and many Raffles College students (including Lee Kuan Yew, the future first Prime Minister of Singapore) became orderlies in the Medical Auxiliary Corps.[48]

Choi Siew Hong joined the local Chinese volunteer unit, along with two college friends. Formed in the last few weeks of fighting, this was called Dalforce by the British, after its commander: John D. Dalley of the Malayan police. Amongst Chinese, it was called the "Singapore Overseas Anti-Japanese Volunteer Army". Both the communists and Kuomintang had been organising anti-Japanese activities since 1937, and encouraged supporters to join.

Some 1,250 volunteered, including at least 1,072 combatants, organised in eight companies of around 100–150 men each. At least three of these lightly equipped units fought and took casualties, notably in the battle for Bukit Timah in central Singapore.[49] The 2nd Company suffered most, taking up to 60 per cent casualties (90 missing out of 150) in the west of the island. Yet half the companies did not see action. For those that did, Chang Teh Cheok remembers some men melting away at the sound of battle "because they were just common folk who did not know how to fight the Japanese". A postwar campaign by Dalforce veterans for back pay enrolled over a thousand claimants.[50]

While the Dalforce experience was variegated, Lee Kuan Yew later claimed that the Chinese who joined Dalforce: "… made Dalforce a legend, a name synonymous with bravery".[51] Later accounts claimed that it was drawn from a broad cross section of Chinese society, from Communists and Kuomintang supporters, to Chinese female dancers and Raffles College students. Siew Hong and two classmates — Yap Siew Choong and Hiew Kiang Mian — were the only Raffles College students to join.[52] All three were from Malaya. Siew Hong recalled how:

> … towards the end of January, we came across an article or advertisement in the newspaper on the establishment of a new Chinese volunteer force … and we decided to join the force for some real action and to do whatever little we could to fight the enemy and defend Singapore. We were also impelled to do so because of the atrocities perpetrated by the Japanese in China. Another reason for us to join the force was to play a liaison role between the British officers and the Chinese recruits who were predominantly Chinese educated[53] … As instructed, the three of us, Siew Choong, Kiang Mian and I reported for duty on 1 February 1942 at a Chinese High School in Kim Yam Road. I was assigned to take charge of the armour and food supplies and designated Quartermaster Sergeant, and my two friends were each assigned to separate platoons. We were issued with [blue] uniforms in which we changed … I was given a revolver and my two friends a rifle each …[54]

Most of those Siew Hong was handing out arms to were communists:

> The Chinese high school which was used as the Headquarters of the communist faction of Dalforce swarmed with new recruits displaying great excitement and raring for action ... the Kuomintang faction of the Dalforce was much smaller in number and was housed near to the centre of the city".[55]

His two friends were sent to the front as combat troops:

> With no more than three or four days' rudimentary training in the use of firearms, the newly formed platoons were dispatched to the front line to join the regular army to defend the island of Singapore. One of my two friends was sent to the Sungei Kranji area and the other to the Bukit Timah area ... There were reports that Dalforce units fought valiantly and some of them made the supreme sacrifice.[56]

As Dalforce became a legend, however, this focussed on the abstract idea of the bravery of poorly armed volunteers, rather than individuals, let alone its British officers.[57] There was a gap between the legend, and the reality that some ex-Dalforce fighters felt largely forgotten. Choi's postwar experience can tell us why this should be so.

After the surrender, Siew Hong destroyed his uniform, and he and his two English-educated college friends returned to Malaya, to their homes. They spent the rest of the war in fear of arrest and execution. Siew Hong recalled that, "I waited until May [1942] when the Malayan Railway was started, then went to Kuantan". His priority was not to be recognised as ex-Dalforce. The Malay District Officer at Kuantan asked him to attend a Japanese-run course in Singapore, but he replied, "maybe I will go in the second batch". Then, in October 1942, a friend asked him to go to Pontianak in Borneo to join their family trading business. "I thought that was a jolly good idea as I would be away from a place where I could be known [Singapore] ..."[58] There he married and had two children.

After the war, Siew Hong was classified "displaced" and flown to Singapore. He worked as a teacher there and in Kuantan. When Raffles College became the University of Malaya, he returned, graduating in 1954 with a First Class honours degree in economics. This allowed him to join the Malayan Civil Service in 1955, working in the Treasury, Ministry of Commerce and Industry, and the Economic Secretariat in the Prime Minister's Department. Finally, he joined the central bank of Malaya, Bank Negara, in 1958, becoming Deputy Governor from 1966–1972.

For Siew Hong, therefore, life returned to its prewar path of learning and using economics, motivated by the trauma of the Depression. He entered a financial and government world which was mainly Malay and English-speaking. Dalforce thus remained "just one week of my life", of little relevance to fellow Malaysian civil servants and bankers. He occasionally met Raffles College Dalforce veteran Hiew Kiang Mian, until Hiew migrated to Australia. The third Raffles College veteran, Yap Siew Choong, died in a truck accident during the Occupation. Although he was awarded the medals that went with being a Dalforce member, the Burma Star and 1939–1945 Star, Siew Hong lost them. He never mixed with other veterans. Regarding its communist majority, Siew Hong remarked, "they were suspicious of me, I am sure, because I was not part of their gang".[59]

Siew Hong demonstrates that the impact of the war on people's lives often depended as much on their response to the Fall, as on the military campaign itself. He felt that "no one has ever shown any interest" in "just one week of my life" in February 1942. His sense of the force's ephemeral nature — like a firefly in the night — contrasts with the holding up of Dalforce as heroes in Singapore. Malaysian nationality distanced him from the Singapore state's decision to emphasise Dalforce's heroism. Choi's English-language education also distanced him from the Chinese-language presentation of Dalforce as heroes, even if Chinese-language books, *The Price of Peace* (1995, later made into a TV series) and *Eternal Vigilance* (1999), were eventually translated into English.[60] What ethnicity you identified with, the ideology you supported in 1942, the country you lived in, the language you were educated in and which your friends spoke, all affected the way you framed wartime experiences. While amongst the Chinese-speaking the volunteers did quickly became a "legend", in English-speaking circles, they remained until recently a relatively neglected army.[61]

What all Dalforce volunteers shared after February 1942, regardless of their party affiliation, was an urgent need to disappear. Eurasians in the local volunteer forces, by contrast, had a more awkward decision. Could they pose as "Asian"? Or did loyalty, skin colour or job mark them out as too close to the British? Victor Grosse, a member of the Eurasian Company of the Singapore Volunteer Corps, chose captivity with Europeans. He went to Changi and then to work on the Burma-Thailand Railway with other POWs. Victor recalled that, after "some demeaning work for a day" to demonstrate to all that Asians were now in charge, he was taken to Changi.[62]

For British and Australians, this "demeaning" continued. Amusement at this Japanese obsession could, and frequently did, lead to a bashing.[63] Don Lee recalled one incident at Kanu Camp no. 2 on the Burma-Thailand Railway:

> … one night in the cutting we were having a ten-minute rest. The Japs were wolfing down bowls of rice and salted fish while we sat around in the light of bamboo fires. The Japs started throwing bits of fish to us. Not a soul stirred and the food lay on the ground. The Nips laughed, but they were furious and I'll bet we paid for snubbing them.[64]

This was at a time when vitamin deficiency and ulcers were pushing many towards amputations or death. The Japanese remained self-conscious about their country's struggle to modernise, and its mission to free Asians from white rule. Superiority had to be demonstrated, not just to POWs, but also to other Asians. The march to Changi — with 50,000 Australian and British soldiers traipsing up to 12½ miles (20 kilometres) on 17 February — provided an early opportunity.

Another of the 2005 forum speakers, Mohd Anis bin Tairan, was then 10 years old. He watched the procession from his attap (palm leaf)-roofed house at Siglap, along Singapore's East Coast Road:

> From City Hall, the prisoners of war were forced to walk to Changi Prison. The Japanese told us village folk to stand by the roadside in order to shame the whiteman, who had once been the big masters, the maharajas, bosses, the most important people. Now they had become the small people, lowly. The white man had fallen. The Japanese had risen.[65]

Anis described how "all the people go to the road side to see what happened to the *orang puteh* [white people] … The Japanese looked proud … But we also bow, not just to the Japanese, but to the prisoners".[66] Don Lee recalled that, despite the risk of punishment, "kindly Malays and Chinese stepped out from the crowds lining the routes and offered drinks and even food".[67]

The memories of Asian civilians such as Anis, meanwhile, are mostly of living under Japanese rule, learning a little of the Japanese language, and of hunger and eating rice-substitutes such as tapioca. For them, the fear of massacre or sexual assault of February to March 1942 morphed into the banality of everyday occupied life, and finally into a period of increasingly desperate shortages in 1944–1945. There was, therefore, not one undifferentiated civilian experience of "Occupation", but rather qualitatively different experiences over the three main phases of terror, mature administration, and decay.[§]

Mohd Anis was directly exposed to the terror of the first phase, in early 1942. Though a Malay child, he was to witness the massacre of Singapore Chinese. On 18 February, the day after Anis saw European POWs march to Changi, Lieutenant General Tomoyuki Yamashita (Commander, Japanese 25th Army) gave a key order. He instructed garrison commander Major General Kawamura Saburo to "*tekisei kakyo no genju shobun*" (dispose of hostile Chinese with severe punishment). The Chinese were to be screened for anti-Japanese elements, and the latter executed without trial.

The Japanese had in mind several types of undesirables. These included Chinese who had been involved in fundraising to support China in its war against Japanese, for instance through Tan Kah Kee's China Relief Fund, or the National Salvation Movement.[68] Also high on the wanted list were Dalforce members.[69] In Japanese memory, the Army command's insistence that the operation be completed in three days — despite appeals by local commanders that this was impossible — added to its arbitrary nature.[70] It is difficult to gauge Japanese soldiers' memories, given the postwar dangers of prosecution or moral condemnation. But some Japanese soldiers and police felt the action was hasty, and the victims far from obviously "guilty". Henry Frei tells the story through the eyes of Private Miyake Genjiro, a Hiroshima conscript in the 5th Division who assisted a similar massacre in Malaya:

> [In central Malaya …] Seventy people were loaded into Miyake's truck, standing up. They had six trucks and in this way could pack 400 people.
>
> They drove to a rubber plantation ten minutes away. There they led the captives into the rubber trees, where their commander stood waiting for them. Sixty Chinese were assigned to Miyake and his comrades.

[§] The intensifying shortages in Malaya were symptoms of the wider disintegration of Japan's imperial system, as its merchant fleet losses became critical from 1944 onwards.

'Now you must obey orders', the commander said. 'You must now kill the Chinese'. Kill. They had to kill them. Miyake and colleagues harboured no hostility against their assigned group. They had been done no harm by the Chinese people, they had no reason to take their lives … They were human beings. People.

To raise their will to kill the people, the officer in charge of them said: 'You are about to kill these people by order of the highest general, the Emperor'. Then he proceeded to cut off the heads of two of them. He did it with his saber [sabre]. The blood came out in a hissing sound — 'shooo!' — and spurted two or three metres into the air, spraying around'.

Another 12 were beheaded, the rest stabbed. A ghastly stench of blood pervaded the rubber trees. All 400 were dumped into a big trench and buried. Miyake's impression was that about half of them were not yet dead, and buried alive.

'The emperor now orders you to kill these …,' Miyake never ceased asking himself: Does the emperor have this right?

Miyake's taste for wide reading and distaste for indoctrination made him an atypical conscript. But the sense of an overcondensed, out-of-control operation in Singapore was pervasive. The very audaciousness of Japanese operations, involving successive waves sweeping further and further into the Southeast Asia, persuaded the army command to insist on the impossible: effective screening in three days.

In the days following 18 February, Chinese in Singapore were concentrated by Japanese military police (*kempeitai*), at screening centres, assisted by army detachments. Up to three layers of screening were meant to select anti-Japanese Chinese for execution with the help of local informers and captured lists, releasing the others with a "passed" stamp. Dalforce survivor Choi Siew Hong recalls how:

> I knew the Japanese would be after me, after those who had joined the force, so, of course, I took off my uniform and threw it away …[71]

Unable to return home to Kuantan, he stayed with a friend in Singapore's Geylang area. He recalled how:

> the Japanese rounded up all the residents of the area and took them to Telok Kurau English School, and very innocently I took my [requisitioned] car that day with some rations and I went with my friends to Telok Kurau … We were rounded up in the afternoon and stayed at night. The next morning they lined us up on a field. I was sitting down there. The Japanese spies pointed out if you could

stand up or sit down. There was a neighbour who was pointed out. We said, sit down! We pulled him down. Those who were taken away I think they were shot. Then in the evening, they let us out.[72]

As Siew Hong was leaving the compound, he was called back by a guard, who mistook his identity disc for a watch. Realising his mistake, the guard let him go.[73] He was lucky. Of all the screening centres, Telok Kurau English School was the one responsible for the largest massacre. On 23 February 1942, it dispatched around 1,500 on 32 trucks. At the 7½ mile point of East Coast Road, they drove a quarter of a mile inland, up a dirt road called Jalan Puay Poon. This road was near Kampong Siglap where Anis lived. The Japanese forced the villagers to dig large trenches, then shooed them away as they set up machine guns. Anis describes how:

> From my house at where Woo Mon Chew Road is today, I heard the machine gun fire start after about nine, and it did not stop until well after three in the afternoon. I was very scared. I dared not go have a look. In the afternoon, there was thick smoke coming from the valley. A horrible stench in the air lasted for several days, and for many days we could not bear to eat.
>
> Only two or three weeks later did my brother and I finally resume in the valley our regular household chores of gathering *daun simpuh*, leaves for the making of *kuih*, or cakes, to be sold by our mother. We saw parts of about ten bodies poking out of the ground. My brother was more scared than me. I was thinking it's scary but they're dead anyway, and we have to work.
>
> I found a Japanese helmet and bayonet there, and I kept them even though my mother told me to get rid of them.[74]

He added, "Mr Ong and my Chinese friends at the Siglap market [near Telok Kurau screening centre], one day they are all gone, taken by truck to Puay Poon".[75]

The area was the scene of a massive exhumation of thousands of victims' bodies from 1962–1966. The press called it the "valley of death" and "valley of tears".[76] The remains of the victims and their personal effects were recovered by the Singapore Chinese Chamber of Commerce.[77] The skeletal remains were placed in urns under Singapore's Civilian War Memorial in 1966. The personal effects were later donated to the Singapore History Museum and some put on exhibition in 2008. Included in the collection were many expensive watches, a doctor's wallet, and a large number of gold false teeth (the latter stored away and not put on display).

The hundreds of items recovered from Jalan Puay Poon indicate the wealth of the middle-class Chinese living in Singapore's Katong area. The occupiers would soon tap this Chinese wealth by a forced community "donation" of $50 million Straits dollars. Meanwhile, doubts remain about how discriminately victims had been singled out. They were selected at Telok Kurau English School as "anti-Japanese" by the Japanese military, police and soldiers, with Chinese detectives assisting. All these were under the operational command of the *kempeitai* (military police) commander Onishi Satoru.[78] During the 1962–1966 exhumations, the discovery of women's earrings, watches, and rings, and children's anklets and bracelets, raises questions. Were some women, or children, caught up in the screening? Did men conceal valuables to safeguard them, or in hope of buying safety? The *sook ching* or "screening" is usually depicted as a massacre almost entirely of men, with women and children sent home.[79]

The massacre that Anis heard engulfed thousands of Chinese with limited rhyme and reason. Credible estimates range from 20,000 upwards, with some Chinese organizations claiming a toll as high as 50,000.** Whatever the final tally, the massacre etched on the Chinese consciousness a sense of intense, ethnically-specific victimhood. As Goh Sin Tub — then a boy and later to become a major Singapore writer and poet, would write, for the Japanese it became "The shame you cannot speak".

Some Chinese fought back. A few members of Dalforce made it to India or Ceylon (Sri Lanka) and enlisted in Britain's Force 136. They were then sent back by submarine or aircraft to liaise with the communist guerrillas in Malaya's jungles. Others joined the communist-led resistance force more directly: the Malayan People's Anti-Japanese Army (MPAJA). There they joined Chinese villagers, and communists such as the 17-year-old Ong Boon Hua. Boon Hua, barely out of Chinese-language and a little English-language education in Sitiawan, Perak, was already a communist organiser amongst workers and students. When Singapore fell:

> in the guerrillas, I became the Fourth Company party representative for only four months. We set up on the day of the fall of Singapore:

** The remains of 20,000 or more are estimated to be buried under Singapore's Civilian War Memorial. It is likely that significant numbers of additional victims were never recovered. For Japanese estimates, see also p. 139 below.

15 February. That day, I led ... roughly twenty persons, we rode bicycles in two groups, from Tanjong Tualang down to Tanjong Malim ... Half way on the journey, the Japanese trucks passing over, shouted Bansai! Bansai! We wondered what had happened ... But we proceed to Tanjong Malim. I was in the army only four months. Then I was transferred out to State Committee [of the Malayan Communist Party, the political arm of the movement] ...[80]

So began an odyssey that would see Boon Hua become communist liaison officer with Britain's Force 136 in 1943, when the latter's senior officers arrived from India and Ceylon by submarine. One of the aliases he took was Chin Peng. Under that name, he would become Secretary-General of the Malayan Communist Party (MCP) in 1947. For many Chinese of his generation, the several thousand anti-Japanese fighters were heroes who, by spilling blood in Malaya, made the communist party "Malayan". Previously, it had been as much an offshoot of China politics as of local concerns. The postwar communist recourse to revolt in 1948–1960 (the Malayan Emergency) would result in the exclusion of these people's memories from state-sponsored "nationalist" stories. Only after the final end of insurgency in 1989, would ex-fighters be able to argue openly for greater recognition in Malaysia. As we will see in later chapters, that argument continued into the 21st century.

The majority of Malaya's civilians, of course, did not escape to the jungle. Many remained on estates and smallholdings. Tens of thousands of Chinese moved onto land on the jungle fringe as squatters, to survive by farming, and to keep their distance from the Japanese. Many of these forged close links with the MPAJA in the jungle. Still more remained in and around the big towns such as Singapore, which was renamed *Syonan-to* or Light of the South by the Japanese.

Anis was amongst this latter category. After seeing the aftermath of the *sook ching*, he had to work out how to survive under Japanese authority. His choices would be made in the context of incipient Malay nationalism, and yet also of the *kampong* (village) spirit of serving immediate family and community interests first, regardless of changing regimes.

One of the influences on the young Anis was the *Kesatuan Melayu Muda* (KMM, Union of Malay Youth), which was established in May 1937 in Kuala Lumpur, and officially registered in August 1938. It was the first Malay organisation to have as its objective the end of British rule. The other main objective was to create a *Melayu Raya* or greater Malaysia, in which Malaya and Singapore would join the Dutch East

Indies. KMM was founded by teacher and journalist Ibrahim Yaacob. Membership was strong among the alumni of Sultan Idris Training College (Tanjong Malim, Perak), who were teachers in Malay vernacular schools. This explained why the KMM had branches in all nine Malay states plus Singapore within a year of founding.[81] Some KMM engaged in prewar intelligence work for the Japanese, believing Japan would give them independence. Between 13–18 December 1941, the British arrested 150 members and held them in Changi Prison.

Upon British defeat, these KMM members were released, and assisted the Japanese administration. But the Japanese were not prepared to give independence, and banned KMM. They preferred to integrate KMM personnel directly into Japanese-controlled units, installing its leadership in volunteer forces: the *Giyugun* (volunteer army), *Giyutai* (volunteer corps), and *Heiho* (volunteer auxiliaries). KMM leader Ibrahim Yaacob was given the rank of Lieutenant Colonel and command of the *Giyugun*. This army also took the same name as its Indonesian counterpart, *PETA* (*Pembala Tanah Air*, Avengers of the Motherland).[82] These were perceived as future national liberation armies by KMM members.

A high number of Malay villages had a few KMM members, many of whom were schoolteachers.[83] The young Anis was influenced by the two KMM members of Kampong Siglap, especially teacher Idris bin Daud Mhd. Shah, whose father was the *penghulu* (village head). Anis remembered that, "on the day he was arrested and imprisoned in Changi Prison, the villagers were surprised to learn of his anti-British activities and co-operation with the Japanese". Idris afterwards accompanied Japanese army officers' visits to villagers "to hear about their problems".[84] After the war, he was tried for "collaboration", but Anis described the KMM's spying for the Japanese as "a tactic for *merdeka*" (independence). The KMM were "not for the Japanese, not for others [colonial rule], but for *merdeka*".[85]

The line between playing community protector — which involved fulfilling some Japanese demands — and being "collaborator" was dangerously thin. None knew this more than Eric Paglar, aged 76 when he spoke to the forum in 2005. His father, Doctor Charles Paglar, was a Eurasian. This small group was in a particularly difficult situation because it was so closely identified with the British. While some Eurasians such as Victor Grosse were members of the volunteer forces and so became POWs, others such as Eric Paglar's father remained at liberty.

Dr Charles Paglar accepted Japanese entreaties to act as a community leader and an intermediary. In 1943, the Japanese then asked for Eurasian volunteers to establish an agricultural settlement at Bahau, on the Malayan mainland. Dr Paglar found himself drawn into this project to relieve pressure on food supplies. Eric saw his father try to help the settlers, but many died of diseases such as malaria. They could not adapt to farming life after having served the British in office work.[86] After the war, Charles Paglar was tried for collaboration and imprisoned during his trial at Pearl's Hill Gaol. At the forum, Eric read from the prayer book his father had kept when alone in gaol: "Saviour of my community. Helper of the poor and suffering. Victor of a glorious struggle. Singer of a noble cause. Now inmate of Pearl's Hill gaol. Such are the honours of my life". Eric recalled how his father had told him that, "I saved my people, my community, now I am being stabbed in the back". Paglar's trial was aborted after the Japanese backed his claim that he had little choice, and he later re-emerged as a leader of his community.

Anis' Kampong Siglap, meanwhile, was not a hotbed for KMM nationalist-collaborators. Other villages, such as Singapore's Kampong Tanglin were more radical. Kampong Tanglin villager Ismail bin Zain claimed that:

> the Malays, they welcomed the Japanese to come to Singapore ... when the Japanese were in Singapore they were very friendly, they were, I mean, very nice to all people, it is not only the Malays, but to all. And you see, the Malays was thinking, you see, that the British was not giving the Malays any, I mean, benefit ... if the Japanese come and occupy Singapore, then the new master may be much better than the British.
>
>   And ... they promised, see, about the co-prosperity sphere, that is for all the Southeast Asia ... Another thing, they also promised, this is what I heard from the KMM people ... to ... give independence ... But when they saw the Japanese brutality after some time they loathed the Japanese very much, you see ... after a few months.[87]

Kampong Tanglin was clearly nationalist before the Occupation, but for Kampong Siglap, Anis tells us that:

> The *merdeka* feeling came during the Japanese time because of the voice of Sukarno, the first president of Indonesia; during the time of books from Indonesia and the special market for them in Singapore.

Also Singapore and Sumatra were under one government during the Japanese time. We would get books and other propaganda and study it. There were old men and people who did not know how to read, so I would read it to them ...[88]

Anis recalled propaganda that, "We are brothers ... [the Japanese] are the elder brother. We are an independent nation. You are under the British or Dutch government. Why don't you live together with big brother, and be an independent nation?"[89]

Anis eventually attended a *Heiho* technical training school at Balastier Road, where, "they trained us to be like a Japanese ... We also had the *botak* [shaven] head ... I studied how to be a gentleman. They taught me Japanese martial arts, judo, kendo, jujitsu. The Japanese were tough. Once we learn, we must know. Prepare. Prepare. Prepare ..."[90] He described what motivated him, "We were very scared. They asked us something. We don't know. Bang!", and the stress on games:[91]

Half an hour would be set aside for exercise in the mornings. Self-defence martial arts classes like judo were also scheduled. A special wooden rifle called the *ju-ken* was used as a weapon to stab parts of the enemy's body which were marked either at the neck, heart or abdomen. A favourite weapon would be the wooden sword called the *kendo* which was used to hit the neck to slice off the head or other parts of the body. This sport required the players to wear armour from head to foot. During the weekends, competitions were held to select the best of the best in these sports and every year, all sorts of sporting competitions and races were organised.[92]

Many young men, like Anis, responded well to some of the more idealistic or physical aspects of Japanese training and education. Yet Anis' elder brother, Said bin Tairan (born 1920), had fought with the British. Anis also described this in terms of pride:

He served in the British army Royal Engineer 34 Company and Royal Artillery — First Malay Battery ME 314 in charge of the air attack searchlights (AA search light). He was trained in Port Dickson Camp as a Malay soldier in Malaya. He served at Bukit Lunchu, South Johor, opposite the Seletar Naval Base in Singapore. He attacked and shot down Japanese fighter planes attacking Singapore. Then he was transferred to the Infantry unit at MacRitchie Reservoir, Thomson Road and managed to capture a Japanese tank. When Singapore fell Lieutenant Arthur Slade, who was in charge of Said bin Tairan's unit, instructed his soldiers to disguise themselves as civilians to avoid capture from the Japanese as prisoners of war.[93]

Anis described how when the Japanese exacted revenge on Malays who had fought for the British, they only looked for the "Malays in the green sarongs [the dress uniform of the Malay Regiment], not those in the blue-black sarong [of the Malays in the Royal Engineers]".[94] Anis' brother in the Royal Engineers was left alone.

Anis recalled how another elder brother, Saleh bin Tairan (born in 1925), joined the Japanese volunteer military units:[95]

> The late Saleh graduated from Victoria School in 1941. He then served in the Japanese Royal Navy (*Giyugun*) as a cadet wearing number E7 based in Seletar. The training was really intensive, tough and dangerous. He was sent to the siren unit as well as… the engineering unit.
>
> From all the training he received, he was able to secure a job as an engineer when Malayan Airways was first set up while also volunteering in the Royal Navy Volunteer Reserve as the leader of the siren unit of the ship he was in charge of. He helped protect the Malaya waters, now Malaysia, during the Confrontation between Malaysia and Indonesia. He then became a lecturer at Singapore Polytechnic.[96]

For Anis and his brothers, joining the military — British or Japanese — was an opportunity to fulfill the Malay military tradition, and to access resources and skills that would sustain themselves, their families, their *kampongs*, and the wider Malay community. They exhibited an instrumental view towards their choice of employer, rather than seeing such decisions in terms of loyalty and collaboration. They also followed the words of Hang Tuah, the Malay martial hero from the 15th-century Melaka (Malacca) kingdom, that it was the duty of Malays to help keep united so that "*takkan Melayu hilang di dunia*" (the Malays will never disappear off the face of the earth).[97]

Anis followed his second elder brother, Saleh bin Tairan, by training for the Japanese volunteer forces. The technical school he attended taught him how to be a mechanic, building trucks for the Japanese auxiliary force, *Heiho*.[98]

Indoctrination was a key element to his education:

> … my fellow workers and I were taught as students to be good Japanese citizens in all aspects of life. For example, when the sun rose in the sky, we were instructed to face the east and recite after the Japanese teacher. The recited words were a kind of oath to pledge allegiance to the Japanese Emperor.[99]

Anis was about to be sent to Japan for further training when the war ended. For him, the impact of the Occupation was critical, "We now started to try to be independent, to have *merdeka*. We had been ruled by the Portuguese, Dutch, English, and Japanese, but now how to be independent? How to have *merdeka*?"[100] Many young Malays felt like this, especially those from the Japanese volunteer armies. They were *pemuda*, nationally conscious Malay youth. These sentiments formed the basis of the Malay Nationalist Party, founded in October 1945 by former KMM leaders, and its youth organisation, *Angkatan Pemuda Insaf* (API, generation of aware youth).

Anis' story reflects the way many Malays experienced the war as a time of heightened nationalist feeling, without this necessarily dictating that they join one side or the other, or feeling that this necessitated violent nationalism after the war. Talking about classmates who joined the radical API group, Mohd Anis remarked, "my word, there were lots of them" in the immediate postwar period. But after the British banned API in July 1947, he "took the advice of my religious teachers who said, 'Now is a time to keep out of politics'".[101] Instead, he started training as a teacher at Sultan Idris Training College. He worked in Indonesia for two years, returned as a Malay language teacher, and then trained Malay teachers at the Singapore Teachers' Training College.

Plate 2.3 Mohd Anis bin Tairan being interviewed by Kevin Blackburn, 2004

Conclusion

For Das, Siew Hong and Anis, the 2005 public forum provided a public platform that they otherwise lacked. The media attention and respect given to veterans in the mainstream of war memory, such as Don, rubbed off on them and ensured that marginalised voices were heard, and broadcast along with the normally more dominant voices.[102] The event acted as a partial antidote for the dominance of national war memories by others, notably white male POWs imprisoned at Changi and sent to work on the Burma-Thailand Railway, and the mainly Chinese victims of Japanese massacres. It also allowed them to voice the more complex realities of occupation, rather than nationalist simplifications. That people such as Das, Siew Hong and Anis feel their memories are marginalised also confirms what French sociologist Halbwachs writes: that we tend to remember the past in terms of groups, not merely as individuals. A community's collective commemoration, symbols, and rituals may validate, ignore or even reshape its members' individual memories.

The tension between the kaleidoscopic variety of individual experiences, and the way groups frame their memories after the event, may grow over time. Collective memories are formed and finessed from selected personal memories, to which most members of a group can subscribe to. As group members interact and recall the past in their day-to-day lives, they do this in social groups based on unit, class, religious, or ethnic ties. This process reinforces some memories while allowing others to fade. Memories are then reshaped according the myths the community wants to remember the past by. In its turn, a community may adapt its "collective memory" over time to suit changing needs.[103] In short, while events happen, memory constantly evolves.[104]

Alistair Thomson in his work on oral history has also noted how some veterans — whose own memories do not fit into the broader collective memory of their veteran group — feel marginalised. Thomson observed that most veterans take their cues from the mythology generated by veterans' organisations. They may even publicly "misremember" so that they can feel a full part of the group, and of its identity-affirming myths. Thomson was exploring how some Australian Anzacs from the First World War felt antagonistic to the legend of the fearless Anzac, while others incorporated it into their own accounts, even where their experience did not entirely conform to the stereotype.[105]

Building upon Halbwachs' work, Paul Connerton notes how commemorative ceremonies can play a key role in providing frameworks for remembering war.[106] Individuals take cues not just from their social group, but also from such social events. In commemorative events, a wider community is reminded of its identity through the way a story is told about the past. Many of these narratives are about personal sacrifice for the good of the wider community. Connerton also argues that these collective memories shape representations of the past in popular culture, such as in books, movies, and television. These may employ similar stories about events, and portray similar common characteristics of the group. Such devices can help to bind the group together. We should not be surprised, then, if some of the wartime generation focus on those parts of their story which can be framed as serving a wider, nationalist purpose: as in Das' and Bhupalan's INA experience.

If memories of war are mainly expressed in groups, this raises important questions. How have the major ethnic groups of Singapore and Malaysia — Malays, Chinese and Indians — interpreted the Fall and Occupation? What if anything has the collective memory been of Das' INA among Indians, of Siew Hong's Dalforce among the Chinese, and of Anis' Malay volunteer units among the Malays? To what degree have the experiences of large groups of people — such as Asian labourers on the Burma-Thailand Railway — been addressed or neglected by their own communities?

Above and beyond ethnic communities, there is also the question of state-sponsored "collective memory". James V. Wertsch has argued that nation-states create historical narratives "grounded in textual resources" for their own purposes. These are created by official bodies of nation-states, and then "consumed" by the public, so that they may even become the dominant "collective memory".[107] In the context of Malaysia and Singapore, how have these states tried to shape "collective memory"? How accurately do these state-level "collective memories" match actual experiences of the wartime generation? How successful have these states been in establishing their preferred stories about the war as accepted "collective memory", in the face of individual and community contestation?

The chapters that follow will show how — notwithstanding state efforts in Malaysia and Singapore up to the 1980s — communities and individuals continued to shape their own memories, and at times to press for these to be accepted or acted upon at national level. Hence, we will continue to detail not just community narratives, but, within them, the personal narratives of people such as Das, Choi, Anis, Ong Boon Hua (Chin Peng) and the wartime generation more generally.[108]

In Chapters 3 to 9, we will look at the relationship between personal memories such as these, and each wider community's "collective memory". Hence, there will be chapters on the Europeans, Chinese, Malays, and Indians. This will allow us to ask how the personal confirms, enriches, and contradicts group memories. How do individual Chinese memories fit with broader community representations of the war (Chapters 4 on the "Overseas Chinese War Hero" and 5 on "Chinese victimhood")? How do Indian communities square heroic stories of the INA with the suffering of workers conscripted onto the Burma-Thailand Railway (Chapter 6)? How do Malay narratives deal with the contrast between Malays who fought the Japanese — for instance in the Malay Regiment — and those who joined Japanese-sponsored groups (Chapter 7)?

Throughout these chapters, we will keep returning to oral history accounts. These allow us to test community (and later state) memory against individual memories. They allow us to restore the true variety of experience. But oral history interviews do more than that. In the words of Alessandro Portelli, they "tell us not just what people did, but what they wanted to do, what they believed they were doing, and what they now think they did".[109] Insofar as people's thoughts determine actions, oral history can cut to the heart of what made history unfold as it did. Hence, the 16-year-old Ms Rasammah Navarednam's passionate embrace of the INA — almost a death wish in the service of romantic nationalism — demands analysis of how she felt at the time. She was trying to mould her life into a wider story of heroic Indian nationalism, one with a pedigree stretching from the Rani of Jhansi, through violent Bengali nationalists, to an imagined future where her unit would spark revolt. In short, it is our job to give an impression not only of what happened, but of what happenings meant to people at the time, and as time unfolded afterwards.

COMMUNITIES

CHAPTER 3

The European Prisoner of War as Hero and Victim

THIS CHAPTER TRACES THE WAY BRITISH AND Australians tried to shape the memory of the Fall and Occupation of Malaya. It details their attempt to turn their defeat, and shame at Malaya's wartime fate, into something that could buttress empire, and provide a balm for the traumas many of them had experienced. It makes sense to start here, because Europeans who had been POWs and internees returned to play a major part in the postwar colonial state, and as such were in a position to try and set the tone for war memory in Malaya and Singapore alike. As decolonisation gathered pace in the 1950s, the local political elites would have to deal with the legacy of European monuments and commemorative practices.

The process of trying to shape war memories began soon after British and Indian troops started reoccupying Malaya, with their arrival in Singapore from 5 September 1945. They quickly set about selecting images of European victories and heroism which they could project to the local population. Soon afterwards, they also began to refashion the public image of the European POW and internee, to be a hero as well as a victim. This work seemed urgent. For the preceding three and a half years had all but destroyed the prestige of the *orang puteh* (white man).

For Europeans, this decline in prestige had been as sudden as it was traumatic. Right down to December 1941, they had continued to live as Malaya's privileged elite of civil servants, masters of business, professionals, planters, and agency house managers: their tropical life-styles graced by *amahs*, cooks, gardeners, and Cold Storage shops. While the war in Europe had brought blackouts, rationing, and the Blitz to London, it actually fuelled demand for Malaya's dollar-earning tin and rubber. Food and the locally brewed Tiger Beer flowed freely, night-time dances continued at Raffles Hotel. The sight of soldiers in khaki on the streets, and aircraft above, lent to "Fortress Singapore" an air of invulnerability.

For the white population, life in this rapidly growing cosmopolitan city of 720,000 had never been better.[*][1] The Cathay cinema had opened near the seafront, and air conditioning had found its way into a few shops and houses.[2] Even the enervating humidity need not trouble Europeans over-much. In the daytime, they could drive by car or ride in a "coolie"-drawn rickshaw; in the evenings, they could sip stengahs (whisky and soda water over ice), or lounge in the cool of a verandah, soothed by scent of frangipani, or the rustle of coconut trees.

There were not much more than 30,000 Europeans in Malaya and Singapore by early 1941, including women and children, out of a total population in excess of four million. Many of the women and children were evacuated before Singapore was surrendered. By then, some of the men had been killed defending Malaya. Several thousand more surrendered after fighting in the Federated Malay States and Straits Settlements Volunteers. After 15 February 1942, the latter were marched to the Changi POW camp. Later, many would labour on the Burma-Thailand Death Railway, alongside POWs such as Don Lee, whose story we told in Chapter 2.

In addition, about 3,000 British civilians, together with a few hundred children, became internees. Most of these were incarcerated first in Changi gaol — with its cells and guard towers — then from May 1944 at Sime Road. At the Sime Road camp, attap-roofed huts were surrounded by a few banana plants, to which internees soon added flowers. Governor Sir Shenton Thomas was among the small number of civilians who, together with senior military officers, suffered the further angst of being shipped off to labour in Japan (in his case) or Formosa (Taiwan).

In this way, a high percentage of prewar Malaya's adult British males became POWs or internees. For them, the war brought utter transformation, from a life of relative privilege to one of gnawing hunger, fear, and a struggle for survival. Defeat and captivity seared memories and eroded confidence. To grasp these surreal somersaults

---

[*] Singapore's population was 560,000 in 1931 and 938,144 in 1947.

in Europeans' fortunes is to go some way towards understanding their actions after liberation.

One of the big divisions in postwar Malaya would be between the "stayers" who became POWs or Sime Road veterans, and those who escaped or were extracted. June Ferguson's family and friends experienced most of this range of outcomes.[†3] Her fiancé and her sister's husband died in the final battle for Singapore. Family friends from Kuala Selangor were interned at Sime Road. Her parents — "Meg" and Captain Jack Ferguson, were planters in Malaya's Kuala Selangor district who were evacuated by ship along with June, in "Singapore's Dunkirk".[4] Decamped to Durban, they longed for home: which for them meant Malaya. In order to get part way back, June wrangled a job as governess in Ceylon in February 1944. Once in Ceylon with her family, contacts with fellow exiles landed a further post with Force 136. June even asked if she could be parachuted into Malaya, only to be "well snubbed". Finally, she was able to sail on one of the first ships into Singapore in September 1945.

June's vessel was packed full of "banana Colonels", as civilian administrators given military rank under the British Military Administration (BMA) were known. As it approached shore, Collyer Quay was buzzing with locals, some bartering cigarettes with the first British to land. Once on dry land, she made a beeline for Sime Road, past still-shuttered shops, in search of her friends from Kuala Selangor:

> At first sight they looked alright, if you forgot the fact that their gym shoes were tied on with string … their shorts just a maze of patches … their eyes like poor wild animals look in a very small cage. Their legs were just stalks … most of the men only wore 'V strings' … Just a bit of cloth held on by a piece of string … Nearly all had beri beri, but how cheerful they were … One brewed 'coffee', another produced soup made of weeds and tapioca … It was just awful though to see white men and women living like coolies, and walking the street on their poor swollen feet, some with no shoes and tattered socks.[5]

Amongst the "banana colonels" and officials was Oswald Gilmour. Gilmour numbered amongst an even smaller fraction of British Malayans.

[†] Later married and subsequently known as June Taylor.

Not only was he one of around 230 (out of around 2,000) white colonial employees still free after the Fall of Malaya and Singapore, but he made it all the way back to London.[6] What had saved him in 1942 was expert knowledge. As a Municipal Engineer in the Malayan Civil Service (MCS), he had been too valuable to spare for military duties, and valuable enough to ship out just before the final curtain fell on 15 February.

Once back in London, it was not long before Gilmour was snapped up by the Malayan Planning Unit (MPU). The MPU had been set up in July 1943 under the War Office, with Colonial Office cooperation, and with some ex-Malayan civil servants amongst its personnel. Colonel Ralph Hone headed the MPU. Colonel Harold Willan was eventually selected to take charge as Chief Civil Affairs Officer Malaya, and Colonel Patrick McKerron as Deputy Chief Civil Affairs Officer, Singapore.[7] The MPU's job was to prepare for reoccupation.

By the time Gilmour joined, a plan was emerging. The aim was to change Britain's Southeast Asian possessions from a mosaic of disparate territories, into a structure that would strengthen Britain's world power. The Federated Malay States (FMS: Perak, Selangor, Negeri Sembilan and Pahang) and Unfederated Malay States (Perlis, Kedah, Terengganu, Kelantan and Johor) would be refashioned into one "Malayan Union". Where before only Malays were citizens in Malay states, now there would be a common citizenship, and a central Executive and Legislature.

It was thought that reconquest, and then temporary rule by the BMA, would provide cover for the Malay sultans to be persuaded to hand sovereignty over to a new central state. The Malayan Union would then provide a platform on which to rebuild the economy. It would also provide the basis for introducing elections from the local level upwards — the first elections in Malaya — so as to engender a new, and multiracial, politics. This would induct "Malayans" — as Malays, Chinese and Indians would slowly become — into the art of self-government. The MPU planners thought the latter would take decades, as the old "plural society" — by which the different communities lived their lives using different customs and languages — eroded.

Singapore's fate was to be different. Prewar, it was the administrative centre of the Straits Settlements Colony, which also included Penang and Malacca. Penang and Malacca were now to become part of the Malayan Union. Singapore would be left as a separate Colony, and as Britain's military base east of Suez. The main reason for this was the

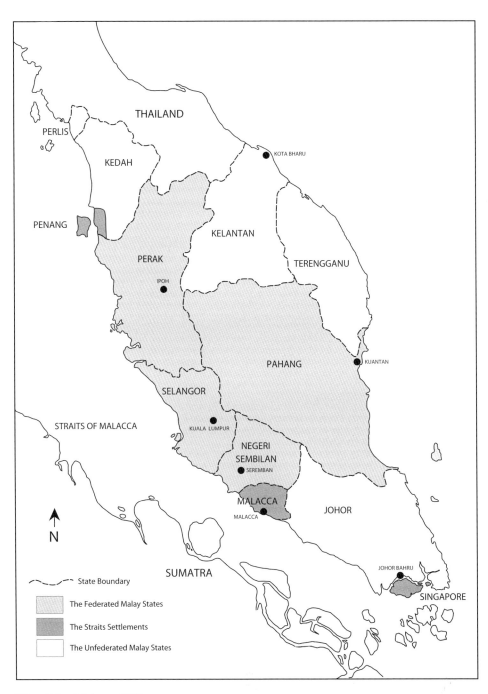

THAILAND

PERLIS

KEDAH

PENANG

PERAK

KOTA BHARU

KELANTAN

TERENGGANU

IPOH

PAHANG

SELANGOR

KUANTAN

STRAITS OF MALACCA

KUALA LUMPUR

NEGERI
SEMBILAN

SEREMBAN

MALACCA

MALACCA

JOHOR

SUMATRA

JOHOR BAHRU

SINGAPORE

N

State Boundary

The Federated Malay States

The Straits Settlements

The Unfederated Malay States

Map 3.1 Malaya, 1941

assumption that the Malays of the peninsula were not ready to accept Singapore's Chinese majority.

The icing on the cake would be a new British Governor-General for Southeast Asia, for which post the ex-Labour Government minister Malcolm MacDonald was selected.[‡] He was to coordinate policy between all British territories in the region, including the protectorate of Brunei and the new colonies of Sarawak (under its own British Rajas before Japanese occupation) and North Borneo (formerly under a British Chartered Company). MacDonald was to foster the long-term bringing together of Malaya and Singapore, if not of all British territories, into a Dominion of Southeast Asia. The latter was not, however, expected for decades, given the far less developed condition of the Borneo territories.[8]

The MPU's work was inextricably linked to the memory of the Fall of Singapore, and the fate of European POWs and internees. On 15 February 1944, MPU members gathered in London "to remember the Fall of Singapore". By the time they gathered on 15 February 1945, the unit had moved to join Southeast Asia Command (SEAC) in India and Ceylon. They were now the potential civil administration for when SEAC reconquered Malaya, and Gilmour was calculating every pipe and part needed to resuscitate Singapore's services. But "the main thing, which we never forgot, was to get our fellow countrymen and the British peoples out of the hands of the enemy, and to see the flag again flying over Malaya".[9] By the Japanese surrender on 15 August 1945, they were preparing for imminent seaborne attack on Malaya, code-named Operation Zipper.[10]

What followed was an exasperating wait for the British to secure an official Japanese surrender in the SEAC region, which stretched from India to Indochina. Japanese generals were summoned to Rangoon (liberated by the British in May 1945). As soon as the Japanese signed a preliminary agreement there, a convoy of 30 or so ships — including HMS *Sussex* as the flagship, HMS *Derbyshire*, and troop, hospital and landing ships — left Rangoon on 20 August. Gilmour was aboard HMS *Derbyshire* as it steamed towards Singapore on "a dead-still sea".

On Sunday 2 September (the day General MacArthur took the main Japanese surrender on board USS *Missouri* in Tokyo Harbour), the

---

[‡] In 1948, the post of Governor-General was replaced by that of Commissioner-General for Southeast Asia, which also covered regional foreign policy. MacDonald filled the new post, staying until 1955.

convoy sighted northwest Malaya. It left a party at Penang. Gilmour's ship finally docked at Singapore on 5 September. He wondered: "Would our defeat in 1942 have destroyed all faith in the white man"?[11] His concern was heightened because the reoccupying force was mainly young Indian soldiers, led by British officers.

Gilmour disembarked at Singapore on the day they arrived, 5 September. This was just a day after the formal, local Japanese surrender of Malaya (onboard HMS *Sussex*), and three weeks after the Japanese Emperor's "endure the unendurable" broadcast of 15 August. As he drove into town, "There were children, who, though too young ever to have seen a white man who was not a prisoner, were waving little Union Jacks".[12] With Changi and Sime Road in mind, Gilmour noted the use of Japanese POWs to prepare for the formal surrender ceremony, to be held in Singapore on 12 September.

> The boot was on the other foot now, and the Japanese were put to work in Singapore. Care was taken that some of that work should

Plate 3.1   Australian ex-POWs watching Japanese POWs labour on Singapore's Padang, September 1945

be where it could be seen by then local people, and one of the most conspicuous places chosen was the Padang, or open area in front of the Municipal Building ...[13]

Gilmour was not alone in his angst about prestige. Ashley Gibson — a former editor of the *Malay Mail* — wrote in May 1945 that "when ex-Malayans gathered together" (in London that year), they agonised over "the impairment of our prestige in S.E. Asia ..."[14] Gibson fretted that it was fellow MCS members, many of whom were civilian internees, who would have to bear the heaviest burden of lost prestige. Ex-MCS man P. Curtis, struck a similar note in a May 1945 report, writing that "one of the earliest and greatest difficulties ... will be the enormous loss of prestige which the occupation of the country by the Japanese who had always been regarded by the Malays as a vastly inferior race will have cost us ..."[15] Curtis wanted the returning British to dramatise the restoration of justice. "I think," he wrote,

> that all Japanese commanders of the present civilian and Prisoner of War camps, and every Japanese who is proud to have committed any acts of atrocity against either civilians or prisoners of war should be tried, sentenced, and executed, in Malaya — and publicly ... I am positive that this ... is the only thing that will be understood by the uneducated classes of Malaya.

Curtis also wanted interned MCS men to re-assume old positions "with all possible pomp and ceremony", starting with "those officials who are now interned in Malaya ... immediately they have recovered their health ..."[16]

Others argued for even more demonstrative action. Flight Lieutenant Harold Hammett was a "banana" Flight Lieutenant, having been a prewar member of the MCS in Johor, and subsequently a POW.[17] He had quickly returned to work. On 1 November 1945, he wrote to the BMA's Johor Headquarters. By speaking to Johor's Asian population, he had learned that "the picture of the mad scramble to Singapore of British civilians and British military forces before the smashing advance of a victorious intoxicated Japanese Army" remained undimmed "in the eye of the people of Malaya".[18] Hammett argued that "A display of British arms — tanks, guns, aeroplanes — would do much to dispel the disillusion ... the R.A.F. could do valuable work by organising large flights of bombers and fighter formations over the country".[19] Since "the part that Britain played in the late war is still not known to the illiterate masses resident in the country", he also recommended telling the story of Britain's victories over radio, mobile loudspeakers, in the cinema, and by illustrated leaflets.

Hammett was especially concerned with countering the propaganda of the communist-led, Malayan People's Anti-Japanese Army (MPAJA). During the three-week hiatus between Japanese surrender in mid-August and the return of the British in early September 1945, this guerrilla force had taken control of many towns, held liberation parades, and tried "collaborators" in kangaroo courts.

The Malayan Communist Party (MCP) had also issued an Eight Point Proposition on 25 August. Point 2 called for "a democratic government in MALAYA with the electorate drawn from all races of each State and the anti-Japanese Army". Point 4 called for freedom of speech, publications and societies. Point 6 added demands for educational and social improvements, a minimum wage, and an eight-hour day.

The progressive tone of these points was in advance of British plans, which only envisaged starting on local elections at an indeterminate date. It was April 1946 before the BMA would make way for civilian administration, in the form of the Malayan Union and the Colony of Singapore.[20] Hammett, meanwhile, warned the BMA about continuing MPAJA activities:

> In disseminating their propaganda they belittle the part that British arms have played in the final victory. It is they, and not the British, who have 'liberated' the peoples of Malaya from Japanese domination. And by what right do they British come back to dominate the country once more?[21]

The MCP were engaged in a semi-peaceful "united front" struggle to gain control of unions, and to influence politics towards early decolonisation. Major G. Walker, of the BMA Department of Publicity and Printing, was therefore keen to take up Hammett's recommendations. He sent crews with documentary films to show Britain's war victories to Malayans.[22]

Hammett's memorandum was also sent to BMA Headquarters at Kuala Lumpur. There Colonel John Dumeresque — prewar General Manager of the Malayan Broadcasting Corporation[23] — was now Director of the Publicity and Printing Department. Dumeresque saw himself as engaged in a long-term propaganda war to restore "British prestige in the Far East", and the military were thinking along similar lines.[24] On 23 September 1945, SEAC Headquarters charged its Political Warfare Division with propaganda aimed at "the restoration of Allied prestige in liberated countries".[25] On the same day, cinemas reopened in Singapore. The first film shown, three times a day at the Cathay, was *Desert Victory*.[26] *Desert Victory* was emblematic of the British — not the Americans or Soviets — reversing the tide of war. Directed by Roy Boulting in 1943, this black-and-white film spliced rousing music over authentic battle footage: a feat which the opening shots told the audience had cost the lives of six cameramen.

In *Desert Victory*, the Germans are shown halted just short of Cairo in Egypt. Then the British recover, and Field Marshal Montgomery is made commander in late 1942. He masses his forces for the second battle of El Alamein. The Home front is shown too, women and men churning out tanks and munitions, so that the conflict is integrated into the story of the war as a whole. Battle follows. More than 200,000 Allied troops and over 1,000 tanks penetrate German minefields in October to November 1942. Victory is won: the first decisive British victory after a string of defeats. This is the beginning of the end for German forces in Africa, and a harbinger of the reconquest of Europe. The stark desert, scale of events, and measured storytelling combine to convey epic conflict.[27]

Colonel Dumeresque's Publicity and Printing Department followed this up with a travelling photographic exhibition on Britain's victories in North African, Italian, European, and Burma campaigns. Commencing in Singapore on 14 January 1946, this toured Malaya during January and February.[28]

To pictures, the British added pageantry. On 6 January 1946, the colonial authorities arranged a ceremony at which the 16 colonial subjects, including Chinese from the MPAJA, Dalforce, Force 136, and three Malay resistance fighters, were honoured. Lord Mountbatten presented the Burma Star and the 1939–1945 Star to them on the footsteps of Singapore's Municipal Building (renamed City Hall after 1951). The eight members of the MPAJA who attended on 6 January were ambivalent about being decorated by a British commander. Amongst them was Chin Peng (alias Ong Boon Hua), who we met in Chapter 2 as the MCP's State Secretary in Perak, and liaison officer with Force 136. He noted that the authorities "had arranged an extensive military programme for us the following day".[29] They were to inspect Singapore's Sembawang Naval Base, Tengah airbase, and Alexandra Barracks. Chin Peng suspected a "propaganda exercise" to "demonstrate what surely faced us should we choose to challenge Britain's post-war right of return ..." The MPAJA members therefore boycotted the tour.[30] In contrast, the three Malay guerrillas were flown over Singapore in a Sunderland flying boat, treated to an aerobatics show at Seletar airbase, and then examined Spitfires, Harvards and captured Japanese aircraft.[31]

The British attempt to frame local efforts as part of one, larger British Empire war effort extended to holding a London Victory Parade on 8 June 1946. A 135-member Malayan contingent was sent, including a few communists (though not Chin Peng).[32] Similar parades were held in Malaya. At Johor Bahru, there was a Victory Parade of 700 British servicemen at which Sir Montagu Stopford, Acting Supreme Allied Commander for SEAC, took the salute. Major General Arkwright, commander of the 2nd Division, and Commodore Freidberger of *HMS Terror* (the Singapore naval base) sat astride horses named after European victories. The General rode "Rhine", the Commodore "Putot".[§][33]

The Malayan Campaign defeats were thus to be eclipsed by victories elsewhere. In Singapore, there was a Victory Exhibition at Happy World Amusement Park. It included a photographic collection called "Victory on Two Fronts". The most prominent photographs of the "East Asia Front" showed the atomic bombs on Hiroshima and Nagasaki. Those on the European front showed British soldiers. Franklin Gimson, the Governor of Singapore, opened it, and 25,000 people visited.[34]

War films were shown on Victory Parade Day, continuing the pattern of showing British heroes from the European theatre. These included the 1942 classic, *In Which We Serve*, directed by Noel Coward and David Lean. *In Which We Serve* showed British sailors from different class backgrounds rallying around their upper-class commander, merging into a team on a destroyer, and overcoming all odds and defeats, in a display of unity, and of national character in adversity, that preordained as-yet-to-be-won victories.[35]

Colonial responses to this propaganda onslaught were mixed. Choong Kum Swee, from Taiping, summed up Chinese opinion in a letter published in the *Straits Times* of 16 June 1946. He noted that "the 'V-Day' celebrations are meeting with a cold response". Choong contrasted this with Chinese readiness to stage large displays of lion dances and plays before the Japanese Occupation, in particular at the 1935 Jubilee celebrations for King George V:

---

§ Putot-en-Auge in Normandy was liberated by the British in August 1944.

The fire of rejoicing so easily kindled in 1935 now has to be fanned artificially. Are we really celebrating a victory won by the blood, sweat, tears and toil of many nations? Or is it just another game in which everyone 'puts on a smile' to please our rulers as in the days of Dai Nippon?[36]

Memorials

The British were aware of the need to do more to bind together local and British memories of the war. By 1946, the colonial authorities had established two committees to help plan memorials for all those (military and civilian) who had died. One would plan for Kuala Lumpur, the other for Singapore. They included members from diverse backgrounds, such as the Malay Regiment, MPAJA, and Eurasian members of the Volunteer Forces. But there was no agreement as to what form commemoration should take: scholarships, monuments, or otherwise. How could the insurgents of the MPAJA and the Malay Regiment, let alone British soldiers and Asian civilians be represented on one memorial? It was also too early after the war to raise significant funds. In 1948, colonial officials in Kuala Lumpur quietly shelved the idea, instead adding the dates "1939–1945" to the existing First World War Cenotaph.

This Kuala Lumpur Cenotaph was located near the main Railway Station (it has since been relocated to Kuala Lumpur's Lake Gardens). The monument was unveiled on 30 March 1924 by Sir Laurence Guillemard, the High Commissioner and Governor. It was one of many, built all around the empire in the 1920s, which echoed the form of the first, imperial Cenotaph, in Whitehall. The latter had been constructed in temporary form in 1919, and then in stone in 1920 as a focus for ceremonies which marked each anniversary of the Armistice (11 November 1918), by which First World War fighting was ended. It took the form of an "empty tomb" at which the fallen could be commemorated. The ceremonies also became linked, in people's minds, with the tomb of the "Unknown Warrior". This contained the unidentified remains of a soldier, which were brought back from France and interred in Westminster Abbey on 11 November 1920.

From 1920, the Whitehall Cenotaph became the location for the main British ceremony each Armistice Day (11 November), to mark the end of the First World War. The ceremony that year included a military parade, the laying of wreaths, the invocation to remember the dead and their sacrifice for the nation, two minutes' silence, and a bugle call. It was now recommended that there should be simultaneous ceremonies all over the empire. Other towns in England, and colonies, soon built their own cenotaphs.[37] Most featured steps up to a central column, which included a wreath carved in stone, and words along the lines of "The Glorious Dead" or (as in Singapore) "Our Glorious Dead". Some were almost identical copies of the original.[38]

Singapore's Cenotaph was unveiled on 31 March 1922 by the Prince of Wales. In this way, Malaya and Singapore joined the empire-wide act of remembrance, which once a year synchronised events in locations as diverse as Canterbury and Kuala Lumpur.[39] Armistice Day (after 1945 renamed Remembrance Day) became the moment when the main towns and cities of the United Kingdom and its empire were choreographed into a worldwide, simultaneous act of commemoration of past battles as well as — of equal importance — invocation to sacrifice in as-yet-to-be-fought struggles of the future.

In Singapore as in Malaya, the post-Second World War committee on commemoration at first favoured building a new, unifying monument or monuments. One suggestion was for a collection near Singapore's Bukit Timah (a central district, which contained its biggest hill). There, near today's Bukit Batok, a Japanese memorial to their war dead had stood from 1942–1945. This *Syonan Chureito* had been a 12-metre high obelisk (pillar) on a small hilltop. The location remained undeveloped, despite the Japanese taking down their memorial in 1945, and removing their dead to Singapore's Japanese cemetery. But there were objections, for instance, that the more numerous Chinese victims would need to be represented in a way sympathetic to their customs. Different communities' religious and cultural customs might demand different formats. Other suggestions for honouring the dead included a tuberculosis hospital, educational scholarships, or a community and arts centre.

The authorities also considered adapting the existing Cenotaph. The idea, as put forward in 1947, was to extend the plinth on the seaward side, and add two urns either side of this. One would contain the ashes of an "Unknown Soldier", the other the ashes of an "Unknown Civilian". At the same time, money would be put aside for educational scholarships. This idea of merging commemoration of Asian civilians and Empire soldiers was put to the public through newspapers and multilingual leaflets. The resounding sound of silence — as the public showed no enthusiasm — killed the idea stone dead.[40]

Plate 3.2 Singapore Cenotaph

Between the failure of proposals for a new memorial ground, or for adding urns to the Cenotaph, no further progress was made. In 1952, the disappointing outcome was a slight change to the Singapore Cenotaph, with the addition to it of the dates 1939–1945.[41]

This meant that the 11 November ceremonies at the Cenotaph continued, though the date, and the form of the monuments, had limited resonance for Asians. In July 1946, Britain's Remembrance Day services were changed from 11 November to every second Sunday in November.[42] Singapore and Malaya followed Britain's lead.[43] Remembrance Sunday gradually came to be used to remember the war dead from all wars. The *Straits Times* of 10 and 11 November 1947 reported that "men of two world wars, men who had fought in Malaya, and men who were in the resistance movement during the occupation", had lined up in front of the cenotaphs.[44] With the failure to build new state-sponsored monuments, remembrance remained symbolically lost amongst all the victorious wars of the British empire.[45]

So Remembrance celebrations continued to be held on the closest Sunday to 11 November each year. Yet the dominance Europeans had enjoyed when the cenotaphs were built was ebbing away. There was a communist-led insurgency in Malaya from 1948 (The Malayan Emergency of 1948–1960), Malay Muslim riots in Singapore in 1950, and rising student, trade union, communist and nationalist agitation. In April 1955, Singapore held its third postwar elections (after those of 1948 and 1951). For the first time, these allowed for elected Singapore ministers to form a local government under a local Chief Minister. This was to enjoy significant, if limited, internal self-government. David Marshall became the first local Chief Minister of Singapore, at the head of a Labour Front-led coalition.

Decolonisation now accelerated, more so in Malaya than Singapore, as counterinsurgency in the jungles succeeded, precisely as agitation in urban Singapore increased. On 31 August 1957, Malaya gained independence. In June 1959, Singapore, under the People's Action Party (PAP), achieved almost complete internal self-government.

In this environment, the Singapore Cenotaph's position along the seafront, close to the main municipal buildings and "Chinatown", made it vulnerable to protest. There was also one vital difference between the war dead of Malaya, and those of Britain and its settler Dominions such as Australia. Most of Britain's dead lay in foreign fields, and as such a cenotaph (empty tomb) offered a suitable focus for grief, along with the "Tomb of the Unknown Warrior" in Westminster. In Malaya, many POWs had died in Thailand, but significant numbers of POWs had also died and been buried locally. As such, there were war graves, and the question of what to do with these.

One of the highest concentrations of such graves was within what had been Changi POW camp. The POWs had created Changi Cemetery there, burying 809 of their dead (as opposed to the several thousand POWs who died on the Death Railway). This being Singapore, however, the dead move. The Japanese had used POW labour to expand Changi airfield. In 1946, most of the old British military barracks in the area were taken over by the Royal Air Force. Now the British wanted to expand Changi military airport. The cemetery was exhumed by the Army Graves Service in 1946. Where should it go? The answer was Kranji Cemetery in the northwest of the island. There they would eventually be joined by other war dead, including from Buona Vista, and even a few from as far afield as Saigon.[46]

Kranji Cemetery was then located well outside the urban areas of Singapore (now the Kranji race course stands nearby). It sat on a large mound of earth, at the bottom of which was a swamp. The area had been the burial ground for POWs at the Kranji hospital for POWs, and for a nearby POW work camp.[47] At first, makeshift wooden crosses were used to mark the graves of the war dead. The Imperial War Graves Commission (since 1960 renamed the Commonwealth War Graves Commission) then used sturdy, square, stone slabs on which the Christian cross was embedded.[48] In addition, the Commission needed to recognise the many soldiers whose bodies had not been found, including those of non-Christians. Their solution was to construct — uphill from the stone markers — 12 giant concrete slabs, each adorned with the names of the dead. These slabs were a covered with a thin roof, which in turn was topped by a structure resembling an aeroplane's tail fin. The overall effect was a massive structure with a surprisingly light and uplifting feel to it.

The official unveiling at Kranji War Cemetery occurred on 2 March 1957. The Duke of Gloucester, representing the Queen, unveiled the memorial to members of the Commonwealth armed forces who lost their lives in the theatre of war, and for whom there is no known grave.[49] Though the names of the dead range across ethnic groups and religions, the wording on the monument retains an imperial echo:

> On the walls of this memorial are recorded the names of twenty-four thousand soldiers and airmen of many races united in service to the British crown who gave their lives in Malaya and neighbouring lands

Plate 3.3 Kranji War Memorial, Singapore

and seas and in the air over southern and eastern Asia and the Pacific but to whom the fortune of war denied the customary rites accorded to their comrades in death.

THEY DIED FOR ALL FREE MEN

The monument itself was a success. Kranji now plays host to ceremonies, notably led by the British on Remembrance Sunday to mark the 11 November, and by the Australians on Anzac Day every 25 April. At the same time, its central structure was inclusive, naming Indians, Malay Regiment soldiers and others whose remains were not recovered. The monument itself served those with no known grave, while the square stone slabs on the slope in front of it marked the graves of Christians. Far from diminishing Kranji's stature, Singapore's independence in 1965 saw the old ceremonies continue, while over time, veterans and their families started making "pilgrimages" to it, and eventually Singaporean schoolchildren also started visiting it on school trips.

The Emergence of the POW as War Hero and Victim

We have already seen how, in 1945–1946, the British projected images of the British war hero to Singapore and Malaya, using imagery from North African and European theatres. Kranji, meanwhile, eventually provided an acceptable focus for fallen soldiers and for commemorative services. But none of this was enough for the British colonial administration of the 1940s to 1950s.

In 1946, the *Malaya Tribune* described the colonial state as "influenced by a Changi Gaol group": former internees and ex-POWs.[50] Within the colonial state itself, Oswald Gilmour recalled that such was the "comradeship in adversity" that "where a name was proposed for office ... immediately it was asked: 'Is he an ex-internee?'"[51] The problem was that the 1941–1942 campaign offered few examples of ex-Malayan Civil Service (MCS) as martial heroes. The only real option was to develop the image of the POW and internee as a hero.[52]

In this context, the colonial establishment began to stress the character POWs had displayed under duress. In the past, when representing British imperial history, POWs had not usually been considered, unless for daring escapes.[53] John MacKenzie writes that in the heyday of empire, "imperial heroes developed instrumental power because they served to explain and justify the rise of the imperial state, personified national greatness and offered examples of self-sacrificing service to a current generation".[54] For the POWs and ex-internees to become imperial heroes, they had to be represented not just as passive victims, but rather as displaying imperial character. This was now done in two ways. First, their captivity was portrayed as part of a wider, moral drama, as a sacrifice which enabled victory in a global war against evil. Second, it was presented as an opportunity to display imperial characteristics, and through that fitness to rule.

As early as December 1945, Lieutenant-General A.E. Percival wrote that many returning POWs had developed "an implicit faith in the ultimate triumph of right over the forces of evil which was threatening the very existence of peace-loving and God-fearing people".[55] Harold Bull, a magistrate in prewar Malaya's Colonial Legal Service and an ex-internee, also articulated the idea of captivity as a moral and imperial sacrifice:

> Most of us recall with a thrill of pride when the Old Country stood alone in the early years of the war, when the power of Nazi Germany was at its height.
>
> We in Malaya had to be sacrificed and bear the well nigh intolerable and terror of 3½ years of Japanese occupation. None of us emerged unscathed, but if Old England had gone under, the consequences would have been too dreadful to contemplate.
>
> And yet because England stood firm, we are free once again, albeit with a legacy of sorrow and bereavement in most cases.[56]

Their sacrifice was vindicated by the British victories projected to the people of Malaya and Singapore in 1945–1946. This implied that Singapore's fall, insofar as it was due to a shortage of modern ships, aircraft and tanks, had been right: a fundamental part of Britain's contribution to defeating evil by winning the battles that most mattered. That echoed Churchill's defence of his allocation of resources, as made in closed session of Parliament in 1942, and later in his memoirs.[57]

This idea of the POW and internee as a necessary sacrifice was then adorned with examples of heroic behaviour. One story was that of internee John Leonard Wilson, the Church of England Bishop of Singapore from 1941–1949. Bishop Wilson was tortured after he was taken on 17 October 1943 from Changi Prison to the *kempeitai* (military police) headquarters in Singapore. There he remained until 13 July 1944. His arrest was part of the aftermath of the "Double Tenth" incident. Starting on 10 October 1943, the Japanese took from Changi

Prison civilian internees whom they wrongly suspected had passed information to Allied commandoes. The latter had sunk seven Japanese ships in Singapore harbour, in an operation launched via boat and canoe from Australia. Of the 57 civilians (54 men and 3 women) taken from Changi Prison and interrogated, 15 men died from torture and one was executed.[58]

A war crimes trial was held for the "Double Tenth" perpetrators. Lasting from 18 March to 15 April 1946, it was one of the first such trials. 21 Japanese *kempeitai* were accused: eight were sentenced to death, seven received long jail sentences, and six were acquitted. The judgement, which was delivered on 15 April 1946, was later broadcast over Radio Malaya.[59] Malaya heard Lieutenant Colonel S.C. Silkin, as President of the Court, declare that the Japanese had engaged in a "deliberate and carefully planned campaign of torture which turned the prisons of the Singapore Kempei Tai into the Belsen of the East". That "Belsen of the East" tag was, given the small number involved, a tasteless invocation of the fate of Europe's Jews. But its lack of perspective speaks volumes about the frame of mind of Europeans in Malaya. Silkin went on to say that the experience of the civilian internees illustrated that the war had been a moral struggle, and that the epitaph of the victims would be, "that they died for an undying cause".[60]

Bishop Wilson emerged from the trials as a hero after the manner of Jesus: the archetypal victim as hero. During the Double Tenth incident, Bishop Wilson had been repeatedly whipped and beaten on a wooden, cross-like structure, his body left swollen and black-and-blue. Yet he cheerfully gave communion and support to other detainees in between interrogations. In October 1946, Bishop Wilson gave a sermon on BBC radio in which he evoked the passion of Christ:

> When I muttered 'Forgive them' I wondered how far I was being dramatic and if I really meant it, because I looked at their faces as they stood around and took it in turn to flog, and their faces were hard and cruel and some of them were evidently enjoying their cruelty.[61]

Two years after the end of the war, Bishop Wilson baptised four Japanese war criminals who were serving sentences at Changi Prison, including one of his own torturers.[62] His experience was viewed by members of the Church of England and colonial establishment as "one of the Christian epics of the century". In 1959, the Rank organisation made a film about his experiences called *Singapore Story*. In March 1969, after many years as Bishop of Birmingham, he returned to Singapore to make the BBC documentary, *Mission to Hell*. Bishop Wilson was given a hero's welcome by the British expatriate community.[63]

While the colonial administration played up the image of being staffed by ex-internees and ex-POWs, the legacy of the latters' experiences was not always positive. They were more likely to suffer from debilitating diseases, low self-esteem, or depression.[64] This was noted by Sir Franklin Gimson, who was Colonial Secretary of Hong Kong when the war broke out. He had been interned there, and was subsequently the first postwar Governor of Singapore (1946–1952).[65] Commemorating the sufferings of imprisonment as heroism therefore had an additional, therapeutic effect for some administrators.

This psychology of the POW as hero and victim permeated many aspects of the restoration of British rule. The statue of modern Singapore's "founder", Sir Thomas Stamford Raffles, had been taken down by the Japanese and kept in a storeroom in Singapore's museum. When it was ceremoniously re-erected on 6 July 1946, the colonial authorities described Raffles as having had "a period of four years 'internment'".[66] The ceremony for the re-erection of statues of empire-builders, Captain Francis Light in Penang on 11 August 1946, and Sir Frank Swettenham in Kuala Lumpur on 16 November, were also seen as metaphors for the return of the colonial administration from internment.[67]

The key piece of pageantry marking this return was a celebration on the anniversary of the Japanese surrender, held on 12 September 1946. On this date in 1945, Admiral Lord Louis Mountbatten, as Supreme Commander of SEAC, had formally taken the surrender of Japanese generals at the Singapore Municipal Building.[68] The ex-internees and ex-POWs had given Mountbatten the "Changi Flag" for this. This was the Union Jack that Lieutenant General Percival's entourage had carried with them next to a white flag at the 15 February 1942 surrender to General Yamashita. It had been kept hidden in Changi during captivity from the Japanese who wanted to put it on exhibition to mark their victory. After 12 September 1945, the "Changi Flag" was displayed at the Municipal Building. When the first Asian mayor of Singapore, Ong Eng Guan, was elected in December 1957, he would have it removed as a symbol of imperialism.[69] The Union Jack that had flown at the Governor's official residence at Government House (today's Istana) had also been concealed, only to be flown there again in September 1945.[70]

The initial idea for a celebration of the 12 September 1946 as Victory Day had been suggested by the leaders of Singapore's Christian churches. Many were former internees held at Changi Prison (1942–1944) and Sime Road Camp (1944–1945).[71] After leading representatives of the churches met in July 1946, Patrick McKerron, Singapore's Colonial Secretary, was informed that they were planning to hold a Service of Thanksgiving for Victory on 12 September 1946. They also suggested that the day be declared a holiday.[72] For former interned clergy, the day represented the time God had broken the years of darkness with light.[73]

This perspective was shared by many former internees, POWs, and former British colonial staff returning to Singapore and Malaya. George Seabridge (the prewar editor of the *Straits Times*), argued in the *Straits Times* of 15 February 1946 that "in retrospect, the gloom … [of captivity] … is pierced by the shining light of those countless examples of one of the finest of human qualities, fortitude in the face of adversity". Fortitude, and imperial grit in the face of adversity, were emerging as the predominant images of captivity.[74]

The colonial government welcomed the idea of 12 September becoming the official "Victory Day". Singapore Colonial Secretary Patrick McKerron even wanted the planned procession to stop at Raffles' Statue.[75] McKerron, a senior member of the prewar MCS, had been evacuated before the fall of Singapore. This had allowed him to join the MPU in London and return as head of the BMA in Singapore from 1945–1946.

Hugh P. Bryson, McKerron's Colonial Under Secretary, was also a prewar MCS member, and a former civilian internee. Bryson was involved in finalising the details of the 12 September commemoration. The key address was by ex-internee Cyril Collinge, formerly leader of the civilian internees in Changi Prison.[76] Token Chinese, Indians, Malays, and Eurasians from chambers of commerce and the Governor's Legislative Council read out vetted speeches.[77] The administration requested that the Chinese Chamber of Commerce close shops, that flags be flown from ships, and "that the day should be celebrated in as many private households as possible though according to the austerity standards required by the food situation".[78] Despite this, the lack of enthusiasm was noticed. Governor Gimson commented that "the Victory celebrations … should in future provide for more representative members of the community than participated yesterday".[79]

Britain's colonial subjects had other things to worry about. The *Malaya Tribune* ran articles in the lead up to Victory Day with titles such as: "A Year of Liberation in Retrospect: Rebuild Damaged Prestige!".

Plate 3.4 *Malaya Tribune* cartoon on postwar conditions, 5 September 1946, frontpage

An editorial asked, "Celebrate What?".[80] The BMA (until April 1946) and then the restored colonial administration were struggling with high crime and low food supplies. Even where efficient — and some unkindly dubbed the BMA the "Black Market Administration" as soldiers flogged off supplies and filched goods[81] — it could not hope to meet unrealistic local expectations, given an acute, worldwide, food shortage in 1946.

What was at stake was, however, much more than theft, rice and frustration. There were opposing views of the significance of defeat, occupation, resistance and liberation, particularly from the MCP. The MCP lost no time in orchestrating a counter-demonstration for 12 September 1946. This was achieved through multiple associations, including the General Labour Union, the MPAJA's Old Comrades Association, and the Women's Federation. As people assembled at Farrer Park for this, they were greeted by no-holds-barred images of Japanese atrocities, and a sombre line of widows, each with a picture of a massacred relative: a husband, son, or brother.

A few thousand attended the colonial administration's procession, some dragooned at official request. An estimated 20,000 flocked to Farrer Park for the MCP-inspired event. The crowd were offered resolutions demanding freedom and racial equality, which it enthusiastically endorsed. The message was clear: the struggle for "liberation" had not ended in September 1945, but continued. The colonial authorities could not control how Singapore's Chinese, Malay and Tamil speakers reinscribed anniversaries and commemorative events with their own meanings.[82]

12 September nevertheless remained an unofficial public holiday and an official school holiday, even in Chinese schools, well into the 1950s.[83] On Victory Day 1952, there was still full imperial pageantry when the High Commissioner to Malaya, General Sir Gerald Templer, accompanied by Commissioner General for Southeast Asia Malcolm MacDonald, opened the "War Memorial Wing" of St Andrew's Cathedral. Dedicated to servicemen who lost their lives in Malaya and Singapore during the war, the wing also had a special plaque which listed the names of fallen MCS members.[84] The occasion was attended by 500 members of the colonial establishment, but evoked little response from the local population.

Celebrating Asians as Empire Heroes

The colonial authorities needed to draw Asians into stories of heroic, but also loyal, wartime heroism. A racial apartheid of commemoration would be sadly insufficient to their needs. They therefore set about elevating the status of some Asians who were both non-communist, and also "loyalist".

The Asian who would be most publicly revered by the colonial authorities was also the most distinctively pro-British. This was the part-Irish, part-Eurasian nurse Sybil Kathigasu, (originally Daly). Kathigasu and her Indian husband operated a wartime medical clinic in Papan, near Ipoh in Malaya's state of Perak. There they secretly listened to the BBC on the radio, and treated anti-Japanese guerrillas by night. For this, the Japanese tortured Sybil and her husband. In November 1943, Yoshimura Eiko, a *kempeitai* sergeant, went further. He hauled Sybil's seven-year-old daughter Dawn up a tree by rope, and threatened to drop her into a fire below. Dawn yelled, "Don't tell mummy. I love you and we will die together. Jesus will be waiting for us."[85] At this point, a Japanese officer intervened, and Dawn survived.

As a result of torture from October 1943 to July 1945, Sybil was left unable to walk. She was later given the British Empire's highest reward for civilian bravery, the George Cross, awarded by King George VI in person at Buckingham Palace in October 1947. Richard Winstedt, a former Colonial official, wrote in the preface to Kathigasu's memoirs, *No Dram of Mercy* (published posthumously in 1954) that: "Mrs. Kathigasu had the blood of Asia as well as Ireland in her veins and was born in Penang, part of Northern Malaya. The white cliffs of Dover and the Sussex downs were alien to her. Yet when the Japanese were yelling paeans on their Emperor's birthday, she from the dust of her verminous cell sang 'God save the King'".[86] Northcote Parkinson, Raffles Professor of History at the University of Malaya, included Sybil in his and his wife's *Heroes of Malaya*, published in 1956 for use in Malayan schools, alongside Templer and historical figures such as Hang Tuah.[87]

The Malayan state of Perak's first war crimes trial concerned Sybil's torturer, Yoshimura Eiko.[88] The court took less than two days before sentencing on 20 February 1946. Lieutenant Colonel Figures, as Court President, told Yoshimura that: "The heroism of the mother and her young child is beyond all praise. To you, who inflicted such unendurable mental anguish upon them, no mercy can be shown. The sentence of this court … is that you suffer death by hanging".[89] The colonial authorities, meanwhile, flew Sybil to London for treatment, and there she wrote her memoirs, recording her devotion to the British Empire. She then suffered from acute septicaemia in a jaw fracture inflicted by a kick while in captivity, and died on 4 June 1949. Her body was returned to Ipoh, where her funeral was a major public event.[90]

The presence of such loyalists is hardly surprising, given the way that British rule, and British civilisation, framed the lives of many successful immigrants before the war. It had provided the legal and economic framework, and for many a language of education, and a source of religious succour too. Another such loyalist was Borneo-born, English-language educated schoolteacher, and wartime nurse, Elizabeth Choy.

Plate 3.5   Elizabeth Choy

Elizabeth was also honoured, this time for helping British civilian internees in Singapore. She and her husband ran a wartime canteen in a hospital frequented by civilian internees, and helped smuggle food and supplies to them. Those she helped, such as Governor's wife Lady Shenton Thomas, and Bishop Wilson, never forgot the Choys' kindness.[91] Elizabeth and her husband were arrested in the Double Tenth incident of October 1943, when Japanese suspected internees and those associated with them of assisting a raid on ships in Singapore Harbour. Like Sybil Kathigasu, she endured months of torture by the *kempeitei*.

Elizabeth Choy, again like Kathigasu, was resolutely pro-British, and so easily embraced by the British administration and press. Along with her husband, she was flown to London in January 1946 to recover. She would spend almost four years there, returning to Singapore by ship on 22 December 1949. In 1946, Elizabeth and her husband received the Order of the British Empire.[92]

Elizabeth Choy was an ideal war heroine for colonial authorities. She was an Anglophile, married, Christian, middle-class woman, and yet also Chinese. Her background as a prewar teacher at the Church of England-run St Margaret's School and St Andrew's School reinforced pro-British feelings.[93] Her first year away from Singapore was spent travelling in Europe. In her second year, she took a course in domestic science at the Polytechnic College in London, and then taught catering at the London Chamber of Commerce. She also studied art under sculptress Dora Gordine, for whom she modelled. Upon returning to Singapore on 22 December 1949, she intended to return to teaching, at St Andrew's School.[94]

After returning, she stood as independent candidate for an elected seat in Singapore's Municipal Council in December 1950, without success. In 1951, she was appointed as a nominated member of the Legislative Council by the Governor of Singapore, Franklin Gimson. Clearly, the English-educated Choy enjoyed greater support in high places than amongst Singapore's Chinese-educated. The British Governor placed her on the Legislative Council to raise issues that concerned women.[95] In April 1955, she again stood for Legislative Council elections, this time for the Progressive Party, and was again defeated.

Elizabeth Choy's period in political life had been brief. But she lived for decades afterwards, giving oral history interviews and occasionally talking to the press. As we shall see in later chapters, both Elizabeth Choy and Sybil Kathigasu were to enjoy a renaissance in fame in Singapore and Malaysia after the 1980s, though with the British component of their stories downplayed.[96]

Changi as a Site of Heroes

Away from state-planned commemoration of heroism, the Changi area was taking on increased significance. The colonial authorities naturally welcomed back visitors who shared their memories of captivity. Former POWs and internees were hailed as returning heroes. Some were taken to the eastern tip of Singapore, to Changi, and given a tour of the area. The visitors' deeds were extolled in the press. In this way, Changi gradually became an historical site of considerable importance. The colonial state did not actively plan this. Instead, the high number of ex-POWs and internees in the administration and prison service, and the natural sympathies of the British military, made it happen without forethought. In conjunction with Changi becoming a sacred historical

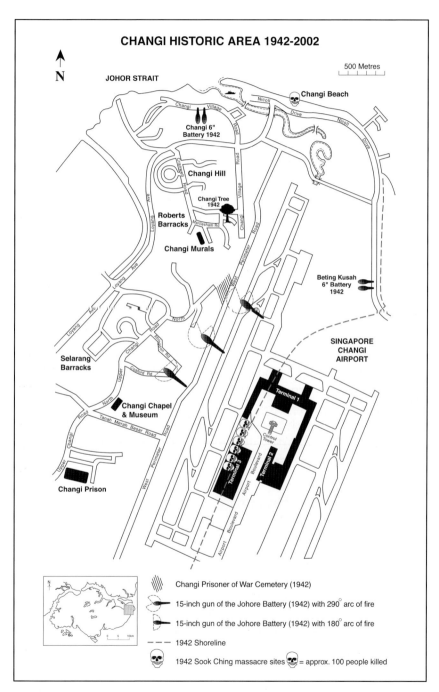

CHANGI HISTORIC AREA 1942-2002

500 Metres

JOHOR STRAIT

Changi Beach

Changi 6"
Battery 1942

Changi Hill

Changi Tree
1942

Roberts
Barracks

Changi Murals

Beting Kusah
6" Battery
1942

SINGAPORE
CHANGI
AIRPORT

Selarang
Barracks

Terminal 1

Control
Tower

Changi Chapel
& Museum

Terminal 2

Terminal 3

Changi Prison

‖‖‖ Changi Prisoner of War Cemetery (1942)

15-inch gun of the Johore Battery (1942) with 290° arc of fire

15-inch gun of the Johore Battery (1942) with 180° arc of fire

--- 1942 Shoreline

1942 Sook Ching massacre sites ☠ = approx. 100 people killed

Map 3.2   Changi Historical Area

Map 3.2 Notes

Prison, POWS, and Internees

Changi Prison was built in 1936 to hold only 600 prisoners. From 1942 to 1944 about 3,000 civilian internees were housed there. The POWs were held nearby, in former barracks. The Australian POWs were stationed in Selarang Barracks (demolished in 1986) and the British mainly in Roberts Barracks (demolished in 2004). Only in May 1944 were some POWs moved into Changi Prison, and even then, they were also housed in huts outside the prison walls. When the old Changi Prison was demolished in 2004, a small part of it was preserved as a memorial. The iconic gates were reassembled on a 180-metre stretch of prison wall which runs parallel to Upper Changi Road North, complete with guard turrets. This was named "Old Changi Wall". There is limited access and visibility.

The Murals

The British POW Stanley Warren painted the Changi Murals between 1942 and 1943 in an indoor chapel at the hospital wing of Roberts Barracks. These depictions of New Testament scenes were restored after the war by Warren, when he visited Singapore in 1963, 1982, and 1988. The building containing the murals is the only remaining structure from the 2004 demolition of Robert Barracks. It is located in the middle of a Singapore Armed Forces base, and as such there is very limited access.

The Chapels

There were also outdoor chapels created by the POWs, but all were destroyed or removed after the war. Instead, a postwar chapel in the prison came to be used by returning veterans and their families from the 1950s. When visits inside a maximum security prison were deemed no longer practical, the Singapore Tourism Board built a replica of the outdoor chapels and a small museum. These were placed just outside of the gates of Changi Prison in 1988. Due to new prison building, the Changi Chapel and Museum moved a short distance to a new location in 2001, as marked on the map.

The POW Cemetery

In 1942, a cemetery was created between Selarang and Roberts Barracks, with one section for the British war dead, and another for the Australians. After the war, the bodies were exhumed and moved to Kranji. This was because of the expansion of Changi RAF airport. The first runway there had been begun by the Japanese in 1943, using POW labour.

Johore Battery

All that remains of the three 15-inch guns of Johore Battery is one underground ammunition bunker. Ironically, this belonged to the only one of its guns that could not and did not turn and fire landward in 1942. In February 2002, the Singapore Tourism Board built a same-size replica of one of these 15-inch guns of the Johore Battery above the ruins of the remaining ammunition bunker. This was opened to the public as a historical site, at Cosford Road. In 2011, the site was turned into a restaurant called "The Bunker", with the replica gun as a backdrop for ambience.

The Changi Tree

Close to Johore Battery stood the "Changi Tree". At 76 metres high, this Sindora (Sepitir) tree towered above the surrounding landscape, and was even marked on maps. In 1942, the British blew its top off, in order to deprive the Japanese of a landmark. In February 2001, the Singapore Tourism Board planted a sapling at the opening of the new Changi Chapel and Museum, a new "Changi tree". This new tree was of the *chengai* (Balanocarpus) species, which gave its name to the area.

The *Sook Ching*

There are two documented *Sook Ching* massacre sites in the Changi Historic Area. On the evening of 20 February 1942, Japanese troops took 70 Chinese males out to Changi Beach and shot them at the water's edge. Four survived because they were mistaken to be dead, and were able to flee later. When POWs from Changi were ordered to dispose of the bodies the next day, they found another Chinese man alive and smuggled him out of the area.

At Tanah Merah Besar Beach, on which Changi Airport is built, Chua Choon Guan and Cheng Kwang Yu have described between 400 and 600 Chinese being machine gunned at low tide on the evening of 22 February 1942. These survivors testified at the 1947 war crimes trials that they had lived because there were too many victims for the Japanese to be able to bayonet them all, in order to check that they were dead. The Japanese are rumoured to have returned every evening for the next three days to machine gun more Chinese.

site, key relics of the POW past also came to be regarded with reverence and placed on display.

The first notable ex-POW welcomed as a returning hero was "Black Jack": Frederick Galleghan. Galleghan was the Lieutenant Colonel in charge of the Australian 2/30th Battalion during the Malayan Campaign. He also commanded the Australians at Changi POW camp after August 1942, when officers above the rank of full colonel were sent to Japan and Formosa. Galleghan, now a Brigadier, arrived by flying boat on 9 January 1948 for a one-night stopover. He was met by three former 2/30th Battalion members who were now part of Singapore's colonial administration. They presented him with a "bouquet" of one egg, soya, and a tin of bully beef. The card on the bouquet read: "Memo: Black Jack — your ration sir". His ex-POW comrades then took him on a tour of Changi Prison.[97]

On 10 January, the English-language press went with the headline: "Kept Without Water 8 Days, But … The Japs Couldn't Budge 'Black Jack'". It told how he had led POWs at Changi prison camp in refusing to sign forms stating that they would not escape.[98] On 1 September 1942, the Japanese had applied pressure by crowding 15,000 POWs into a small square meant for no more than 1,200: the "Selarang Barracks Square incident". The press had these men left without water, a creative take on reality, which was that they had access to one or two taps connected to a small water tower. The press also had the men heroically holding out for eight days. In reality, dysentery soon made its appearance, and on 5 September the POW commanders had ordered their troops to sign the "no escape" forms.

The return of Black Jack also reinforced memories of the execution of "Corporal" Rodney Breavington, who had been executed in conjunction with the Selarang Barracks Square incident. What we know for sure is that the Japanese executed four men on Beting Kusah Beach, at Changi, on the morning of 2 September 1942: two POWs from the Australian Army's Ordnance Corps (Breavington and Private Gale); and two POWs from the British Army (Privates Waters and Fletcher). They were executed for trying to escape, probably with the additional aim of pressurising the POW commanders to order their men to sign the "no escape" pledge.

Beyond this, the story becomes opaque. Breavington and Gale appear to have escaped in May 1942. By one account, they were captured after rowing 200 miles from Singapore in a small boat. The

English privates seem to have made separate escape attempts. Waters escaped from a work camp on Singapore, and was recaptured immediately.[99] But the story took on a life of its own amongst the postwar expatriate population. Versions circulated that all the prisoners had escaped together. Breavington emerged as the self-sacrificing hero. Facing a Japanese firing squad on the beach, he is said to have pleaded with the Japanese to let the others go, saying he ordered all the privates to escape with him. Another version has Breavington pleading only for his Australian "mate" Private Gale.[100]

Breavington came to be appropriated by colonial and military officials, as embodying the heroism that they read into their own experiences as prisoners. In fact, martyrdom in Changi was the exception. Most POWs who died did so on the Burma-Thailand Railway. Only about 850 POWs out of the estimated 87,000 that moved through the holding camp at Changi died there, most from battle wounds or tropical diseases.[101] The execution of Breavington along with three other POWs was the only event of its nature there.[102]

The testimony of an apparently authoritative witness added further pathos to the evolving story. Reverend J.N. Lewis Bryan, the Assistant Chaplain-in-General, Far East, gave the four men absolution before their execution. He wrote a powerful account for a 1947 issue of the magazine *British Malaya*.[103] In this, Bryan gets most of the four POW's names wrong. He conjures up "Cpl. Breavington reading the New Testament open in his hands" as he was shot, having told Bryan, "I have my New Testament here, sir, and I am going to read it while they shoot me".[104] Bryan is the only witness to these theologically satisfying last acts.

A poem written by another witness, and called "Corporal and His Pal", provided a slightly different version of the story. Its verses did emphasise that Breavington "placed his trust in God", but now he is not clutching the New Testament, but rather has, "One arm around his mate" and "His free hand held a picture of the one he loved most dear":

> His rugged face grew stern; 'I ask
> One favour ere I go
> Grant unto me this last request
> That's in your power to give.
> For myself I ask no mercy
> But let my comrade live'.

The poem then held up Breavington as an example of heroic death:

Example, yes — of how to die,
And how to meet one's fate.
Example, true — of selfless love
A man has for his mate.
And when he reaches Heaven's Gate
The Angels will be nigh,
And welcome to their midst, a man
Who knew the way to die.[105]

The poem is redolent of Anzac glorification of mateship. It again recasts the story. Most accounts from the officers who were made to witness the executions indicate that Breavington did not say he ordered just Gale from the Australian Ordnance Corps to escape, but the two English privates as well.[106]

Closely linked to the Breavington story was the war crimes trial and execution of Lieutenant General Fukuei Shimpei. Fukuei was the Japanese officer in charge of POWs in Singapore at the time, and was believed to have given the orders for the execution. The 13 previous Japanese war criminals given the death sentence had been hanged in Changi Prison, with limited witnesses. Fukuei was singled out for more public treatment. On the morning of 27 April 1946, Fukuei was dressed in uniform, but without insignia of rank. He was taken from Changi Prison to Beting Kusah Beach, where the POWs had been shot, and where ten Australian soldiers stood ready to witness his execution. He was tied to a post. A hood was placed over his head, a white circular target over his heart. The firing squad shot nine bullets. On 28 April, the front page of the *Straits Times* reported that "A red patch of sand on Changi beach early yesterday marked the spot where a Japanese General met his death as a war criminal. Lieutenant-General Fukuei Shimpei joined his ancestors …"[107]

The mythology of Breavington thrived in press stories, poetry, and his dramatic war crimes trial. Breavington's body was reburied at the Kranji War Cemetery in Singapore after the war. For this, his true details had to be recorded in stone. On the stone, "Corporal" Breavington now became "Private" R.E. Breavington.[108] His Australian defence service file suggested that he was officially a private, despite witnesses testifying that he was a corporal who pleaded he had ordered the privates to escape.[109] He could not, of course, have given such an order, since he only escaped with Gale.

Did Breavington hold a Bible at his death, or his mate and a picture of his loved ones? Did he plead only for his Australian mate, or for all the POWs with him? Did he claim to be a corporal to give credence to his "orders", or has some wartime field promotion escaped all records and memories?[110]

Whatever happened, the legend's growth reflected the wider focus on Changi as a site associated with captivity as heroic, and the need Europeans felt for examples of heroic behaviour. The different re-workings also show attempts to make him fit specific narratives of heroism, notably those of the Church and of the Anzac tradition.

The colonial administration soon realised how important Changi as an area was becoming to the POW and internee story. In the 1950s, it showed a growing concern with preserving parts of the POW land-scape and creating symbols of the POW past. This was in sharp con-trast to sentiment upon liberation. In 1945, the squalid attap huts that had housed many POWs in Changi, and the services for them, had been swept away. Malcolm MacDougal, an Australian ex-POW who had a contract for this, called their destruction "a funeral pyre of many things best forgotten" in order that the grounds "looked cleansed and renewed".[111]

As early as 1952, however, there was a desire to revive some fea-tures of captivity. That year saw the re-erection of the Changi Lychgate. This had stood over the entrance to the British POW cemetery at Changi, until the latter's remains were relocated to Kranji. The lychgate had been constructed by Royal Engineers in December 1942 from the hardwood of a Changi tree (a type once abundant in Singapore). When the Changi POW Cemetery was exhumed, the lychgate of the British section was put into storage. It was re-erected at St George's Church, Tanglin Army Barracks, on its tenth anniversary, on 14 December 1952.[112]

Among the structures dismantled in 1945 had been the outdoor chapels, mostly constructed of wood. There were several of these at Changi POW camp.[113] Just one of these outdoor chapels survived. Members of the Australian Army had sent the Roman Catholic chapel to the Australian War Memorial, in Canberra. There it lay in storage, until re-erected decades later at Australia's Duntroon Military College.[114]

With not one of the wartime chapels ostensibly remaining in Singapore, where could returning POWs and internees pay their res-pects to the dead, and give thanks for survival? From 1953, an answer presented itself. When they returned to Changi, they would often be

Plate 3.6 Changi Chapel as built by the Singapore Tourism Board. Modern construction built in the Changi Museum, to echo the original outside chapels of the wartime POW camp

Plate 3.7 Changi Prison before demolition in 2004

shown around the prison by senior prison personnel, some of whom were ex-POWs or internees, or had links with ex-captives. When Changi Prison had resumed its role as a maximum security civilian prison after the war, there had been strong pressure from Christian ministers for a chapel to be established for the prisoners. A hospital ward was converted, and on 9 August 1953, it was dedicated.[115] At the end of the standard tour given, the prison officers now took ex-POWs and internees to this new chapel.[116]

Members of the British military forces and civil administration stationed in Singapore, and visitors, subsequently helped to refurbish Changi Prison Chapel as a shrine to the POW past. Representatives of some of the battalions and units that were captured in 1942 began to put plaques with their unit insignia on the walls. On 18 August 1957, it was formally dedicated as a memorial chapel to the 905 POWs and civilian internees who died in the camp. "The Memorial Changi Prison Chapel Visitors Book" created for the occasion opens with a "dedication of the fittings to the memory of prisoners of war and internees who died in the precincts of Changi Prison".[117] Present and signing their name were representatives of the colonial administration, the Commonwealth armed forces, and the British, Australian and Dutch consuls in Singapore. In attendance was also the Singapore's Church of England Archdeacon, Robin Woods.

William Goode, the Chief Secretary of Singapore from 1953–1957, also visited the chapel at its rededication. He had been a prewar MCS member and part of the Singapore Volunteer Corps, becoming a POW and working on the Burma-Thailand Railway.[118] A few months after his visit, Goode was appointed the last Governor of Singapore (1957–1959).[119] Goode's presence was symptomatic of a colonial administration pervaded by ex-POWs and internees. The Governor of Singapore at the time, Robert Black (1955–1957), had also been a member of the prewar MCS, and a commissioned officer in the Intelligence Corps of the British Army at the fall of Singapore. He spent the war as a POW in Japan.[120]

Sir Robert Scott, British Commissioner-General for Southeast Asia from 1955–1959, was also an ex-captive. A member of the British consular service in China (1927–1947), he had been sent to prewar Singapore to coordinate the Ministry of Information's regional propaganda. He fled Singapore on 13 February 1942 in HMS *Giang Bee*, a 30-year-old Chinese coastal steamer commandeered by the Admiralty. When it sank, he rowed to a Japanese destroyer to plead for help, only for it to sail off. Desperate days on an island were ended by capture. As a civilian, Scott was interned in Changi Prison, and later at Sime Road. During the "Double Tenth" incident, he was one of the first to be arrested, on 10 October 1943, and one of the last to be returned after torture, on 28 February 1945. Scott was another of the "ideal-type" of heroic prisoner, his obituary claiming that he "established a moral and intellectual ascendancy over his prosecutors [at his own trial by the Japanese as a spy]".[121]

A message from Scott had been broadcast from post-liberation Singapore as early as 8 September 1945, while he was still severely ill. In it, he told his audience of his torture, and of how even in the darkest hours:

> They knew, as I knew, that the dawn must come one day, and that the citadel of the Empire had been saved. One day, yes one day, the forces of freedom would pour forth from that citadel and drive away the darkness and the hatred from the soil of Malaya ... [and as his closing words] ... Britain stands for freedom.[122]

Remembering their past as prisoners created cohesiveness among the British colonial administration and armed forces. Ceremonies held at Changi in remembrance reinforced this. In 1952, former internee Reverend A.J. Bennitt wrote that:

> The fact that reunions of the ex-P.o.W.'s and internees go on proves that there was something there we do not want to forget — perhaps a depth of friendship we do not often meet in ordinary life, because we could no longer pretend to be different from what we are, perhaps lessons learned of courage and patience and integrity which we shall never forget.[123]

This process of using war memory as an instrument of colonial state building waned as decolonisation accelerated. But the memorials established to the prisoner as hero and victim endured into the post-colonial world. Changi Prison Chapel is a striking example of this endurance.

In 1988, the Chapel in the Prison was, for security reasons, closed to visitors, even though it continued intact until the prison's demolition in 2004. But the Singapore state, realising that a place of pilgrimage was still required, erected a replica based on the attap hut chapels that had been built outside of the prison during the war. The replica sat just outside of the prison. In 2001, the construction of a new prison building opposite the old one meant that the replica could not stay. The Singapore government responded by moving it just down the road, and housing it in the middle of a new, purpose-built museum complex. Ex-POWs and former internees have thus continued to return on "pilgrimages" to Singapore and Malaya, and to this new "Changi Chapel and Museum".[124]

The refurbishment of the chapel inside Changi Prison had continued into the 1960s. In 1963, the Australian Returned and Services

League made a donation including pews. The British expatriate population held a memorial service at the chapel, which was re-dedicated to ex-POWs and internees on 5 May 1963 by ex-internee, Methodist Bishop Hobart Amstutz.[125]

The "Changi Chapel" was, by this point in time, joined by an equally emotionally charged POW site. For it had only seemed, in 1946, as if all the wartime chapels had been destroyed. Unknown to most people, one indoor chapel still stood. This was the Chapel to St Luke the Physician, housed in the old Roberts Army Barracks. In it were life-sized murals, paintings of scenes from the New Testament. These had been completed in 1942–1943, on the walls of the dysentery wing in Block 151.

The artist was Stanley Warren, a prewar film poster artist for Grenada Cinemas who had joined the Royal Artillery in 1940, aged 18. Posted as an observation post assistant, he found himself in Malaya, drawing the topography and Japanese targets. On 15 February 1942, he became a POW, and was put to work building the approach roads for the new Japanese monument at Bukit Batok, the *Syonan Chureito*. The prisoners also built their own attap-roofed, open chapel nearby, and Warren was asked to decorate behind the altar. This he did with his first two chapel murals: a Malay Madonna and child, and Jesus' "Descent from the Cross" into the comforting arms of a man dressed as a British army medic. Warren's charcoal images created a stunning immediacy, by compounding British with Malayan details, and Christian iconography with contemporary figures, some of which he modelled on his comrades.[126]

Warren contracted amoebic dysentery — common amongst prisoners — and his kidneys started failing. By now in a critical state, he was taken to the Roberts Barracks Hospital in Changi POW Camp. Come August 1942, he was in the dysentery wing where, "One day ... lying in a ward above St Luke's", he "heard the sound of hymn-singing from below" to the accompaniment of a small organ "and he was so inspired that when he had recovered enough strength to walk; he came down and joined the choir and the Guild of Servers. Later, as a thanksgiving for his partial recovery, he said he wished to paint a series of murals on the walls of St Luke's".[127]

This he did, at first in the short bursts his health allowed, using scrounged paint, and billiard chalk for blue. As he worked, POWs would come and sit along the walls, watch, and make small talk. Sometimes Japanese and Korean Guards would do the same, resting their rifles against the Chapel Walls. There, in the half-light of the Chapel, with the fragrance of frangipani blooms drifting up from the altar, Stanley completed five murals.[128] They were: The Nativity Scene, The Last Supper, The Crucifixion, The Ascension, and St Luke the Physician.

First completed, in time for Christmas 1942, was The Nativity Scene. In this, the three wise men are depicted as of oriental, Middle Eastern and European origin, while the ox sports an Asian-style hump. Mary's face is softened into tender lines, while Joseph throws his hands up almost in astonishment. The work is part religious icon, part contemporary, and yet almost cartoon-like in its bold lines, expressions and surprising details.

The Crucifixion had a much bolder message. In it, both Jesus and the "slaves" who fix him to the cross are shown reminiscent of famished POWs. This leaves the possibility that even perpetrators — who for the POWs would be Japanese — deserve compassion. The Crucifixion mural bears the legend: "Father Forgive Them, They Know Not What They Do". The Last Supper, meanwhile, features little more than a stool for a table, and dishes and a circular vessel modelled on the bowls used to wash bedridden prisoners. In the foreground, Stanley drew his own sandals.

In completing these murals, the still fragile Stanley missed his unit going to the Burma-Thailand Railway, with its much harsher conditions. He was still there in Easter 1943, when the choir processed from the Chapel door, bedecked in white shirts and singing the hymn "The strife is o'er, the battle won". The hymn's message could hardly have been more mistimed. Many more of the POWs would soon be trucked off to the Burma-Thailand Railway.[129] The Chapel itself closed in May 1943, when the Japanese airforce took over the building. The murals were partially covered over with distemper, and that of St Luke part destroyed.[130]

After the war, the murals were at first only part visible beneath the distemper, and known to a limited circle of British servicemen. James Lowe, a young airman who arrived at Changi airbase in December 1948, recalled that "we were told the wartime history … and never to forget the terrible happenings there, we were then shown the Murals, by which I was really moved".[131] It was 1958–1959 before the murals became more widely "rediscovered". The RAF Changi magazine *Tale Spin* ran an article picturing two of them, and then the *Daily Mail* in Britain championed a search for the artist, who was "discovered" teaching in London.[132] The British military coaxed Warren back to

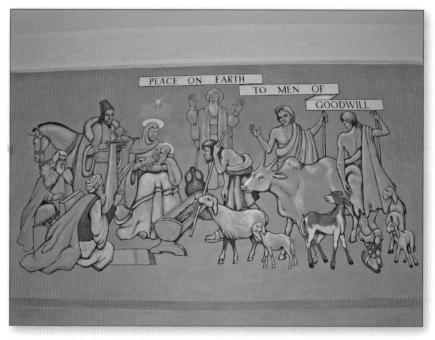

Plate 3.8 The Changi Murals: The Nativity Scene

Plate 3.9 The Changi Murals: The Last Supper

Plate 3.10 The Changi Murals: The Crucifixion

Plate 3.11 The Changi Murals: Australian tour party

restore three of the murals (The Crucifixion, The Ascension and The Last Supper) in December 1963 to January 1964 — he wept when first alone with them again — and he returned in 1982 (The Nativity Scene) and 1988.[133]

After the "rediscovery", a pamphlet was produced for visitors. This used the same phrases as those heard by fresh arrivals to the military base, such as James Lowe:

> The Murals, now restored are visited by many who come to Changi. Some see them and recapture the grim days of the occupation when they were themselves prisoners at Changi. Others see them as a reminder of the faith and courage, which overcame evil and enabled them to survive it. For all who take the opportunity to see the Murals there is one enduring message of the victory of the powers of light over those of darkness.[134]

This narrative of the past thus skewed the intention behind the murals. Warren created them to illustrate a sense of humanity shared by all, including the Japanese, and hated war. He had not envisaged a theme of "triumph of good over evil", and continued to believe that war could scarcely be justified, if at all.[135]

Nonetheless, the story of the Changi Murals was told and retold — in the twilight of colonialism — to illustrate the idea of "fortitude through adversity". Upon the announcement that the British would withdraw from the bases, there were suggestions in 1968 and 1971 that the murals should be removed to England.[136] After all, St Luke's first Padre, Padre Chambers, had written in his diary — before premature death in 1945 — that "I would urge that St Luke's be retained as a memorial chapel … it would be a great comfort to the relatives of the fallen".[137] Removal proved impractical, and the Singapore authorities promised to preserve them for posterity. Given the Chapel's location in a military area, access has in reality become increasingly circumscribed over time — becoming by appointment only and even then in very restricted periods. Fortunately, copies of the murals were made for the Changi Chapel and Museum which opened nearby in 2001. So though the authentic site is all but lost to the general public, at least some shadow of it is accessible.

Conclusion

After the return of the British in September 1945, war memory was manipulated by the colonial state in an attempt to restore its badly battered prestige. Initially the main focus was on remembering campaigns in which the British Empire had been successful. This gave way to the notion of remembering the POWs and civilian internees not just as victims, but as heroes as well.

With large numbers of the colonial administration having been incarcerated by the Japanese, former civilian internees were portrayed as living proof that the "sacrifice" of occupation had been redeemed by freedom, that good had triumphed over evil, and that the British imperial character and fitness to rule had been demonstrated even in captivity. Some Asians, notably those who had been British Empire loyalists, were associated with this imagery of prisoner as hero.

These images had both a propaganda value to the colonial state, and a personal and therapeutic value to individuals, some of whom had also endured beatings or even prolonged torture. It was further reinforced when the state responded to growing visits by ex-POWs and internees (and their families) to Changi, amongst other things by the dedication of a Changi Chapel within the prison, and by the "rediscovery" of the Changi Murals and attachment to them of messages the author never intended.

These sites were inherited by the Singapore Government upon independence in August 1965, and its care of them will be discussed in more detail below, in Chapter 10. The late colonial period thus bequeathed to the postcolonial world the enduring image of the POW as war and imperial hero as well as victim. In addition, it left key commemorative sites such as Changi Chapel and Kranji War Cemetery, whose use and emotive force has continued to present day. This leads, however, to the question that will be explored in the following four chapters, namely: who were the heroes and victims that the Asian population of Malaya and Singapore remembered in their own ethnic communities, away from British officialdom?

CHAPTER 4

The Chinese War Hero

FOR MALAYA'S CHINESE POPULATION, THE OCCUPATION was the worst of times, and the best of times; a time of humiliation, and yet also of transcendent heroism.[1] It was the worst of times: a nightmare in which civilians were massacred by Japanese soldiers, survivors had to obey the perpetrators, bow to them, befriend them as employers, and learn their language, and when ebbing fear after 1942 was matched by intensifying shortages and hunger. Yet it was also the best of times for testing what the human spirit is capable of. It provided an opportunity for blood sacrifice, when "Overseas Chinese" (*hua qiao*) staked their claim to be not just sojourners, but also Malayans, or at the very least *ma lai ya hua qiao*.[2]

From 1937, the Overseas Chinese community, though still divided by dialect, class and ideology, had become increasingly united in one thing: its hatred for Japanese aggression towards China. It had provided funds for China's defence, and then, from 1941, men and women willing to fight for Malaya, willing to pay "The Price of Peace".[3] For some, that price would include capture, torture, and death.

This era would, therefore, provide a pantheon of "heroes", ranging from ordinary people caught up in extraordinary times, to natural leaders; and including both supporters and enemies of the Malayan communists. Above all, they would include several thousand members of the eight MPAJA (Malayan People's Anti-Japanese Army) Regiments, and tens of thousands of its civilian supporters. On the one hand, these included the rank and file, villagers who gave food, and the likes of pineapple seller Chan Peng Kun, who joined the MPAJA aged 19 in 1943. Chan survived the occupation, only to go into the jungle again in 1948 to fight the British in the Malayan Emergency. He was captured and hung on the orders of the latter in 1949.[4] On the other hand, there were leaders such as the inspirational Li Fuk (alias Tu or Du Lung Shan). Li Fuk was a young teacher in a Chinese-language school, who recruited former schoolmate Ong Boon Hua (alias Chin Peng) to the Anti-Enemy Backing Up Society (AEBUS). AEBUS raised funds and carried out anti-Japanese activities in prewar Malaya. Later, Li Fuk was trained for behind-enemy-lines action by Britain's 101 Special Training School in Singapore, and in July 1942, became leader of the MPAJA in Perak. This would become the MPAJA 5th Regiment. In common with the majority of the MPAJA's and MCP's most senior leaders of 1942, he did not live to see the end of 1943. He was captured, and ultimately beheaded.[5]

Chapter 5 will deal with the postwar struggle to come to terms with the Chinese civilian losses, with a special focus on commemoration of those killed in the Japanese massacres of February to March 1942. This chapter deals with the Chinese attempt to identify and celebrate heroes and martyrs, paying special attention to three groups. These are: Dalforce or the "Singapore Overseas Anti-Japanese Volunteer Army", which fought alongside the British on Singapore in February 1942; the MPAJA; and the Chinese who joined Britain's Force 136, and in that capacity liaised with the MPAJA, especially as represented by Lim Bo Seng.

Chinese in Force 136 numbered less than a hundred, Dalforce was around 1,250, and the MPAJA's eight regiments several thousand, with a multiple of that number offering support.[6] To put this into perspective, Malaya's 1947 population was roughly five million, slightly less than half of these being Malays, 38 per cent (1,885,000) Chinese. Singapore's population, swollen by wartime refugees, was 938,144 by 1947, more than 70 per cent of them Chinese. So even in 1947, the combined Chinese population for both Malaya and Singapore was less than two and a half million.[7]

This chapter will trace how early emphasis on unity amongst Malaya's Overseas Chinese — on how all groups came together to resist the Japanese from 1941 — dissolved into competition over who to emphasise as heroes. The decisive turning away from the emphasis on unity would come in 1948, as the communists again took to the jungle, in the Malayan Emergency. The battle over which of these groups to hold up highest for reverence, and which to push to the margins, therefore came to be as much about postwar politics as about interpretations of the war. It became embroiled with the wider struggle to define what the "Overseas Chinese" were, who most deserved to lead them, and what sort of postcolonial state was desirable.

The most significant split over memory came to be between communists on the one hand, and non-communists on the other. The MCP wanted to remember their MPAJA fighters as the real heroes, and 15 February 1942 as the beginning of their resistance. Non-communist "Overseas Chinese", often led by business leaders with Kuomintang sympathies, wanted to deflect attention to acceptable non-communist heroes. As we shall see, Lim Bo Seng — businessman, Nationalist Chinese Colonel, and British Force 136 officer — would emerge as the latter's most prominent choice.

Non-communists soon started to spin Lim Bo Seng's story as if it was mostly detached from that of the MPAJA, as if his Chinese colleagues in Force 136 were heroes largely autonomous of the communists. In reality, most Force 136 officers initially relied upon MPAJA support to help them upon their return to Malaya at various points from 1943 to 1945. Lim Bo Seng himself only stayed free a matter of a few weeks after he left the safety of the MPAJA's Blantan Camp in Perak.[8]

An MPAJA leader from the 2nd Regiment (Negeri Sembilan), Shan Ru-hong, has angrily dismissed the British and Lim Bo Seng narratives as "The Force 136 lie":

> After the war there was talk of the real fighters against the Japanese being Force 136. This lie was spread by the pro-British elements. It was a gloss over the shameful British history ending with Percival's surrender … It was to create British heroes … The following needs repetition …
>
> 2. The Malayan Communist Party took up the task of national liberation … The Malayan People's Anti-Japanese Army … fought a bitter and difficult underdog war against the Japanese and developed from small to big, from weakness to strength until there were in all eight independent regiments which in the three years and eight months destroyed five to six battalions of the fascist troops and finally with the help of supplies from the allies defeated the Japanese colonial rule and liberated the people …
>
> 3. It was when the Malayan People's Anti-Japanese Army had grown strong and the war against the Japanese aggressors intensified that the British army sent from India the so called Allied Davies group [Force 136, including Lim Bo Seng] …
>
> 5. Facts are stronger than lies. History cannot be wiped out. We must tell the truth about the Malayan anti-Japanese war.[9]

In this way, real war was followed by a fight to control its memory. This became more and more politicised over time because, to tap support, postwar leaders needed to harness the emotions and memories of tens of thousands of Chinese — English- and Chinese-educated, China- and Malaya-born, rickshaw pullers and businessmen alike. This broad mass had intense needs and hopes: for the proper commemoration of loved ones; for retribution on war criminals and compensation; and for the comforting feeling that others had achieved revenge-by-proxy upon the Japanese. There was a swirling of emotions of love, hate and anger in the Chinese community that needed satiating, as seen in novels such as Miao Xiu's *Huolang* (*Waves of Fire*) of 1960.[10] The collective memory of the war, however amorphous, was a powerful force, and one that different political groups, and champions of various groups of veterans, hoped to harness to their own needs and purposes.

As we shall see, this would involve not just the emphasis of some and neglect of others, but also the imaginative re-interpretation of what people such as Chin Peng and Lim Bo Seng had done, of the context they had worked in, and of their very identities and hopes. People may have been heroic at the time, but postwar "heroes" were also refashioned to be icons of the sort of "Malayan" different parties and groups wanted to remember.

The "Great East Asiatic War"

These battles to fashion suitable heroes also need to be framed in the context of Overseas Chinese's understandings of "the war". For them, this began in July 1937, in China. It was not the "Second World War" or "Pacific War", but a "Great East Asiatic" or Patriotic War for China. When the postwar Malayan press ran stories of local resistance, they often accompanied these with accounts from China. Next to stories of massacres of Chinese in Malaya were stories about those in China. This wider Sino-Japanese conflict would see four million Chinese soldiers and 18 million civilians perish.

Postwar Chinese leaders would repeatedly draw upon the memory of this wider war, and of its Japanese atrocities. After the formation of the People's Republic of China in 1949, the state there would also depict the communists as the only force capable of launching effective counterattacks. There emerged a mainland Chinese nationalism that viewed the "story of anti-Japanese resistance as the founding impulse of the new nation". Recollection of wartime atrocities by communist leaders "allows them to re-enact, in textbooks and elsewhere, the great victory that originally legitimised their rule",[11] and forged a united and strong China.[12]

The Sino-Japanese War also brought Chinese nationalism to a previously apolitical peasantry. This process was set in motion by the indiscriminate violence that the Japanese army visited upon peasants, particularly in the brutal "*soto*" (mopping-up) operations. When moving into rural areas, the Japanese could not easily distinguish guerrillas from civilians, so they killed large numbers of civilians in order to cow the population. This gave the impression that the Japanese were at war with the Chinese people as a whole.[13] To use a Southeast Asian expression, Japanese tactics brought "the frog out of the coconut shell", making China's peasant masses believe that they had a life and death stake in events and forces beyond their villages and fields.

In the early postwar period, the Chinese community of Malaya and Singapore also venerated the guerrilla heroes of China, and mourned the victims of Japanese atrocities inflicted there. The Occupation also seems to have helped to bring the Southeast Asian frog out of the coconut shell: in the sense of making more Chinese there see that they needed to operate beyond their business, clan, dialect and other community groups. Wang Gungwu has observed that in Singapore and Malaya,

> the Japanese made no distinction whether a Chinese was a patriot or not; all Chinese faced the same kind of terror and fear ... the effect of this on the collective memory consolidated the sense of Chinese nationalism and forced a Chinese cultural identity on everyone, no matter how long the Chinese had been in the country.[14]

What this left was the question of what form this more politicised sense of Chinese identity would take. Would it result in a greater sense of China-based nationalism, or at least of ethnic-based identity as the basis for involvement in Malayan politics? Or would the groups who wanted to forge a new "Malayan" identity — such as the ideologically very different MCP leaders, and business leader Tan Cheng Lock — succeed in making Chinese think in more cross-communal terms? Would the communists, who had led the most successful resistance forces, be able to turn this to political advantage and emphasise their troops as the main heroes? Or would business elites, and English-language-educated Chinese leaders, be able to ally with the British to allow non-communist heroes to dominate the public stage?

Chinese Unity and Divisions: Dalforce

Soon after the war, Chinese writers honoured the Chinese irregular unit present at the fall of Singapore. This was variously known as the Overseas Chinese Volunteer Force or similar titles by local Chinese, and as Dalforce. The latter derived from the name of the John Dalley of the Malayan Police. Dalley put together a band of 1,250 Chinese (including at least 1,072 combatants) to help defend Singapore in 1942. Dalley headed the unit, with Major Hu Tie Jun as Deputy Commander.

After the war, Dalforce was initially presented as a heroically dedicated unit that had brought together Chinese "of all walks of life" and so represented a time of unprecedented unity between the rival supporters of the Kuomintang and the Communist Party.[15] The leaders of these parties had temporarily put their differences aside from December 1941, when the British belatedly asked for Chinese help.

One of the earliest postwar attempts to present a public image of Dalforce was by Mah Khong, Chairman of the Dalforce veterans' group. In December 1946, he wrote an account of the unit's exploits for Singapore's Chinese Affairs Department. He wanted to persuade the authorities to give back-pay for all of the Occupation, which the British felt Dalforce, as irregulars, did not warrant. He wrote that,

> although we differed in sexes, religious creeds, political ideas, yet since Malaya is our second home where we have been born and bred, we felt it necessary for us to resist the invasion of the bestial enemy … [Dalforce was formed from] … various elements — some having been the promoters of political causes, some having been editors, or managers, some having been teachers of schools, some having been students and co-eds of Raffles College, some having been young partners in shops, some having been industrious labourious peasants, hawkers, old women, young dancing girls.[16]

Mah Khong painted a vision of Overseas Chinese unity in the face of the Japanese threat. Yet despite his primary audience being British, he still presented his comrades as having fought in the "second front" in the Sino-Japanese War, against "the enemy that opened the line in the south to frustrate the efforts of our fatherland".[17] Veterans emphasised that they were fighting for *zuguo*: the "fatherland" or "motherland", meaning China. When referring to the wartime achievements, Chinese-language literature continued to write of *nan qiao* (southern sojourners) or *hua qiao* (Chinese sojourners). The use of *qiao* (sojourner) indicated

strong attachment to China, and that the term "Malayan Chinese" —
though growing in popularity — had not yet triumphed.[18]

More substantive accounts soon followed Mah Khong's. Dalforce
veteran Chen Ping Bo published his story in the Chinese-language *The
Great War and the Overseas Chinese: Malayan Section* (*Da Zhan Yu Nan
Qiao: Malaiya Zhi Bu*), which appeared in January 1947. This epic book
was published by Tan Kah Kee's China Relief Fund. In his chapter,
Chen declared that the goal of Dalforce had been "to fight the enemy
ourselves at the overseas front of our motherland". Chen also emphasised unity, saying that "the Volunteer Force consisted of Communists,
Nationalists, clerks, labourers, dancers, students, and various other
types ..."[19] He thus echoed Mah Khong, and Dalforce Deputy Commander Hu Tie Jun's *Singapore Chinese Volunteer Army: The Battle of
Singapore, 1942* (*Xing Hua Yi Yong Jun Zhan Dou Shi: 1942 Xing Zhou
Boa Wei Zhang*).[20]

Writers further recalled that Dalforce was one section of the
Chinese Anti-Japanese Mobilisation Council. This was set up under
businessman and community leader Tan Kah Kee, at a meeting held in
the Singapore Chinese Chamber of Commerce at the end of December
1941. Why had the British asked for united Chinese help so late?
Because of their suspicion that the communists and Kuomintang were
both dangerous, both offshoots of "alien" or overseas (Chinese, non-
Malayan) politics, and both anti-colonial in temperament.

Tan Kah Kee's 1946 *Memoirs of an Overseas Chinese in Southeast
Asia* (*Nan Qiao Huiyilu*), describes the origins of the Mobilisation
Council. It was established in December 1941 after Chiang Kai-shek
and Shenton Thomas, the Governor of Singapore, appealed to the
Chinese to unite. The first meeting at the Chamber of Commerce established sections under Tan Kah Kee's leadership, notably for Labour
Service, General Affairs, Subscription, Propaganda, Militia or district
watch, Financial, and Secretariat. Ng Yeh Lu (alias Wee Mong Chen),
a communist just released from prison with other political prisoners,
successfully put forward a motion of "arming the people".[21] Ng Yeh Lu
and fellow communist Lim Kang Sek (alias Lin Chiang Shih) were given
command of the resulting Popular Armed Units Section.[22]

Simultaneously, Lieutenant Colonel Dalley of Special Branch was
organising "Dalforce" under instructions from Malaya Command Headquarters.[23] The Popular Armed Units Section agreed to encourage volunteers to join Dalforce. Dalforce's strength eventually came to 1,250,
organized into the equivalent of eight companies. This consisted of

seven companies of 150, with an additional "Dare to Die" 6A company of 120. One additional company had just 40 members when looming defeat caused the British to disband it. There were also 40 staff members at Dalforce headquarters at the Nanyang Normal School along Kim Yam Road, including a propaganda section.

At least three Dalforce companies, totalling 450 men or more, went into action on Singapore Island alongside British, Australian, and Indian troops in February 1942.[24] As the first volunteers left for the front on 4 February, they sang:

> Arise, arise, those who do not want to be slaves. Build a new Great Wall with your flesh and blood.[25]

In the postwar years, Dalforce would be eulogised as the most fearless fighters.[26] Veterans Mah Khong, Hu Tie Jun, and Chen Ping Bo gave accounts of driving the Japanese back. Mah Khong described how even before the Japanese came over the Johor Straits, "in the deep midnight we struck back the enemy's patrolling fleets" and later when the Japanese attacked Singapore in the northwest, "we repulsed thirty rubber vessels". Other troops are blamed for Dalforce having to retreat. When the Japanese landed on the night of 8 to 9 February 1942, "we attacked the landed enemy troops fighting vehemently till day-break"; but "owing to the loss of the defence line of other allied forces we were finally compelled to advance to the defenceless 15th milestone quarter of Jurong Road".

Mah Khong also described how Dalforce's Second Company came to suffer the unit's highest casualties. On the Lim Chu Kang Road, the Second Company "advanced to the twelfth milestone to fight a vehement battle with the enemy so valiantly that for a time we advanced five miles and the enemy was repulsed". The veterans claimed that after the authorities "decided to forsake" Singapore, "our forces still continued holding weapons to fight the most bloody battles".[27] Veterans also claimed to have slowed down the Japanese advance by several days.[28]

In addition, where white troops had run, they claimed to have fought on some occasions almost to annihilation. He Wei Bo, leader of the third platoon, Second Company, described attack and counterattack near the Lim Chu Kang Road. After the Australians began to retreat and Japanese troops advanced:

> Bullets went flying in the direction of the enemy troops. I tossed a hand grenade which sent them scuttling for safety. My comrades and

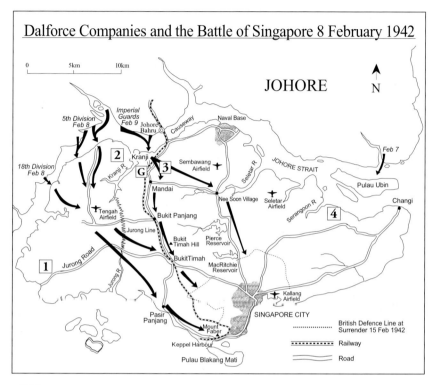

Dalforce Companies and the Battle of Singapore 8 February 1942

KEY

1   Dalforce Company at Jurong 18th milestone.

2   Dalforce Company at Lim Chu Kang 19½ milestone and attached to the 2/20 Battalion, Australian 22nd Brigade.

3   Dalforce Company at Causeway Sector

4   Dalforce Company at area between Serangoon River and Pasir Ris. (Also referred to as the Company at Hougang by Hu Tie Jun).

G   Chang Teh Cheok's Overseas Chinese Guard Platoon.

Map 4.1   Dalforce Deployment in the Battle for Singapore, February 1942

I yelled at the top of our voices as we rushed forward to fight the enemy. A couple of Japanese soldiers fell ... By the time the enemy troops advanced again we had used up almost all our bullets. Left with no alternative, we backed off slowly and made contact with the Aussie soldiers ... I was slightly injured in my left arm. Surrounded by the enemy troops, the Aussies took the offensive. Our team followed suit.

Luck was not with us. Several of our comrades were captured and summarily executed. One by one, they collapsed under the hail of bullets with blood gushing from their wounds. I fainted at the sight and two of the dead men fell on top of me. Their blood, still warm, splashed on my body as if to wash away all our humiliation. As I lay there motionless, I thought of my dear mates and how they died in glory for Singapore. I vowed to avenge their deaths if I survived …

He Wei Bo did survive, crawling out from under two stinking corpses hours later.[29]

Though neither Japanese nor Australian accounts corroborate the most dramatic claims for Dalforce's impact, there is no doubt that some units took heavy casualties.[30] After the war, a Singapore Chinese Affairs Department study of 1946 confirmed that "all reports state that in spite of being badly armed and inadequately trained, they fought bravely". Casualties of the most badly mauled companies were from 30 to 60 per cent (the latter for the 2nd Company, see p. 33); and an estimated 300 were killed in action in total.

They were told to disperse on 13 February 1942, so there were no prisoners of war. Many fled into Malaya after the Fall of Singapore. He Wei Bo, for instance, swam the straits to Singapore's north and then lay low for a short time in a Malayan pineapple plantation. Others, mainly from the unit's communist members, joined the MPAJA. Some were killed by the Japanese when their identities were discovered. The number of people in the postwar Overseas Chinese Volunteer (Dalforce) Association soon reached 600, half of the original complement of Dalforce. Even allowing for those who survived but never joined the Association, the unit clearly took heavy casualties.[31]

Percival's Challenge

The images of Dalforce heroism and a Chinese community united in resisting the Japanese were strong. Not all British commanders shared this exalted view. In February 1948, Lieutenant General A.E. Percival, who commanded British forces at the Fall of Singapore, wrote that "many of the Asiatics were of a type unsuitable for training as soldiers", and there was "great difficulty in filling the Chinese sub-units in the existing Volunteer organisation". This unwillingness "was in no way due to lack of available material or to lack of effort on the part of the military authorities", but "due chiefly to the lack of unity and of forceful leadership which existed among the Chinese population". Percival concluded that "the Chinese population ... lacked homogeneity and centralised leadership ... the sense of citizenship was not strong nor, when it came to the test, the feeling that this was a war for home and country". He argued that the "Asiatic population" showed no sense of "service to the State in return for the benefits received from membership of the British Empire".

Percival also resorted to stereotyping, remarking that "Asiatics tend to take the side of the more powerful". He had also limited the demolition of facilities since he "feared that the sight of destruction being carried out well behind our lines would induce them to help the enemy rather than ourselves". Percival's words oozed the sort of colonial distrust of prewar Chinese that had delayed British calls for their help.[32]

Percival's despatches were published in Malaya and Singapore in February 1948. On 27 February, the Chinese-language newspaper *Nan Chiau Jit Pau* (*The Southern Seas Chinese Press*) reported that the Chinese had been raising funds for the Chinese government since 1937, and had mounted crippling trade boycotts on Japanese businesses. The editor wrote that "Not a word is said of Tan Kah Kee's leadership in organising the Relief Fund Committee and the Mobilisation Council and neither is anything mentioned about the merits of thousands of local people who sacrificed themselves during the operations". Yet these Chinese efforts had proceeded even during times when the British government had sought to curb anti-Japanese activities, to avoid jeopardising its own policy of appeasing Japanese concerns, so as to make a two-front war (Europe and Asia) less likely.

The editor of the *Nan Chiau Jit Pau* wrote that "before the outbreak of the Pacific War, the Malayan Chinese anti-Japanese sentiment was very high and they were quite united in the stand against the Japanese, but they could not engage themselves effectively in anti-Japanese activities because the British Government then was not willing to clash with Japan". He argued that "after the inauguration of the Mobilisation Council, three thousand people enlisted themselves immediately to be armed, but on account of the British Government's delay in issuing arms they were not organised until the Japanese forces landed in Singapore in the beginning of February".[33]

On 3 March 1948, Tan Kah Kee, *Nan Chiau Jit Pau*'s owner, wrote a public letter to the Secretary of State for War in London. Published in the morning edition of the Chinese-owned *Malaya Tribune*, the *Morning Tribune*, of 5 March, this stated that:

> on behalf of the Chinese community I wish to register my strongest protest against the various references to the Chinese in Lt.-General A.E. Percival's despatch and I wish to ask for suitable amendments to the despatch and an apology to the Chinese community

Tan Kah Kee's letter asserted that "in peace-time the Government had consistently denied the Chinese the opportunity to serve in the army, but on 1 February the British Government decided to hand 1,000 rifles to a group of Chinese youths flying the Chinese flag popularly known as the "Dalforce" and sent them to the Lim Chu Kang Sector". Tan further argued that:

> if the Chinese were really inclined 'to take up the side of the more powerful', then how are we to explain China's resistance against the Japanese, which lasted for 8 years, and the heroic sacrifices of the MPAJA? ... even before the fall of Kuala Lumpur, Chinese youths had begun to organise guerrillas to harass the advance of the Japanese. These guerrillas later developed into the Malayan people's Anti-Japanese Army, which became famous for its heroic struggle with the Japanese.[34]

Chinese opinion united. The editorial of the *Morning Tribune* wrote that "on the one hand the General's critical eye is blind towards defects that pertained to European military elements", and "the despatch is careful not to give offence in this direction", but "the General does not permit himself this caution when pronouncing judgements upon the part played by the local population, particularly the Chinese". The *Morning Tribune* complained that, "If any evidence is required that the British military authorities had no sympathetic understanding of the people in whose country they fought, it is amply demonstrated in Gen. Percival's comments ... [that] many of the Asiatics were of a type unsuited for training as soldiers". This was "a myth which, however, convenient politically for Colonial powers, has been irretrievably shattered by the recent war".[35]

An apology was given by the Governor of Singapore, Franklin Gimson. But Percival's own explanation to the Singapore press was glib.

In the House of Commons, the Secretary of State for War sidestepped the issue, saying that the despatch only reflected "the personal opinions of the author".[36] The colonial authorities in Malaya and Singapore, meanwhile, were unenthusiastic about the public commemoration of Dalforce. They did not endorse the Overseas Chinese's view of the fall of Singapore, which had Dalforce and its Chinese guerrilla fighters at the forefront as an expression of the nationalism that the Chinese community felt towards China.

The Colonial State and Dalforce

If Malaya's Chinese had known what colonial authorities really thought about Dalforce in 1947–1948, they would have been furious. E.C.S. Adkins, Secretary of the Singapore Chinese Affairs Department, regarded them as mainly "recruited from hot-headed communists", so that after the war "a number of them have become gangsters, but this is hardly surprising given their antecedents". He argued that Dalforce members should be given limited compensation, just as the MPAJA had. Adkins noted that "The M.P.A.J.A. were, very wisely, paid off and disbanded soon after the re-occupation".[37] The idea was to quickly celebrate then forget the wartime contributions of Dalforce and the MPAJA.

The British therefore gave recognition to Dalforce's achievements more out of expediency than admiration. After MPAJA demobilisation on 1 December 1945, the authorities held a ceremony at Singapore's Municipal Building on 6 January 1946. At this, members of anti-Japanese resistance guerrilla groups were personally given the Burma Star and the 1939–1945 Star by SEAC Supreme Commander Mountbatten.

The majority of those honoured were from the MPAJA. Wang Siang Pau was the lone representative of Dalforce. He dressed in Dalforce's uniform of indigo blue shirt and trousers and khaki yellow cloth for headgear, in contrast to the khaki and three-starred beret of the MPAJA.[38] The Chinese Affairs Department went to the black market to get Wang's uniform made because there were none in existence.[39] A few months later, the authorities sent Mah Kong and On Yong How, the most fluent English-speaking Dalforce members, to the 8 June 1946 London Victory Parade.[40]

The Overseas Chinese community pressed for more to be done to commemorate their wartime experience. On 3 February 1946, a joint meeting was held of the Singapore Chinese Chamber of Commerce and the Singapore China Relief Committee. This decided that a memorial should be erected to Chinese who had defended Singapore, together with those who had lost their lives in the Occupation. Their preferred site was on top of the ruins on a hill in Butik Batok, where the Japanese formerly had their memorial to their war dead: the *Syonan Chureito*.[41]

Tan Kah Kee's suggestion for an Overseas Chinese memorial "was stalled off temporarily" because the colonial administration wanted a memorial that emphasised the unity of all races that had fought under the British Empire.[42] The Chinese demand for a memorial that would affirm their identity was sidetracked into a proposal for this "Combined War Memorial". Tan Kah Kee "objected to the scheme on the grounds that there are conflicting religious interests".[43] Within a few years, it became apparent that there was no enthusiasm for another war memorial with imperial overtones.[44] In the meanwhile, a separate proposal for a collection of monuments at Bukit Timah got nowhere by 1952, for reasons which included lack of funding, and a loss of impetus as early ideas for memorials fell to the wayside. Instead, the colonial authorities quietly changed the wording on the Singapore Cenotaph for the war dead from the First World War, adding the dates for the Second World War. The First World War cenotaphs in Kuala Lumpur and major towns in Malaya were similarly re-enscribed.

This did not satisfy Dalforce veterans, partly because of an obdurate attitude by the colonial authorities. Despite the 6 January and 8 June 1946 public ceremonies in Singapore and London, the authorities resisted acknowledging that Dalforce members were formally part of British Imperial forces in 1942. They regarded them as irregulars, who did not therefore require back payment for the entire war. The veterans conducted an ultimately unsuccessful campaign, demonstrating outside public buildings from 1946–1947. They insisted that the British should acknowledge that they were not "irregulars", but had been under Malaya Command.[45] Veterans claimed that Colonel Dalley had told them at disbandment in 1942, that "you are certainly to receive the same treatment as the British Regular Army".[46] As a compromise, in 1947, the British agreed to give the veterans seven and a half months' back pay.

Dalforce veterans represented by Hu Tie Jun also demanded a separate Dalforce war memorial in the Jurong area. This was rejected in favour of the abortive combined war memorial.[47] The large number of communists in Dalforce also contributed to British doubts about officially honouring their heroes.[48]

Dalforce was kept in the public eye by the controversies over back pay and the lack of a proper memorial. Its veterans continued to bring to light their exploits in the news. One of the most extraordinary stories was that of Madam Cheng Seang Ho (alias Cheong Sang Hoo).[49] Madam Cheng was a 66-year-old grandmother when she joined Dalforce in 1942. She and her husband Sim Chin Foo (alias Chum Chan Foo) fought alongside British and Australian forces at Bukit Timah on 10–11 February 1942. Madam Cheng told the Singapore press in 1948 how her comrades tried to hold back the Japanese "in their last stand at Bukit Timah firing their last shots from behind shell-torn tree trunks". Afterwards, "with a handful of survivors", she "escaped through the jungle and reached the mainland", but her husband "slipped into Singapore city". She described how a few months after the fall, she went back to Singapore. The two fighters were briefly reunited and worked as labourers. But there was to be no happy ending. Her husband appears to have been caught by the Japanese military police, the *kempeitai*, and "tortured to death". He is recorded as having died on 1 September 1942.[50]

Madam Cheng's story remained the exception to the rule that female fighters are given scant mention in Overseas Chinese literature on the war.[51] In July 1948, the Chinese Affairs Department issued her a letter of appreciation. This had photographs of herself and her husband, and was signed by E.C.S. Adkins, Colonel Dalley, and colonial officials. The letter stated, in both Chinese and English, that:

> This is to certify that Madam Cheong Sang Hoo of Singapore together with her husband and children voluntarily joined the Dalforce during the critical days of the Japanese Attack in 1942. Madam Cheong fought the Japanese gallantly and risked her life by going to the front at the battle of Bukit Timah where her comrades died one after the other. This engagement certainly dealt a hard blow to the Japanese. Although advanced in years Madam Cheong was courageous enough to fight for the cause of righteousness.[52]

Madam Cheng was not satisfied with a private letter. On 2 March 1957, she attended the official unveiling of the Kranji War Memorial: the memorial to the 24,000 war dead from British Imperial forces in Southeast Asia who had no known grave. Madam Cheng's husband's name, Sim Chin Foo, was one of the 134 names of the Dalforce war dead listed on the memorial. Just as Governor Robert Black stepped up to the monument to lay his official wreath, Madam Cheng, by now aged 81 and clad in a worn samfoo, stepped out from the crowd. She stumbled her way up to the centre of ceremony, at the Cross of Remembrance, and began "to wail for the dead".[53]

Plate 4.1 Cheng Seang Ho at the opening of the Kranji War Memorial, 1957

By this stage, events had overtaken the campaign to publicly honour Dalforce. The outbreak of the Malayan Emergency in June 1948 had made Dalforce more suspect than ever in British eyes. They could see that it had represented a moment of Chinese unity against Japan. But equally its members had included large numbers of communists, who were now enemies branded "bandits" and (from 1952) "terrorists".

What would Dalforce's response to the Emergency be? On 3 July 1948, Lim Siew Pheng, the Secretary of the Dalforce veterans association, indicated that "the majority of Dalforce members, who number about 800 today, would not bear arms in the present emergency even if the Government asked them to do so".[54] The Dalforce Ex-Comrades Association had a name redolent of the MPAJA's Ex-Comrades Association. Its offices were in the same building as the communist trade unions, the Pan-Malayan Federation of Trade Unions (PMFTU) and the Singapore Federation of Trade Unions (SFTU). Lim Siew Pheng was at pains to point out to disbelieving colonial authorities that "we are not communists and have nothing to do with them". He protested that "neither have we any connection with the S.F.T.U. or the P.M.F.T.U., although we did share the same building". Lim insisted that, "We took up arms to fight the Japanese. The war is over, and our anti-Japanese activities are also over".[55]

   In this context, the authorities were unlikely to support commemoration of an organisation that had included large numbers of communists. Chinese-language writers continued to affirm that Dalforce had driven back and delayed the Japanese, losing up to half their men, while in public, the colonial and early postcolonial state increasingly drew a veil over it.[56] But, while the Emergency made the authorities more ambivalent about Dalforce, that was nothing compared to the hostility it provoked towards commemoration of the largest group of anti-Japanese fighters: the MPAJA.

The Malayan People's Anti-Japanese Army

The Malayan Emergency was declared by the British between 16 (locally) and 18 (nationally) in June 1948. At this point, all of the MCP's senior military officers were MPAJA veterans, and 60 per cent of MPAJA veterans joined the insurrection.[57] On 23 July 1948, the MPAJA Ex-Comrades Association was duly banned along with all MCP-affiliated organisations.[58] Official opposition could now be expected to any commemoration of communist organisations.[59] The Emergency thus drove communist remembrance underground, culminating two years of struggle over how to remember the war and liberation. For the battle over memory had commenced in earnest almost as soon as the war had ended.

   Commemoration of the MPAJA was coloured by its communist background from the beginning. In 1946, the MPAJA Ex-Comrades Association's publication *Blood Memorials* (*Xue Bei*), featured poems and eulogies highlighting the communist backgrounds of fighters. The authorities banned it after 1948, and banned it remained until republished in 1997 in Hong Kong.[60] Here is *Xue Bei* praise for a war heroine:

> Fighting the Japs was the so brave Communist.
> She was tall and sweet,
> Her age was twenty eight,
> Tortured by the cruel M.P.
> But it was all in vain,
> She mentioned not a name,
> Then one day, at a time,
> She …
> Faced the sentence of death,
> Though she is gone now, she grows with us,
> Always in our memory.[61]

After June 1948, "Bandits", as the state initially called communist fighters,* could no longer innocently be remembered for their part in the Overseas Chinese anti-Japanese effort. Yet that is how most Chinese had remembered the MPAJA in the immediate postwar years, and into the 1940s and 1950s.

Hai Shang Ou's *The Malayan People's Anti-Japanese Army* (*Malaiya Renmin Kangri Jun*) was published in December 1945. Hai wrote that "the MPAJA guerrilla forces recreated and used the tactics adapted from the experience in China". His book quickly gained the status of semi-official MPAJA military history, with its statistics reproduced in later publications.[62] Tzu Szu's December 1945 *Anti-Japanese Heroes in Southern Johor* (*Kangri Yingxiong Zai Rou Nan*) went further. It described numerous, heroic *nan qiao* (southern sojourner) guerrillas in the MPAJA Fourth Regiment, in a way that became almost formulaic. Joining the MPAJA and embracing communism transformed the individual. The story of an anonymous rubber tapper will suffice to give the tone. He was illiterate, but "thanks to MPAJA training in bringing out his natural talents that had remained dormant as an exploited worker in the capitalist system", soon became a leader and instructor, analysing strategies and international affairs. Tested in battle, he "fought to the last drop of blood".[63]

When the British returned in September 1945, they were therefore confronted with an MPAJA that was popular among swathes of the Chinese community. Even the conservative sections of the Chinese press serialised stories of guerrilla heroes. The *Nanyang Siang Pau* ran a ten-part serial in September and October 1945. This featured 23-year-old Overseas Chinese *nu zhanshi* (female warrior) Cheah Swee Seng, modelled after legendary Ming warrior Ge Nen Niang. The story commences with Cheah leaving a Chinese independent school in Kuala Lumpur to join the guerrillas. Initially, she does not even know how to handle a rifle, but soon she is a crack shot, and proficient with hand grenades. As the story unfolds, Cheah leads up to 30 armed women against the Japanese.[64]

In the shadow of the war, the authorities therefore had little choice but to allow the MPAJA to be commemorated in this open, eulogising fashion.[65] But they were also wary of the MPAJA, and anxious to see it

---

* The government officially redesignated them "Communist Bandits" or "CTs" from 1952.

Plate 4.2 MPAJA 4th Regiment demobilisation parade in Johor Bahru, 1 December 1945

demobilised.[66] This was done in December 1945, when most MPAJA men handed over weapons, received $350, and were awarded the Burma and 1939–1945 Stars.[67] The War Office considered withholding medals because they were led by communists, but Mountbatten warned of "internal repercussions amongst the only people of Malaya who fought for us".[68] A further ceremony, in front of Singapore's Municipal Building, was organised to recognise the contribution of anti-Japanese fighters in general. On 6 January 1946, Lord Mountbatten, as Supreme Allied Commander SEAC, awarded the leaders of anti-Japanese forces with the Burma Star and the 1939–1945 Star. Eight Chinese MPAJA leaders, three non-MPAJA Malay guerrillas, four Force 136 and Kuomintang Chinese guerrillas, and one Dalforce fighter, were decorated.

The stories of the eight MPAJA leaders who received military awards were retold by the press as heroic tales.[69] Some of the MPAJA guerrillas would be further honoured when they were sent to the 8 June 1946 London Victory parade as part of a 135-man Malayan contingent.[70]

Ironically, some of those honoured — in Singapore and in London — would go into the jungle again in 1948, and be hunted down.[71] The most prominent of the eight in Singapore were Chin Peng and Liew Yau, both Central Military Council leaders of the MPAJA.[72] Chin Peng would become MCP Secretary General in 1947, and lead many MPAJA veterans back into the jungle to fight first the colonial authorities, and then the independent government of Malaysia. He would only finally negotiate a peace with the latter in December 1989.

Liew Yau was a graduate of Special Training School 101, who had set up and led the MPAJA's First Regiment (Selangor). Both Chin Peng and Liew Yau were twice captured by the Japanese, and twice escaped. Liew's last escape was a sensational jail-break from prison in Kuala Lumpur. There was, however, nothing heroic about his end. After being betrayed by his own bodyguard, he was shot dead by British security forces on 16 July 1948, at a hideout near Kajang. When he died, his place as Regiment leader was taken by another of the eight decorated in January 1946: Chan Yeung Pan (Chou Yang Pin). Chan's fate was even more inglorious. He would betray his former comrades, and help the administration hunt some of them down. In MCP parlance, he went from hero to "running dog". Another MPAJA leader to receive medals on 6 January was Liao Wei Chung (alias "Colonel Itu"), who had been a commander of the Fifth Regiment (Perak). He was arrested at the start of the Emergency and banished to China, where he would die in the 1980s.[73]

In January 1946, though, these grim destinies lay in a distant, if not quite unimaginable, future. The anti-Japanese guerrillas posed for photographs with British officials on the steps of the Municipal Building. Some smiled as they received their awards from Mountbatten, who wore a decoration he had received from Chiang Kai-shek. At the evening reception at Government House (today's *Istana*), Mountbatten spoke to every fighter, using a few words of Mandarin he had learned for the occasion. Afterwards, the MPAJA returned to Raffles Hotel, booked for them by the British. Things only soured the next day, when the MPAJA contingent refused a military tour.[74]

After June 1948, public commemoration of MPAJA fighters such as those recognised in January 1946 became unacceptable. Colonial officials noted in July 1948 that as "former members of MPAJA are main components of insurgents now fighting against the Government in Malaya", recognition of wartime efforts was not possible without a "most detailed screening" of any particular MPAJA fighter.[75] Even non-communist MPAJA veterans, such as Ho Thean Fook, felt their past was best kept quiet. Ho observed that all members of the MPAJA were suspect, basking in "tainted glory". Ho later wrote that "only when the famous Berlin Wall, separating East Berlin from West Berlin, was brought down and the communist ideology disintegrated in the Soviet Union where it all began, did I start to write about it".[76]

The group representing the MPAJA veterans was the MCP-controlled MPAJA Ex-Comrades Association. It was formed on 8 December 1945 with Liew Yau as President. A total of 6,800 MPAJA veterans joined.[77] John Davis, who had fought alongside the MPAJA as a member of Force 136, wrote that the MPAJA Ex-Comrades Association "is nothing more than a satellite political organisation of the Malayan Communist Party".[78] Chin Peng viewed the MPAJA veterans group as a vehicle to continue the MCP's struggle against British colonialism.[79]

Indeed, the MCP was almost certainly already plotting the humiliation of British authorities by the time the January 1946 ceremony took place. The MCP wanted to mark 15 February 1946: the first post-liberation anniversary of the fall of Singapore. This offered the first major date on which MPAJA veterans might commemorate their fallen. According to the MPAJA's Chinese-language newspaper, the *Combatant's Friend* (*Zhan You Bao*), however, the MPAJA organisers were not interested solely in commemoration. They also saw this as a continuation of labour unrest and of other activities intended to challenge the colonial authorities.

The *Combatant's Friend* announced that, "Four years ago on February 15th, British imperialism against the wishes of all Malayans shamefully bowed before Japanese Fascism and surrendered ... As a result the five million people in Malaya suffered numerous deaths and loss of property and lived in agony during three years and eight months. This we shall never forget".[80] On 14 February, the MCP-affiliated *New Democracy* (*Xin Min Zhu Bao*) ran an article called "Never Forget the Painful Lessons of 15th February". The first lesson of the resulting occupation was:

> [the] sense of urgency to gain freedom and fight for democracy ... Secondly, the day marks the defeat of the British whose army betrayed the trust of Malayans, and left our people in the lurch. It

made our people for the first time realise the importance of unity and to fight for ourselves … Our victory eventually demonstrates that the strength of a united community is formidable, and we are all that we ever need to defend ourselves.[81]

The MPAJA Ex-Comrades Association's Lin Ah Liang applied for permission to hold a procession in Singapore on 15 February 1946. Before the war, Lin Ah Liang had been a *Sin Chew Jit Poh* journalist. When the Occupation began, he worked undercover for the MPAJA until caught, tortured, and sentenced to death. His life was saved by the Japanese surrender.[82] Lin was now a member of the MCP's Singapore Town Committee, as well as an MPAJA Ex-Comrades' Association's leader.[83]

The colonial authorities saw the proposal to mark 15 February as an attempt to humiliate them. The date had been a holiday during the Occupation, and the MCP also proposed that 15 February 1946 be a holiday. Mountbatten issued a statement, affirming the banning of the proposed rally and procession. The statement read that "whilst expressing the fullest sympathy with the desire to commemorate the fall of the Japanese fascists", he felt "that the most appropriate date would be September 12, the date of the formal surrender of the Japanese in Singapore".[84]

Mountbatten privately told London, that "a few Extremists are preparing to arrange celebrations for that day" and "it is obvious that this small minority is trying to embarrass us by every means and is hoping to arouse contempt for the administration. We must clearly resist such efforts".[85] Colonial officials concurred that "a less appropriate date could hardly have been chosen".[86] Victor Purcell, Principal Adviser on Chinese Affairs to the BMA, wrote, that "if the mass of labourers could be persuaded to associate the British defeat in 1942 with their present sufferings, a great point would have been gained in the campaign to discredit the B.M.A". The present sufferings referred to wages falling behind postwar inflation, and still serious food shortages.[87] Thus, the scene was set for a showdown.

At around 10am on 15 February 1946, Lin Ah Liang emerged from the MPAJA and MCP headquarters on Queen Street. He led 250 demonstrators to a field opposite St Joseph's Institution at Bras Basah Road. The field is now occupied by buildings of Singapore Management University. Once at the field, the marchers came face to face with 45 police, who ordered the assembly to disperse. The demonstrators refused, and responded with sticks, crowbars, and bottles. Finally, the police fired into the crowd. One demonstrator died on the spot, another in hospital, and 19 were injured. Amongst the latter was Lin Ah Liang, who was also arrested.[88] The authorities recognised these events as a "trial of strength which took place between the British Military Administration and the Communist Party" from which "a feeling of confidence has been restored in the power of the Administration".[89]

The authorities also came down hard on attempts to mark 15 February in Malaya. In Labis, the police fired on a large crowd, killing 13 Chinese and hitting one Indian, who died later. At Mersing, the demonstration was stopped before it even began, though on 20 February, 250 Chinese did manage a protest against the earlier banning. Once again, police fired into the crowd, this time killing two.[90] There were also serious clashes between demonstrators and police in towns such as Malacca and Penang.[91] *New Democracy* claimed that 5,000 people gathered in Malacca alone.[92]

To the wider Chinese community, the 15 February demonstration was not "a trial of strength", but an almost sacred anniversary. Letters to *New Democracy* asked: "are we chickens and weeds?" The implication was that the British had fired on the people as if they were animals for slaughter and pests for eradication.[93] Even the conservative Chinese-language newspaper, the *Nanyang Siang Pau*, expressed sympathy for demonstrators.[94] While the leaders of the Chinese business community, such as the Chinese Chamber of Commerce in Penang, had been unwilling to back the banned 15 February demonstrations, the authorities' response now made them sympathetic.[95] Tan Kah Kee used a speech to argue that:

> people all over Malaya had just wanted to commemorate the painful incident of the day of 15 February when the Japanese invaded Singapore and commenced their occupation of the country. Better would have been expected of the British government than mobilising armed troops to stop such activities of the people, even to the extent of firing into unarmed crowds.

He added that the "way the British army have killed our people in this incident only reflects that they have treated us all with contempt ..."[96]

15 February was marked in another, quieter, but also more enduring way: by the erection of memorials. A large meeting was held in Kuala Lumpur to erect a monument to the MPAJA war dead.[97] At Umbai, just south of Malacca, the MPAJA Ex-Comrades' Association

erected a prominent monument to leaders of the Malacca MPAJA who had been killed in 1945. Their memorials and grave markers, in a Chinese cemetery on a hillside, carried the three stars of the MPAJA. Some of their tombstones blended the traditional and the communist. They were created in the Chinese Daoist (Taoist) armchair style, so the spirit of the deceased could recline and rest, but in addition, had the Communist hammer and sickle emblazoned at the top.[98]

Reflecting the strong Chinese character of the MPAJA, the commemoration of their war dead mixed traditional Chinese funeral practices from Buddhism and Daoism (Taoism) with communist symbolism. The grave tablets had a prayer written on them in Chinese characters. At their foot were the usual stone ledges for joss sticks and food offerings to be made to the deceased's spirit.[99] Many of these early monuments were in specifically Chinese community space, such as Chinese cemeteries.[100]

From 1945–1948, there were public reunions of MPAJA veterans at these sites, which celebrated the MPAJA fallen as the quintessential Chinese war heroes. The most notable was for the unveiling of a stone monument bearing the inscription *Jiu Yi Lieshi Jinianbei*: September 1st Martyrs' Memorial. This commemorated 18 communists — leaders and bodyguards — who were killed in a Japanese ambush on 1 September 1942. This high-powered group had been meeting near the Batu Caves, on the outskirts of Kuala Lumpur. 17 men and one woman died, betrayed to the Japanese by their own leader, Lai Teck. Lai Teck had been the Secretary General of the MCP, but before the war had also worked with the British Special Branch. During the war, he was quickly arrested and turned by the Japanese *kempeitai*. Lai Teck's treachery would send the majority of the MPAJA's senior leaders to their death in 1942–1943, though it did not seem to affect Britain's Force 136 officers. The traitor himself would flee in 1947, just when it seemed his identity was about to be revealed.

The "September Martyrs", meanwhile, were a focus for the traumas of resistance and the large numbers of MPAJA who had been betrayed. But they were also associated with heroic stories of the leaders' attempts to break free from encircling rings of the Japanese and their auxiliaries. The MCP and MPAJA now erected, near the Batu Caves on 1 September 1946, a memorial, a simple stone column inscribed with Chinese characters. The monument was said to mark the spot where the bodies of those ambushed and killed were dumped, after the Japanese had cut off their heads for display along Jalan Ampang in Kuala Lumpur.

The 1946 ceremony, held on Sunday 1 September, was even attended by Hugh T. Pagden, who had been Adviser on Chinese Affairs to the colonial administration as recently as April 1946. Pagden laid a wreath at the memorial in his personal capacity, at the invitation of members of the MPAJA Ex-Comrades Association, with whom he was friendly. Pagden did try to get an antagonistic colonial Public Relations Department to cover the occasion because he felt that it would create goodwill amongst equally suspicious ex-MPAJA members. He observed that the negative reaction was "characteristic" of colonial administration opinion.[101]

Colonial opposition ensured that later ceremonies in 1946 and 1947 needed to be quieter affairs. But colonial suspicions about the commemoration of the MPAJA's war dead hardened into suppression once the Malayan Emergency was declared. After the Ex-Comrades Association was banned in July 1948, and there were no longer public reunions of MPAJA veterans. Reunions were now held in exile, in China or Hong Kong, where a significant number of MPAJA veterans had been banished or fled to. An active group of MPAJA veterans in China and Hong Kong maintained contact with each other under the umbrella organisation *Xinma Qiaoyou Hui* (Singapore and Malaysian Returned Chinese Association). Sometimes they would publish Chinese-language accounts of their war exploits after their get-togethers, though even these were then banned in Singapore and Malaya.[102]

Communist commemoration in Malaya went into the jungle in 1948, and into villages on the forest frontier, along with the communists who took up arms again. In June 1949, the MCP's Central Committee fixed 1 September (sometimes referred to as "9-1") as "Revolutionary Martyrs Day". Henceforward, it joined other communist days such as Women's Day, 1 May, the July "anniversary" of the MCP's foundation, and the November anniversary of the Russian Revolution. It was 1 September that came to be used most for commemoration. It had everything, a glorious battle against the odds, large-scale martyrdom, and escapees whose survival proclaimed it a communists' "Dunkirk". The Emergency redoubled this anniversary's potency. In 1949, leaders in South Johor even claimed to have assembled 700 for a September event, despite the previous year's celebration being disrupted by British attack. Tension was high, people wept, berated British crimes, and gave supplies, "An old lady even donated her sixteen year old son to the Liberation forces as a revenge against the red-haired devils, who killed her elder son and burned down her house ..."[103]

The 15 September 1952 edition of *Freedom News* — the MCP's underground newspaper — shows a continuing elaboration of the September Martyrs' memory. It recounts the September Martyrs' battle in detail, down to ever more desperate attempts to break Japanese encirclement, and Comrade Siu Hong shouting "Long Live the M.C.P." before "he breathed his last".

The fallen were named in publications and at meetings, and comrades exhorted that the incident proved to all the party's "iron will" and "dare-to-die revolutionary spirit". Comrades were told that "they must also call to memory those other numerous martyrs", party and non-party, who had sacrificed themselves in the anti-Fascist and "the anti-British struggle".[104] In September 1956, *Freedom News* further exhorted that, "All our compatriots should join us in observing silence" for the martyrs.[105] The 1 September Martyrs' Day in this way took on features not dissimilar to British ceremonies on Remembrance Day: the reading out of the names of the fallen, a silence, the invocation to remember their sacrifice and take it as an example, and the gathering (when possible) around a memorial which could be taken to symbolise not just specific deaths, but the war dead in general.[106]

Chapter 9 will tell the story of how, after the December 1989 peace, a new September Martyrs memorial would rise up in Malaysia, with ex-comrades then able to celebrate "9-1" in public again. That, however, is running far ahead of our narrative. We left open, public commemoration in 1948, when the communists' remembrance went underground. From this point on, they also began killing "running dogs", which included from 1949 members of the newly formed Malayan Chinese Association (MCA), police, informants, and others deemed to be assisting the British. Some of these "running dogs" were shot, grenades were thrown at MCA shops, and sulphuric acid splashed on informants, in an attempt to "police" the population. The Malayan Emergency developed into a civil war amongst Chinese as well as an anti-colonial war. The attacks on the MCA in particular cut down any remaining Malayan Chinese unity on commemoration. To commemorate wartime MPAJA — no matter how heroic — would be to commemorate a party which had a grenade thrown at Tan Cheng Lock at an open meeting in April 1949 (he suffered a splintered bone and lost two pints of blood), or which had a schoolteacher shot in the head in broad daylight in 1952 for teaching against the Party in Penang.[107]

What, then, filled the public void in Malaya and Singapore?

Lim Bo Seng

We have seen how many Chinese wartime heroes, from the MPAJA and Dalforce, were regarded with suspicion by the colonial authorities before 1948, and with hostility afterwards. At the same time, non-communist Chinese — notably many businessmen, and sympathisers with Kuomintang Governments in China and later in Taiwan — sought alternative heroes. It was in this context that Lim Bo Seng came to be memorialised as an Overseas Chinese *Yue Fei* type of patriot.[†] He would be held up as an example of a successful businessman and doting father who risked everything, putting *zuoguo* (fatherland) above family and self.

Lim Bo Seng had been born in Nan-Ann, Fujian Province, in China on 27 April 1909. He was the first-born son of the wealthy Singapore merchant Lim Chee Gee. The latter brought his son to Singapore aged about 16, in 1926. By January 1930, when his father died, Lim was studying at Hong Kong University. Cutting his education short, he rushed back to Singapore. Though just 20, he now headed the family's Singapore-based Hock Ann biscuit and brick manufacturing businesses, and assumed his father's position on the board of the Singapore Chinese Chamber of Commerce.[108] Becoming a key supporter of the Kuomintang Party, he helped to revive its fortunes in Singapore in the 1930s.[109] With a need to keep the colonial authorities onside, he also maintained close relations with Special Branch in Singapore.[110]

When Japan attacked China in July 1937, the Chinese of Malaya and Singapore established a "Nanyang Chinese National Salvation Movement" and the "Singapore China Fund Relief Committee", both headed by Tan Kah Kee.[111] As a patriot and community leader, Lim took a leading role in the labour arm of the National Salvation Movement. He encouraged boycotts of Japanese businesses, and fundraising for China, notably getting workers at the Japanese-owned Dungun iron ore mine to strike in 1938. At this stage, the communists organised their anti-Japanese efforts separately and competitively in Anti-Enemy Backing Up Societies (AEBUS) of the sort the schoolboy Ong Boon Hua (alias Chin Peng) joined.

[†] Yue Fei was a patriotic 12th-century Southern Song Dynasty general who fought brilliantly and sometimes against overwhelming odds, only to suffer false accusations and execution. He is used as a model of martial ability and loyalty in Chinese literature.

Then came 8 December 1941, and the Japanese attack on Malaya. The British now, belatedly, dropped opposition to calling on their Chinese colonial subjects to help. In December 1941, Kuomintang, communists and other Chinese unified their efforts. They established the joint Chinese Anti-Japanese Mobilisation Council under Tan Kah Kee. This Mobilisation Council was to coordinate help for the defence of Singapore. It seemed natural that Lim should take charge of its Labour section, helping to secure 2,000 to 3,000 labourers a day for defence and civil works.[112]

With the Japanese closing in on Singapore Town in February 1942, Lim knew that he would be a prime target. But the docks were a chaos of bomb damage and would-be refugees, all seeking the last berths out. He arranged a steamer, but with so many who would be marked men to fit on, it was difficult to justify taking a large family, including his wife, Gan Choo Neo, four sons, and three daughters. Besides, what was safest? He feared it was "too risky for women and children" to leave. Japanese planes had sunk ships. He would later confide the pain of separation to his diary, but for now he must go, and they must stay.[113]

So Lim left Singapore on 12 February, zigzagging via a series of ships and ports to Sumatra, Ceylon, and finally India. Once in India, he was no ordinary refugee: he remained a well-known community leader, China-loyalist, Kuomintang supporter and anti-Japanese organiser. As such, he journeyed to Chungking (Chongqing) on 6 April 1942, to meet with the Chinese Kuomintang government in their capital of free China. They made him a Colonel, and sent him back to India to organise Chinese seamen into military service. Almost inevitably, this new mission meant going to the seaport with the largest concentration of stranded Chinese seamen: Calcutta.[114]

Hence, it was that Lim came to be in Calcutta in June 1942. Colonel Basil Goodfellow, and Captains John Davis and Richard Broome could hardly believe their luck. They were also in Calcutta, working for the eastern arm of Britain's "behind-enemy-lines" service: the Special Operations Executive. Now dubbed Force 136, the eastern unit needed Malayan Chinese to accompany its European officers back to Malaya. They knew that some communist Chinese that they had trained in Singapore's 101 Special Training School had established the MPAJA. Now they wanted sound — that is non-communist — men to liaise with MPAJA guerrillas. Such Chinese officers would also be able to use false papers to reconnoitre and visit inhabited areas: things that would be suicidal for white Europeans. They asked Lim: was he up for it?[115]

Lim confided to his diary that: "This was something after my heart. Since 1937, I have tried in my small ways to contribute to our war effort and this offered me an opportunity to continue work".[116] But he was also a Nationalist Chinese Colonel. So he flew to Chungking and secured permission to join Force 136, to be their Regional Liaison Officer with it, and for Chungking to provide recruits. The cooperation was agreed between the British and Nationalists at an official level. Others Lim Bo Seng approached shared his view that this work could contribute to China's wider struggle. Fellow SOE veteran Tan Chong Tee had also gone from Singapore to Chungking, and remembers thinking "yes, I must support Lim Bo Seng and help him in his noble task — national salvation".[117] Recruiting offices were opened in Chungking and Kunming, and Lim Bo Seng found himself scuttling between Chungking, SEAC headquarters in Kandy, and training centres in India.[118]

In this way, British officers of Force 136 added Chinese who were mostly of Nationalist sympathies to pro-British Chinese they had already recruited. These could return to Malaya with the British, to liaise with the MPAJA, and establish independent intelligence networks as well. The intention was to harness these various networks later for sabotage, and as the eyes and ears of any future reoccupation of Malaya.[119] There were months of training before the recruits would be ready. But finally, from May 1943, the men began to arrive on Malaya's coast by submarine.

As a leader, Lim had a longer wait. It was October 1943 before he found himself crossing the Indian Ocean in a Dutch submarine. As "Tan Choon Lim" (his operational name), he set out with his deputy, and Claude Fenner. Lim Bo Seng left the Dutch submarine on 2 November 1943. At this point, fact and legend start to diverge. Over the years, Lim and his colleagues' activities would increasingly be presented as those of Chinese Force 136 officers acting semi-autonomously, heroically trying to extend their own intelligence network in Perak's towns. Lim Bo Seng's friend and recruit, Tan Chong Tee, has written a book, *Force 136*, on the Chinese in that unit. Inevitably, this makes the Kuomintang recruits central, though it does include limited space on the MPAJA they contacted. By 1998, however, Clara Show's entertaining and popular comic book, *Lim Bo Seng: Singapore's Best-Known War Hero*, would tell the story with no mention of the MPAJA whatsoever. The latter had been airbrushed out.[120] Clara Show's presentation was a logical culmination of the gradual sanitisation of Force 136: the separation of their story from that of communists.

What really happened? Just what did Lim Bo Seng achieve, and with what motivation? Operation Gustavus had started with a May 1943 operation, which went in near Sitiawan in Perak because Force 136's British officers already knew some of the communist guerrillas in the area. Force 136's infiltrated officers duly met the MPAJA. They were, however, then kept at arms' length, only meeting Perak State Secretary Chin Peng as late as September. Meanwhile, a few infiltrated Chinese officers of Force 136 set up businesses or secured jobs — for instance establishing a fish business and variously becoming a rice seller and a waiter — as a front for their independent network in the towns. They were reinforced by later landings.

Lim's aim in November 1943 was to land in Malaya, receive information from the already established network, give advice to local agents, and then return to India. His strengths were primarily as an organiser, and as the chief liaison point with Chungking, rather than as a field officer.[121] On 2 November 1943, Lim Bo Seng and Chang Hui-Tsuan duly arrived at their rendezvous point near Pangkor Island, off north Perak. Their Dutch submarine surfaced, and waited for Broome, who was supposed to arrive from the mainland by junk. But Broome did not come. Japanese activity had made it too dangerous for him to travel to the coast, and he was also ill.

When a tiny junk did appear, its occupant was the Perak State Secretary — and MCP Liaison officer with Force 136 — Chin Peng. Transfer to the submarine was via folding boat. By some accounts, Chin Peng went below to the submarine's boardroom, and was soon in deep conversation with "Tan Choon Lim" (as Lim introduced himself). Chin Peng's detailed account also has the two men standing on a moonlit deck, with Tan Choon Lim irritating Chin Peng by endless nationalist hectoring.[122] The upshot was that Lim decided to go into the jungle with Chin Peng, rather than straight to his own contacts. Perhaps the impulse to see real fighters propelled him? Perhaps Chin Peng said it was too dangerous to drop another Force 136 man into an area now swarming with Japanese.[123] What we do know is that Lim remained safe in the MPAJA's Blantan Camp from November 1943 until early March 1944. While there he acted as translator during the negotiation of a Force 136-MCP agreement (31 December 1943 to 1 January 1944). This "Blantan Agreement" saw the MCP promise to help the British, in return for supplies and training.

Plate 4.3   Lim Bo Seng with Force 136 colleague John Davis

As Lim Bo Seng resided in Blantan, the Force 136 network in local towns came under increasing strain. By March 1944, it was beset by lack of funds, disputes over roles, and personality clashes. Lim decided to leave the Blantan to raise more money, and to help resolve problems. Unfortunately, the Japanese were stepping up their attempts to catch spies in the area. Lim was arrested at a roadblock on 27 March 1944. He had been betrayed, under torture, by a colleague captured the previous day, who in turn may have been betrayed by an agent arrested beforehand. Lim and Force 136 colleague Tan Chong Tee were imprisoned. They were tortured, but according to the latter, neither yielded more than outdated or harmless information.[124] Lim died, of dysentery, on 29 June 1944, and was buried outside Batu Gajah gaol, near Ipoh.

Chin Peng, whose memory of British Force 136 officer John Davis was warm, was less generous in his opinions of Lim Bo Seng. For him,

Lim was typical of the Kuomintang types in Force 136, lacked tact (Chin Peng was far too astute to lecture an opponent at length), and had met his end due to indiscipline amongst the intelligence network he had hoped to boost. Safe when in communist hands, he had been arrested a short time after leaving Blantan, as the entire Force 136 network in Perak unravelled. According to Chin Peng, this would leave Force 136 overwhelmingly reliant upon MCP help. The subtext is clear: Force 136 is a side story, Lim Bo Seng a minor figure, and neither should detract from the real story of the MPAJA.

Lim Bo Seng's mission had failed. But he was brave, and he was not only non-communist himself, but admired by his fellow Nationalist Chinese in Force 136. In addition, he had his reputation as a leader of prewar anti-Japanese organisation. Hence, the postwar colonial authorities identified him as an untainted war hero, in contrast to their suspicions about Dalforce, and even greater doubts about the MPAJA. By April 1946, the administration was "building up Lim Bo Seng as the Singapore Chinese war hero".[125] This was assisted by the return to Malaya of several of Lim's British Force 136 counterparts, such as Broome and Davis. Pagden, the colonial authorities' adviser on Chinese affairs in Singapore, wrote in Colonial Office files that:

> Lim Bo Seng was a supporter of the KMT and an outstanding man. A Chinese patriot, he was also a British patriot and one of the really great men. Cultured and well educated, with considerable business interest, he yet was trusted by and had a great influence with labour and it was he who kept labour working in the docks during the bombing.[126]

This early veneration was spurred by the emotional journey of his body from its original, prison-side grave, back to Singapore. Lim's remains were disinterred at the Batu Gajah gaol on 3 December 1945, then placed in a coffin at Ipoh Town Hall, ceremoniously draped in the Chinese nationalist flag. Chinese and British officers paid their respects, and Lim's Force 136 comrade, John Davis, laid a wreath next to the coffin. It then proceeded to the station trailed by mourners. In a broadcast across Malaya, Richard Broome, by now with the Chinese Affairs Department in Singapore, told the public of Lim's exploits. The coffin then journeyed to Singapore by train, stopping en route at Kuala Lumpur, so that its Chinese could pay their respects.[127]

On 7 December 1945, the train finally arrived in Singapore. There, Lim's coffin was carried to Armenian Street for public viewing, then to

Lim's family residence on Upper Serangoon Road. A further memorial service was held, at the Tong Teh Library where Singapore's Kuomintang had its headquarters. Present were Richard Broome, Hugh Pagden, and a representative of Colonel Victor Purcell, Chief Advisor on Chinese Affairs in the BMA of Malaya, as well as prominent Chinese.[128] The coffin remained for one month of mourning, until 13 January 1946.

On 13 January, the coffin made its final journey. First it went to an official ceremony at Singapore's Municipal Building. When the hearse arrived, Lim's Chinese comrades from Force 136 placed the coffin on a dais, so that the public could pay their last respects. Chinese representing guilds and unions gathered on the Padang opposite. Patrick McKerron, the BMA's Chief Civilian Affairs Officer, represented the colonial state. He was accompanied by Broome who spoke in Chinese about his friendship with Lim. Colonel Chuang Hui-Tsuan, Lim's Force 136 Deputy commander, also spoke. But he broke off mid-speech, too upset to continue, and took his place as a pallbearer alongside other ex-Force 136 members. The coffin was removed to an armoured carriage, with the British 2nd Durham Light Infantry providing a Guard of Honour. On the way to its final resting place on a hillside overlooking McRitchie Reservoir, British armoured cars drove alongside.[129]

Within a few weeks of the funeral, Colonel Chuang Hui-Tsuan would announce on behalf of the Kuomintang Chinese government that Lim had been promoted posthumously to the rank of Major-General.[130]

These events showed how both the British and the Kuomintang in China embraced Lim Bo Seng as a hero. At the end of speeches at the Municipal Building, the construction of a Lim Bo Seng Memorial was mooted. The government decided to shift the suggested site from the park where Lim Bo Seng was buried, to the more accessible position it now occupies: on Singapore's Esplanade, near the Padang and Municipal Building.[131] A design by architect Ng Keng Siang was approved in July 1952. The monument featured a 15-foot high pagoda on a four-and-a-half-foot base, in the shape of the Victory Monument built in Nanking by the Kuomintang.[132] The pagoda was mainly of concrete lined with marble, capped by a bronze roof.[133] Four lion statutes, cast in China, guarded the four corners of the pagoda.[134] The $50,000 cost was mainly raised by a private Lim Bo Seng Memorial Committee.[135]

By the time this memorial was unveiled in 1954, Lim Bo Seng was increasingly being held up not just as the Chinese patriot he was, but also as a Malayan patriot. On 27 June 1951, Colonel Chuang Hui-Tsuan, had "hoped that the memorial would serve to encourage

Plate 4.4 Opening of the Lim Bo Seng Memorial, 1954

people here to be as loyal to this country [Malaya] as was Major-General Lim".[136] Lim Bo Seng's changing position to Malayan hero reflected the reorientation of the Chinese. In 1949, the Malayan Chinese Association (MCA) had been formed as an overarching organisation of Chinese associations.[137] In 1952, the MCA entered a coalition with the United Malays National Organisation (UMNO), which was leading Malaya to independence. Members of the Chinese elite, such as Colonel Chuang, engaged in a twofold struggle: to persuade the authorities that the Chinese were loyal to Malaya and deserved full citizenship; and to persuade most Chinese to think of themselves as Malayans rather than citizens of China.[138]

In the 1950s, the British authorities were as eager as Chinese leaders to portray Lim Bo Seng as a "true Malayan", for emulation. On 3 November 1953, at the foundation-laying ceremony of the Lim Bo Seng memorial, Malcolm MacDonald (British Commissioner-General for Southeast Asia), declared that "the pagoda which will arise here will commemorate the life and death of a true Malayan hero ... the inspiration for his deeds was his love for his adopted country, Malaya. He was a shining Malayan patriot and it is fitting that his memorial should stand here on the waterfront in Singapore. He died that Malaya might live". MacDonald hailed Lim as "the most effective member of the Mobilisation Council in Singapore".[139]

The Lim Bo Seng memorial was unveiled on the tenth anniversary of his death, 29 June 1954, with 400 attending. Lim Keng Lian, Chairman of the Lim Bo Seng Memorial Committee, gave the key address. He declared that Lim "identified himself with the defence of this country when the war broke out", and that "it is not an overstatement when we say that Major General Lim had worked for the prosperity of this country helped in the defence of this country and died for this country. His death has brought glory to the people, especially the Chinese in this country". He finished by saying that "we are very grateful to the Government of Singapore for allotting two of the most beautiful sites on the Island for his grave and memorial in order that our patriot might still live among us and forever remain an inspiration to the 3-million Chinese in Malaya to express in deeds and not in words only, their loyalty and love for this country".[140] Lim Keng Lian told the press that "the inspiring example of Major-General Lim Bo Seng should clarify for us once and for all how a true Malayan should live and when duty calls, should die". The memorial's plaque describes him as "a martyr to the cause of a liberated Malaya".

When the Lim Bo Seng Memorial was unveiled, the Chinese press saw the occasion as an opportunity to express its loyalty to Malaya. In an editorial entitled "The Spirit of Lim Bo Seng", the *Nanfang Evening Post* wrote that "the spirit of heroism of the late Major-General Lim Bo Seng is representative of the Malayan Chinese especially the China born and has put to shame those politicians who used to accuse the Chinese of not being loyal to Malaya and looking to China as their real home". The editor added that "when Malaya his second home was invaded he gave his all to the country and sacrificed his life bravely ..."[141] The *Singapore Standard*, a Chinese-owned, English-language newspaper owned by the wealthy Aw family, described Lim Bo Seng as "a martyred Malayan Chinese hero".[142]

Northcote Parkinson, Raffles Professor of History at the University of Malaya, also selected Lim Bo Seng for inclusion in his 1956 book for schoolchildren, *Heroes of Malaya*, which his wife Ann helped to write. They wrote that "had Lim Bo Seng's chief loyalty been to China, he could have stayed at Chungking and worked there for the Chinese cause. But he had became a true Malayan, and wanted to free Malaya from the tyranny of the Japanese". The most charitable interpretation of the Parkinsons' story is that they were unaware of just how Lim Bo Seng had become involved in Force 136, and of how far he remained Chungking's man thereafter.[143]

Lim's popularity as a heroic figure continued into the postcolonial period. Just days after Singapore achieved self-government, there was a wreath-laying ceremony to remember him. This marked the 15th anniversary of his death, on 29 June 1959. It was attended by former members of Force 136, his wife, and one of his daughters. There Colonel Chuang Hui-Tsuan said that "it is no over-statement to say that Maj-General Lim died for this country".[144] Chuang regarded Lim as a "martyr" now not just for Malaya, but also for the emerging nation of Singapore.[145]

With the establishment of Malaysia in September 1963, Lim Bo Seng was appropriated as a hero for that nation-state, which briefly incorporated Singapore. Lim Bo Seng as a non-communist Overseas Chinese hero proved acceptable to the Federal government in Kuala Lumpur. That government had continued to face the remnants of communist insurrection after independence in 1957, and from 1964–1965, suffered armed incursions due to "Confrontation" by Indonesia. In July 1965, at a wreath-laying ceremony on the 21st anniversary of his death, Malaysian Deputy Prime Minister and Defence Minister

Abdul Razak bin Hussein, called Lim "a great patriot who made the supreme sacrifice … a good example to all Malaysians in the fight against confrontation".[146]

In the 1950s–1960s, as the role of the Chinese Malayan war hero was increasingly falling to Lim Bo Seng, even his widow took on public significance. There was a press sensation when Gan Choo Neo was found unconscious in her Palm Grove Avenue house on 5 October 1955, having taken an overdose of aspirin. When she regained consciousness, she was charged with attempted suicide. She left Singapore on 26 October for Perth. This facilitated six months of treatment under a psychiatrist before return, with any question of prosecution now seemingly put aside.[147]

Lim Bo Seng's status in Chinese memory remained secure. There was his grave at MacRitchie Reservoir, his monument near Singapore's Padang, and a place for him as a safe "Malayan" and Singapore patriot in textbooks. His career even attracted research that claimed (in the 1970s) that he and not the British had been the most effective link with Chin Peng. Another piece of mythmaking, as Chin Peng declared himself closer to John Davis than any other European, and viewed "Tan Choon Lim" with "scepticism", and as a wartime failure.[148] Lim also featured in a steady stream of articles, representations in Chinese-language (*The Price of Peace*) television dramatisations, and in English-language media.

Hence, the legend of Lim Bo Seng, increasingly stripped of its links to the MPAJA, continues to resonate. It would be a hard heart that was not moved by the diary entry in which he records the "tear-stained faces" of his children as he leaves them in Singapore in 1942, or the "parting words" others make him say to Choo Neo:[149]

> My duty and my honour will not permit me to look back. Every day, tens of thousands are dying for their countries … You must not grieve for me. On the other hand, you should take pride in my sacrifice and devote yourself to the upbringing of the children. Tell them what happened to me and direct them along my footsteps.
>
> [Excerpts from *The Price of Peace: True Accounts of the Japanese Occupation* also quoted as the concluding words of Clara Show's *Lim Bo Seng*, of 2009.][150]

The latter words prefigure his death in an improbable way given that he was at this time contemplating leaving for India and possible safety, and are not supported by his diary. But if anything, his diary is more powerful. He writes of "My dear Neo" and you see him wrestle with his conscience, as he realises that while staying might only attract attention to his family, once left behind, their survival would rest on the hope that the Japanese "would not vent their wrath on [a] defence-less woman and children".[151] In the end, his simple sentiments of love, duty, and sacrifice are what reverberate, regardless of the reworkings of his story for more banal political ends. The "agony of separation" his diary records for February 1942 could stand for the agony of separation endured by thousands upon thousands of Malaya and Singapore's Chinese.

Conclusions

In conclusion, we can see that the way the Overseas Chinese in Malaya and Singapore remembered wartime heroism was strongly influenced by the power of the colonial state and its control over public commemo-ration. The Chinese communist-inspired guerrilla movement with its insistence on having 15 February as the commemorative date for war memory was suppressed by the colonial state. Its commemoration went underground, increasingly focussing around commemoration of the 9-1 (1 September 1942) incident. By encouraging the celebration of Lim Bo Seng, the colonial state then used him as an alternative, acceptable way of publicly remembering Chinese war heroism.

Just as importantly, Lim Bo Seng's story was malleable enough to accommodate the new identities that the Chinese assumed as the inde-pendent nation-states of Singapore, Malaya, and then Malaysia emerged. He could transform from "Overseas Chinese", through "Malayan" to "Singaporean" hero, according to need. Dalforce was, by contrast, a small organisation that operated only for a couple of weeks and con-tained communists. The MPAJA, meanwhile, transmogrified into the MNLA (Malayan National Liberation Army) in 1948–1949, at war not only with the British, but also with Kuomintang supporters and the MCA. As we will see in Chapters 9 and 10, the case for public remem-brance of communist guerrillas could not even start to be made again until the end of insurgency in Malaysia — and of the international Cold War — after 1989.

The struggle over who to mark as heroes was not, however, the only or even the most heartfelt one amongst the Chinese. New monu-ments to the MPAJA have been built in Malaysia since 1989, albeit in Chinese memorial parks. In Singapore, the Lim Bo Seng Memorial still graces the central civic district. But less than 100 metres away is another, even more emotionally charged monument. This is the Civilian War Memorial, erected in 1966–1967 in the memory of Chinese civilians massacred during the war. If you stand with your back to both the Singapore River and the four-metre high Lim Bo Seng Memorial, you may just see the top of the 67-metre tall pillars of the Civilian War Memorial. The arrangement of these two memorials reflects the polarities around which the Chinese have perceived themselves, as heroes and as victims. The following chapter explores the other side of this polarity: the Chinese as victims.

CHAPTER 5

Chinese Victimhood

CHINESE MEMORIES OF THE WAR CRYSTALLISED AROUND three main types of experience: those of the hero; the everyday victim; and the "inspections" and massacres of 1942.

The previous chapter has already dealt with those who were elevated to the status of anti-Japanese heroes: community leaders such as Tan Kah Kee; Dalforce; MPAJA fighters; and Lim Bo Seng.

At a more mundane level, stories of "everyday victims" soon featured in newspapers and books. Some memories appeared over and again until they became stock images, namely: the Japanese demand for a $50 million "donation" to expiate anti-Japanese actions; being slapped by sentries; growing food substitutes such as tapioca; securing jobs with the Japanese; learning to speak a little Japanese language; increasing shortages in 1944–1945; and the contrasting "good Japanese" employer or officer. For a few, there was also memory of a scheme to alleviate the hunger experienced in Singapore: the establishment of a successful agricultural settlement — *New Syonan* — at Endau in Johor.[1]

These memories blended fear, hunger, initiative and occasionally some admiration as well. Such everyday experiences were touched on in Chapter 2. We can also see some more of their range and ambivalence by looking, in a little more detail, at an individual such as Goh Sin Tub. His experiences took in a wide range: from initial fear of bombing, through determination to survive, to admiration of some Japanese values.

Later in his life, Goh Sin Tub could remember sheltering under the stairs of the family home in Emerald Hill in December 1941, as the first bombs fell on Singapore. Yet he also recalled that the Occupation "fast forwarded me into instant manhood". The young Goh sold bread from house to house to help his family survive, before landing a job with a Japanese company as a trainee typewriter mechanic. Along with

Raffles College students Lee Kuan Yew and Choi Siew Hong, Goh was one of the generation of "42 who were toughened and prematurely matured by the war.

Goh was, however, not satisfied with mere survival. He studied Japanese at evening school, advancing to a Japanese teacher training institution. Another Malayan Chinese, Chin Kee Onn, would write in 1946 that just a few more years of this might have seen "Nipponisation" — of ceremonies, language and manners — take firm root in Malaya.[2] The young Goh embraced Japanese civilisation:

> Through the genuine and contagious idealism of our newfound mentors ... our hearts began to beat in sympathy and we too felt a touch of that heroic spirit: *Yamato-Damashii* or *Nippon Seishin* (the Japanese Spirit), even Bushido, the way of the warrior. Young minds must find causes ... [and] things more precious were being inculcated ... phrases such as ... '*isshokenmei*' (with all one's life might)

Yet even for someone like Goh, partly spellbound by slogans such as "Asia for the Asians", respect for teachers could never erase the searing images of February 1942. This was the memory of the "savages that descended upon us", and of the "inspections" and massacres. Hence, the torn intimacy of his postwar poem "My Friend, My Enemy", in which he confides to his Japanese teacher that "you see as I see, you understand the things done ... A shame you cannot speak".[3]

Inspections and Massacres

The shame that could not be spoken would overshadow the memory of anti-Japanese heroes, and of "everyday victims". It consisted of the "screening" or "inspection" of Chinese in the days following the fall of Singapore, and the massacre of tens of thousands that these inspections facilitated.

These Japanese actions were based on the assumption that the conquest of Malaya and Singapore was, at one level, a continuation of the war against China. For the Japanese, the surrender of the British only removed one enemy. The other — the anti-Japanese Chinese — had to be dealt with swiftly. On 18 February 1942, therefore, the commander of the 25th Army in Malaya, Lieutenant General Tomoyuki Yamashita, gave the order for *genju shobun* (severe punishment) of the Chinese population. Yamashita's subordinates knew *genju shobun* to require *shukusei* (purging or cleansing). In Chinese, this is rendered *sook ching* (*su qing*): the name the events would come to be known by in Malaya.[4] Society must be "cleansed" or "purged" of anti-Japanese, and those identified executed without trial. *Genju shobun* operations had been first developed in Japanese-occupied Manchuria in the 1930s. These procedures were adopted by the Chief of Staff of North China Area Army in 1938–1939, Tomoyuki Yamashita.[5] By 1942, now in Malaya, he had under his command three Japanese divisions — the 5th, 18th and Imperial Guards. All had been blooded in *shukusei* operations in China.[6]

These *shukusei* operations had by 1942 become routine when areas were newly occupied in China, and also a standard response to guerrilla action. In theory, they remained military, intended to methodically remove "anti-Japanese" elements, as well as to purify the surviving Chinese of their anti-Japanese mentality. In practice, there were usually insufficient troops to permanently occupy new areas, and those available lacked the time, and local intelligence, necessary to accurately identify who was anti-Japanese. The result was that selection was at best semi-discriminate, and sometimes whole villages were slaughtered.[7]

It is, therefore, no surprise that Yamashita gave an order for a *genju shobun* on 18 February 1942, to apply throughout the entire Malayan Peninsula. The screening duly started where the Japanese were most concentrated, in just-fallen Singapore. Thereafter, the focus of intensity would work its way up the Malayan peninsula.[8]

In Singapore, the sheer scale of operations demanded a high degree of organisation. Male Chinese were asked to report to screening centres set up around the island. It was to one of these, at Telok Kurau English School, that demobbed Dalforce veteran Choi Siew Hong went on 19 February (pp. 38–9). From them, those selected as actually or potentially anti-Japanese were trucked to beaches, boats, and isolated spots to be bayoneted or shot. Hence, it was that on 23 February, the ten-year-old Mohd Anis bin Tairan (p. 39) heard the machine gun fire, and smelt the smoke, from the biggest of these massacres, near Siglap in the east of Singapore. This site alone would later give up the remains of more than 1,500 victims.

Meanwhile, in mid-February, some British soldiers and local volunteers were still holed up on Blakang Mati,[*] awaiting removal to POW camps. Sited a few hundred metres off Singapore Island, they noticed

---

[*] Malay for "Behind Death". The island was renamed Sentosa or "Isle of Tranquillity" in the 1970s, when it was turned into a tourist attraction.

launches emerging from the latter. Looking through their field bino-culars, they saw groups of two or three, tied together back to back, being shoved into the water. Machine guns raked the bound figures as they bobbed up and down, staining the ocean red. Over the following days, victims washed ashore, 108 in one location, and more than 500 for Blakang Mati as a whole. Most were adult Chinese males. Many wore Singapore Harbour Board armbands. There was the occasional Malay, and a few women. One of the latter had two babies tied to her. British and Indian troops tried to bury the corpses, but some could not be freed from the island's barbed wire fences. By the time these troops left Blakang Mati, on 27 February, the stench of putrefying bodies could be smelt on the hills of Fort Connaught, high above the seashore.[9]

By this point, Singapore's *sook ching* was complete. The *Syonan Times* of 23 February 2602 (that is, the former *Straits Times*, and 23 February 1942 by western reckoning), declared that:

> the recent arrests of hostile and rebellious Chinese have drastically been carried out in order to establish the prompt restoration of the peace of *Syonan-Ko* (port of *Syonan*) and also to establish the bright Malaya.
>
> Chinese in *Syonan-Ko* have hitherto been in sympathy with propaganda of Chungking Government, the majority of them sup-ported the aforesaid government and taken politically and econo-mically the same action with Britain against Japan and moreover they have positively participated in British Army, in forming volun-teer corps and still have secretly disturbed the military activities of the Nippon Army as guerrilla corps or spies they, in spite of being Eastern Race, were indeed so-called traitors of East Asia …
>
> Thus it is important to sweep away these treacherous Chinese elements and to establish the peace and welfare of the populace.[10]

Though a few did survive the execution grounds, the predominant memories in Singapore would not be of killing. Dead men do not remember. Rather, they would be the memories of surviving the erratic screening; and more poignantly, the memories relatives and friends had of those who never returned.

The nature of these memories had two results. First, amongst Singapore Chinese, the incident became known as the *jian zheng shi jian* (identification parade) incident. Second, the most painful legacy would be that of absence: absence of identifiable remains to bury, honour, and burn offerings to. The scale of events meant that many

Plate 5.1 Remains from the 1960s Chinese Chamber of Commerce exhumation of the Singapore *sook ching* massacre sites

Chinese families — there were almost certainly less than 350,000 adult Chinese males in Singapore in February 1942[11] — were affected.

The Japanese military's Tokyo Investigation Committee claimed, after the war, that the number massacred was not more than 5,000, as executioners exaggerated numbers to fill quotas.[12] But they were trying to minimise their guilt. In the war crimes trial into the massacre after the war, Lieutenant Colonel Hishikari Takafumi, a war correspondent at Yamashita's headquarters, recalled conversations on the number killed. Lieutenant Colonel Sugita Ichiji had told him that "it had been planned to kill 50,000 adult Chinese", though other officers confessed that "it had been found to be impossible to kill the whole of the 50,000 people, as after half that number had been killed, an order was received 'to stop the massacre'".[13] That would suggest anything up to 25,000 victims.

Whatever precise number died in Singapore, it represented a large-scale massacre for such a small Chinese population, and was only the beginning of a Malaya-wide *sook ching* which would culminate in Penang, in April. In between, Yamashita's *genju shobun* command would grind its way northwards along Malaya's west coast. First the operation jumped the narrow stretch of water that separated Singapore from the Malay State of Johor. On 28 February 1942, no less than 2,000 Chinese were slaughtered in the town of Kota Tinggi. After the war, eyewitnesses would tell Dr Chen Su Lan that "children were thrown into the air and fell on the bayonets ... Pregnant women had their bellies split open ..."[14] On 4 March, another 300 were massacred at the Chinese village of Gelang Patah, in the Pontian district. Nearby was Benut, then with a population of around 1,000. On 6 March, "the men were packed in the market and the women in a Malay school ... [the women] were raped, and all were slaughtered". During late February and early March 1942, the list of massacres grew: Johor Bahru, Senai, Kulai, Sedanak, Pulai, Rengam, Kluang, Yong Peng, Batu Pahat, Senggarang, Parit Bakau, and Muar. After the war, the Chinese press claimed that in Johor alone, 25,000 Chinese were massacred. Again, while precise numbers are beyond reach, the brutality and large scale of events are beyond dispute.[15]

By mid-March, the main focus had advanced north of Johor, to the settlement of Malacca and the state of Negeri Sembilan. On 16 March, the Malacca *kempeitai* executed 142 Chinese civilians on a remote beach near Tanjong Kling. Informers had helped to identify the suspects as active in the China Relief Fund.[16]

On 18 March, it was the turn of Joo Loong Loong, a village of around 1,000 Chinese in Negeri Sembilan. On that day, *Kempeitai* Major Yokokoji Kyomi had his men assemble the villagers in the school hall, with a machine gun at the entrance. In Yokokoji's postwar crimes trial, one witness recalled what happened next:

> After a short while those assembled were split into batches of about 15 to 30 persons. Each batch was in turn marched about 800 yards from the school where they were bayoneted ... there were only 10 survivors ... About two hours after the killing the accused made a speech in the market of Titi warning the people that they must co-operate with the Japanese administration or be killed like the people of Joo Loong Loong.

The ten survivors would live to bear witness against Major Yokokoji in a war crimes trial of December 1947, and some would see a postwar memorial erected in nearby Titi. But as for their village, it disappeared from the map.[17]

One Joo Loong Loong survivor recalled how her daughter-in-law was "attacked" before being killed. In another village, this time further to the north, near Kuala Lumpur, a young Cantonese girl saw two lorryloads of Japanese arrive and disembark. They were led by a Chinese "traitor":

> I was cooking ... Three soldiers with rifles came into our house while the rest fanned out through the village. They burst in and grabbed me. My parents tried to rescue me but my father was kicked in the head. Blood went everywhere. I struggled as hard as I could, but I got kicked in the head too. I still have the scar, see? Then my panties were ripped off and one of the soldiers undid the front of his trousers. While the others held me down, he stuck his thing into me. I had no idea what he was trying to do ... I was only fifteen and hadn't even reached my first period ... They did it on the kitchen floor, right in front of my parents and brother ... For the next three years, I was constantly haunted by that last vision of my parents, especially my father's blood on the ground.

She was dragged off, ending up a comfort girl in the Tai Sun Hotel opposite Pudu Gaol (near the present Times Square in Kuala Lumpur), along with former Dance Hall hostesses from the Great Eastern Dance Hall. Her Comfort Station had eight Chinese, three Sumatran Malays, two Koreans and a Thai. Malays and Indians were generally spared such sexual slavery. Both Kuala Lumpur and Singapore had 20 or more such stations established (in addition to pre-existing colonial era brothels), and they were set up in other garrison towns as well.[18]

The massacres, meanwhile, reached Penang in earnest in April. There, Japanese *kempeitai* chief Major Higashigawa Yoshinoru had received the *genju shobun* order in March. He rounded up several thousand Chinese in early April, leading to their torture and death over the following months.[19]

After April, "cleansing" was used only sporadically, to counter anti-Japanese guerrilla activity in particular locations. In such cases, the *kempeitai*, Japanese soldiers and local auxiliaries would launch an operation restricted to the affected area. This happened in August 1942, when a Malay resident at Sungei Lui, a mainly Chinese village near the Bahau settlement in Negeri Sembilan, was killed. Tan Chu Seng told an October 1947 war crimes trial how:

> I was in the first row of the first batch of eight persons ... We were taken to an attap hut in the centre of the village ... they rushed at us from the back with blood curdling cries. I dodged them when my turn came ... The bayonet went through my right upper arm. I fell immediately and saw my brother-in-law bayoneted ... the bayonet going through his chest.

The Japanese poured kerosene over the hut and set fire to it. Tan Chu Seng escaped from it later, but his village, formerly home to 350 people, was no more.[20]

Even where communities did not disappear, bodies did. Those that washed ashore on Blakang Mati, the British buried the best they could. Others the Japanese tried to bury, as the young Mohd Anis bin Tairan found when gathering *daun simpuh* leaves at Siglap in 1942 (pp. 39–40). He discovered "parts of about ten bodies poking out of the ground".[21] Even when bodies were rediscovered, anything up to decades later, it was often impossible to identify individuals. In short, the key memories for postwar Chinese would be of the inspections, and of those who disappeared. The key dilemma would be how to deal with the terrible absence that resulted: the absence of bodies, of identification, and the consequent inability to reunite ancestors with the graves of their predecessors, and with the living who wanted to pay their respects, and to burn offerings for the dead.

Early Postwar Remembrance

After the war, Malayan resistance to the Japanese continued to be viewed by the Nanyang Chinese as part of broader resistance to the Japanese in China.[22] Their deep feeling of belonging to China found expression in the deathscapes they created when they came to commemorate the *sook ching*.

The initial impetus for this commemoration came with the recovery — in the two to three years after the war — of bodies of massacre victims by local communities. The bodies were reburied in mass graves at the site, or in nearby Chinese cemeteries. In Negeri Sembilan, this resulted in a central committee being set up. In May 1947, the Negeri Sembilan Chinese Relief Fund Committee (which had before the war raised money for China) formed a central committee of 29 people, with 15 subcommittees for remote outlying areas. The aim was to rebury the estimated 5,000 Chinese massacred in the state.[23] It proved to be a protracted process. Mass graves were still being discovered right into the 1980s. In 1982, the mass graves of 1,474 Chinese villagers killed at Joo Loong Loong and 600 Chinese from Kuala Pilah were uncovered and their remains reburied under large memorials in Chinese cemeteries.[24]

In 1947, meanwhile, the Chinese Chamber of Commerce for Malacca sponsored a Malacca War Victims Memorial Committee. This collected remains, including of those who had died on the beach at

Plate 5.2 The 1980s exhumation of the mass graves of the *sook ching* massacre in Negeri Sembilan (I)

Plate 5.3 The 1980s exhumation of the mass graves of the *sook ching* massacre in Negeri Sembilan (II)

Tanjong Kling. Among these were people who had been active in the Kuomintang and the China Relief Fund. They were reburied under a large memorial erected at Bukit Cina,[†] the principal Chinese cemetery of Malacca. On top of the memorial was sculpted a white 12-ray sun against a blue background. This was the pattern on the flag of the ruling Kuomintang Party of China, and also on China's national flag from 1928–1949. Chiang Kai-shek, the President of China and Generalissimo of armed forces, was asked to compose an epitaph, and chose "Models of Loyalty and Virtue" written in Chinese.[25] The memorial was unveiled on 5 April 1948 by Sir Edward Gent, the High Commissioner of the Federation of Malaya. In attendance were Tan Cheng Lock, and Ng Pah Seng, China's Consulate-General to Singapore. Other memorials were also decorated with symbols of nationalist China. In 1946 at Mentakab, in Pahang, the memorial to the Chinese war dead was built with a *pai lou* (a ceremonial entrance gate, removed in the 1980s), topped with the white 12-ray sun of the Kuomintang.[26]

The war memorials springing up around Malaya often described *sook ching* victims as *nan qiao* (southern sojourners) or *hua qiao* (Chinese sojourners), indicating continuing attachment to China. Early postwar Chinese literature, meanwhile, described the dead as martyrs who had died for *zuguo*, the "fatherland" or "motherland".[27] The *sook ching* commemorative space which perhaps best expressed this Chinese nationalism and identity was that built in Johor Bahru. In August 1947, the town's Chinese community built Malaya's largest *sook ching* memorial. It commemorated no less than 2,000 Chinese civilians who were massacred there in 1942. Their remains were reburied under a large monument just outside of the town centre, next to existing Chinese cemeteries along Jalan Kebun Teh.

The Jalan Kebun Teh monument was constructed so that mourners enter the memorial park through a *pai lou*: a three arched gateway. This *pai lou* was emblazoned at its top with the white 12-ray sun of the Kuomintang. As for the *pai lou* itself, its arches represent the three islands of immortality. The Johor Bahru gate is also decorated with symbols and prayers to ward off evil spirits. From the Song Dynasty, Chinese had used *pai lou* gates to protect entrances to places of commemoration, such as tombs. In Republican China, Sun Yat Sen's

---

[†] Bukit means hill in Malay, and Malacca's Bukit Cina rises sharply from the surrounding town.

Plate 5.4 Jalan Kebun Teh *sook ching* massacre Memorial

mausoleum had such a gate, as does Chiang Kai-shek's in Taiwan. Many overseas Chinatowns have a *pai lou* at their entrance. Singapore's Chinese-language Nanyang University also had a large *pai lou* at its entrance when constructed in the 1950s.[28]

The use of forms commonly associated with Chinese culture and memorial parks also made these monuments apt places for key commemorative occasions, such as *Qing Ming* (All Souls' Day) when the Chinese traditionally visit their ancestors' graves to pay their respects, and to burn offerings.

At the Johor Bahru memorial, the victimhood of the Overseas Chinese was also couched in traditional Chinese metaphors and legend. The memorial has inscribed on it 51 names of the China Relief Fund who were killed. There are Chinese verses composed by Li Szu-yuan. These compare the Japanese — and the Chinese they massacred in Malaya, Singapore and China — to the massacres of Chinese civilians by the invading Manchus at Yangzhou and Jiading (Yang-chou and Chia-ting) during 1645. That is, when the Manchus consolidated China's Qing Dynasty. The Malayan Chinese feeling of victimhood thus mirrored the mainland Chinese nationalist sense of victimhood, ranging from perceptions of Manchu dominance, through British imperialism, to Japanese atrocities of 1937–1945.[29] Naturally, the Kuomintang and Chinese nationalist elements would have less salience after 1949 — with the establishment of the People's Republic of China — but commemoration of war victims in Malaya remained in distinctively Chinese cultural space, and couched in specifically Chinese traditions.

Singapore Chinese Organise for Assistance, Revenge, and Commemoration

The Chinese quickly began to organise at all-Malayan and at Singapore levels, as well as at state level. In Singapore, traditional Chinese associations banded together on 22 February 1946, the first postwar anniversary of the massacres. They established the Chinese Massacred Victims Dependants Association, "to look after the dependants of those whose fathers or sons were screened and butchered by the Japanese in the early part of 1942".[30] The organisation also helped victims' families to obtain hawker stall licences at markets so that they could eke out a living.

There were also public ceremonies for victims whose remains could not be found. Some Chinese believed that those who died violently, or otherwise did not receive offerings of food at their graves, would become "hungry ghosts". These neglected souls would be released to wander for two weeks from the 15th day of the seventh lunar month, which was celebrated as the "Festival of the Hungry Ghosts".[‡] On this day, around Malaya, pavilions would be set up decorated in golds and reds, their tables laden with incense and offerings of food. Stages for performances for the living and dead would be assembled. These beliefs and rituals, loosely associated with Daoism's emphasis on ancestor worship, and with popular Buddhist beliefs, gave edge and form to some of the gatherings which began to be held for the missing.[31]

One of the first of these gatherings was held on the fifth anniversary of the massacres, in the last week of January 1947. Hundreds of relatives gathered on a small hill overlooking the biggest known massacre, at the 7½ mile point on East Coast Road at Siglap, Singapore.[32]

Another remembrance ceremony was organised by the Singapore Women's Mutual Aid Victims Association for just after Chinese New Year, on 23 February 1947, at Edward Gardens in the Singapore town

---

[‡] *Zhong Yuan Jie* using Hanyu Pinyin.

area. Two to three hundred relatives gathered. Wives and daughters chanted: "Where can we go in search of the remains of our beloved relatives. Will their souls please return to us where ever they drift?" The aim was "to purge the souls their sufferings". Couplets in Chinese characters on white banners were placed at the two sides of the stage for the ceremony, reading:

> Never would we have known that a matter of identification would turn out to be a mirage of injustice. Though we might have surrendered and pledged ourselves to the invader we were still not spared.

On stage was an enormous wreath of white mourning flowers arranged in the Chinese character for "hate": *hen*.[33]

Rumours now spread that massacre victims' relatives had heard wails from unmarked graves all over the island. This led to a further three-day event, culminating on 23 December 1947. "Chinese Spiritualists", according to journalist Sit Yin Fong, had "peered into the underworld and were thoroughly alarmed by what they saw: thousands of naked hungry and discontented ghosts roaming about the earth, their wrath threatening calamity to the land". The priests said that "these forgotten, tortured souls had to be appeased and driven away from the earth, to wherever they should go". The High priestess Miaw Chin of Hoon Sian Keng temple in Changi was given the task of "screening" the ghosts for despatch to heaven or hell. It was claimed that Miaw Chin had been selected for this task by none other than "Hood Chor" (Kuan Yin), the Goddess of Mercy.

"For three days and nights great piles of food, paper clothing and money were offered in sacrifice", burnt for the dead, near the Siglap massacre site. This culminated on Tung Chek (*Dong Zhi*, Winter Solstice), when Chinese families would get together.[§] Towards the end of the ceremony "a thousand women asked: "How did the spirits of our men-folk fare after death?" The white-robed Miaw Chin — holding a black whip to chastise evil spirits in one hand and the "Keys to Hades" in the other — fell into a trance, assuming the voices of victims, who called out their names and fates, and were identified by relatives. Nor were the perpetrators forgotten. Some of the relatives brought paper

---

[§] *Dong Zhi* (Tung Chek) is the Winter Solstice, which in Singapore falls in December.

models of naked Japanese soldiers being disembowelled by horse-faced devils, in the court of Eam Lo Ong, king of hell.[34]

These feelings of loss, hate and anger found an outlet not only in these familiar rituals, but also in the notion of *xuezhai*: "blood debt". This was the debt Chinese were duty bound to exact payment of from the Japanese for spilling innocent Chinese blood. "Blood debt" was well-established in Chinese history. It had been used to signify that when a member of one clan or family is killed by another, the aggrieved family or clan has to settle this blood debt through revenge killings, or by compensation. Hence the saying that "blood must atone for blood".[35] By using the term, the Chinese presented themselves as an aggrieved clan demanding retribution. This idea initially found its outlet in hopes that war crimes trials would result in large numbers of executions of those Japanese who had planned and carried out massacres.

The relatives of victims initially expected that War Crimes Trials would address their need for payment of the blood debt. They were to be sorely disappointed. In the 1947 War Crimes Trials in Singapore, just seven Japanese officers were charged with carrying out massacres. These were Lieutenant General Nishimura Takuma, Lieutenant General Kawamura Saburo, Lieutenant Colonel Oishi Masayuki, Lieutenant Colonel Yokota Yoshitaka, Major Jyo Tomotatsu, Major Onishi Satoru, and Captain Hisamatsu Haruji.[36] The sentences only compounded the sense that too few were being held responsible. On 2 April 1947, Kawamura and Oishi were sentenced to death, but the five other officers received only life imprisonment.

The colonial authorities were acutely aware that the results were immensely unpopular. One member of the War Crimes Investigation Team wrote that:

> Acquitting these Gestapo Japs, whose reputation is notorious in this area has got no possible propaganda value for us. We are on our last legs as a Colonial Power. The eyes of the world, mostly very hostile eyes, are turned on our Empire, eager to make the most of any unrest among subject peoples. The people trust us. They look upon us as clean and upright people, unsoiled by crimes of brutality, who have come to right their wrongs and to punish the wicked who have hanged and burnt and buried alive their husbands and sons. All we can offer them are legal quibbles propounded by lawyers in Singapore.[37]

The War Crimes Investigation Team in Singapore continued to search for more suspects, with little result. As a token, in March 1948, the British prosecutors in Singapore put Major Mizuno Keiji on trial

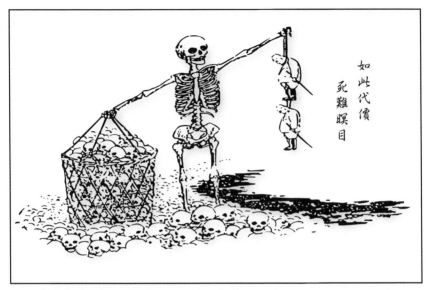

'At such a price the dead cannot rest in peace' *Nanyang Miscellany*, vol.1, no.6, April 1947

Plate 5.5 Cartoon of the scales of justice, *Nanyang Miscellany*, 1947

for his part as a *kempeitai* commander. Mizuno was, however, a minor figure, and as such only received life imprisonment.[38]

Local colonial officials were at pains to demonstrate that war crimes officers were trying to arrest culprits. In May 1947, General Sir Neil Ritchie, Commander-in-Chief South East Asia Land Forces, stressed that "owing to the work of the S.E.A.L.F. War Crimes Organisation in Singapore, 110 Japanese had been tried for crimes in the Singapore town area. Ninety-eight of these or 89 per cent were tried for crimes against the Chinese. Ninety per cent of those sentenced to death had been found guilty of crimes against the Chinese".[39] The Overseas Chinese Appeal Committee was underwhelmed, demanding the "execution of all seven Japanese" and "the arrest of all those who participated in the screening of the Chinese at the various concentration camps".[40] Dalforce veterans also condemned the trial verdicts. The Overseas Chinese Volunteer Army veterans association requested the death penalty for the five Japanese defendants who had only been given life imprisonment.[41]

The Overseas Chinese Appeal Committee (later reconstituted as the Singapore Chinese Massacred Appeal Committee) consisted of 37 prominent Chinese. It was formed after the trial with the objective of securing death sentences for all the Japanese convicted. Tay Koh Yat, from the Chinese Chamber of Commerce, was Chairman. When the sentences were confirmed 71 days after the Court's judgement, Tay stated that "we will not be satisfied until these Japanese have paid for their crimes with their lives". Tay urged hangings before the Chinese community in order to visibly atone the blood debt. Failing this, Tay suggested that ten members of the Committee should witness the execution of the two convicted: Kawamura and Oishi.[42] The British ultimately allowed six members of the Committee to see the hanging of these two officers.

Some relatives also wished to see the Japanese hang, and two female relatives did eventually attend.[43] 29-year-old Li Poay Keng, Chairman of the Singapore Women's Mutual Aid Victims Association, which consisted of 1,000 widows and female dependants of victims, was there. So was Madam Ong Goh Kee, a 45-year-old widow. Li Poay Keng had lost her brother-in-law and uncle. Madam Ong's 22-year-old son had been killed. Li remarked that all the widows in her association "would have welcomed the opportunity of seeing the Japs die ... women who were normally afraid of such a spectacle, became fearless through their travails". Li claimed that "some of the widows had gone through so much suffering and were so bitter, that they had expressed their willingness to act as the executioners".[44] Both women, along with the six Chinese Committee members, witnessed the death sentences carried out on 26 June 1947. After the hangings Li said, "I'm not satisfied. I want to see their faces to make sure they are dead". Ong asked, "Are they dead? I'm not so sure."[45]

It was Chinese women who were most vocal about blood debt. Miss Li Poay Keng emphasised that Chinese "women have changed after the war".[46] They had had families torn apart and independence thrust upon them in earning a living in the absence of husbands and sons. The Singapore Women's Mutual Aid Victims Association wrote an open letter of protest to the colonial authorities. Published in the Chinese-language press, this complained that "when the British government came back, we were anticipating some answers from them" and had the "hope that the injustice we suffered could be redressed".[47]

The growing image of the Chinese united as war victims pushed women's experience to the fore. In the 1946 Singapore Chinese-language comic book on the atrocities, *Memories of Painful Grievances* (*Chan Tong De Huiyi*), the cover features an artist's impression of a Chinese mother lying prostate, a Japanese bayonet thrust into her body just above her vagina, her blouse ripped off, her breasts exposed. Beside her a small child cries into his mother's hair. In the background a Japanese soldier is running off with a bag of the family's valuables. Inside are equally graphic images, of naked Chinese women being sexually enslaved as "Comfort Women".[48]

The latter grievance had become an issue in its own right. In September 1945, the Kuala Lumpur branch of the Kuomintang prepared a report for submission to the British Military Administration of Malaya. According to this:

> Young Chinese girls and women were drawn from respectable families by force, and together with a large number of prostitutes, were shipped to such places as Java and other occupied territories to fill the Military Comfort Houses. To meet the requirements of these Comfort Houses, it was estimated that a few thousands of young Chinese women of respectable families were kidnapped from their respective homes.[49]

This was raised again when N.I. Low and H.M. Cheng published their *This Singapore (Our City of Dreadful Night)* in 1947. The authors wrote as if addressing the Japanese war criminals on trial, and the surrendered Japanese POWs still in Singapore. Low and Cheng recounted how on 6 March 1946, 15 girls who had "served as 'comfort' girls" in Java returned by ship to Singapore harbour. One girl asked, 'Will my father have me back?'"[50]

Sexual enslavement also featured prominently, alongside the massacres, in the Chinese-language documentary movie, *Blood and Tears of the Overseas Chinese*. This was shown up to three times daily in Singapore to commemorate the first anniversary of the end of the war, in September 1946.[51] After the end of the 1940s, however, the issue subsided. It only revived in the 1990s, when other Asian women — notably Koreans — started to demand compensation. The main focus of women's grievances soon became that of having lost their husbands or sons.

The feeling that the blood debt had not been paid remained acute. Japan's recovery from the 1950s, economically and diplomatically, provided repeated reminders of this unfinished business. One of these reminders came with the reopening of the Japanese Consulate in Singapore. Ken Ninomiya, the new Consul-General, arrived on 18 October 1952. Within weeks, he was receiving letters about "blood debt". On

26 November 1952, the Chinese press reported that the Victims Association had invited the Japanese Consul-General to see the exhumation of massacre graves. These exhumations did not go ahead at the time, but a list of 8,000 names of people killed by the Japanese had been just compiled after several years of research.[52]

The colonial administration, meanwhile, suppressed information about the release of war criminals responsible for the 1942 massacres. In August 1951, these had, along with other war criminals held outside Japan in British territories, been repatriated back to Japan's Sugamo Prison. In 1955, the British government, after lobbying from Japan, commuted all the life sentences of Japanese war criminals to 15 years.[53] This meant many would soon be eligible for release on parole for good behaviour. For the releases, the British Foreign Office requested that there be "no publicity for the reduction of the sentences".[54] On 23 September 1955, the first release was that of Onishi Satoru, who was responsible for sending 1,500 Chinese in the Katong area to their deaths at Siglap. He was regarded as one of the most junior prisoners in rank, and without publicity in Malaya, his release went unnoticed there.[55]

Both the British Foreign Office and the Singapore colonial authorities had to agree before the release of such prisoners. Despite being under pressure from Japan to free convicted Japanese war criminals in Sugamo, the British Foreign Office remained cautious. The Governor of Singapore was consulted before recommendations for parole were approved. British authorities feared that further releases could fuel anti-colonial feelings. On 18 March 1956, the Governor of Singapore, Sir Robert Black, witnessed a mass rally of 25,000 people at the Kallang airport being whipped into an anti-colonial frenzy by political speeches about *Merdeka* (independence). The rally was intended to demonstrate local feeling prior to Constitutional negotiations due to commence in London in April.[56] Black was aware that these negotiations might fail. Singapore's Chief Minister David Marshall was likely to ask for total internal self-government not excluding internal security. In the light of rising communism, student activism, and labour riots of 1955, the Colonial Office had decided not to yield the latter. Black therefore advised that all releases be postponed until later in the year "in view of the delicate situation in Singapore".[57]

Foreign Office officials were also worried.[58] They noted that,

In April 1947, when the sentences on Yokota, Jyo and Hisamatsu were pronounced the Chinese press in Singapore raised an outcry at the alleged leniency of the life sentences imposed on them ... anti-Japanese feeling ... might be revived by an announcement that three of the men sentenced to life imprisonment for their part in the Chinese massacre case were to be released simultaneously nine years later.[59]

In September 1956, Yokota Yoshitaka was paroled for medical reasons, and Hisamatsu Haruji released because he was junior in rank.[60] Mizuno Keiji was released on 23 December 1956, followed by Jyo Tomotatsu on 25 December 1956.[61] In releasing them, the Foreign Office stressed that "in view of the possible effect of the reductions upon the Chinese population of Singapore, it is hoped that there will be no publicity ..."[62] There was none, and as a result, no reaction in Malaya and Singapore.

There was also the issue of Japanese government recovery of the war graves of those Japanese war criminals who had been executed at Singapore's Changi and Outram prisons.[63] Colonial officials agreed that "we obviously cannot object to their removing the remains ..." On 20 February 1954, the colonial authorities therefore gave permission for exhumations, while stipulating "that there be no ceremonial and as little publicity as possible".[64] The Japanese government completed exhumations at Changi Prison on 17 March 1955.[65] However, the unrepentant nature of the Japanese government of the 1950s about wartime atrocities was evident. On 30 March 1955, a small 70-centimetre tall memorial was surreptitiously erected to these war criminals in the old Japanese cemetery of Singapore, describing them as "135 martyrs" who "gave their lives to the emperor". The return of the remains to Japan was reported in the press, but — to the relief of officials — as a minor story.[66]

It seemed as if the emotions which surrounded "blood debt" had subsided. Japanese Premier Kishi Nobusuke stopped off at Singapore and Malaya from 24 to 26 November 1957.[67] Japan was now recovering after the 1951 Peace Treaty, and colonial officials were aware that its trade and aid might be helpful. Robert Scott, Britain's Commissioner-General for Southeast Asia, "wanted to establish that time had marched on to the point when a Japanese Prime Minister could again pay an official visit to Malaya without ... incurring any overt hostility ..."[68] There were no protests.[69] At the end of the visit, Kishi invited the Prime Minister of Malaya, Tunku Abdul Rahman, to Japan; an offer that was taken up May 1958.[70]

Superficially, it seemed as if the dark undercurrents of the "blood debt" were being overtaken by the economic needs of the present and the passage of time.[71] In June 1958, Japan Airlines made its inaugural flight to Singapore. Sumino Yoshimasa, Assistant Editor of the Japanese newspaper, *Mainichi Shimbun*, reported that "I felt that the people of Singapore would still be feeling the sting of war when the Japanese militarists overran this tropical paradise", but "I was most pleasantly surprised as no anti-Japanese sentiment remains ... everywhere I went, with whomsoever I conversed, I discovered to my great joy that the people of Singapore have forgotten the past and are all eager to join with Japan in the building of a new Asia".[72]

Sumino's confidence was misplaced. People could accept Japanese trade, but personal anger — directed at any Japanese who had been involved in the 1942 massacres — festered. It was brought to the surface by the August 1958 visit to Singapore of Ogata Shinichi. Ogata had been a Japanese police chief during the Occupation. He was now Director of the Higher Education and Science Bureau in the Japanese Ministry of Education. In August 1958, Ogata made a brief stopover in Singapore. He had not been involved with the *kempeitai*, but to the Singapore public, his association with the Occupation police evoked memories of the *kempeitai*. His presence acted as a lightning rod for the suppressed anger of relatives of the massacred. When it was made public that Ogata was in Singapore, Chuang Hui-Tsuan, Secretary of the Singapore Chinese Massacred Appeal Committee, organised hundreds of victims' relatives to besiege Ogata at Paya Lebar Airport. They intended to hand him a "blood letter" to "demand repayment" of the "blood debt". Chuang, whose brother had been killed by the Japanese, put up banners inscribed (in Chinese), "The Blood of Singapore Civilians Cries For Vengeance".[73]

Chuang's crusade continued after Ogata departed. An official cocktail party was held for businessmen at the Japanese Trade Fair in Singapore, on 10 December 1958. Chuang appeared. The Japanese leader of the business delegation, K. Nakanishi, bowed in embarrassment, as Chuang told his audience that "businessmen trading with Japan should never forget the Japanese atrocities ..."[74]

The Chinese press also took up the issue of Ogata's visit to Singapore. On 6 August 1958, *Sin Chew Jit Poh* asked, "When can the 'identification parade' blood debt of 100,000 Chinese be paid up?"[75] A *Nanfang Evening Post* editorial explained that:

the Singapore people suffered innumerable hardships for 3 years and 8 months and have had no opportunities to ventilate their pent up emotions; it is only natural that they want to let off steam now that an important figure of the Syonan-to period comes to their very doors.

The editorial said that without all the graves of the dead being known, "the 'blood debt' of the past can no longer be reckoned and cleared … we only hope that this director of the Bureau of Higher Education in Tokyo can relate to his people the atrocities of the Japanese militarists and the resentment of the Singapore people, so that the Japanese will understand and repent".[76] The issue of still-missing bodies was raised by Chuang during Ogata's August 1958 visit. "We want him [Ogata] to show us the actual spots where thousands of Chinese were massacred … We want to re-bury these victims". Chuang said that his "committee had a vague idea that a large number of Chinese were massacred in the Siglap area, but there were many other places and none knew the actual spots".[77]

Thus, at the closing of the colonial era, the blood debt issue was still potent. Malaya became independent on 31 August 1957. Singapore attained full internal self-government in June 1959. Singapore subsequently gained full independence first as a part of the new state of Malaysia on 16 September 1963, and then in its own right on 9 August 1965. The new nation-states inherited the old blood debt problem. Where the colonial authorities worried that the issue might be exploited to further fuel growing anti-colonialism, the new states feared it could fan the flames of Chinese chauvinism, be used as propaganda by the remnants of communist insurgency, or damage trade, aid and investment with Japan. For the postcolonial governments, however, the issue also became embedded in the broader one of nation-building.

Blood Debt and Nation-Building in Singapore

How could the sense of victimhood be channelled into forms that would unite, rather than divide, the Chinese with other ethnic groups? This issue was brought into sharp focus in 1962, with the exhumation of the largest massacre site, that in Siglap in the east of Singapore. In February 1962, sandwashing operations in the Siglap area exposed five mass war graves. The Chinese Chamber of Commerce then began to exhume what the press dubbed the "valley of tears" or "valley of

even to the Japanese themselves ... it is our responsibility to tell them. So, when the exhumation of remains and collection of evidence have come to a certain stage, we must send a mission to Japan to reveal the true facts to the Japanese government and people".[87]

While the Japanese Consul-General in Singapore understood Chinese bitterness, Japanese politicians did not. They feared that offering compensation to the Singapore Chinese could open the floodgates to other claimants.[88] Lee Kuan Yew, Singapore's Prime Minister, raised the issue in Tokyo on 25 May 1962. Japanese Prime Minister Ikeda Hayato expressed "sincere regret for what had happened", but Lee later noted in Singapore's Parliament that Ikeda's comments were probably an expression of politeness, rather than of willingness to address the issue.[89]

Back in Singapore and Malaya, the ongoing recovery of bodies featured almost daily in the Chinese press. In March 1962, the *Nanyang Siang Pau* wrote that "after 21 years the people of Singapore still shudder at the mention of the identification parades".[90] The press coverage began to mobilise the Chinese of Singapore (more than 74 per cent of its population) behind the blood debt campaign. This also became politicised. The governing People's Action Party (PAP) under Lee Kuan Yew was wrestling for power with a breakaway group, who had formed the *Barisan Sosialis*. Though still easily the biggest single party, the PAP's majority in Parliament had, in the weeks after the breakaway in mid-1961, been reduced to one. The Opposition *Barisan Sosialis*, who the PAP painted as pro-communist, seemed to have a real chance of undermining the PAP, if not of eventually securing power itself.

The PAP feared that the *Barisan* might use communal issues to increase its support.[91] Leaders of the Malay minority also feared that *Barisan* might turn Singapore into a "little China", by playing on the Chinese sympathies for their homeland.[92] Whatever the motivation, on 26 February 1962, *Barisan* expressed support for the Chinese Chamber of Commerce's compensation demand.[93] Chamber President Ko Teck Kin, meanwhile, announced that it wanted to make sure "the elected Government shares joy and sorrow with the people and should not shirk the responsibility of demanding compensation from Japan".[94] In parliament, the *Barisan* asked Lee Kuan Yew's government to seek compensation.

Lee could not afford to lose the votes of Chinese speakers. Yet he did not want to act as advocate for a narrowly Chinese issue. Alex Josey, Lee's aide and confidant, wrote that on the blood debt issue, there was a danger that there would be Chinese "capitalists and communists in harmony against the popularly elected Government".[95] Lee therefore adopted the cause, but also adapted it. Lee told parliament, on 14 March 1962, "that the people of Singapore, as whole, suffered by these massacres", and that "it is our view that atonement should be made to the people of Singapore collectively".[96] The government was reframing an historically rooted claim for compensation because of massacres of Chinese, into a "national" claim based on generalised suffering. This involved blurring the focus, to include all locals as "everyday victims" of occupation. While massacre victims were overwhelmingly Chinese, "everyday victims" — of food shortage, casual brutality and the general hardships of war — were from all ethnic groups.[97]

Meanwhile, the government had to work out a way of dealing with the thousands of exhumed — and overwhelmingly Chinese — massacre victims. The need for a suitable memorial and resting place was becoming acute. This issue gave the Government a way of influencing the Chinese Chamber of Commerce, and the associations for relatives. In granting a licence to exhume massacre victims in 1962, the government pushed the Chamber to adopt the government's national vision of common suffering. The Chinese Chamber of Commerce also agreed that any compensation the Government secured would not go directly to the families of victims, but to the government to spend in the national interest. On 27 July 1962, the *Sin Chew Jit Poh*, owned by the rich Aw family, wrote that "this is not a matter which concerns the Chinese Chamber of Commerce or the Chinese community only, but rather a matter which concerns the entire society. It therefore deserves the support of all the people in the State".[98]

The Chamber of Commerce now added six prominent persons from other ethnic groups in Singapore to its action committee.[99] It later called a meeting of 1,000 representatives, from 600 organisations, for 21 April 1963. Lee Kuan Yew told that meeting that his was a nationalist government which spoke for all the people. He said that the previous compensation claim for British property damaged by the Japanese "was settled by a colonial government that did not represent us, and never understood the depth of our feeling at the atrocities and humiliation an occupying invader inflicted on us".[100] Lee added that they would build a memorial "to an unhappy incident in which many tens of thousands of all races died at the hands of a brutal invading army". He was combining empathy with an attempt to harness Chinese feeling to a national framework. He thus reassured his audience that, "it was my duty to make known the depth of the feelings of the people to the Japanese Government" but cautioned that the "amount of trade, technical co-operation and industrial development that they could take part in Singapore and Malaysia would be out of all proportion to any gesture of atonement they can make".[101]

As part of its balancing act, the Government tried to direct commemorative efforts away from the creation of any prominent Chinese cemetery.[102] For at this point ideas included reburial in a large Chinese cemetery and park, with a Chinese memorial, possibly in the Siglap area. Lee Kuan Yew had even agreed to a Chinese-style park in March 1962, when caught offguard in parliamentary question-time by the *Barisan Sosialis*. The government then offered land in the west of the island, at 15½ mile Choa Chu Kang Road. The Chinese Chamber of Commerce rejected Choa Chu Kang by August 1962, asking for a central site instead.[103] On 13 March 1963, the government therefore offered a memorial site in the heart of Singapore, on Beach Road. In return, the victims' remains would be interred under a monument dedicated not to "Chinese" Massacre victims, but to all Singapore civilians who were killed during the Occupation. This new site was accepted by the Chinese Chamber of Commerce.[104]

The wider context for this was that the PAP had, since its inception in 1954, argued that full independence could only come by Singapore joining with Malaya. The PAP, in common with all the main Singapore parties, saw the island's inhabitants gradually becoming "Malayans", who would speak some Malay as a national language, and enjoy an incipient "Malayan culture". The desire to secure federation with Malaya strongly coloured Singapore's approach to nation-building.

This was especially so, because the Malay-dominated Federation of Malaya was initially reluctant to consider uniting with mainly Chinese Singapore. Until 1961, the Federation resisted British and Singapore politicians' pleas that they should embrace Singapore. But in May 1961, Malayan premier Tunku Abdul Rahman suddenly and publicly offered the prospect of a wider federation. In reality, he did so in large part in order to try and puncture the left wing and communists, and so to ensure Singapore could never go communist. He acted following a humiliating PAP defeat in the April 1961 Hong Lim by-election.[105]

With a constitutional review for Singapore due by 1963,[**] Malaya's ruling party, UMNO, now perceived a real danger that Singapore might

---

[**] The 1957 agreement for internal self-government provided for a review, which was due by 1963.

lurch to the left, and also seek independence alone. The spectre of an independent, radical socialist or even communist Singapore was even more frightening than that of merger with its awkward and predominantly Chinese neighbour. By late 1961, negotiations for a wider federation — to be called Malaysia — were well underway. Malaysia — comprising Malaya, Singapore, Sarawak and Sabah — finally came into being on 16 September 1963.

Even without this looming federation, the PAP, with its English-educated core, was determined to forge a "Malayan" identity, which party intellectual (and Minister for Culture, 1959–1965) Sinnathamby Rajaratnam envisaged as *rojak*. *Rojak* is a local salad that mixes diverse ingredients with one unifying sauce.[106] The PAP styled itself as a multi-racial party. In addition, Lee Kuan Yew and the PAP did not want the Federal Government in Kuala Lumpur to think that it was in any way the communal instrument of Singapore's large Chinese community. This was doubly important, as the dominant party on the Malayan mainland was the Malay nationalist UMNO. It was significant that the predominant Malay-language newspaper also favoured a multiethnic approach to commemoration. In August 1963, the *Utusan Melayu* snapped that "members of the Chinese community are not the only victims of Japanese atrocities", because "the Malay community has also suffered".[107] Indian leaders of Singapore echoed this sentiment.[108]

The Government therefore persisted with its approach of mixing Chinese commemoration with a more general remembrance of everyday victims from all communities. Lee Kuan Yew's next big opportunity to emphasise this came at the groundbreaking ceremony for the new memorial, on 15 June 1963. Speaking in the heart of Singapore's civic district, Lee Kuan Yew told his audience that

> over 20 years ago, in February 1942, we went through a cataclysm experience ... Part of our agony was a sudden disappearance of tens of thousands of our young men, mostly civilians, and some volunteers. Most of them who disappeared were Chinese, but there were also Indians, Malays, Eurasians, Ceylonese and others. Even two Sikh families were massacred.

At this ceremony, Buddhist, Daoist, Hindu, Sikh, Muslim, Christian, and Jewish clerics were on hand, representing the religions of all Singapore's major ethnic groups. Lee declared that he was "dedicating this ground to the memory to those of all races and religion who died in Japanese-occupied Singapore". He also reaffirmed that while the

Japanese should make atonement to all races, the Japanese "can contribute to our industrial growth" with their "technical know-how and industrial equipment".[109]

Lee Kuan Yew's government was conscious of the danger that the blood debt could become divisive, and so decided to help lead the campaign in constructive directions. Lee stepped in to head the campaign when the Chinese Chamber of Commerce called for a mass rally of over 100,000 people to demand $50 million (US$17 million) in compensation, as restitution for the "tribute money" that the Japanese had forced the Chinese community to pay in 1942. Lee Kuan Yew later wrote that Ko Teck Kin, President of the Chinese Chamber of Commerce, "knew that the PAP government would be unhappy as long as it was purely a Chinese issue, so he persuaded the chambers of commerce of the Malay, Indian, Eurasian and Ceylonese communities to join in the mass rally".[110] The public call by the Chinese Chamber of Commerce produced the largest demonstration ever in Singapore. More than 120,000 gathered at the Padang outside City Hall on 25 August 1963, to demand that Japan apologise and pay compensation for its blood debt.[111]

The rally was organised by the new, multiracial, All-Community Action Committee, which called upon all ethnic groups to go to the Padang on 25 August. Despite this, the rally was overwhelmingly Chinese.[112] Representatives came from across Malaya. The Chinese Chambers of Commerce from the Malayan states of Selangor, Perak, Malacca, Kuantan, and Johor all sent representatives...[113] There were even special free Chinese newspaper issues for 25 August, which depicted the exhumed bodies of the massacre victims, juxtaposed alongside pictures of the mutilated bodies of Chinese women from the 1937 Nanking massacre.[114]

On 25 August, Lee Kuan Yew told the assembled crowd that he had himself been at the concentration centres in 1942:

> As I was queuing up at Weld Road-Jalan Besar Concentration Centre in February 1942, the scrutineers at the gate looked at my physical size and asked me to join some people on a lorry ... Somehow I felt that lorry was not going to carry people to work. I asked them to let me go back to get my belongings ... I never returned to the exit point until they had changed sentries and scrutineers. When they did, I walked out and they allowed me to go home.
>
> Those who went into that lorry never came back. Such was the blindness of their brutality ... They made me and a whole generation like me determined to fight for freedom ... From that time onwards, I decided that our lives should be ours to decide.

He thus located himself as one of the "everyday victims" who could and nearly did, join the ranks of the massacred, and also firmly linked the massacres to the fight for independence. Yet he also made it clear that, above all, Singapore needed Japanese investment and skills to help in its industrialisation. Lee's oratory tapped emotion and logic, preparing feelings for the sort of compromise he might extract from Japan.[115]

Lee Kuan Yew remained alert to the danger that his opponents would try to steer the blood debt campaign in other directions. The day before the rally, the Government warned pro-communists who might "intend to create trouble under the cover of the 'blood debt' mass rally".[116] Security was tight. According to Alex Josey, Lee Kuan Yew had "a revolver in his pocket when he addressed the silent crowd".[117] Lee's reported aim was to "take over the movement so that he could contain and control it".[118] He was planning a snap election in September 1963. Though he supported the blood debt campaign in public, however, in private he said that he had "done his utmost to play it down". When Singapore merged with Malaya to form Malaysia in September 1963, the government gladly handed related negotiations with Japan over to the Malaysian Prime Minister, Tunku Abdul Rahman.[119]

Even before Malaysia was inaugurated, campaigners had started couching their campaigns in multiracial, Malaysian terms. One of the key resolutions of the 25 August 1963 meeting was that "the people of all races of Malaya, Sabah, Sarawak, and Singapore should join together in united action against Japan to press for a satisfactory settlement of the 'blood debt'".[120] A short boycott of Japanese goods by the Chinese Chambers of Commerce of Malaysia was implemented in September.[121] This prompted intervention by Lord Selkirk, the British High Commissioner, who, with the British Foreign Office, persuaded Japan to begin negotiations with Malaysian Prime Minister Tunku Abdul Rahman in October 1963.[122] The Malaysian Indian Congress also backed the campaign from October.[123] The Japanese government response, in 1964–1965, was to stall negotiations.[124] In Japan, the issue was known as the "Singapore Blood Debt Problem", or *Shingaporu Kessai Mondai*.[125]

If Japan hoped that a Malay-dominated Malaysian government would let the issue subside, they were to be foiled by events. Singapore's brief period in Malaysia provoked 1964 race riots on the island, and also tension with the federal government. On 9 August 1965, Singapore left Malaysia, and became an independent state. As such, the government had more need to address its majority Chinese sensitivities, and less need to be sensitive to mainland Malay views. The Singapore government restarted talks with Japan. Finally on 25 October 1966, the Singapore and Japanese Foreign Ministers announced that Japan would provide $50 million as a gesture: $25 million of this as a grant; $25 million as a loan. Lee Kuan Yew had persuaded Japan to view this as an investment, rather than as formal compensation. There was no Japanese apology, but the Singapore government chose to view the matter as closed. Lee privately slapped down Chinese Chamber of Commerce demands for more. The latter were angry that the settlement only included $25 million as a grant, not the $50 million targeted, and had been accepted without consultation with them. But they were told not to pursue the issue as it would harm much needed Japanese investment at a time when the country badly needed to accelerate economic development.[126]

The Civilian War Memorial Takes Shape

The October 1966 settlement was timely. The last Singapore exhumations had been completed in August 1966, and the Beach Road memorial site was now ready. On Tuesday, 1 November 1966, more than 600 large funeral urns, each filled with the bones of up to 30 victims, were lowered into a cavern under the finished monument. Named the Civilian War Memorial, this stood guard over thousands of massacre victims, with the Singapore Chinese claiming up to 20,000 interred there.[127][††] On 15 February 1967, the monument was officially opened, and dedicated to all the civilians of Singapore who had been killed during the Occupation. Prime Minister Lee Kuan Yew attended the opening, and prayers were said by leaders of the Inter-Religious Council representing the Muslim, Buddhist, Christian, Hindu, Jewish, Sikh, and Zoroastrian faiths. The crowd comprised in large part elderly Chinese women who, according to Daoist and Buddhist rituals, made offerings to dead relatives.[128]

The Singapore government had much to be pleased about. It had got the monument dedicated to all civilian war dead. It had influenced

[††] The number of victims in the urns is almost impossible to pinpoint given the advanced state of decay and disintegration of many of them. See the proximate endnote for discussion of this emotive issue. The lack of an authoritative list, and of a monument which actually names the victims, is one of the most gaping holes in Singapore's history and commemoration.

the physical design of the monument and memorial park, towards which it contributed half of the costs. The other half was raised by the Chinese Chamber of Commerce.[129] Before government involvement, there had, by contrast, been proposals for a monument similar the memorials to Chinese massacre victims in Penang and Malacca, as erected in 1947–1948. These consisted of a single pillar with a Chinese inscription written on one side, usually located in Chinese memorial gardens, or near mainly Chinese settlements.[130]

With government involvement, government land, and financial backing from 1963, a competition had been rapidly organised to find a new design for a "Memorial to Civilian Victims of the Japanese Occupation". Already the emphasis had switched to commemorating all ethnic groups, but the conditions still emphasised the visual and symbolic importance of the victims' remains. The instructions were that designs should manifest solemnity, simplicity, and mould the memorial into the surrounding gardens while maintaining its dominance. There should be a vault, sanctum, or accessible space for the storage of the urns, and their viewing by the public.

By May 1963, the judges had shortlisted three entries from more than 20.[131] The winning entry, by Swan and Maclaren, had an arch formed by sweeping columns, said to reflect "a local architectural mood". But it was criticised as lacking adequate public access to the vault which would hold the urns. The design included a central "flame of remembrance", and the whole was to be surrounded by a pool or pools of reflection, to be lit up at night.[132] Early plans also called for the sweeping concrete arches to have plaques attached, each naming an area or areas where there had been exhumations, which would have made the link to massacre sites explicit.[133] Several other designs made the space for viewing the urns a more central, dramatic feature.

An exhibition of the designs was opened in the Victoria Memorial Hall in June 1963, just after Lee Kuan Yew attended the ceremonial soil-breaking ceremony.[134]

At this stage, there was still the possibility that remains would be cremated, and so ideally require a small enough number of urns to allow display in the monument precincts. But there were always those within the Chinese Chamber of Commerce who felt victims' remains should be laid to rest as they were. Subsequently, there were also objections that the remains might include people whose beliefs precluded cremation. That meant vastly more urns, making display more problematical. In addition, the technical demands of the sweeping arches may have

Plate 5.6 The Winning Design for the Civilian War Memorial, by Swan and Mclaren, 1963

proved challenging. For whatever reason, Swan and Maclaren were kept on as architects, but the design modified. First of all, the increased number of urns were to be placed underground, which dramatically reduced the visual impact of the memorial and gardens as a burial site. The new monument would have the appearance — not the reality — of a cenotaph or empty tomb. There would be no visible element of grave or urn, bar a single, symbolic sculptured bronze urn to be placed discreetly at the base of the monument. Second, the sweeping arch of columns was replaced by four upright columns, which converged towards each other as they soared into the sky. In October 1965, before construction began, the Chinese Chamber of Commerce had to get the government to approve this final design.[135]

The move to four pillars also allowed them to be read in symbolic terms, as one pillar for each of Singapore's main ethnic groups (Chinese, Malay, Indian, and either Eurasian or more generally all others). By October 1966, the Singapore Government was telling the public that "these columns, being close together, symbolise the four separate streams of culture merging into a single entity which is the basis of Singapore's unity".[136] This structure made the monument appear as two pairs of

Plate 5.7 The Civilian War Memorial, Singapore

chopsticks rising into the sky. This gave rise to the colloquial name the monument subsequently gained in Singapore: the chopsticks.

The metamorphosis of the monument from sanctuary and display-scape for Chinese massacre victims, to abstract monument to all civilian dead, also reflected in its inscription. In 1965, the Chinese Chamber of Commerce invited Pan Shou — journalist, educationalist, poet and calligrapher — to compose an inscription. Pan Shou had been Secretary-General of Singapore's private, Chinese-language Nanyang University (Nantah) from 1955–1960. As such, he had been tainted by government criticism of that institution's early years.[137] His job was to compose verses which would tell how the monument arose out of the discovery of numbers of mass graves, from 1962 onwards. Pan Shou's epigraph evoked the need for peace, and stated that the four columns stood for "loyalty, bravery, virtue and righteousness which are reflected in the traditional harmony and solidarity of the multi-racial, multi-cultural and multi-religious Singapore". It added that "No one can list all our multi-racial compatriots who were killed in the massacre". This echoed government emphasis on unity emerging from common suffering, but the ending delivered an emotional punch:

> May the souls of the civilian victims of the Japanese rest in eternal peace and accept this epitaph dedicated to them by the people of Singapore.
> Tears stained flower
> crimson-like
> And blood tainted the blue ocean
> Ye wandering souls who
> rise with the tide
> Shall guard this young
> emerging nation.

The final verse came close to evoking the Chinese image of "Hungry Ghosts" — souls without a grave or ancestors to pray for them — who in this case would "guard" the young nation. It is an almost exact echo of a gesture in late 1947, when some Chinese "burnt a sacrificial paper ship, bearing to these sea spirits supplies of rice, firewood and charcoal".[138] Pan Shou's final stanza was a graphic image of victims and future generations bound together, and emotionally supercharged at a time when Lee was trying to ensure the blood debt issue remained closed, and that Japanese investment should increase.

When the monument opened, Pan Shou was shocked to find the verses were not there.[139] They were, it is true, rather long, describing the history from exhumation to monument at length. In their stead were sterile words representative of the PAP approach, with its English-educated core of leaders, and preference for precise, technocratic language:

> This memorial was erected by the people of Singapore through the efforts of the Chinese Chamber of Commerce and the action of the Government from funds donated by the Government and the people of Singapore. It was unveiled on February, 15, 1967, by the Prime Minister.[140]

Government involvement had resulted in a shift from an inscription which blended specifically Chinese sentiments and images into an invocation to nation-building, to a statement of dry fact.[141] These changes contradicted the initial impetus for the monument, which had been to properly rebury the exhumed remains, in order to "appease the souls of the victims of Japanese atrocities".[142]

The Prime Minister gave the key speech at the dedication ceremony on 15 February 1967. He used the occasion to cement his preferred image of monument, as representing the common suffering of all the people of Singapore:

> This piece of concrete commemorates an experience which in spite of its horrors, served as a catalyst in building a nation out of the young and unestablished community of diverse immigrants. We suffered together. It told us that we share a common destiny. And it is through sharing such common experiences that the feeling of living and being one community is established.[143]

Rhetorically, Lee Kuan Yew completed the shift from a community memorial to massacre victims, to a national monument dedicated as much to "everyday victims". The Singapore press picked up on this national use of the Civilian War Memorial. In an editorial entitled "The Blood Debt" on 6 February 1967, the *Eastern Sun* emphasised that all communities had suffered. Hence, "the Chinese had a bad time when Japanese soldiers burst into their homes and committed all manner of atrocities". For the Indian community, "Japanese soldiers would drive up to estates in the night and forcibly took away the male Tamil labourers amidst the wailing and shrieks of their women folk. Thousands

of these Tamils were sent to Thailand to build the death railway and
most of them did not return". For the Malay community, "mosques
were desecrated and Malay victims were forced to commit acts against
their religious conscience".[144] All the races were seen as united in remembering national suffering.

The 15 February 1967 unveiling ceremony of the Civilian War
Memorial initiated an annual 15 February commemoration. Early ceremonies were organised by the Chinese Chamber of Commerce, and
attended by a senior Singapore Cabinet Minister, by the Japanese Ambassador, and by representatives of the diplomatic corps. In attendance
were large numbers of Chinese, but the Chinese Chamber of Commerce
was also careful to invite members of their Malay and Indian business
counterparts.[145] The Singapore settlement of the "blood debt" compensation package in 1966 and the erection of a monument to civilian war
dead in 1967 thus established a pattern of national-level commemoration, in which community and nation were welded together and made
into an abstract, national whole. This was now encapsulated in the
Civilian War Memorial, and in the annual ceremony held there every
15 February.

Blood Debt and Community Remembrance in Malaya/Malaysia

The situation in Malaysia could scarcely have stood in greater contrast.
There most massacre victims' remains had been recovered from 1946–
1948 and marked by memorials, mainly in Chinese cemeteries. These
monuments represented an Overseas Chinese rather than a Malayan
or Malaysian identity. The settlement of the "blood debt" thus did
not initiate any national ceremony, as it was viewed as a Chinese issue
within a "plural society". In contrast to Singapore's multicommunal
parties, peninsular Malayan politics remained dominated by the Alliance,
whose three main parties each represented one communal group: the
United Malays National Organisation (UMNO) for Malays, the Malayan Chinese Association (MCA) for Chinese, and the Malayan Indian
Congress (MIC) for Indians. The balance between these was maintained
by elite accommodation, and toleration for their respective languages
and cultures, while acknowledging overall Malay predominance.

This system did not favour an inter-communal approach to commemoration, as in Singapore. As such, the Chinese Chambers of
Commerce there did not involve members of the other communities in

Plate 5.8   15 February Ceremony at the Civilian War Memorial in Singapore

agitation. The Associated Chinese Chambers of Commerce of Malaysia passed a resolution in September 1963 that Japan should give $130 million, $10 million for each Malaysian state and settlement. After Singapore got a settlement in October 1966, they concluded that Japan had settled with Singapore and not Malaysia because Singapore "had made too much noise".[146] From late 1966, they therefore began to make as much noise as they could in the direction of the Malaysian government. As negotiations reached a climax, victims' relatives began turning up at the offices of Chinese Chamber of Commerce in the hope that they would receive compensation.[147] They seemed unaware that any such claim would be paid to the Malaysian government, and not through their traditional associations and chambers.

In January 1967, Japan offered just $25 million, against the $130 million demanded.[148] Tunku Abdul Rahman was anxious to settle, as Japan was now Malaysia's second largest export market after Singapore, and its second largest source of imports after Britain.[149] In January 1967, he criticised the Associated Chinese Chambers of Commerce for demanding $130 million.[150] He presented payment as "money paid out of the goodness of their heart for war damages ... it all happened so long ago and the British have collected all there is to collect. However, if we accept it as a goodwill gesture, we can use the money for development, like the setting up of a university college in Penang".[151] In May 1967, Japan's Premier Sato Eisaku agreed that two freighter ships and capital equipment worth $25 million would be given. On 17 August 1967, the Japanese requested a last-minute "no further claims" clause. That was dropped, after the Chinese Chambers of Commerce threatened to boycott Japanese goods.[152] On 21 September 1967, Japan and Malaysia finally signed a "Goodwill Payment Agreement" outlining settlement of the "blood debt" as the two cargo ships and money for capital works.[153]

Conclusion

The contrasting approaches of the governments of Malaysia and Singapore had a major impact on how the Chinese community in each country commemorated victims. In Malaysia, a plural society, and the existence of communal political parties favoured Chinese deathscapes, ideally suited to Chinese patterns of mourning and cultural norms. The cost of that pattern was that such commemoration had relatively little impact at the national, cross-communal level.

In Singapore, the state stepped in to reshape the Chinese community's public remembrance. The result was a deathscape — the Civilian War Memorial — which retained little that was specifically Chinese, and annual ceremonies on each 15 February that were "nationalised". The Civilian War Memorial was used to emphasise common suffering, and to highlight 1942 as the moment when the determination to be free was born. The cost of this approach was greater dissonance between the needs of the victims' families — for a place to mourn relatives and a familiar and comforting cultural framework for this — and the form of state remembrance. So abstracted from events was the final monument, that a bypasser could easily mistake it for a cenotaph (empty tomb), rather than the actual burial site for thousands of massacre victims that it was.

For Chinese in both countries, the sense of "blood debt" was ultimately ameliorated, rather than satisfied. The inability to identify many of the recovered bodies, combined with the tiny number of Japanese convicted — let alone executed — for their role in the *sook ching*, left a sense of unexpiated "blood debt". The final Japanese offers of loans and grants, to Singapore in 1966 and to Malaysia in 1967, were accepted by the respective governments as convenient excuses to drop the matter. By now, the governments were anxious that history should not get in the way of maximising Japanese investment and involvement in their countries' modernisation.

As we shall see in Chapters 9 and 10, the image of Chinese victims continued to exercise the public in both countries into and beyond the 1980s. But by then, the main question would no longer be how to extract Japanese payment of a "blood debt", but rather, what weight such victims would play in each countries' national history and ceremonies.

CHAPTER 6

Indian Nationalism and Suffering

ON 4 JULY 1943, SUBHAS CHANDRA BOSE spoke in Singapore's Cathay Building. There he accepted the Presidency of the Indian Independence League (IIL), and the allegiance of the Indian National Army (INA). At that point the INA, raised from British Indian Army soldiers captured in Malaya and Singapore in 1941–1942, was at a low ebb. Its initial leader, Captain Mohan Singh, had struggled to keep disparate groups united, and had fallen out with his Japanese sponsors. But S.C. Bose had been elected the President of the Indian National Congress for 1938 and 1939, and with his words could evoke a different order of nationalist passion. Besides, the Japanese now felt a more urgent need for allies, as the tide of war turned against them. Already, in January 1943, Japanese Premier Tojo Hideki had promised Burma and the Philippines that they would be given independence within a year. By 6 July, Bose was standing on the steps of Singapore's Municipal Building, alongside Tojo, taking the salute from an INA march past.

Japan would finally grant Burma "independence" in August 1943, and the Philippines in October 1943. For India to follow their example, it must first be liberated from British rule, and to that end Bose was determined to revitalise the INA and launch it at India's borders alongside the Japanese. Bose believed that Indians would have to arm themselves, and seek help where they could, if they were to remove their obdurate British masters. In prewar India, he had expounded the need for radical action, violence if necessary, and this had brought him into conflict with Gandhi. Put under house arrest by the British in July 1940, he had given the colonial authorities the slip in January 1941. Crossing the Indian border to Afghanistan dressed as the Pathan "Ziauddin" — with salwar, leather jacket and newly grown beard — he had travelled on to Kabul. Then as "Orlando Mazzotta", he had conti-

174

nued by train to Moscow. From Moscow he flew to Berlin, where the Germans allowed him to raise a small Indian Legion. Finally, he was inspired by Japanese successes of 1942 to make his way to Tokyo, travelling by submarine and aircraft from February 1943.[1]

By now, Bose was convinced that democracy alone might be insufficient to revive the fortunes of Indians, and that in the first instance a great leader would be needed.[2] In Singapore, meanwhile, the IIL and INA leaders had called on the Japanese to send them S.C. Bose. Once in Singapore, Bose acted the part of the celebrity nationalist to the full. He electrified the crowd at the Cathay Building on 4 July 1943. In Chapter 2, we saw how just one ex-British Indian Army soldier, K.R. Das, responded to Bose. Das had been cool about the first INA, as led by Mohan Singh. Of Bose, however, Das wrote that "In some inexplicable way, the imagination of every Indian, man and woman, was fired by the mere presence of Netaji [leader]. He became the only symbol of hope for subjugated Indians".[3]

Before this moment Das, who as a boy had listened to Gandhi and Nehru at rallies in India, had seen himself as tarnished. Having joined the British Indian Army for the paypacket, he saw himself as a mercenary.[4] Now, under Bose's spell, he felt that joining the INA, in September 1943, restored his dignity.

Das went on to become a 2nd Lieutenant in the INA, and a trainer, though he never did make it to the frontline in Burma. Nevertheless, he remembered the war, the INA, and especially Bose with warmth. For Das, Bose transformed not just the elite and volunteers, but the Indian rubber tapper on the plantations, and "every Indian". The INA broke down class divisions, and the isolation of the tapper on the estate, to allow a new level of community organisation.

Even more dramatic than Das' story was that Chapter 2 told of Rasammah Navarednam (later known by her married name of Mrs Bhupalan). Though a 16-year-old from a respectable family, she too rushed to join the INA in mid-1943: signing up for its all-female unit — the Rani of Jhansi Regiment. After the war, she remembered — in fact spoke as if it still existed for her in the present — her passionate devotion to the Netaji, and her equally passionate desire to fight for India. Her dream had been that the shedding of female blood — perhaps including her own — might spark a final rebellion and liberation. Only the failure of the Japanese, and the male INA regiments, in the battle for Imphal and Kohima of April to June 1944, denied her this most fervently desired fate.[5]

Plate 6.1   Subhas Chandra Bose inspecting the Rani of Jhansi Regiment

The likes of K.R. Das and Rasammah Navarednam, along with thousands of ordinary INA fighters, linked the story of Indians in Malaya with the wider tale of nationalism in India. Indeed, the Provisional Government of Free India (*Azad Hind*) was formed in October 1943, in Singapore, under Bose's leadership

After the war, a nationalist Indian elite in Malaya and Singapore would mould this story, of the Indian nationalism of the INA and its leader S.C. Bose, as the dominant collective memory of their community. By 1993, Romen Bose, then a 22-year-old Singapore journalist, could write that, in 1942–1943,

> another arm rose in greatness that even the Imperial Japanese Army recognised ... as true patriots ... [which was] ... an historic movement that came to shake the very foundations of colonial rule and imperialism in the Indian subcontinent and throughout Southeast Asia ... Indians throughout Asia and especially in Southeast Asia can be proud of having forefathers that belonged to a movement that although failed, created in its aftermath a struggle for freedom that makes its impact felt, even today.[6]

For Bose, the INA story was not one that faced outwards only, to India, but one that looked inwards as well, to postwar decolonisation in Singapore and Malaya:

> The desire for independence and need for self-determination showed Singaporeans the way ahead towards self-rule. Thus, it was in no way insignificant, that on the very steps of City Hall, where Subhas Chandra Bose declared the creation of a new and free India in 1943, that, twenty years later, on those very same steps, Prime Minister Lee Kuan Yew would be declaring ... the fledging state of Singapore.[7]

This chapter examines the power of this INA myth.[*] We say "myth", because the exaltation of the INA involved selective amnesia about the experiences of those who refused to join the INA; of those who were conscripted to work for the Japanese; and of "everyday" survivors and victims. As we shall see, the experiences of the everyday victims, conscripted labourers, and POWs who did not join the INA, together represented larger number of Indians than joined.

G.J. Douds and Peter Stanley have highlighted the inhuman treatment given to Indian POWs who refused to join the INA. Many were sent to work in appalling conditions in New Guinea, with high death rates.[8]

The INA was complicit, through its political arm, the Indian Independence League (IIL) — in the even greater suffering imposed on civilian Indians. The chaos of war, and the particular chaos on the Burma-Thailand Railway, make precision over numbers of Indians sent to the railway elusive. But we can easily establish the general dimensions of this disaster. Estimates range from 73,502 Asian labourers of all ethnicities from Malaya (24,470 dead) to 78,204 (40,000 dead). Around 70 per cent of the total (between 50,000 and 56,000) seems to have been Indian. By these figures, the death rate was somewhere between 32 and 51 per cent. The lower of those two rates is almost certainly too low, since it leaves large numbers of labourers unaccounted for, at least some of whom will have died. This toll was not restricted to adult males, as with Western POWs. As many as 40 per cent were aged between 12 and 18, and women were present too.[9]

---

[*] By myth, we mean a story created out of selective and sometimes remoulded memories, and having a didactic or moral purpose.

The best that could be said is that the IIL acquiesced in the Japanese forcing tens of thousands of Indian rubber estate workers to join labour gangs on the "Death Railway". Members of the INA and IIL assisted in recruitment, though no doubt with varying degrees of willingness and foreboding. At first the Indian workers were lured with the promise of contracts as short as four months or less, with good conditions. As rumours filtered back of ill-treatment in crude jungle camps, the Japanese then refused to let existing labourers go at the end of their contracts. As recruitment stepped up, the Japanese subsequently started to lean on the IIL and the *kirani* (supervisors on estates) to procure larger numbers of "volunteers".[10] Even those tactics could not produce the increasing numbers needed as 1943 wore on, so the Japanese resorted to press-ganging. Mooniandy Ramasamy could vividly recall the trauma of such kidnapping nearly 50 years later, in 1991:

> I was working on the Kuala Selangor Estate. One day I was walking along the road towards Bukit Rotan near my house. A Japanese military lorry stopped, and the soldiers said something to me in Japanese. I could not understand them. The soldiers forced me to get in the lorry. There were already thirty other people there. I was wearing only a pair of shorts and sandals. I begged them to let me go home to put on a proper shirt … instead they sent me directly to Kuala Lumpur and loaded me onto a freight train for Siam. There we started by cutting dense jungle. The Japanese did not give me a proper shirt or blanket for seven months. I had to work in the jungle and sleep on the bamboo floor in a hut, half naked and without any blanket.[11]

Once on the railway, Indian labourers suffered some of the highest death rates of any group, rates which resulted in Australian POWs such as Don Lee being ordered to tip cholera victims into ravines by the cartload, or burn bodies without checking too closely if anyone was living. British POW Arthur Lane described arriving by barge at one camp 132 kilometres north of Kanchanaburi, to find it packed with "emaciated men and women, some with children clinging to their hands". For him:

> The sight was enough to cause a fit man to throw up. There were men with great ulcers chewing away their arms and legs, others totally blind being led by others practically unable to support themselves, let alone assist others. Women suffering from ulcers and palagra [pellagra], mostly in a state of undress, which didn't matter, they had lost all resemblance to women and their bones showed through in the same places as the men.

Plate 6.2   Emaciated patients in a hospital hut at Nakom Paton, on the Burma-Thailand Railway

Lane's men were sent to bury cholera victims, disposing of roughly 2,000 rotting corpses in seven pits. The Japanese, who sometimes abandoned cholera-ravaged camps rather than risk infection, rewarded the POWs with two days' rest. The Asian labourers, lacking the military structure, unit camaraderie, and medics of the POWs, descended into squalor more quickly. Again, in contrast to Western POWs, who left rows of graves, most Indians who died ended up in pits such as those Lane's men dug, or in unmarked, mass graves.[12]

The suffering did not end in Thailand. After the war, thousands of survivors, often destitute, or physically and psychologically scarred, returned from working on the Burma-Thailand Railway, women were left without husbands, and several thousand children without parents.

There were, therefore, many images of the war which Indians could have chosen to emphasise: ranging from the 16-year-old Ms Navarednam's euphoric, teenage nationalist fervour, through Mooniandy Ramasamy's sudden kidnapping, to the bodies that still lie in unmarked graves, somewhere along the Burma-Thailand Railway. These experiences bequeathed a set of contradictory memories and emotions, with the period seeing both elevation from the sneering condescension of prewar colonial society, and yet simultaneously the most complete degradation of thousands of Indians sent to Thailand. Taken together, the images of the Netaji and the railway labourer, of pride restored and of dignity shredded, form an oxymoron.

In the postwar years, it was the exhilarating experience of the nationalist movement that emerged triumphant in public memory. By contrast, little was remembered — in public — of the experiences of Indians who refused to join the INA, and of the thousands of labourers sent to Thailand. The community need for uplifting images trumped the disparateness of individuals' memories.[13]

The INA and Commemorative Days

Indian troops comprised the largest component of the 130,000 British Empire personnel who helped to defend Malaya. By the time Singapore was surrendered in February 1942, 55,000 Indian soldiers had become POWs in the theatre.[14] According to Peter Ward Fay's interpretation of documents at the India Office, of the captured Indian soldiers, 40,000 offered to join the INA, while 15,000 remained POWs.

The biggest single act of recruitment came on 17 February 1942, at Farrer Park in Singapore, when 45,000 British Indian Army POWs were asked to join by the INA organiser, Captain Mohan Singh. Mohan Singh was an officer in the 1st Battalion of the 14th Indian Punjab Regiment. He had been captured by the Japanese at the beginning of the campaign, at the Battle of Jitra, on 12 December 1941. He fell into the hands of the Japanese intelligence unit (F-Kikan) led by Major Fujiwara Iwaichi. Fujiwara had been recruiting Indians and Malays since before October 1941. He also sympathised with Japan's theme of "Asia for the Asians" and so local nationalism. As the first British Indian Army officer to defect to the Japanese and then work closely with Fujiwara, Mohan Singh become the natural leader of the first INA.[15]

According to his memoirs, Mohan Singh asked the 45,000 Indian POWs crowded into Farrer Park on 17 February,

> to raise hands if any one from amongst them would like to volunteer to join this force and fight for the liberation of his country. There was a spontaneous response from all the soldiers. Along with the raising of hands, thousands of turbans and caps were hurled up in the air ... soldiers jumped to their feet ... with prolonged shouts of *'Inqilab Zindabad'* (Long Live Revolution).[16]

Fay claims that just 5,000 of these 45,000 Indian POWs in Singapore absolutely refused to join this first INA over the next year and a half, compared with the 40,000 who were willing. The 10,000 taken prisoner on the Malayan mainland were not asked. When the INA was officially formed on 1 September 1942, however, the Japanese would arm only 16,000. They only became more generous with the arrival of S.C. Bose, and formation of the second INA, in 1943. Fay notes that 18,000 Indian civilians in Malaya and Singapore joined the INA after Bose's arrival.[17]

The INA quickly decided that it needed dates to celebrate its formation and mission. They ignored dates associated with their first foundation. The 17 February 1942 address by Mohan Singh at Farrer Park, and the formation of the first INA division on 1 September 1942, were overlooked. This was because the first attempt suffered from factionalism and communalism, and ended in failure when the Japanese disbanded most of it. There were also reservations about Mohan Singh, not least because he was not the most senior officer from the surrendered British Indian Army.

The first INA lacked a leadership charismatic enough to galvanise nationalist feelings over and above communal divisions into Muslim, Hindu, Sikh and other sub-identities. K.R. Das remembered 60 years later that, unlike Subhas Chandra Bose, "Mohan Singh, although a sincere man, was not a popular leader in India. He had support in the army, but no support among the South Indians in Malaya, who were thinking, "he is not a Nehru so why support him?"[18] The first INA collapsed in December 1942, when Mohan Singh was placed under arrest for refusal to follow Japanese orders, and after his demand for the INA to be treated as an allied army.

The dates chosen to commemorate the Indian experience were, therefore, associated with the second INA as developed in 1943 from the remnants of the first, under Subhas Chandra Bose's leadership. It was his charisma that made many Indians feel they were part of a fervent, united nationalist movement. Bose had the advantage of being a well-known prewar nationalist, having been elected President of the Indian National Congress Party in 1938 and in 1939. His idea that India's independence could only be achieved through armed struggle ran counter to Gandhi's views, so Bose had eventually resigned from his position as president. His subsequent arrest by the British, and remarkable escape to Nazi Germany had added to his lustre.

Bose first arrived in Singapore, by aeroplane, on 2 July 1943. He received a rapturous welcome from previous INA members and the Indian community. An IIL spokesman welcomed Bose, declaring that "he ranks with such illustrious sons of India as Mahatma Gandhi, Maulana Azad, and Pandit Nehru. Throughout his life, Subhas Bose has been in the thick of the fight against the British".[19] Soon, Bose was being called *Netaji*, meaning leader. He had used the name in Europe, following the German *Führer* for Hitler and Italian *il Duce* for Mussolini.[20] *Neta* meant leader in Hindi, and *ji* was used to soften the word so that it had a more endearing ring to it.[21] Mahatma Gandhi was often referred to as "Gandhiji". Thereafter during the war, the coming of Bose to Singapore was commemorated as "Netaji Week".

On 4 July, Bose accepted the Presidency of the IIL and the allegiance of the INA at the packed meeting at Singapore's Cathay Building. Behind Bose, there was a large flag of Japan and the saffron, white, and green tricolour: the flag of the Indian nationalist movement. When Bose entered the hall, the assembly rose to its feet. This was "followed by many an unrehearsed shrill, and from all parts of the house men rose to their feet and repeatedly called for '*ki jais*' [*ki jai* — long live] to Subhas Bose, Rash Behari Bose, Mahatma Gandhi, Maulana Abdul Kalam Azad, Pundit Jawaharlal Nehru and the whole galaxy of Indian national heroes". At the end, "refrains from national songs sung by Indian girls came from the crowd in the form of prolonged cries of "Long Live Revolution" and "Long Live Hindustan" and "Long Live Dai Nippon".[22] On 6 July, Bose, with Japan's Premier Hideki Tojo at his side, reviewed a parade of the INA outside the Singapore's Municipal Building — which the Japanese called *Tokubetsushi* Building. Both leaders, Japanese and Indian, returned the troops' salute.

On 8 July, the existence of the INA, or *Azad Hind Fauj* (Free India Army) as it was now called, was announced to the world by Bose. The aim was to march on India, until they could hold a victory parade in the Red Fort, the seat of power in India before the British Empire. Bose suggested that the INA would build upon the fall of Singapore: "When the brave soldiers of Nippon set out on their march in December 1941, there was but one cry which rose from their lips, 'To Singapore, to Singapore.' Comrades! My soldiers! Let your battle cry be, 'To Delhi, to Delhi [*Chalo Delhi*]'".[23]

On 9 July, Bose addressed 60,000 at Singapore's Padang. He stood in front of a platform adorned with a huge picture of India, roses, a life-sized portrait of Mahatma Gandhi, and the words, "Welcome Srijut Subhas Chandra Bose". In his speech, Bose proclaimed that "there is no nationalist leader in India who can claim to possess the many-sided experience that I have been able to acquire", and that without help from outside, "it is impossible for anyone to liberate India" because "all the efforts that we could put forward inside India, would not suffice to expel the British from our country".[24] Thus ended the first "Netaji Week", which was subsequently marked annually during the war.

Out of the enthusiasm of "Netaji Week", the women's regiment was formed on 12 July 1943, as the "Rani of Jhansi Regiment". This force of several hundred was led by Captain Lakshmi Swaminadhan, a doctor from India who had lived in Malaya since 1940. It was named after a heroine of the 1857 uprising, Rani Lakshmi Bai (1835–1858), the young widowed queen of the principality of Jhansi. She instituted military training for women and led troops against the British in several battles.

Bose mentioned having women in the army as early as his 9 July address, and again to Lakshmi that night. Bose said in his speech that in the pursuit of total mobilisation, "I want also a unit of brave Indian women to form the "Death-defying Regiment" who will wield the sword which the brave Rani of Jhansi had wielded in India's First War of Independence in 1857".[25] By Monday, 12 July, Lakshmi had put together the first 20 women, recruited from the Women's section of the IIL. On 22 October 1943, the day after Bose declared the establishment of a provisional government for Free India — or *Azad Hind* — a military camp of the Rani of Jhansi Regiment opened. The regiment never did go into action, but it was brought to Burma to assist the INA. Ironically, its main practical achievement there turned out to be assisting with medical care. As INA casualties increased, regimental soldiers near hospitals were called on to help, in addition to the minority of the regiment specifically trained as nurses.[26]

The key event for public commemoration, meanwhile, became the declaration by Bose of the *Azad Hind* Government (Free India Provisional Government) on 21 October 1943, again at the Cathay Building. This time Bose stood on a stage behind which a large Indian tricolour and the Nazi flag flanked the Japanese flag in the centre. The national anthem, *Jana Gana Mana* ("Thou Art the Ruler of All Minds"), was played. This is today's Indian national anthem, which calls Indians of different faiths and languages to unite. A cabinet headed by Bose was sworn in. The nationalist rhetoric of the *Azad Hind* Government was astutely designed to create enthusiasm among all surrendered Indian soldiers, and all civilian Indians, regardless of differences. The aim was to convince them that they were now at the centre of the Indian independence struggle.[27]

Almost immediately, this declaration of the *Azad Hind* Government, on 21 October, provided the main day for commemoration. The 21st of every month after 21 October 1943 was marked. This usually took the form of a mass rally at which members of the INA (*Azad Hind Fauj*), and the women of its Rani of Jhansi Regiment, as well as the IIL civilians, would affirm allegiance to the *Azad Hind* Government. Eventually, 232,562 Indians in Southeast Asia would acknowledge allegiance in writing. Most of these were from the roughly 700,000 Indians in Malaya and Singapore, although Indians in Burma and Thailand also offered allegiance.[28]

At these monthly 21st day celebrations, schoolchildren would sing *Vande Mataram* as the Indian tricolour was run-up flagpoles at mass rallies.[29] *Vande Mataram* was traditionally used at Indian Congress Party meetings. Then, after the Indian national anthem was played, leaders would recount recent progress.[30] In a 21 February 1944 statement given out by an *Azad Hind* Government spokesman, each achievement was recounted on a monthly basis. He declared that one month after 21 October 1943, the Free Indian Provisional Government had already been recognised as the government of India by the Axis governments. At the end of the second month, it had gained stable financial backing. By the third month, it had transferred its headquarters nearer to the frontline in Burma. At the end of the fourth month, its troops had amassed strength "culminating in the offensive against the British and the sensational victory on the Arakan Front".[31]

Not satisfied with marking the 21st of every month, the movement also started to celebrate Bose's birthday. The Indian community already celebrated Gandhi's birthday annually with "a mammoth procession and rally at Farrer Park".[32] The first celebration of Bose's birthday came on 23 January 1944.[33] Celebrations on 23 January 1945 included a military review at the INA's Singapore camp, sports events in which Rani of Jhansi members and school students competed, and a mass rally at Waterloo Street Padang, where senior INA and IIL members reaffirmed allegiance to Bose. On this day, an article in the official newspaper, *Azad Hind*, proclaimed that "Netaji himself represents all that is noble and great in India".[34]

There was also commemoration of Bose's arrival in Singapore during the first week of July 1943, in "Netaji Week".[35] By the 1945 "Netaji Week", the INA had been involved in fighting on the Burma frontier, culminating in entry into India during the March 1944 offensive at Imphal. That return to Indian soil was brief. Two token INA divisions had been all but annihilated with the main Japanese forces. Bose returned to Singapore in the wake of this. "Netaji Week" for 1945 started with Bose addressing a mass rally of 10,000 on 4 July. The *Azad Hind* Government's national flag was raised, the national anthem sung, and participants reaffirmed their pledge to the government and determination to fight for India's freedom.[36]

The fighting on the India-Burma border also provided fallen soldiers to commemorate. On Sunday 8 July 1945, at 11am, Bose laid the foundation stone of the "Memorial to the Unknown Warrior of the *Azad Hind Fauj*", at Singapore's Padang. Situated near Connaught Drive, the memorial was finally unveiled in the evening of 23 August 1945. The words which had adorned the banner of the *Azad Hind* newspaper and documents were inscribed on the monument in Urdu. These were *Itteaq* (unity), *Itmad* (faith), and *Kurbani* (sacrifice). These words harked back to the first INA of Mohan Singh. They were the motto adopted at the first major meeting of the IIL held at Bangkok in June 1942.[37] Present at the unveiling and wreath laying were Major-General M.Z. Kiani and Major-General S.C. Alagappan of the INA, Dr M.K. Lukshumeyah as Vice-President of the IIL, and other leaders.[38]

Even before the INA memorial was completed, it became the focus of mourning for Singapore's Indian community. The cause of this premature use was news that Bose had died in a plane crash at Taipei, on 18 August. He had been trying to escape capture after the surrender of Japan on 15 August. Singapore and Malaya remained under Japanese control until 5 September when British forces returned. On 26 August 1945, meanwhile, wreaths were laid at the INA memorial in honour of Bose. A large group gathered at the memorial and speeches on Bose's life were made by Major-General M.Z. Kiani and Major-General S.C. Alagappan of the INA, and IIL members. The Japanese newspaper, the *Syonan Shimbun*, reported that "during the ceremony which lacked nothing in solemnity and dignity, many husky warriors — Sikhs, Punjabis, and others from the Central Provinces — soldiers who had taken part in the actual war operations were seen to shed tears as they saluted for the last time a giant portrait of Netaji which occupied a prominent position in front of the War Memorial".[39] Thus, at the end of the war, the INA and the Indian community had successfully created not only commemorative dates to remember Indian nationalism, but also a memorial at which to recall their war memory as Indians.

The Colonial State and Postwar Indian War Memory

British forces returned to Singapore on 5 September 1945. On the evening of 6 September 1945, the INA memorial was dynamited by what the British press described as "Loyal Indians": sappers of the 5th Division of the British Indian Army.[40] It was not clear whether British officers ordered this desecration, or if the Indian sappers acted of their own accord. There were Indians in the British Indian Army who despised the INA for having betrayed their martial tradition of loyalty to the crown, and as having chosen to fight other Indians of the British Indian Army.[41] Lord Mountbatten, Commander in Chief in Singapore in September 1945, later said that he had not even heard of the monument at the time.[42] On the other hand, in the normal course of events, Indian sappers would have at least sought British officers' approval.

Regardless of who ordered the monument destroyed, the result was far from gratifying to the newly returned British authorities. Pilgrimages to the INA memorial were renewed in early 1946, even though the monument now consisted of little more than a low base with rubble heaped on top.

The first time a postwar ceremony was organised to mark the establishment of the *Azad Hind* Government was on 21 February 1946. Indians recommenced their monthly commemoration of Bose's declaration of the *Azad Hind* Government. A crowd of 200 gathered around the base of the INA memorial. Indians laid wreaths and erected a makeshift wooden plinth that bore the words "Army War Memorial" in English, under a large photograph of Bose. The police dispersed the gathering, tore down the plinth, and took away the wreaths. Surprisingly, given the shooting of 15 February marchers only days before (pp. 116–8), there were no arrests. Compared to Chinese who attempted to commemorate 15 February, the Indians had got off lightly.[43]

Despite the suppression of the 21 February 1946 event, attempts were made to mark the 21st of subsequent months. Encouraged by a newly created *Jai Hind* Committee of Indian nationalists, some Indians would hoist the Indian flag in their houses, businesses and temples.[44] Worse still, from the British point of view, Indian independence leader Jawaharlal Nehru made an official visit to Singapore and Malaya, and laid wreaths at the INA memorial site on 19 March 1946. After paying tribute to the INA there, Nehru visited sick INA veterans at the Bidadari Camp, and attended a meeting of INA and Rani of Jhansi veterans at Jalan Besar. There he was presented with a photograph of Bose, and with an Indian national flag that had been used by the INA.[45] The reception committee had deliberately made the wreath laying ceremony a part of Nehru's official programme. On 19 March 1946, Nehru addressed 50,000 people of all races at Singapore's Jalan Besar Stadium.[46]

Nehru's visit reinvigorated local Indian nationalism. Nehru was virtually Prime Minister in waiting, given British promises to accelerate India's independence. In the eyes of the local population, the visit re-legitimised the INA as a political organisation pursuing nationalism, rather than as collaborators. Nehru's official tour, from 18 to 26 March 1946, included events at which he met INA veterans. Many of these turned out in their old uniforms, or at the least in their INA badges.[47] Nehru even arrived in Kuala Lumpur on *Azad Hind* Day, 21 March 1946, to be greeted by a guard of honour of Rani of Jhansi veterans led by Janaki Thevar, together with male INA veterans.[48] Given the status of Nehru and proximity of Indian independence, the British deemed it wise to not to interfere.

Many of the INA and Rani of Jhansi veterans were idealistic young men and women. The Rani of Jhansi leader of Nehru's guard of honour on 21 March, Janaki Thevar,[†] had been one of the first to join the regiment. She had signed up in August 1943, after seeing Bose address a mass rally at the Kuala Lumpur Padang. She had lied about her age, as recruits needed to be 18 years old, and Janaki was then just 17. Her reluctant father only signed permission forms when the regiment's leader, Lakshmi, turned up at the family house. Janaki later became second in command.[49]

Nehru was able to get tacit confirmation from the authorities that the veterans of the INA and its supporters would not be punished, as they had been first and foremost nationalists.[50] Previously, in February 1946, he had sent several Indian lawyers to assist Indians imprisoned by the British on charges of collaboration.[51] Nehru described the purpose of his visit as giving "psychological relief" to the Indian community.[52] Prior to his visit, the British could have suppressed INA activities; after it, they had to tolerate such public events. The local *Indian Daily Mail* wrote in March 1946 that "every Indian felt a cubit added to his stature as he welcomed Nehru".[53]

[†] Thevar is sometimes transcribed as Devar or Davar. After marriage and honours she was later known as Puan Sri Datin Janaki Athi Nahappan.

At a celebration of *Azad Hind* Day on 21 April 1946, J.A. Thivy, the former secretary of the *Azad Hind* Government, demonstrated the freedom of speech that ex-INA members now had. Addressing an assembly of the Selangor Indian Association in Kuala Lumpur, Thivy spoke stridently of the INA saying that, "The war has awakened Indians to a sense of unity and they are now conscious of their own rights".[54]

On 21 June, there was another conspicuous celebration of the establishment of the *Azad Hind* Government, this time at the destroyed INA memorial. Indians came from all parts of Singapore and Malaya to lay wreaths and observe a two-minute silence, followed by a lecture by Sri Brahmachar Kailasam, the joint secretary of the Indian Relief Committee, the Malayan organisation which had been set up by Nehru to help Malayan ex-INA personnel who were displaced.[55]

The colonial authorities also stood by when the Hind Volunteer Service was established. This verged on being a paramilitary organisation, consisting of young men and women who had trained to fight for the independence of India in the INA's youth section. The Hind Volunteer Service (HVS) was a department of the Malayan Indian Congress, a political party established on 5 August 1946, along the lines of the now defunct IIL. The organisational structure of the Malayan Indian Congress (MIC) copied that of the IIL, having a strong centre and a branch system. It was founded to carry on the Indian independence movement and anti-colonialist struggle, as well as to represent Indian interests more generally.[56] The MIC's principal creator was none other than J.A. Thivy, who had previously been secretary of the *Azad Hind* Government. He was assisted by many former members of the INA and IIL.[57]

The HVS became part of the youth section of the MIC. It staged rallies in uniform, advocated Indian independence, and ran camps. The committee in charge described how, during the war, HVS members had already received part-time "military training to become soldiers of the INA". Its governing body described how "their training has inculcated in them the knowledge of one people and one Nation despite the varying class caste and creed distinctions". Adult leaders feared that: "With the end of the war, these trained youths have to go back to a humdrum life which will bring disaffection and dissatisfaction, unless some programme is placed before them". The HVS was intended to appeal "to their sense of discipline and consciousness of unity and nationalism" and "prepare them for the role of that type of citizens who can be entrusted with the destiny of their homeland or country of adoption".[58]

This nationalist sentiment grew stronger whenever the 21st of the month occurred. On 21 July 1946, *Azad Hind* Day, schoolchildren laid wreaths at the remains of the INA memorial. J.A. Thivy told the crowd that "The fact that month by month you are observing *Azad Hind* Day proves that though the form may be destroyed yet the spirit lives. It is the spirit of the *Azad Hind* martyrs that is urging us all forward in our struggle for independence today".[59] In July 1946, the Indian community held wider "Netaji Week" celebrations, including meetings at which schoolchildren sang songs in praise for Bose. There were also processions to the INA memorial remains.[60]

These *Azad Hind* Government day celebrations grew in size as the Indian community mobilised itself in the MIC. On 21 August 1946, they included a procession from Race Course Road to the INA memorial at the Padang. Led by former INA and Rani of Jhansi veterans, participants shouted "*Azad Hind Ki Jai*", "*Nehru Ki Jai*", and "*Netaji Ki Jai*".[61] Speaking in Hindi, ex-INA officer Ananda Singh told the procession that "a replica of the INA and IIL organisations is now in the making — The Malayan Indian Congress ... the one service we could render to Netaji as a token of our respects and allegiance is to join forces in the Malayan Indian Congress" in order to revive the time when "Hindus, Sikhs, Muslims nay Indians of all creeds and colour — rallied around Netaji and worked for the common cause, that of making India free and to fight for the freedom of the India".[62]

On 21 September 1946, 500 paid homage at the INA war memorial remains. Speeches were given, led by Lieutenant Janaki Thevar of the Rani of Jhansi Regiment, still barely out of her teens.[63] The grandest celebration of *Azad Hind* Day came on the 21 October 1946, on the third anniversary of the declaration of the *Azad Hind* Government. There were mass meetings all over Malaya. Indians in Singapore held an evening rally at Farrer Park, opened by J.A. Thivy, as MIC Chairman. This followed an afternoon wreath laying ceremony at the INA memorial, organised by the HVS.[64] A 13-foot high wreath was placed at the site by the Seletar *Jai Hind* Committee.[65] At Farrer Park, Thivy's speech echoed the theme of unity of all Indians through continuing the nationalist rituals established in the war, and in reincarnations of wartime organisations in new forms, such as the MIC.[66]

Former INA and IIL men also had access to newspapers. Govindasamy Sarangapany was an ex-officer of the Publicity Department of the

IIL. In an editorial for the *Indian Daily Mail*, he wrote that for Indians, "there is no date more important than that the Twenty-First Day of October 1943", and "not merely the 21st day of October only, but the 21st day of every month ..."[67] He contrasted the new assertive attitude of Indians in Malaya with his memories of prewar humiliations:

> In the pre-war days, Indian labourers on the Estates had to undergo a lot of indignities. The haughtiness of the European managers and their Assistants based on their so-called colour-superiority, had gone to extreme lengths. Those labourers who refused to get off their bicycles in time on the august approach of the Manager or his Assistants, were invariably punished. They were fined or even paid off from the Estate altogether for 'insubordination or misconduct'.[68]

Sarangapany concluded that, "With their inferiority complex gone, they are to-day demanding complete equality with the whites. They are determined not to tolerate anybody's racial arrogance and haughtiness".[69] British officials in the Department of Labour noticed that Indian estate workers no longer accepted the derogatory term "coolie". In September 1946, Innes Miller, Deputy Chief Secretary of the Malayan Union, told all Resident Commissioners and Heads of Departments that, "no use of this word should be made; the terms 'labourer', 'workman' or 'workers' should be adequate to meet the needs of every case".[70]

It is hardly surprising that Indians wished to express gratitude towards Bose for their political awakening, and for their pride at participating in the movement for India's independence. The spell that Bose's personal charisma had cast lingered long after his death. As well as marking *Azad Hind* Day on every 21st, many Indians also celebrated Bose's birthday on 23 January 1947.[71] MIC Chairman Thivy further proposed that Indians build a permanent memorial to Bose, a building that would be the MIC headquarters. Thivy "felt that Netaji himself would have wanted it that a memorial dedicated to him should be alive with human activity".[72] A Netaji-MIC building might provide a "living" replacement for the destroyed INA memorial. At the first annual meeting of the MIC in Kuala Lumpur during June 1947, it was resolved that a "Netaji Memorial" be built at the cost of half a million dollars.[73] Donations of over $6,000 were made. The most symbolic came from Janaki Thevar, a former Rani of Jhansi commander, who gave her gold bangles. The main room of the building which would house the MIC in Kuala Lumpur was eventually called Netaji Hall.

By 1947, the regular processions on the 21st to the INA memorial were grating on the colonial administration.[74] In July 1947, J.A. Gagan, President of the War Prisoners (Singapore) Association, wrote to the Colonial Secretary to complain. Gagan made his members' disgust clear:

> It is with the strongest feelings that some few months after their release [liberation from the Japanese in September 1945] members of this Association observed a small mound of rubble next to the cenotaph surrounded by wreaths and a monthly memorial service to the traitors thereby commemorated being held. It is requested that this pile of rubble be removed and that these monthly processions be forthwith banned, since they are nothing less than an insult to the memory of our fellow prisoners who died and a gross affront to those who survived ill treatment at the hands of members of this Army [INA soldiers were regarded as brutal guards at the Changi prisoner of war camp].[75]

The ex-POWs also feared that the widely reported desire of the Indian community for a permanent memorial to Bose and the INA would result in the re-erection of the destroyed memorial.[76] Hugh P. Bryson, the Under Secretary, and Patrick McKerron, the Colonial Secretary, shared the repugnance of the President of the War Prisoners (Singapore) Association.

Bryson and McKerron did not, however, want to antagonise an incoming independent Indian government. McKerron thought, "it unlikely that this 'INA nuisance' will be perpetuated much longer now that India has got her independence". He was also confident there would be no attempt to rebuild the memorial, adding: "I understand that the Indian community propose to purchase a private home as a memorial".[77] Bryson replied to Gagan affirming "that no I.N.A. memorial on the ground near the cenotaph has been or will be authorised. Nor has any application to erect a memorial on Crown Land to Subhas Chandra Bose been received".[78]

The celebration of Indian nationalism, however, intensified as India's independence grew nearer. Even as Bryson was telling ex-POWs that the processions would die down, the Indian community was again celebrating "Netaji Week".[79] MIC Chairman Thivy once again used a Netaji Week speech to call for donations for a permanent memorial to Bose,[80] so as to "enshrine Netaji in the hearts of this generation and the generations yet to come".[81]

The local Indian community was emboldened by support from leaders in India. In the lead up to the 21 March 1947 *Azad Hind* Day celebrations, Gurubaksh Singh Dhillon, one of three who had been accused in the first of the INA trials in India of November 1945 to May 1946, had a message published in the *Tamil Murasu* and the *Indian Daily Mail*.[82] Dhillon advised that "Indians in Malaya should not forget Netaji's teachings" because "the flag of Indian freedom was unfurled in Malayan soils and Premier Attlee's statement promising transfer of power to Indian hands" was "the culmination of the struggle started in Malaya ... Let Indians in Malaya consider themselves as members of a free nation and behave as such".[83]

Indian independence and partition on 15 August 1947 demon-strated the power of the Indian community vis-à-vis the colonial state. Many Indians living in Malaya and Singapore could now be citizens of an independent India, if they chose. In Singapore, celebrations began at nine o'clock on the 15th, when the INA Free India flag was raised by Thivy at the Waterloo Street Padang, on the grounds at St Joseph's Institution. This was also where the first Rani of Jhansi camp had been established. In attendance was Colonial Secretary McKerron, who gave a speech welcoming Indian independence. At 11.30am, Thivy and former IIL and INA members proceeded to the INA memorial to lay wreaths. Sarangapany addressed thousands of Indian labourers at Short Street, declaring, "This greatest event fulfils the prophesy made here in Singapore four years ago by our great leader Subhas Chandra Bose. Netaji had confidently predicted that 'India shall be free — and before long'. To-day that prophesy had come true, and sooner than any one of us expected".[84]

Indian War Memory and Malayan Nation-Building

After 15 August 1947, commemoration of the *Azad Hind* Government changed. The colonial officials were correct in assuming visits to the INA memorial would decline. There was a growing feeling in the Indian community that yearly commemorations on 21 October should replace monthly events.[85] The nationalist agenda began to change too. Just before India's independence, MIC Chairman Thivy urged fellow Indians to see themselves as Malayans. In his July 1947 "Netaji Week" address, he urged cooperation with other ethnic groups to gain independence saying, "when we look at the larger picture of Malaya we find that

there should be a general give-and-take that forms the basis of any constitution and which in reality marks the birth of a new nation. For only
a nation in Malaya can look after the future of Malaya". Thivy used
commemoration of Bose and the INA to back this vision of the different communal groups joining together to strive for independence:

> The greatest assurance Netaji gave the cause of freedom in Malaya was
> when he categorically refused the Japanese request to use INA troops
> for the suppression of the Malayan People's Anti-Japanese Army.
>
> So we had an almost paradoxical situation where across the lines
> of the Japanese quest for spheres of influence two freedom forces
> never interfered [with] each other in the pursuance of separate policies
> towards the same goal of freedom.
>
> This was Netaji's glimpse of the future ... The groundwork of
> the plan that he had when he was with us becomes clearer day by
> day.[86]

Despite the increasing theme of Malayan nationalism, attachment
to India remained strong. When Gandhi's ashes were scattered across
the corners of India in March 1948, it was arranged to have some immersed at the Singapore seaside within metres of the INA memorial.[87]
Thivy received Gandhi's ashes in Singapore on 15 March 1948. They
were kept at Victoria Memorial Hall, where 5,000 people paid homage
in just one day.[88] The ashes then toured Malaya, before returning for
immersion on Saturday 27 March 1948, in the sea just off the Padang.[89]

Rituals that affirmed connections with India continued, but with
decreasing frequency. After August 1947, the wreath-laying ceremonies
at the INA memorial settled down to two a year: on Bose's birthday on
23 January; and *Azad Hind* Day on 21 October. These ceremonies were
arranged by the Singapore branch of the MIC: the Singapore Regional
Indian Congress. Thivy usually presided.[90] By the 1950s, however, these
visits appear to have ceased altogether. On 23 January 1950, Bose's
birthday celebrations did not include a wreath-laying, only a meeting
of the Singapore Regional Indian Congress at Race Course Lane.[91]

The 1950s saw an increasing focus on Malaya. Thivy touched upon
this when he was about to return to India in July 1950. At a farewell
meeting in Kuala Lumpur, he said that "Indians outside India ought
not to participate in and introduce party politics of India here. There
could only be one politics for us and that is to do everything in our
power to develop feelings of brotherhood and good-will with the other

communities in this country and to help in the attainment of Malaya's self-determination". He addressed a complaint that the MIC "was part and parcel of the Indian National Congress", saying that it "was not in any way affiliated to the Indian National Congress and the MIC was purely working out the destinies of Indians in Malaya ..."[92]

Ironically, it was Nehru and members of the Indian parliament who revived interest in Singapore's INA memorial in the mid-1950s. This happened in the lead up to centenary celebrations of India's First War of Independence: the 1857 Indian Mutiny-Rebellion. In March 1956, H.V. Kamath, a member of India's Lok Sabha (House of the People), asked the Indian government to add one new item to its centenary commemoration plans. These already included the erection of a monument at the Red Fort for INA soldiers, and bringing the last Mughal Emperor Bahadur Shah II's remains home from Burma. Kamath asked that the Indian government request the Singapore government to allow the reconstruction of the INA monument.[93]

The reaction to this idea revealed how the INA memorial could now stand not only for Indian nationalism, but for Malayan nationalism as well. Sarangapany, as editor of the *Indian Daily Mail*, wrote that "we have no doubt that it will gladden the hearts not only of Malayan Indians but of all people of Malaya who have been inspired by the sacrifice and heroism of the INA men and their leader Netaji Subhas Chandra Bose and whose own liberation and emancipation from colonialism has been hastened by INA martyrdom". Sarangapany believed "that India's freedom has set the spark to the freedom struggles in various Asian lands including Malaya ..." Re-erecting the monument "will also help Malaya preserve the memory of Netaji who gave to this country such inspiring slogans as *Nichhawar sub karo; bano sab fakir* (Sacrifice everything, you're your all)". Sarangapany concluded, "Malaya's true freedom is still not achieved because our leaders and people are reluctant to sacrifice their all ... the INA memorial if reconstructed will inspire and guide them along the right path".[94] Indian war memory had been harnessed to the need for Malayan nation-building, and for the Indian need to secure their place in that process.[95]

Nehru and the Indian government did not take up the idea of requesting that the INA memorial be re-erected.[96] Lord Mountbatten, meanwhile, continued to insist its destruction had been "the right thing for all".[97] That the site of the destroyed INA memorial was beginning to be represented more as part of Malayan nationalism was not surprising. The MIC of the 1950s was increasingly preoccupied with finding a role in the proposed Malayan nation.[98] In 1948, very few Indians had been able to qualify as citizens, but 1952 legislation meant that over 60 per cent of Indians in Malaya became eligible. This and other measures were intended by the British to help build a multiracial, conservative, political coalition, to which the British might safely transfer control of Malaya. By 1953, the Indian press agreed that "it is fully appreciated that the Indian workers are no longer to be considered as immigrants to this country and they are now an integral part of the Malayan community with a permanent interest here".[99] Indians in Malaya rightly sensed that the colonial administration, and the major political parties which represented the Malay and Chinese ethnic groups, were increasingly open to multiracial cooperation.

After negotiations, the Central Working Committee of the MIC announced on 17 October 1954 that it would formally join the Alliance. The Alliance had been formed in 1952 from the United Malays National Organisation (UMNO) and the Malayan Chinese Association (MCA). From February 1952 onwards, it had won the vast majority of seats in Malaya's municipal elections.[100] In April 1955, the MIC officially became part of this multiracial Alliance. With the help of its partners, it won two seats in the first national elections in Malaya, held in July 1955. These seats were secured despite the Indian population in these two seats being a minority. The MIC then secured two cabinet posts, the most important being the Labour Ministry.[101]

The MIC that went into the Alliance had IIL and INA veterans in senior positions. The two most significant early presidents of the MIC, John Thivy (1946–1947) and K.L Devaser (1951–1955), were former IIL members. Devaser had been one of the Malayan IIL members at the 15 June 1942 Bangkok meeting of Indian political organisations that made the INA the IIL's armed wing.[102] Three early prominent general-secretaries were either INA veterans or former members of the IIL, namely: Lieutenant Appu Raman (1947–1949); S. Govindaraj (1949–1952); and K. Gurupatham (1952–1955).[103]

Most former IIL members and INA veterans in the MIC responded positively to the August 1954 call of the MCA's Tan Cheng Lock "to join the Alliance to enable it to speed up the evolution of Malayan independence ..."[104] Tan had a history of embracing Indian war memory in order to encourage multiracial cooperation. He had appeared at the MIC's Netaji Week celebrations on 5 July 1947, in Malacca. There he had described Subhas Chandra Bose as "one of history's immortals", and added that "self-government for Malaya was assured but it could only be realised by the co-operative efforts of all races in the country".[105] J.A. Thivy, the MIC leader, stood on the platform alongside Tan. For his praise of Bose, Tan received strident Chinese criticism for supporting someone who had been an ally of Tojo and Hitler.[106] Yet Tan believed that the experiences of nationalism and common suffering of communities during the Occupation "should ... 'unite them strongly', rather than divide."[107]

There was division in the MIC over whether to accept Tan's 1954 offer to join the Alliance. Some ex-IIL members and INA veterans, such as Sarangapany (who had served on the MIC Central Working Committee in 1947 and 1950), were opposed. They believed, based on the Indian subcontinent's experience of communal politics, that the MIC should not support communally-based political parties. Sarangapany was one of a number of members who saw it not as a political party but as a community umbrella organisation for Indians.[108] They wanted genuinely nationalistic parties before independence was achieved and believed only intercommunal rivalry, not nationalism, would emerge if independence was achieved through an alliance of communal parties.[109]

The MIC leadership felt differently. Secretary-General and INA veteran, Gurupatham, in partnership with MIC President Devaser, headed the MIC Central Working Committee of five members in negotiating with the Alliance during 1954.[110] INA veteran, K.R. Das, head of the MIC's youth section for the state of Selangor, assisted his former INA comrade Gurupatham in the push to join the Alliance.[111]

The bitter divisions in the MIC over the Alliance led to some adept, if not questionable, political footwork. When the resolution to join the Alliance was taken at a meeting of the MIC's All-Malayan Indian Congress Committee on 17 October 1954, in Kuala Lumpur, the leadership only had representatives of 11 of the 54 branches present. Of the 55 delegates attending in the morning, only 45 were present in the afternoon when the vote was taken. Of these, 16 abstained and only 29 voted in favour. These 29 votes came from just three MIC branches, mainly those in Kuala Lumpur, while those against it came from eight. From the MIC branches, 230 delegates were entitled to attend as each delegate, according to the MIC constitution, was supposed to represent 100 members. There were 23,000 members of the MIC.[112] The only delegate from Singapore, John Jacob, an INA veteran, opposed the resolution, while the Penang Branch of the MIC was not even told of the decision.[113]

Many in the MIC never forgave Devaser for this high-handedness. Sarangapany began to run a campaign against Devaser saying the latter was a North Indian acting against the interests of the majority Tamil South Indian population. This spelt doom for Devesar's re-election chances in the yearly elections for the MIC presidency.[114] On 28 March 1955, Devesar said he would not stand. As a parting shot, he told MIC members that: "Any Indian who is sincere in outlook and loyal to this country must develop a truly Malayan outlook".[115] On 1 May 1955, a virtual unknown, V.T. Sambanthan, who was seen as representing South Indians, won the MIC presidency.[116] He was not a former member of the IIL or an INA veteran. Despite support in his election victory from Indians who wanted the MIC to leave the Alliance, Sambanthan kept it in, earning the reputation as one of the "founding fathers" of independence. Sambanthan, using his influence as a new broom to sweep away the Devaser clique and pay heed to South Indians, was able to do what Devaser could never have done. He stopped the proposed resolutions to take the MIC out of the Alliance.[117] Sambanthan even won over the influential Sarangapany round to the idea of staying.[118]

The exhortations to foster a united Malaya also came from India. In January 1955, Nehru exhorted Indians to look to the country they resided in for their future.[119] During his visit, Nehru was reputed to have described the MIC's entry into the Alliance as "a significant step forward in the Malayan people's quest for self-government".[120] The following year at Indian Independence Day celebrations in Malaya, R.K. Tandon, the Indian High Commissioner, told Indians "to give their full devotion loyalty and industry to Malaya".[121]

The English-language voice of the Indians of Malaya, the *Indian Daily Mail*, reversed its Indian subcontinent-centred views of the 1940s, and asked in 1956: "is it advisable for them to continue celebrating the Indian national or political anniversaries?" The newspaper's editor Sarangapany concluded that it was not: "As Malaya is rapidly marching to independence, we are extremely anxious that nothing should be done which will prolong their fence sitting".[122]

Among the Indian nationalist elite, then, the Occupation continued to be celebrated as a time of national awakening for Indian nationalism and — over time — for Malayan nationalism too. The emphasis gradually shifted from the former to the latter, but throughout they looked back on the Occupation as a time of empowerment. This vision of empowerment caused, if not necessitated, a degree of amnesia about the depth and breadth of Indian suffering in the war.

Forgetting the Suffering of Indian Labourers on the Burma-Thailand Railway

An *Indian Daily Mail* article of January 1951 told readers that:

> … Asians in Malaya have no unpleasant memories [of the war], which are nursed only by Europeans … Asians are actually proud of the Japanese and can never forget their quick and mighty victory over the Western powers in the early part of the war in the East. It proved for the first time in the modern era that Asians have enough resources to regain their freedom and to be masters of their own destiny.[123]

In 1952, the *Indian Daily Mail* further told readers that "Malaya should be eternally grateful" to Japan for allowing the local Asian population to take up administrative positions formerly held by British.[124] In 1956, Sarangapany wrote in the same paper that, "It was their [Japan's] contention that they had launched a war to liberate Asian peoples from the Western yoke" and that the Japanese "were true to their word, they restored sovereignty to the local peoples". He added that "unfortunately this democratic process was halted when the war started to turn against Japan", but "it cannot be denied that Japan inspired the peoples of Asia to agitate for freedom and self-government. In the case of India, the Independence Movement under Netaji Subhas Bose, did a lot to hasten the day of her freedom". Sarangapany mentioned Burma and Indonesia as also being inspired to achieve independence after the Japanese set up local regimes under Ba Maw and Sukarno.[125]

In the 1950s, the *Indian Daily Mail*, perhaps the most prominent Indian newspaper of the time, had virtually nothing to say about the tens of thousands of Indian labourers who had died on the Burma-Thailand Railway. Their plight attracted even less attention that it had in the 1940s. One reason why commemorating the suffering of Indians was crowded out was that most members of the INA did little to stop the Japanese from forcing Indian labourers to go to Thailand, or to protest against workers' exploitation. INA propaganda of the time portrayed the Japanese as Asian brothers liberating Indians. Indeed, some INA leaders encouraged Indian estate workers to go to Thailand to meet the Japanese demand for labour.

Only a few were conscientious enough to air the issue after the war. Ram Singh Rawal, a former INA member who was active in the IIL in Thailand, expressed shame in his memoirs. He recalled how some INA comrades assisted Japanese recruitment of uneducated Indian rubber estate workers, delivering them into "cruel devilish hands", with "hell-like" results. Those who survived, he wrote, were "disabled and invalids as a result of malnutrition, beating, jungle sickness, cancers …"[126]

Oral history work in the 1990s by historian Nakahara Michiko indicates that Bose travelled along the railway, and met Indian labourers, en route to the Burma front. Indian labourers talking to Nakahara thought it likely that Bose and his entourage knew the real conditions, regardless of any Japanese attempts to hide these. They expressed dislike for the INA and Bose, some suggesting that both cooperated in recruitment and management of Indian labour.[127] An Indian independence movement publicist, M. Sivaram, has described how shocked he was by a rail journey he made in 1943, from Bangkok to Singapore. He was struck by the unprecedented sight of crowds of

> semistarved Indian children in loincloths gathered at every railway station begging for alms … with their lifeless eyes, sunken cheeks, stomachs bulging out like balloons, and arms and legs that were merely dry sticks. They sang Japanese songs to rouse the sympathy of the Japanese officers in the military compartment and begged for alms in all languages …[128]

As Sivaram went south, he saw trains crowded with Tamils passing in the opposite direction, headed for the Burma-Thailand Railway:

> Each wagon carried a hundred of these people. Men, women, and children were huddled together in the sweltering heat of the goods wagons, while the younger fellows perched themselves precariously atop … The sight of these unfortunate people, crowding rice depots at the railway stations, was indeed heart-rending — a jostling bunch of humanity in hunger and distress, shouted at, cursed and slapped by everyone.[129]

A minimum of 182,000 Asian workers served on the railway overall, with a maximum of around 80,000 at any one time.[130] One Japanese source from the end of the war suggested that 73,532 labourers were transported from Malaya. Out of that number, it said that 24,490 (more than 33 per cent) died, 12,269 returned, and 4,662 deserted. That left nearly half, or 32,081 unaccounted for. This early estimate was incomplete, and the "unaccounted" reflected the sometimes hellish conditions on the railway line. Japanese sometimes abandoned the most diseased camps, and many workers, in the face of exploitation or rampant disease, fled.[131]

British figures from September 1945, based on more complete documentation, put the number of labourers from Malaya higher, at 78,204 and the number of known dead at 29,634, giving an absolute minimum death rate of 37 per cent.[132] The British also acknowledged, however, that many of those initially listed as missing had died. Bearing this in mind, another estimate suggests that 40,000, or 51 per cent, could have died.[133] If the Indian proportion of the above totals matched the 70 per cent recorded amongst those repatriated in 1945–1946, that would imply that a minimum of 17,000 Indians, and a maximum nearer to 28,000, perished on the railway.

Even if we accepted the minimum number, the toll was horrific. But statistics show us something more: that as an Asian labourer, your chances of survival depended on capricious chance, rather more than individual agency. Surveys on postwar rubber estates showed that the death rate for batches of labourers varied wildly, depending on which camp you went to, on whether cholera broke out, and sheer luck. Of 11 rubber estates surveyed in Perak, 545 Indian workers out of 1,146 returned. Yet one estate had an 88 per cent return rate, while for another it was 13 per cent. The Labour Department report also noticed that "one of the effects of the wholesale drafting of labour to Siam and the heavy death toll was the number of widows and orphans among the Indian estate workers". A survey done by the United Planting Association of Malaya recorded 5,730 known widows with 6,975 children, and another 2,366 orphaned.[134]

In late 1945, the British established displaced persons camps at Sungei Patani, Jitra in Kedah, and along the Isthmus of Kra in Thailand, to help facilitate the return of workers from the railway. A British official noted that of the 16,000 victims who passed through the Jitra camp alone, more than 10,000 were Indians. They had become "disease ridden skeletons … suffering from ulcers and other skin ailments", and had "hardly had clothes to their back let alone any worldly possessions". The same official was told by doctors at the Sungei Patani camp that one hundred per cent of the people being treated had some form of skin disease, with 38 per cent suffering from malaria, ulcers, and anaemia. He described how "in one camp alone there were 90 orphans; they had either been left behind when their parents were carried away to the north or else left alone in the world when their mothers and fathers died beside them in the Siamese labour camps and had been brought south by friendly countrymen".[135]

Colonial officials regarded repatriating these labourers as "a matter of considerable political importance, particularly as it would be most undesirable to antagonise an Indian Government already unsympathetic to British Colonial interests". They stressed that "it would be disastrous to British prestige" if the perception continued that Asian labourers were kept in the camps, "while a large number of Malayan exprisoners have been evacuated".[136]

When the victims of the Burma-Thailand Railway did return to the rubber plantations of Malaya, their communities struggled to support the permanently disabled, widows, and orphans. In March 1946, the All-Malayan Estates Asiatic Staff Association established a relief committee and emergency fund to assist widows and orphans.[137] Singapore's Ramakrishna Mission also took in Indian children orphaned by the railway, up to its limited capacity: its Bartley Road boys' home took 86; its Norris Road girls' home 48.[138] There were desperate calls from the Indian community, press, and Indian government, for the colonial authorities to provide more help.[139]

In August 1946, one of the returned Indian labourers wrote an open letter in the Indian press. In it, he asked for the proceeds of the sale of the Burma-Thailand Railway to the Thai government to be distributed to the many Indian widows, orphans, and other railway victims. He lamented that, "Wherever you go in the streets, in the markets, in the stalls, in shops ... you find only Indian labourers, men, women and children begging about with hungry looks and pathetic appearance being half or nearly naked. Some go about dressed in gunny bags".[140]

By August 1946, 26,000 of 30,000 Malayans formerly awaiting repatriation had been returned from Thailand. Of the 26,000 repatriated, 19,000 were Indians, 5,000 Chinese and 2,000 Malays, with small numbers of Eurasians and Gurkhas.[141] This meant that Indians comprised more than 70 per cent both of those awaiting repatriation in November 1945, and of those who had been returned by August 1946.

The colonial government agreed to provide assistance, so that widows, orphans and disabled would receive ten dollars per month.[142] Indian leaders complained that not many Indians would receive assistance, because of the large number of dependants of the deceased who were in India, and of Indian labourers who had gone back to India. The assistance was also limited to those with no other source of income. Many of the repatriated estate workers had returned to their rubber plantations to take up employment, and were thus excluded.[143]

The Burma-Thailand Railway also had a noticeable impact on the Indian population of Malaya and Singapore. When the 1947 census was conducted, it was discovered that the Indian population had declined from 621,847 in 1931 to 599,616 in 1947. Other ethnic groups had increased in number. It was calculated that in normal circumstances, the 1947 figure might have been as high as 800,000. The census superintendent, M.V. del Tufo, listed three reasons for this:

(a)   The deaths in Siam and elsewhere of Indians employed of serving as members of forced-labour battalions or of military or semi-military bodies;

(b)   The fall of the birth rate due to the absence of husbands;

(c)   The increase in the mortality rate (and in particular in the rate among infants and the aged) due to malnutrition resulting from the absence of the able-bodied bread-winners.[144]

All three reasons strongly related to the exodus of workers to the railway. Colonial figures also revealed that in 1947 compared with 1938, the number of Indian labourers in government employment had decreased from 33,070 to 23,074, on rubber estates from 214,323 to 158,357, and in mining from 7,061 to 4,724.[145]

If we accept the figures of Malaya's Census Superintendent on the numbers of Indians who died on the railway, and the total number affected by illness, loss of relatives and other indirect effects, the grand total exceeded the number who joined the INA.

By the 1950s, there was some criticism that Indian leaders were allowing the experience of the rubber estate workers to be forgotten, particularly when it came to claiming compensation. In November 1954, Mrs E. Somasundaram, Vice-President of the Selangor Progressive Party, felt that the MIC was neglecting the issue. She called for part of the funds from the sale of the Burma-Thailand Railway to Thailand to be distributed not to just the POWs who had worked on the line, but also the Indian labourers, so that they could start farms. Organisations of other communities, such as the Chinese, were collecting information to put forward affected members' claims. Somasundaram was scathing about the MIC response, alleging that "some months ago when this matter was actually brought up to the General Secretary of the MIC about the time when the Chinese stated collected statistics, the Congress was not interested and did not pursue the matter perhaps because it would be of benefit only to 'South Indians'".[146]

Indian political organisations mostly remained aloof from the demands of the victims of the Burma-Thailand Railway for compensation.

Only a very small number of the Asian victims were eligible for assistance in January 1948 when the first phase of the allocation of money from the sale of the line to the Thai government was begun. This was because many of the dependants and infirm labourers were managing to support themselves, however meagrely.[147] Since returning in 1946, they had had to find work, any kind of work. By 1954, the number of widows and orphans in Malaya and Singapore who were eligible for the ten dollars relief money had dwindled to 802 because of the stringent requirements imposed by the colonial government.[148]

The colonial authorities deliberately excluded active Asian labourers and their dependants from receiving any compensation as of right: as opposed to assistance to those with no other means of support. The Colonial Office preferred the funds to go to Malayan Railways for the loss of its rail lines when the Japanese tore up sections of the East Coast line, and sent these materials to Thailand.[149]

In 1955, under political pressure, the British government did agree to give money from the second phase of the sale of the Burma-Thailand Railway to ex-POWs who had worked on the railway. Once again, however, there was no compensation for Asian victims, only assistance for those in need. Put bluntly, it was easier for wealthier Western ex-POWs to qualify for compensation, than it was for poor Indian estate labourers to secure lower levels of assistance.

It was the leaders of the trade unions who took up the Asian labourers' claim. In December 1947, the Singapore Federation of Trade Unions petitioned British Governor-General Malcolm MacDonald. The petition requested that payment be made to families and injured workers according to the Workmen's Compensation Act of Malaya.[150] The colonial state remained deaf to such pleas. For the Indian workers sent to the railway, there was to be no reworking of their experience into heroism, only a sense of victimhood that the leaders of their own community preferred to push to the margins. Poor Indian rubber estate workers did not have the political clout of ex-POWs, who were well represented in the colonial administration.

As a response to only the ex-POWs receiving compensation, a new organisation was formed in 1958: the "All Malaya Association of Forced Labourers".[‡] Indian political organisations were conspicuously absent from the setting up of this organisation.

[‡] The full title was the "All Malaya Association of Forced Labourers and Families of Forced Labourers of the Siam-Thailand Death Railway".

Renewed impetus for compensation came in 1961. John Boyd-Carpenter, the British Minister of Pensions, declared in the House of Commons in April 1961 that the total amount of benefits for the Far Eastern POWs from the sale of Japanese assets and the railway was £4,816,473.[151] Asian labourers believed that if the POWs received compensation, so should they.[152] In August 1961, the group submitted a letter to Tunku Abdul Rahman, Prime Minister of Malaya, the British High Commissioner to Malaya, and the Japanese Ambassador. Copies, which detailed treatment of Asian labourers, were also sent to the American, Burmese, Thai, and Indonesian embassies, the Malaysian Ministries of Justice and Labour, and all Sultans and Mentri Besar.

This mass distribution came out of frustration, after similar letters to the Japanese Embassy had been ignored the year before. The association stated that it "cannot see why Japan cannot pay compensation to the Malayans, as compensation was paid to the Allied prisoners of war who were forced to labour beside them".[153] The Siam-Burma Death Railway Association demanded $2,000 for the dependants of each person who died on the railways, and $1,500 for those who survived. The letters requested that the governments of Malaya, Britain, and Japan negotiate over the issue.

The problem was that the Association failed to mobilise enough of the estimated 23,000 people whom it had identified as survivors of the railway and their dependants. Membership of the association generally remained just under 2,000 until the early 1970s, when it started to decline as it became clear there would be no settlement from Japan. The organisation was wound up in 1973, with membership at just 841.[154] As a result, there never would be any compensation payments for Indians who worked on the railway. Nor is there (as of early 2012) any significant memorial or commemorative site for the Indian labourers who died, not even any equivalent to the neatly tended graves, such as those the Commonwealth War Graves Commission maintains around the world for POWs.

Right into the 21st century, for elite and urban Indians, the dominant memories remained those of INA-inspired national awakening. The memories of the railway held by the rubber estate workers remained largely forgotten, because of the power of the Indian nationalist elite drawn from the INA, and subsequently running the MIC, to have its memories held up as the dominant ones for Indians. While public remembering of the Occupation centred on the national awakening brought about by the INA, however, researchers looking at "history from below" through oral history interviews with labourers have recorded the prevalence among them of traumatic memories. Ravindra K. Jain, a sociologist doing fieldwork on Indian estate workers in Negeri Sembilan in the 1960s, noticed how their memories remained very strong, despite being largely excluded from public remembrance.

Memories of the railway experience also divided the educated Indian elite who helped run the plantations, called the *kirani*, from the labourers. Labourers recalled how *kirani*, many of whom who were enamoured of the INA, assisted the Japanese in recruiting them. Some had little choice but to help the Japanese, as Japanese officials dealt violently with any opposition. Nevertheless, Jain concluded that "it may legitimately be claimed that the large number of Tamils among the labourers being taken to Siam was due in no small measure to the help which the Japanese instantly received from the *kirani* ..." Many rubber plantation labourers believed that Indian managerial staff had "wholeheartedly co-operated in rounding up able bodied men for despatch to Siam".[155] However little choice some of these *kirani* really had, labourers' memories awarded them a share of the blame.

Most of the estate labourers that Jain talked to who joined the INA also tended to do so not out of political idealism, but for more mundane reasons. Many joined because the alternative was the railway. Thus, the war memories of labourers, the *kirani*, and the Indian political elite, continued to be marked by significant differences and tensions.

Conclusion

The Indian community's memory of war illustrates the idea of Raphael Samuel and Paul Thompson that "what is forgotten is often as important as what is remembered" in sustaining collective memories of the past.[156] The memories of the poor Indian rubber estate workers on the Burma-Thailand Railway and the ill-treated Indian POWs who refused the join the INA are not images that Indian community leaders believed would unite the community. Images of INA veterans fired with nationalism to liberate India could be channelled by political leaders into support first for Indian nationalism, and then for Malayan nationalism. By contrast, wretched images of forced labourers would only disturb and unsettle the community, as well as foster divisions. The experience of the Indian community thus also highlights Halbwachs' notion of collective memory being fashioned in groups, giving rise to a dominant memory which can crowd out alternatives.

The result is that, while writers such as Romen Bose still trumpet the INA, and a large plaque was erected at the site of the INA memorial in 1995, for Indians, there remains unfinished memory work. This concerns the "everyday victims" and everyday survivors, nationalists who nevertheless opposed the INA, railway survivors, and the thousands of Indian labourers who died in Thailand.[157]

The latter, in particular, have suffered relative neglect. Dead men cannot write, and cannot record oral history interviews. We can only glimpse their agonies through the eyes of appalled onlookers, such as Singapore Chinese medical student Tan Choon Keng. Tan was a medical orderly on the railway when he was told to burn some huts whose inhabitants had cholera.[158] "But, Sir," he replied to his Japanese superior, "these people are still alive". Given no choice, Tan and his team poured oil on the attap hut, and the beds but not the bodies, of 250 mainly Tamil labourers who lay dying:

> … We poured crude oil all over the roof, the wooden walls and the sleeping planks. We did the job very quickly. I dared not look into their eyes. I only heard some whispering 'tolong, tolong' [help] … God forgive me … All Asian labourers, with their wives and children. They could not walk, all their nails blackened. As the fire engulfed the hut I could not hear them crying out because of the loud crackling noise of the burning wood. The heat was very intense and we ran and ran. After this incident I used to say to myself. Is there a God on earth?[159]

In conclusion, Indian war memory parallels Chinese war memory, which made the transition from being focused on China to being used in the 1950s to encourage the Chinese to support the emerging idea of a Malayan nation. In contrast, however, remembering Indian war suffering was pushed into the background, as it brought to the surface memories that might divide the Indian community, whereas Chinese suffering was seen as a unifying force.

CHAPTER 7

Malay Warriors and *Pemuda*

Kimigayo (Japanese)	*Kimigayo* (English)
Kimigayo wa	May your reign
Chiyo ni yachiyo ni	Continue for a thousand, nay eight thousand generations,
Sazare-ishi no	Until the pebbles
Iwao to narite	Grow into boulders
Koke no musu made	Lush with moss

"STUDENT RESEARCHERS ... TOOK NOTE OF THE EXCITEMENT shown by respondents when they were asked to comment on ... school life under the "rule of the samurai" ... some of them would burst into impromptu humming of a few bars of Japanese songs".[1] While adult Malays had to deal with shortages of rice, salt, sugar and clothing, unwelcome exhortations to "grow more food" for sale, or unpaid service in the local *Jukeidan* (law and order force), many of their children took readily to Japanese education.[2] At 8 o'clock every morning, Japanese time, teachers and students would assemble on the school field. Facing Tokyo, they sang the Japanese anthem *Kimigayo*. *Kimigayo* is all solemnity and emotion, part-hymn, part ode to the Emperor, proceeding with slow, wave-like rises and falls. The song was capped off with *saikere*, a deep, reverent bow. That done, the school day could begin.

At language, technical and other Japanese specialist schools — including those giving short courses to administrators — there was also military drill. Students found gardening added to the curriculum, both for the good of the soul and because of shortages — and heavy emphasis on Japanese *seishin* (spirit). Students might also learn sumo-wrestling or other Japanese games, or (for Malays) *silat*. The aim was not just to impart useful knowledge, but to mould mind and body: to obey, and for ongoing struggle with Western forces. A struggle-based ethos prevailed, in which willpower was expected to overcome obstacles, and the individual was taught to subsume their needs and identity in those of the collective.[3]

This education was underpinned by a vision of "Asia for the Asians", in which Japan perched atop a hierarchy of Asian peoples. This was paternalist, with Malay sultans being left in place in their peninsular states, and the advancement of local administrators to places vacated by Europeans.

Chapter 2 (pp. 39–40) looked at these events through the eyes of Mohd Anis bin Tairan, who in 1942 was a 10-year-old living in an attap-roofed house at Siglap, on Singapore's east coast. He remembers 1942 as a time of British defeat and Chinese tragedy in the *sook ching*, but also as a time of opportunity for Malays.

Anis had been born amidst increasing Malay nationalism. In the 1920–1930s, many Malays felt threatened by Chinese population growth and economic success. British desires to increase Chinese rights further fuelled Malay fears that they might lose their predominance in the peninsula. These coincided with the growth of new types of Malay. More Malays were being formally taught as teachers — at Sultan Idris Training College at Tanjong Malim (founded 1922) — and the burgeoning Malay press meant more journalists.[4] Malay Associations sprung up which, in 1939 and 1940, held the first pan-Malayan meetings of Malay Associations. The sultans also became more assertive of their rights, and that their British Residents were just advisers — as the treaties stated — not colonial overlords. Some exerted pressure for a Malay military force, which helped to persuade the British to form the Malay Regiment in 1933–1934. In addition, young teachers and journalists formed more radical associations, including the *Kesatuan Melayu Muda* (KMM, Union of Malay Youth). The latter had branches all over Malaya within a year of foundation in 1938.

The KMM included recent immigrants from the Netherlands Indies, who encouraged an anti-colonial tone. As such, a few of the KMM were contacted by, and helped, the Japanese in 1941. After British defeat, others, such as the KMM-affiliated village head in Anis' village, were given responsibilities.

For a few months after British defeat, the Japanese gave the KMM free reign to extol Malay nationalism and a *Melayu Raya* (Greater Malaya or Indonesia). Soon, however, they decided it was better to keep such fervent men on a short leash. They banned KMM in June 1942, and integrated many of its leaders, first into Japanese departments then, from late 1943, into Japanese-controlled volunteer forces.

This Japanese recruitment of Malays exacerbated a paradox of war memory. On the one hand, Malay nationalism would recall with pride the Malays who fought against the Japanese. The Malay Regiment would be held up as heroes. Service in British Empire forces, in the Federated Malay States Volunteer Force, and with the relatively small number of Malay anti-Japanese guerrillas linked to Force 136, would all be written into official accounts. Decades later, Anis could recall with pride how one of his elder brothers, Said, served in Royal Engineer 34 Company and the Royal Artillery. This service paved the way for Said's success in later life.

Yet many Malays served in Japanese-raised and commanded forces, especially from December 1943. Malays joined the *Giyugun* (volunteer army), *Giyutai* (volunteer militia), and *Heiho* (support corps attached to the Japanese military). The *Giyugun* also went by the same name that the Japanese-raised militia in Indonesia used: PETA (*Pembela Tanah Ayer*, Defenders of the Fatherland). Close to the end of the war, its training was stepped up, and Malays were belatedly allowed to discuss the possibility of independence.

While one of Anis' elder brothers joined the British forces, another joined the naval branch of the *Giyugun*. Anis expressed pride in the service of both brothers. Malays such as Anis viewed such diverse service as different ways in which individuals achieved common aims: helping their families, their *kampongs*, and the wider community of *Melayu* (Malays). Hence, he saw the war as boosting Malay military opportunities, regardless of which side offered these.

First and foremost, however, he remembered how the Japanese boosted the ongoing growth of Malay nationalism. He recalled his *kampong* having at least two prewar KMM members, one the village head's son. These cooperated with the Japanese on behalf of their communities. He also recalls hearing,

> the voice of Sukarno, the first president of Indonesia [on the radio] … Also Singapore and Sumatra were under one government during the Japanese time. We would get books and other propaganda and study it.

The Japanese called on Anis and his schoolmates to regard Japan as an "elder brother" who would bring more freedom. He responded with enthusiasm. At his *Heiho* technical training school at Singapore's

Balestier Road, he learnt to make and repair trucks, but much more than that:

> they trained us to be like a Japanese ... We also had the *botak* [shaven] head ... I studied how to be a gentleman. They taught me Japanese martial arts, judo, kendo, jujitsu. The Japanese were tough. Once we learn, we must know. Prepare. Prepare. Prepare ...[5]

He particularly loved *kendo*, a martial art using a wooden sword.[6] This variety of experiences, notably of serving both sides, created tensions for postwar memory. How could Malays deal with the fact that Malays served in the KMM and Japanese organisations on the one side, and yet in the Malay Regiment on the other?

Hang Tuah and the Malay Martial Tradition

One main framework for recalling the war, shared by those who served against and with the Japanese, would come to be that of Malay martial tradition. The war came to be seen as having boosted the ongoing recovery of this long-suppressed tradition. A martial tradition can be defined as a military culture or ethos, evolved over time. It can entail a warriors' code of honour. This often implies a wider conception of how soldiers fit into their culture and society.

Anis was inspired by this tradition. At *Heiho* School,

> as well as the Japanese martial arts, we also learnt the Malay martial art of *silat* in the style of our warrior hero, Hang Tuah. At last we had a chance to be warriors that we dreamed of as young men ... Many of us would not have been given that chance if not for the fall of the whiteman at Singapore. Only a few Malays were trained by the British in the military, just one of my brothers. But it was common with Japanese schooling. I learnt to be a truck mechanic and a warrior, my other brother too in the Japanese navy. We imagined ourselves as if we were Hang Tuah's men.[7]

Postwar writers insist that the "Malay martial" tradition, dating to feudal times, was strengthened by experiences in the war, and later in the Malayan Emergency of 1948–1960. Dol Ramli, a senior bureaucrat in the Malayan Ministry of Information (and Director of Broadcasting, 1961–1975), places the Malay Regiment in this tradition. His history of the Malay Regiment states that, "in pre-European days, the Malay could hold his own against anyone, man to man", but "against the better-equipped, better-armed European soldier ... the Malay, like other Asians of the day, found himself at a disadvantage". Ramli addressed colonial criticism of the Malays not being a "martial race". When the Regiment was founded in 1933–1934, it was as an "experimental company", as the British harboured doubts that the Malay had "martial" qualities in the modern sense, as opposed to cobwebbed memories of piracy and feudal warfare.[8]

Ramli countered that this "feudal" tradition still resonated. Traditionally, "the Sultan gave orders through the Bendahara (Chief Minister) to the various Malay rajah and chiefs to rally and lead their men — feudal retainers — who assembled their own arms and equipment". Ramli continued that "what training there was in the military arts was purely an individual concern". Warriors would be privately trained in *silat*, or martial arts, by private teachers or masters.[9]

The Malay martial tradition resonated through folklore, which continued to extol Hang Tuah as the archetypal Malay hero. Hang Tuah's story originated in the *Hikayat Hang Tuah* (*Story of Hang Tuah*). In this, he is a warrior of the 15th-century Sultanate of Malacca, just before it fell to the Portuguese in 1511.[10] His exploits as Laksamana ("admiral" or military leader), may be a compilation of stories of several warriors. Hang Tuah is, therefore, a distillation of the military hero as the Malacca court wished it to be, embodying loyalty, discipline, and honour. This is exemplified by Hang Tuah's fight to the death with his closest friend, Hang Jebat.

In the story, Hang Tuah is wrongly accused, and the Sultan of Malacca sentences him to execution without investigation or trial. Hang Jebat consequently rebels against the sultan, in defence of his friend. The twist in the story is that Hang Tuah does not thank Jebat. He is so loyal that he is prepared to fight Hang Jebat to the death. He holds fast to the discipline and loyalty implicit in the service owed to his sovereign. According to the *Hikayat Hang Tuah*, the Bendahara (chief minister) had not executed Hang Tuah as instructed. When the sultan learned this, he pardoned Hang Tuah, as the only warrior capable of defeating Hang Jebat. In their climactic struggle, Hang Tuah and Hang Jebat duel with kris, swords the size of long knives. Hang Tuah runs Hang Jebat through, leaving him to die a slow and agonising death.[11]

The *Hikayat Hang Tuah* was handed down from generation to generation, in rural areas through oral storytellers.[12] Thus, most Malays would have been familiar with Hang Tuah's most famous utterance: "*Takkan Melayu hilang di dunia* (the Malays will never disappear off the face of the earth)".[13] It was echoed by another saying, that *Biar mati anak: jangan mati adat*: "Better your children die than your traditions". Hang Tuah's phrase became associated with the need for unity in the face of challenges to Malay identity and primacy.[14] As war approached, the image of Hang Tuah was adopted by Malays who fought alongside, and against, the British Empire.

A Legion of Hang Tuahs: The Malay Regiment

The most romanticised Malay unit that fought in 1941–1942 was the Malay Regiment. It was mainly from this that there emerged a strong war memory of the "Malay warrior" who expressed by proxy the character desired for Malay manhood as a whole. An iconography of the Regiment grew up, in which it was seen as one of the earliest manifestations of Malay nationalism.[15] In 1941, Malays protested when the Department of Information and Publicity attributed its creation to colonial officials.[16] In Malay memory, the "fathers" of the Regiment were Alang Iskander Shah (Sultan of Perak); Tuanku Muhammad ibni Shah Yamtuan Antah (Yang di-Pertuan of Negeri Sembilan); Raja Sir Chulan (Raja di Hilir Perak); and Abdullah bin Dahan (the Undang Lauk Rembau). When M.C. ff Sheppard wrote a regimental history in 1947, he described "their dream" as coming to fruition on 1 March 1933 when the British set up an experimental company of 25 men at Port Dickson.[17]

The title Malay Regiment was used from 1 January 1935, and it was understood to be only for the defence of the Malay States, not service overseas. The first Malay officers were commissioned in November 1936. As British fears of Japan increased, so did the Regiment. It was one battalion of four rifle companies by October 1938, with a Vickers machine-gun support company. On 1 December 1941, the 2nd Battalion was formed, bringing the regiment's strength to about 1,400.

Captain Noor Mohamed Hashim, a Malay member of the Legislative Council, and a former officer in the Malay Company of the Singapore Volunteer Corps, hoped that this would lead to the Malay Regiment being deployed in combat, so bringing back to the fore the Malay military tradition.[18] This sentiment was shared by *Warta Malaya*, a Malay newspaper under KMM influence which styled itself as *penyambung lidah bangsa Melayu* (defender of the Malay race)[19]

The Malay Regiment incorporated distinctly Malay martial traditions as well as British regimental practice. Its regimental motto came

Plate 7.1 Lieutenant Adnan Saidi

Plate 7.2 Malay Regiment in traditional dress uniform, around 1941

straight from descriptions of Hang Tuah as *Taat dan Setia* — "loyal and true". Written on the badge of soldiers was both *Taat dan Setia*, and *Rejimen Askar Melayu* (Malay Regiment), rendered in the religious script of the Malay language: Jawi. The badge also featured two Malay kris, and two Malayan tigers supporting "an oriental" crown.[20] The colours of the regiment were green, red, and yellow. Green was the Malay colour for Islam. There was a regimental mosque, with strict observance of prayers, and a month's leave and train ticket home at Ramadan.[21] Red was the colour used to denote bravery and courage, as well as the heroism and loyalty of Hang Tuah.[22] It could also denote the British connection. Yellow represented the connection to royalty, in the form of the Malay sultans, members of whom made regular visits to the Regiment.[23]

The soldiers did not swear allegiance to the British monarch, but only to the colonial government of the Malay States. Officials recognised that the soldiers would "regard their first loyalty to their sultans".[24] In the prewar years, many Malays had looked first to their sultan and his state for their identity, rather than to any wider Malay community or *bangsa Melayu*.[25] This *kerajaan* (royal power of the sultan)-based Malay identity was reflected in occasional proposals to have future battalions of the Regiment named after individual Malay States, and recruited on a state basis.[26]

Such proposals were rebuffed, however. British District Officer M.C. ff. Sheppard insisted that the Regiment promoted pan-Malayan unity, writing in 1939 that "… the Regiment is proving a powerful and indeed the only genuine unifying influence among the Malay people … no quality of oratory or literary heroics could have proved half as convincing … The silent barrier between men of different states disappears in the Regiment".[27] The regimental information booklet for 1941 "strongly stressed in the regiment that all ranks belong to the Malay race and represent their country as a whole …"[28] 80 per cent were recruited in the four Federated Malay States (FMS) of Perak, Selangor, Negeri Sembilan and Pahang, 20 per cent from the Unfederated Malay States (UMS) and Straits Settlements.[29] The Regiment took its place amongst other institutions which from the 1920s fostered a pan-Malayan sensibility, including the Malay College Kuala Kangsar (the "Eton of the East"), and the Sultan Idris Training College at Tanjong Malim.

The Malayan Campaign (1941–1942) provided the Regiment's "first blood".[30] On the Malayan Peninsula, individual companies, together with British forces, engaged the Japanese in a number of

Battle of Pasir Panjang near Singapore Town

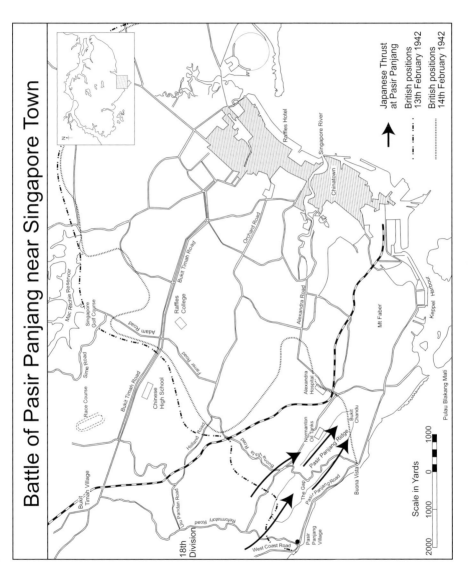

Map 7.1   Battle of Pasir Panjang, 13–14 February 1942

Japanese Thrust at Pasir Panjang

British positions 13th February 1942

British positions 14th February 1942

Scale in Yards

2000   1000   0   1000

Mac Ritchie Reservoir

Singapore Golf Course

Race Course

Bukit Timah Village

Bukit Timah Road

Sime Road

Adam Road

Chinese High School

Farrer Road

Holland Road

Ulu Pandan Road

Reformatory Road

West Coast Road

18th Division

Pasir Panjang Village

The Gap

Normanton Oil Tanks

Buona Vista Road

Buona Vista

Pasir Panjang Road

Pasir Panjang Ridge

Bukit Chandu

Alexandra Hospital

Alexandra Road

Pulau Blakang Mati

Mt Faber

Keppel Harbour

Chinatown

Singapore River

Raffles Hotel

Orchard Road

Bukit Timah Road

Raffles College

N

encounters. The climax came with the Malay Regiment's role in the Battle for Singapore. During the last few days, the Regiment's two battalions were united. Together, on 13–14 February on the west coast at Pasir Panjang, they bore the brunt of the Japanese 18th Division's final advance towards Singapore Town. Malay Regiment soldiers held their positions until — in some cases — killed or overrun. The classic story from this encounter would become that of Lieutenant Adnan, who carried on firing his Lewis gun until shot down, hung upside down from a tree, and bayoneted while reportedly still alive.[31]

In the postwar years, the Regiment's men would be presented as displaying loyalty, bravery and unity at the Battle for Pasir Panjang: as distinctive martial qualities that boys in the emerging nation-state should emulate.[32] The soldiers were also presented as fighting for the "Malay race". The Battle of Pasir Panjang therefore gave the Malay Regiment a key commemorative date. 14 February became "Malay Regiment Heroic Day".[33] On this anniversary, its commanders would sometimes quote the account which the General Officer Commanding during the Malayan Campaign, Lieutenant-General Percival, wrote in 1949:

> The attack was made by the Japanese 18th Division and was preceded by a two hour artillery, air and mortar bombardment ... On this (13 February) and the following day the Regiment fully justified the confidence which had been placed in it and showed what *esprit de corps* and discipline can achieve.
>
> Garrisons of posts held their ground and many of them were wiped out almost to a man. It was only when it was weakened by heavy losses that the regiment was forced to give ground.[34]

In a foreword to the Malay Regiment's official history, written in July 1946, Percival also recounted that "by their stubborn defence of the Pasir Panjang Ridge at the height of the Battle of Singapore, they set an example of steadfastness and endurance under the most difficult conditions which will become a great tradition in the Regiment and an inspiration for future generations".[35] This eulogy would be regularly quoted.[36]

Malays As Colonial Volunteers and Anti-Japanese Guerrillas

Malay martial tradition was also invoked in other Malay forces that fought in 1941–1942. These included the Malay infantry companies in the part-time Straits Settlements Volunteer Forces and FMS

Volunteer Force, and Malays in the Malayan Royal Naval Volunteer Reserve, together totalling a few thousand.[37] For the Straits Settlements Volunteers alone, there were four Malay companies from Singapore, Malacca and Penang, totalling 24 officers and 544 other ranks. Half of the 1,450 Malay naval ratings, meanwhile, were killed or missing, many dying in the sinking of the *HMS Panglima* and *HMS Laburnum*.[38]

One group of Malay volunteer officers who surrendered to the Japanese refused to renounce their oaths of loyalty. They were executed on 28 February 1942. The story of one these officers, Captain Raja Aman Shah of the 3rd Battalion, FMS Volunteer Force (Negeri Sembilan), would become legendary. This was largely due to his loyalty and self-sacrifice, but also because he had prominent brothers-in-law. These were the first Prime Minister of Malaya, Tunku Abdul Rahman; and Raja Lope, the first Malay Chief of Staff of the Malaysian Armed Forces.[39] *

Captain Raja Aman Shah was executed, with up to 90 other volunteers (mostly Malays), on 28 February 1942. The story of his captivity was written by Mervyn C. ff. Sheppard. Sheppard was an Anglo-Irishman, and one of the last of the British scholar-administrators. He joined the MCS in 1928, rising to District Officer and immersing himself in Malay culture. Captured as a Company Commander in the FMS Volunteers in 1942, he spent the rest of the war as a POW. From 1939 onwards, he devoted himself to writing about Malay culture, becoming Malaya's first Keeper of the Archives from 1958, and the first Director of the National Museum of Malaya. Eventually he converted to Islam, completed the haj, and finished his life as Tan Sri Datuk Haji Mubin Sheppard. Above all this, he became the leader of the veterans' Ex-Services Association. In this role, he researched stories eugolising Captain Raja Aman Shah as "a paragon of loyalty", and published them in the popular press in the 1960s, with the aim of increasing public support for veterans.[40]

Raja Aman Shah, meanwhile, was a member of the Perak royal family, who had also married the daughter of the Sultan of Kedah, Tunku Baharom. This made him the brother-in-law to Tunku Abdul Rahman. Raja Aman Shah was one of a small number of Malays who had been promoted from the Malay Administrative Service to the elite Malayan Civil Service (MCS). When the FMS Volunteer Service

---

* Captain Raja Aman Shah had married Tunku Abdul Rahman's sister Tunku Baharom. He was also the brother of Raja Nor Zahan, who was the wife of Raja Lope.

mobilised on 1 December 1941, he could, as the District Officer of Port Dickson, have remained in his job. Instead he took up arms. On 10 January 1942, when FMS Volunteers were given the option of returning home, he again chose to fight.[41] His company fought in Johor and Changi. When defending the McPherson area on the morning of 15 February 1942, his British company commander Major Cockman was killed. Captain Raja Aman Shah then took part in fierce hand to hand fighting, taking a rifle from a badly wounded lance corporal under him and firing until his trench was overrun.

He was captured, and quickly released. Later, however, KMM members told Malay volunteers that the Japanese wanted them to report at Farrer Park. Alerted to the danger by some KMM members, such as Mustapha Hussain, only 400 of 1,000 Malay soldiers turned up. Raja Aman Shah was one of nine Malay officers from the volunteers and Malay Regiment who reported.[42]

KMM members made frequent visits to the detained men. During one of these, Mustapha Hussain urged the Volunteer and Malay Regiment men to renounce their oaths and play down allegiance to Britain. Many refused. Mustapha Hussain, in a quiet part of the room, tried to convince Raja Aman Shah in particular to leave with him, as he had "fought valiantly to the last weapon", while others could be rescued later.[43] Raja Aman Shah refused to leave without his men. After Mustapha Hussain left, he told them, "That was my brother. He brought me a permit for me to go back to Perak with him. I wanted all to be freed with me, but that was not allowed: so I decided to stay and see this through with you. If god wills, we shall all be free: if not then let us die together".[44]

Around 90 of these prisoners were executed on Bedok Hill, in Singapore. Some of these were not Malay. There were two Chinese Volunteer Force officers, and 25 members of the Chinese company of the Malacca Volunteer Corps (Straits Settlement Volunteer Force). Chan Cheng Yean, one of the Chinese officers, was not killed in the hail of bullets at the massacre site, and escaped after the Japanese left. He was one of Sheppard's informants, along with Malay soldier Haji Ibrahim bin Hassan, who was released for giving the "right answers". From these witnesses, Sheppard fingered the KMM's Ibrahim Yaacob as instrumental in the deaths of the Malays, supposedly telling the Japanese "that they were pro-British and anti-Japanese, and would exercise a dangerous influence if they were freed".[45] Mustapha Hussain also implies that Ibrahim Yaacob played a role in the decision to execute Captain Raja

Aman Shah.[46] Mustapha Hussain was the founding Vice-President of KMM. His memoirs show a circumspect attitude to Japan, and emphasise how he saved large numbers of Malays from Japanese retribution in early 1942. Despite this, he lost two brothers to the MPAJA.[47]

Decades afterwards, Tunku Abdul Rahman would describe frantically driving from Kedah to Singapore twice in February 1942, determined to save his brother-in-law, Raja Aman Shah. He remembered with bitterness the indifference of KMM leaders Ibrahim Yaacob and Ishak Haji Ahmad Muhammad, and their scornful question: "Why did your brother-in-law fight for the British?"[48] His anger intensified when he learnt the full story from the Chinese survivor and other Malays.[49] So a chasm opened up between Malays who had fought with the British or carried on their jobs quietly during the Occupation, and those members of the KMM who cooperated wholeheartedly with the Japanese. This would make it very difficult, when Tunku Abdul Rahman later became Prime Minister, to fully integrate KMM and Malays who had served in Japanese-sponsored volunteer armies into national memories. During the postwar period, the emphasis would instead come to fall on Malay soldiery that was anti-Japanese, and on those who loyalty remained with the British.

Other Malay troops who refused to cross sides included the regulars of the Johor Military Forces, which by 1942 had expanded to about a thousand men.[50] This helped to hold the Japanese back from the Tanjong Labah airfield, near Batu Pahat, on 23 January 1942. In 1946, the Johor Military Forces were reduced to guard duty at the sultan's palace, with just 128 men,[51] and some joined the Malay Regiment.[52] On 1 July 1962, Johor erected a monument in memory of the unit's war dead in Johor Bahru. It was dedicated by the sultan, wearing Johor Military Force uniform. It consisted of two twin pillars in green, the colour of Islam, with a wreath cast in bronze at its top. In attendance was Tuan Haji Mushir Arif, President of the Ex-Services Association.[53]

Finding Malays who could qualify as "anti-Japanese" heroes in the mould of the MPAJA — that is fighting on throughout the Occupation — was more difficult. Given that some Malays saw the Japanese as anti-colonial friends, and others could eke out a rural living with relatively low levels of interference, there was little impetus for widescale resistance. Nevertheless, some Malays did engage in guerrilla activity. A small but significant number served in, or supported, covert anti-Japanese resistance units associated with Britain's Force 136. The main

Malay units in Force 136 were in the *Askar Setia Melayu* (Loyal Malay Regiment), in the jungles of northwest Malaya. These contained about 120 men. In addition, Malay District Officer Yeop Mahidin formed a *Wataniah* (defenders of the fatherland) unit in west Pahang, of 244 men. Finally, there was *Anak Melayu Setia* (sons of loyal Malays), a unit of about 20.[54]

These units totalled less than 400, compared with several thousand in the MPAJA, but included significant postwar Malay figures. Raja Lope, the future Chief of Staff of the Malaysian defence forces, joined *Askar Setia Melayu* after the disbanding of the Malay Regiment.[55] Abdul Razak bin Hussein, the first Deputy Prime Minister and Defence Minister of Malaya in 1957 and later a Prime Minister of Malaysia, held the rank of captain in *Wataniah* in Pahang.[56] Tunku Abdul Rahman aided Malays in Force 136, especially when his nephews Tunku Yusuf and Tunku Osman parachuted into Kedah in June and July 1945, to join *Anak Melayu Setia*.[57]

Malays became more open to helping these small guerrilla units as living conditions deteriorated.[58] Despite de facto attachment to British forces, the main motivation of Malay supporters and fighters remained the livelihood of Malays. The term *setia* (loyalty) in these units was understood to mean loyalty to the Malay race. In *Askar Setia Melayu*, recruits also used *setia* to indicate loyalty to the Sultan of Kedah. In at least one instance, this extended to acting against MPAJA pretensions. In August to September 1945, *Askar Setia Melayu*, in cooperation with Malays from a disbanded *Heiho* organised by Tunku Abdul Rahman, prevented the local MPAJA from occupying villages.[59]

Malay Nationalists in League with the Japanese

We have already seen how Malays found themselves arrayed on different sides. Some stuck steadfastly to their units or the British. In the case of Captain Raja Aman Shah of the FMS Volunteers, *setia* cost him his life. But KMM leaders had a different notion of where the call of Hang Tuah should direct them.

KMM leaders Ibrahim bin Yaacob, Mustapha Hussain, Ahmad Boestamam, Dr Burhanuddin Al-Helmy, and Ishak bin Haji Mohammad saw Occupation as an opportunity. Ibrahim and Ishak Haji Mohammad took jobs in the Japanese Propaganda Department. When the Japanese raised the *Malai Giyugun* (volunteer army) and *Giyutai* (volunteer corps) in 1943, KMM leaders exhorted Malays to join. The Malay nationalist magazine, *Fajar Asia* urged that, "Malay pemuda [youth] must seize this excellent opportunity to show the world that within their breasts flows the blood of Hang Tuah who once reminded us: 'Malays shall not vanish in this world'".[60]

The Japanese initially had no intention of giving Malaya — with its valuable tin and rubber and the strategic port of Singapore — independence.[61] Still, Malay nationalists made the most of the cooperation extended to them. Ibrahim Yaacob became titular head of the *Giyugun*, and Onan Haji Siraj head of the *Giyutai*.

Ibrahim Yaacob saw these forces as future nationalist armies that might also help to unite Malays.[62] Members of the *Giyugun* and *Giyutai* were trained in a manner similar to that of Japanese soldiers, with the *Giyugun* numbering thousands at its peak. The auxiliary corps or *Heiho* was even larger.[63] Membership of the KMM reached 10,000 before the Japanese banned it in June 1942, because it advocated independence too strongly. The Japanese then urged KMM leaders and members to join Japanese-run organisations, and sent some Malays to Japan for further training.[64]

Fajar Asia and *Semangat Asia* published stories about characters who joined the *Giyutai, Giyugun,* and *Heiho* in the "struggle for the motherland" in "hope of achieving victory for their race in the future".[65] *Semangat Asia* exhorted devotion to *"Negara Hang Tuah"* (Hang Tuah's country).[66] KMM leader Ishak bin Haji Mohammad wrote a number of such articles, and poems "brought to the fore the subject of Malay nationalism and the struggle for independence ..."[67] Even Masuri S.N., later Singapore's premier Malay poet, contributed.

Mustapha Hussain, vice-president of KMM, and a man with no illusions about the dark side of the Occupation, subsequently wrote that:

> although the Japanese Occupation was described as one of severe hardship and brutality, it left something positive, a sweet fruit to be plucked and enjoyed only after the surrender. Before the Occupation, Malays were just learning to understand politics and were just beginning to press for freedom and Independence. But Japan's clarion call of 'Asia for Asians' gave Malays a new breath of confidence and stirred in them a resounding love for 'country and people'. This was nationalism; from their efforts towards Independence began to flower.[68]

The lesson of the war was that Malays must stay united. These feelings had intensified when the British proposed the Malayan Union in early 1946. The Malayan Union was intended to be accompanied by grants of citizenship to large numbers of Chinese. In response, a Pan Malayan Malay Congress was held from 1–4 March 1946. Hang Tuah's dictum *Takkan Melayu hilang di dunia* (the Malays will never disappear off the face of the earth) was voiced.[100] It was this sense of the *bangsa Melayu* under threat that spawned UMNO, which emerged from a second Congress, in May 1946.

UMNO's early focus was on organising demonstrations, and then political discussions with the British in order to replace the Malayan Union. That was achieved with the inauguration of the Federation of Malaya (*Persekutuan Tanah Melayu*) on 1 February 1948. The latter secured the sovereignty of the Malay sultans, and an effective Malay veto over future political developments, as well as restricting the number of non-Malays who would become citizens.

While the Federation ended the acute political threat, the Emergency intensified military danger from mid-1948. The Malay Regiment would gradually expand until it reached seven battalions by independence in 1957. In addition, tens of thousands of Malays joined the police in regular and part-time posts. This was aimed at countering the growing, MCP-led and mainly Chinese insurgent army, which peaked at an average of 7,292 in 1951. Trains were derailed, and rubber trees slashed. In reality, the MCP tried to limit any targeting of Malays, and raised a mainly Malay 10th Regiment of its Malayan National Liberation Army (MNLA) in Pahang. In many ways, the Emergency looked like a civil war amongst Malaya's Chinese. But the impression was of intensifying threat to the Malays as well, at least until the insurgency visibly eased between 1952–1954. Even after the formal end of the Emergency in 1960, remnants of the MNLA clung on at the Malayan-Thai border, until a final peace was negotiated in December 1989.[101]

Elements of the MNP were close to the communists, and in 1948, some went into the jungle with them. For UMNO, the Emergency was also seen in communal terms, as threatening a resurrection of the reign of terror of the Chinese-dominated MPAJA of August–September 1945. This scenario, according to UMNO, could be averted by following Hang Tuah's call for the Malays to be united politically in terms of UMNO representing the *bangsa Melayu*. It could also be averted by promoting Malay martialism, represented by the mythical warrior figure of Hang Tuah, as epitomised by their representations of the Malay Regiment and its exploits.

UMNO therefore had multiple reasons for rejecting the Republican and KMM dates for commemorating the war, in favour of the Malay Regiment's preferred dates. These included the anniversary of the foundation of the regiment (1 March), and of the Battle of Pasir Panjang (14 February 1942).[102] The Malay Regiment had a useable, heroic and nationalist past, and a politically conservative and safe present.

From 1952, the British tried to position the Malay Regiment in more non-communal terms, as the core of an emerging, multiracial Federation Army. This had the potential to disturb the Malay Regiment's place in Malay nationalism. In 1953, the Legislative Council agreed to expand the Regiment to nine battalions, with an additional mixed-race Federation Regiment of three battalions, and mixed-race supporting units.[103] The British had initially suggested raising a purely Chinese Regiment (to make recruiting of Chinese easier), but the Rulers would accept only a mixed battalion. This was "only on the understanding that each Federation Regiment battalion is offset by an additional battalion of the Malay regiment".[104] In December 1952, the editor of *Utusan Melayu* warned that the Malay Regiment was the "protector of the Malay race", rejecting any idea that it might lose its separate identity within the rapidly evolving Federation Military Forces.[105]

The British accepted that the Regiment would remain ethnically distinct, and even used this to inculcate an attachment to the notion of a "Malayan nation". In 1949, officials noted that "the High Commissioner [Sir Henry Gurney, 1948–1951] attaches great importance to the training of young Malays in the Regiment as a form of 'national service' and as the surest way by which they can be inspired by the ideas of service to the community and the desire to undertake the defence of their own country".[106] Colonial propaganda stressed that "throughout the Emergency the regiment has fought gallantly and while killing terrorists it has also killed one of the Communists' big lies — that the Communists are fighting for the people of Malaya. The men of the regiment are the people of Malaya".[107]

With independence on 31 August 1957, the commemoration of the Regiment was also expressed in a national Malay-language film: *Sergeant Hassan*. Filming commenced in December 1957 so that it could be released for the first anniversary of independence, on 31 August 1958. The biggest box-office star in the Malay film industry, P. Ramlee,

Plate 7.3 *Sergeant Hassan* poster

starred and wrote the screenplay.[108] Posters carried the Malay Regiment's endorsement.[109] Some filming was done at its Port Dickson camp, with hundreds of soldiers appearing in battle scenes.[110] Credits included Corporal Rashid and Sergeant Pon, with two of its British officers named as "co-stars".[111]

The film premiered in Kuala Lumpur on 26 August 1958, showing nationwide from *Merdeka Day* (31 August). The premiere was attended by the King of Malaya; the Deputy Prime Minister and Defence Minister Dato Abdul Razak bin Hussein; the Chief of Staff of the Army, Major-General F.H. Brooke; and Colonel Raja Lope, Assistant Chief of Staff. Colonel Raja Lope was also one of the original members of the Regiment's 1933 experimental company.[112]

The Central Band of the Malay Regiment played at the première. A Malayan Film Unit documentary called *The First Year* showed first, beginning with "a rededication of the spirit of Merdeka as expressed in the handing over ceremony" of 31 August 1957.[113] Of the film itself, Dato Abdul Razak bin Hussein, said that "*Sergeant* ... symbolised the fighting spirit and gallantry of the men of the Royal Malay Regiment who fought and died for Malaya". He added that "it was now 13 years since the Second World War ended but for ten years the regiment had had no respite, for they had been continuously on active service engaged in the task of suppressing Communist terrorism".[114]

P. Ramlee starred as Hassan, one of two stepbrothers who join the Malay Regiment. The movie begins in June 1930, with a Malay boy standing next to the grave of his father, a rice padi planter who had worked hard for a wealthy landowner. The rich landowner Pak Lebai (Pak meaning father, and Lebai religious leader) is a kind and generous man, who adopts the orphaned Hassan. It seems like an image of a traditional Malay *kampong* (village), with *gotong royong* (community self-help and sharing). But this is disrupted by Pak Lebai's son Aziz. Aziz plays the prodigal son: a vain, spoilt, jealous child, constantly taunting and belittling the gentlemanly Hassan. Only the girl Salmah remains Hassan's friend when the whole village believes Aziz's smears on Hassan's character.

In the village, Hassan struggles against Aziz's machinations. By contrast, Hassan's attributes as a model Malay can flourish in the Malay Regiment. He is an excellent marksman, adapts to a disciplined, rugged life, and is loyal. He is promoted to Sergeant, while Aziz remains a private. Aziz is there because of the glamour of the uniform. By contrast, Hassan joins only after villagers taunt him as a coward, because his father wants him to stay at home to help. The reverse proves true. Hassan's reluctance to leave is a sign of the loyalty that will make him a good soldier.

After the Japanese attack, Hassan saves Aziz's life from a Japanese sniper. Hassan's graciousness and commitment to the unity of the group are subsequently demonstrated by his gentlemanly attitude towards Aziz when they are both POWs. Just before escaping, Hassan tells his commanding officer, "please take care of Aziz for me". In the jungles, Hassan makes contact with British officers leading anti-Japanese Malay guerrillas, who also appear to be former members of the Malay Regiment. Hassan not only helps to attack Japanese installations, but persuades the British commander to make an ultimately futile attempt to rescue his friends from a POW camp. He then convinces the officer to rescue Salmah's father who is due be executed for listening to a secret radio set. Later they also rescue Hassan's adoptive father Pak Lebai,

Salmah, and Hassan's fellow villagers, all of whom have been imprisoned due to the treachery of a certain Buang.

In Malay, *buang* means to discard or throw away. Buang represents everything the Malay is encouraged to reject. He has sold out the community, ingratiates himself with the Japanese, and even wants a Japanese uniform. He uses his connections to intimidate villagers and demand special treatment and sexual favours. After the Japanese surrender, Buang is cornered, and fights it out one-on-one with the returning Hassan. After defeating Buang, Hassan makes the only political speech of the movie:

> Let us hope that there will not be another Buang in our motherland. Because those like him will only serve to destroy our generation. Yes, it is true that our race is still young and weak. I do not care about all that. My only wish is that our race remains united.[115]

Aziz, chastened by his experiences as a POW on the "Death Railway", returns to ask Hassan's forgiveness. Aziz tells Hassan that he too was an adopted son, and had wanted to inherit all Pak Lebai's wealth. Hassan forgives Aziz, the village applauds, and the movie ends with unity restored.

The stress on the unity of the *bangsa Melayu*, beyond mere *kampong* and state, is significant.[116] P. Ramlee was an UMNO supporter.[117] In *Sergeant Hassan*, the Malay Regiment is a metaphor for the *bangsa Melayu*. Its men come from different Malay States, and are depicted as defending their country, not the British Empire. By contrast, the film could hardly have cheered anyone with sympathies for the KMM and Japanese-sponsored militias. The *Giyugun, Giyutai*, and *Heiho* per se are absent, but the collaborator Buang is an anti-hero. Nor was this the first such presentation of those who cooperated as Buang-types. In the Shaw Brothers' other Malay war movie of 1958, *Matahari*, the female heroine, Matahari, played by Maria Menado, remains loyal to the British, and is pitted against a nasty adversary played by Salleh Kamil who collaborates with the Japanese and wants her as his sex slave. Matahari, the village head's daughter, flees to start an anti-Japanese guerrilla army. Eventually she triumphs and the Salleh Kamil character is defeated. This theme of the villain who collaborates with the Japanese against the village also featured in early postwar Malay literauture. Ahmad Murad bin Nasruddin's novel, *Nyawa Di-Hujong Pedang* (*Life at the Tip of the Sword*, 1946), had one Said as its villain. Said informs upon the hero,

Yazid, for working for the MPAJA near Ipoh. Yazid is arrested on the eve of his wedding with Juriah (whom Said covets), and tortured.[118] Yazid is about to be beheaded when news arrives that the war is over. In line with the theme of Malay unity, the released Yazid unsuccessfully tries to save Said's life from the MPAJA's execution squads.

Nyawa Di-Hujong Pedang resulted from a British Information Department contest to encourage Malay novels, winning the first prize.[119] The author, Ahmad Murad bin Nasruddin, initially suppressed his own war background.[120] It was not until the 1986 edition that it was revealed that he had been the editor of the Japanese-sponsored English-language newspaper, the *Perak Shimbun*. This tendency to avoid mentioning wartime activities, the "Biodata Blackout Syndrome", afflicted Malaya and Singapore more generally in the 1940–1960s.[121] Many Malays omitted parts of their wartime record from postwar organs such as *Who's Who in Malaya*.

"Blackout Syndrome" was not, however, the preferred technique for explaining Malay Regiment men who joined Japanese organisations. M.C. ff Sheppard took a more combative approach in his history of the Regiment.[122] Sheppard was told by several veterans that they had joined Japanese-sponsored forces. Bandar Omar told him that, "ex-members of the Malay Regiment were wanted badly by the Japanese to join their 'Gyutai'..."[123] Bandar evaded this fate by joining a travelling Malay opera company. Sergeant Major Ismail Babu recalled that:

> On 1.12.43, I was called by Japs Military Officers and was forced to join their volunteer Force known as the 'Giyu Tai'. On 8.12.43, I was sent for training to Kuala Lumpur together with the following members of the Malay Regt: Lieuts Ismail Tahar, Ibrahim Alla Ditta, RQMS Mohd Noor, 64 Sgt Amat Idris, Sig Sgt. Ahmad and Cpl Mat Saman.[124]

Ismail was given the rank of *Giyutai* captain. He passed information on Japanese troop movements to the Chinese MPAJA, then left to join the Malay units of Force 136 as soon as these started operations in Kedah. He rejoined the Regiment after the war, when he was presented with the M.B.E. (Military Division) for service in the Malayan Campaign. According to Sheppard, such everyday resistance from within rendered the *Giyutai* feeble, with "desertions from the ranks ... assisted and encouraged by the Malay officers" rising to a peak of 60 per cent, while some members "improvised the symptoms of venereal disease" and others changed names and moved. In this way, he focussed on those whose stories could be presented as embodiments of *setia*, even when coerced into service under the Japanese.[125]

In 1958, there were public celebrations of the Malay Regiment as a cornerstone in nation-building, which laid the foundation of Malaya's, and later Malaysia's *Hari Pahlawan* (Warriors or Heroes Day). When the Malay Regiment was made the "Royal Malay Regiment" by the King on the occasion of its Silver Jubilee on 1 March 1958, it was suggested that there should be a "Warriors' Day".[126] The first anniversary of independence in August 1958 was seen as the best occasion for a first *Hari Pahlawan* and military tattoo. The latter featured 200 Malay Regiment soldiers arranged at the *Merdeka* Stadium in Kuala Lumpur to form the word "*merdeka*". A crowd of 25,000 watched, including Prime Minister Tunku Abdul Rahman.[127] General Secretary of the Ex-Services Association, Mohamed Yazid, declared that "*Hari Pahlawan* is to commemorate the dead in the battle against Communist terrorists and also the Malays who have given their lives for the country in fighting for independence since 1511".[128]

The first *Hari Pahlawan* tattoo thus marked a step in the process of welding all conflicts, critically including the Malayan Emergency, into one for the sake of commemoration. The day was initially proposed to the Defence Minister Abdul Razak bin Hussein in November 1957 by a delegation of the Ex-Services' Association. Led by its deputy president, Hussein Chik, this suggested the day should replace the ceremonies held on Remembrance Sunday, 11 November. These had been held at the Cenotaph — like Singapore's built on the model of empire-wide cenotaphs — since the 1920s. First built to mark the fallen of the First World War, its ceremonies had been updated to recognise soldiers who died in the Second World War and the Malayan Emergency. The initial Ex-Services' proposal was for Remembrance Day to be replaced by "Martyrs' Day", to be held every 31 August. By March 1958, the idea had evolved into *Hari Pahlawan* (Warriors Day), to be remembered in August, but with no fixed day.[129]

Throughout the 1960s, the achievements of the Malay Regiment continued to be celebrated on several days. The first was the "Malay Regiment Heroic Day", commemorating the Battle of Pasir Panjang, each 14 February. The second was the "birthday" of the regiment, marking its founding on 1 March. The third was *Hari Pahlawan*, in August.[130] Sheppard, meanwhile, continued to popularise the regiment's achievements. He eulogised its soldiers as national heroes in the press,

Plate 7.4 The life-sized image of Hang Tuah at the National History Museum in Kuala Lumpur (1996–2007)

and claimed that he was "responsible for forming the first ex-Malay Regiment Old Comrades Association".[131] On 13 February 1967, the 25th anniversary of the Battle of Pasir Panjang, Sheppard published feature articles in the English and Malay papers. These concluded with the statement that "the Battle of Pasir Panjang Ridge, which culminated in the Battle of Opium Hill (Bukit Chandu), on Feb. 13, and 14, 1942 deserves to be held in honoured memory for all time, in the archives of the Malay Regiment and in the history of our nation".[132]

The men of the Malay Regiment were eulogised as the successors of the tradition of Hang Tuah, and Sheppard worked to ensure that Hang Tuah's story was also widely known. In 1949, he published an illustrated English-language version of the *Hikayat Hang Tuah*, targeted at schools. This was repeatedly reprinted, and in 1954, he sold the movie rights to Shaw Brothers.[133] Two years later, in 1956, *Hang Tuah* was in the cinemas, starring P. Ramlee.[134] In 1957, Sheppard opened yet another article on the Malay Regiment with the words: "Few races in the world today possess a hero who has remained the undisputed paragon ... for five centuries ... The immortal name of Hang Tuah conjures up in the Malay of today, just as it did long ago in Malacca, the epitome of courage, courtesy, loyalty and resource ..." Describing the Malay warrior from Malacca to the Emergency, he concluded: "The spirit of Hang Tuah is still very much alive, and so long as it continues to flourish his famous dictum 'Never shall the Malays vanish from the earth' will remain unchallenged".[135] In 1961 another film, called *Hang Jebat*, retold the *Hang Tuah* story from Hang Jebat's perspective.[136]

Both UMNO and the Malay Left continued to seek favour with Malay veterans. Ahmad Boestamam was active with the Malayan Ex-Services Association.[137] In November 1955, Boestamam told a large gathering of former Malay members of the Malay Regiment, the special constabulary, and the British Army, that "You rallied to the aid of the government when it was in need. Now in time of difficulties, it is only proper that the government alleviate your suffering". One Malay Regiment veteran complained that "After seven years of service, we were discarded when the Government gained control of the Emergency".[138] Veterans, from the Emergency as well as 1941–1942, formed a constituency too important to be ignored.

Tugu Negara

By 1958, the veneration of then Malay Regiment, and other anti-Japanese fighters was secure. *Hari Pahlawan* would persist. At first, it was marked on 31 August, Malaya's Independence Day.[139] However, after the end of the Malayan Emergency on 31 July 1960, *Hari Pahlawan* transferred to each 31 July.[140]

What was lacking was a monument to act as a focus for such commemoration. The Cenotaph was a colonial monument. There was a strong desire to have something more specific to Malaya, its culture, and the martial tradition of Hang Tuah and the Malay Regiment. Each successive Remembrance Sunday, more Malays, and less Europeans, were marching past the cenotaphs in Kuala Lumpur, Taiping, Penang, Malacca, and Ipoh. Increasingly the sultans were laying wreaths at these monuments, alongside Malay Regiment officers who had lost a comrade or relative in the Emergency or in 1941–1942.[141] In Kuala Lumpur, Raja Lope regularly laid a wreath on Remembrance Day for his wife's brother, Captain Raja Aman Shah. Sometimes, Raja Lope's wife, Raja Nor Zahan, would do it.[142] The Tunku also had a wreath laid at the Cenotaph in Kuala Lumpur for Captain Raja Aman Shah, as the husband of his sister, Tunku Baharom.[143]

Prayers at Remembrance Day were increasingly heard not only from Christian ministers quoting from the Bible, but also from Muslim preachers citing Islamic verses. The greater focus on paying respects to the Malay war dead also raised delicate issues. On Remembrance Day 1958 at Ipoh, the Sultan of Perak and his Mentri Besar did not attend as usual "on advice of the Religious Affairs Department" which said "that it is against Islam to pay obeisance to a stone monument and this was being followed since Islam is now the state religion".[144]

The changing nature of Remembrance Day ceremonies combined with two events to prompt a rethink on the centrality of the cenotaphs. First, the official end of the Emergency on 31 July 1960 prompted Tunku Abdul Rahman to question whether a monument specifically fitted to commemorate this conflict was called for.[145] Second, the old Cenotaph site in Kuala Lumpur, near the central railway station, was to make way for new road systems. So at the very least, the Cenotaph would have to be relocated, and new memorial grounds would be required.

The plan that emerged was to relocate the Cenotaph to the Lake Gardens, on a prominent slope near central Kuala Lumpur, and adjacent to a new National Mosque and Parliament. This would create a powerful complex of national buildings. In addition, a new monument there was to have a particular focus on the Emergency. The Public Works Department suggested forms which included space to display Emergency memorabilia, and which did not include human statues, in order to avoid offending Muslim sensibilities. Their final design was for two giant, intertwined vines, moulded in concrete. One would be green, and the other, clad in white Langkawi marble, would rise higher, symbolising the triumph of democracy over evil. At the base of the vines would be an 11-point star of gold mosaic tiles, representing Malaya's 11 states and settlements. The whole structure would be encircled by a reflective pool.

In fact, the mosque was eventually built at a more accessible location, and the final monument bore little resemblance to the initial design. The change came about when Prime Minister Tunku Abdul Rahman visited the United States in August 1960. He was driven past the United States Marine Memorial ("Iwo Jima Memorial") at Arlington (near Washington, DC), as designed by Austrian-American architect Felix De Weldon. It featured six troops, five Marines and one naval corpsman, raising a flagpole topped with the American flag on Okinawa's Mount Suribachi in March 1945. It was a "realist" monument, based on a famous photograph.[146]

In October 1960, the Malayan Cabinet agreed to commission Weldon to design a monument on the model of the Marine Memorial. On the night of 31 July 1961, Tunku Abdul Rahman, as Prime Minister, made a national radio address marking the first anniversary of the end of the Emergency.[147] In this, he revealed the intention to build the new monument, to serve "as an inspiration for all Malayans and particularly to the younger generation, a true and enduring symbol of the national spirit of the Malayan people". It would cost $1 million, the government contributing $200,000, as he felt that "everyone would like to contribute his share to express personally his feeling of national pride and gratitude to those who had died".[148] Shaw Brothers, whose company had made *Sergeant Hassan*, kicked off contributions with a $5,000 donation.

The Tunku now had in mind a blend of the original concept — the triumph of democracy over evil — combined with the Arlington form. Felix de Weldon was sent photographs of individuals posed in Malay security force uniforms. Using these, he fashioned a massive black granite monument featuring seven figures. Of the seven, one holds a flag, two stand guard with guns, and one cradles an injured comrade. Underneath this heroic group of five are two prone figures, representing "the defeated forces of evil". Weldon had been sent photographs in 1962, in which the two dead soldiers are more obviously wearing different uniforms. Despite this, he briefly assumed that the two prone figures were those of martyred government soldiers.[149]

The monument was to be dedicated to security force personnel who died in the Emergency. The Cenotaph was, meanwhile, to be relocated nearby, slightly further down the slope. The monument itself was to

Plate 7.5 *Tugu Negara*

be surrounded by a reflective pool, and flanked by a crescent-shaped, white pavilion, with gold domes to left, right and centre. The pavilion's ceiling would eventually be painted with the emblems of the Malayan and Commonwealth units which served in the Emergency. The central dome was to contain a document with the names of all those who had died, and a crypt underneath would house a flame of remembrance.[150]

The monument was also to reflect the Malay-dominated nature of the state, and Malay predominance in local forces which resisted communism. The granite base would feature inscriptions in English and Malay, but not Chinese or Tamil. The Malay version of the inscription is in the relatively inaccessible Jawi script. It reads: "Dedicated to the heroic fighters in the cause of peace and freedom. May the blessing of Allah be Upon Them". The accompanying plaque, this time in roman-ised Malay as well as in English, extols "the warriors who died defending the sovereignty of the country …" and claims that the monument "represents the triumph of the forces of democracy over the forces of evil".

Up to this point, annual Remembrance Day ceremonies continued to be held at the Kuala Lumpur Cenotaph. This gradually had added to it the dates for new conflicts, until it read "To Our Glorious Dead 1914–1918, 1939–1945, 1948–1960". Finally, in November 1961, the Cenotaph was packed away ready to be moved to Lake Gardens, where it would join the new National Monument complex.[151] It was re-erected there in September 1963, even as the new National Monument (*Tugu Negara*) and gardens were being built next to it.[152] While the National Monument itself was specifically to be dedicated to those who had fallen during the Emergency, the Lake Gardens complex and Cenotaph are dedicated to the dead from other conflicts as well.

In July 1965, the seven bronze statues of figures started to be put into place on the *Tugu Negara*. The seventh figure, holding the flag, was said to represent leadership, with the facial features modelled on the young Tunku Abdul Rahman.[153] There were criticisms that the soldiers looked Western, with their hats resembling the "slouch" hats of the Australian and New Zealand forces. In fact, they represented the hats and uniforms of the Malay Regiment's jungle fighting dress. This uniform had been immortalised for the Malay community by the movie *Sergeant Hassan*.

The National Monument was officially unveiled by the King of Malaysia on 8 February 1966. Tunku Abdul Rahman said that "It is my hope that this monument will be an enduring reminder of the victory of good over evil and serve as a constant symbol of the eternal truth — come what may, the cause of right and justice will always triumph in the end".[154] The Tunku reiterated that the monument was a "symbol of the double victory of the Malayan people — the triumph of right over evil and the unshakeable faith we have in our country". Thereafter, the Malaysian government took important visitors to the National Monument complex, but they would lay a wreath not on the National Monument, but in front of the nearby Cenotaph, which signified the war dead from all wars. Japanese Foreign Minister Shiina Etsusaburo visited the complex in October 1966, and laid a wreath at the Cenotaph, as did Japanese Prime Minister Sato Eisaku in September 1967.[155] It was *Tugu Negara*, however, which became the main focus of *Hari Pahlawan*, now held on the first Sunday after 31 July.

Conclusion

National war memory had come to focus heavily on the Malay Regiment soldier, as well as on all Malays who served against the Japanese, and increasingly on all those who served in the security forces in the Emergency too. The special place in commemoration of the Malay Warrior, and specifically of the Malay Regiment, was trebly assured. Its formation was seen as an act of nationalism. Its performance in 1941–1942 offered a safe, conservative, anti-Japanese example of the best of the Malay martial tradition. Finally, its role as the major Malay combat unit in the Emergency cemented its position as guardian of the Malay race, and of Malay predominance within Malaysia's multi-communal political system.

Malay war memory thus emerged with a similar form to that of Indian war memory, in the sense that memories of martialism are seen as expressions of nationalism. Memories of Malay victims are conveniently forgotten or pushed out of the public memory by images of soldiers of the Malay Regiment fighting the Japanese. In the time of Prime Minister Tunku Abdul Rahman, there was also no national commemoration of the martialism of the Malays who were on the side of the Japanese, such as Ibrahim Yaacob and the members of the KMM. This was no surprise given the suppression of many of the Malay Left organisations during the Malayan Emergency, and Tunku Abdul Rahman's own antagonism towards the leaders of these organisations following the Japanese killing of his brother-in-law, Captain Raja Aman Shah. Even during the Prime Ministerships of Abdul Razak (1971–1976) and Hussein Onn (1976–1981), it was unlikely that Malays who sided with the Japanese, such as Ibrahim Yaacob, would see their martialism commemorated. Razak had helped the British through the Malay guerrillas associated with Force 136. Hussein Onn, who had joined the Johor Military Forces as a cadet, served as a captain in the British Indian Army during the war, seeing action in the Middle East, and working in the intelligence branch of the British military headquarters in India.

Malay nationalist *pemuda* who had openly promoted a nationalist agenda during the occupation, such as Ibrahim Yaacob and the KMM, were not commemorated in the early years of independence.

In addition, Malay commemoration became entangled with that of the Emergency, especially after the unveiling of the *Tugu Negara* and surrounding memorial gardens in 1966. The *Hari Pahlawan* ceremonies were relocated here and came to fall near or on every 31 July, meaning that the central focus of ceremonies for Malaysia's fallen was a monument that presented communists as "evil", as the enemies of democracy whose defeat was necessary for true freedom. Since many of the communist insurgents of the Emergency period had also been anti-Japanese fighters of the MPAJA, the monument and the narrative it represented made it all but impossible to incorporate majority Chinese memories of "war heroes" into any national narrative.

The *Tugu Negara* also reflected Malay predominance, in focussing attention onto a Malay martial tradition, and its triumph in the Malayan Emergency through the actions of the Malay Regiment, fighting alongside Commonwealth troops. The MCP so hated the *Tugu Negara* that in August 1975 — when they were sending small insurgent columns down the peninsula — they attempted to blow it up.

This focus on warriors and heroes, and selection of specifically Malay warriors who had fought against the Japanese, leads to the question of Malay victims. What, if anything, did the state do in the memory of Malays who were the victims of Japanese actions, including forced labour and everyday coercion? That is the subject of the next chapter. Beyond that, it leads to the question of how far, if at all, Malaysia was able to adjust over time to better incorporate non-Malay memories in commemoration, and to acknowledge the variety of memory which had been forgotten, or suppressed, in the bitter years of the Cold War and Emergency. Those questions will also be the subject of Chapter 9, on Malaysian War Memory and Nation-Building.

CHAPTER 8

Malay Victims

THE POSTWAR EMPHASIS ON EXEMPLARS OF THE Malay martial tradition crowded out memories of Malay victimhood. Quite apart from "everyday victims" of the Occupation, and of shortages, these victims included Malays forced to labour on the Burma-Thailand Railway, and those sent to New Guinea and other locations.

Amongst these forced labourers were a number of veterans from the Malay Regiment, FMS Volunteers, and other prewar, British-led forces. The experience of such victims remained peripheral to state-sponsored remembrance of the war, with its central focus on warriors as exemplars of desirable Malay characteristics. Hence, in the movie *Sergeant Hassan*, about two brothers who join the Malay Regiment, the hero's brother Aziz is said to have been sent to the Railway. But his experience there is not shown in the film. There is just one sentence mentioning that he has come back from the railway when he is reunited with Hassan. It is an offscreen *deus ex machina*, the experience of which transforms the petulant Aziz into a more honourable Malay prior to his return to the *kampong*. Sheppard's history of the Malay Regiment, meanwhile, concentrates on the Regiment's achievements, while quietly folding an account of those who were sent to the railway into a fraction of one page.[1]

It is these Malay "victims" that this chapter focuses on.[2] How many Malays were involved in forced labour? British figures from September 1945 put the total number of civilian labourers sent to the Burma-Thailand Railway at 78,204, and the known dead at 29,634. This gives a minimum death rate of 37 per cent.[3] With a proportion of the missing also acknowledged as probably dead, the British estimated that up to 40,000, or 51 per cent of the total, might have perished.[4]

How many of these were Malays? We can get a rough measure by looking at the figures for those awaiting repatriation from Thailand to Malaya at the end of the war. One British report, from November 1945, records 23,000 Malayans awaiting repatriation. Of these, Malays numbered around 2,000, as against 4,000 Chinese and 17,000 Indians.[5]

That suggests that of the 78,204, slightly less than nine per cent, or just under 7,000, might have been Malay, of whom up to half might have died. In addition, Malays were despatched to locations such as Sumatra and New Guinea. To put this in perspective, more than 70 per cent of railway labourers were Indians. On the other hand, there were only around 1,400 Malays in the Malay Regiment, less than 400 in guerrilla forces affiliated to Force 136, and in the low thousands in the volunteers and Johore Military Forces.

The experiences of these Malays victims were not, of course, entirely forgotten. We have already noted that Aziz, in *Sergeant Hassan*, is presented as a Malay Regiment soldier who is sent to the railway after surrender. The fictional Aziz had some basis in the experience of real members of the Malay Regiment, as M.C. Sheppard discovered when he interviewed veterans after the war.

Lance Corporal Tan Manap of "A" company of the 1st Battalion told Sheppard that, "During the Japanese regime I was forced to go to Thailand as a forced labourer ... I stayed in Siam for about two years ..."[6] Private Mohd Yunus Bin Jamal of "C" Company of the 1st Battalion recalled that after February 1942:

> I suffered my wounds for nearly six months and ... happened to go to Ipoh and here I was seized with nearly three hundred other men and were packed straight to Siam. We detrained at Banpong ... and reached a place called Koriang Batu where we were forced to build roads and cut down big trees. After working here for nearly two months I managed to escape but was caught again and put into another Jap Camp.
>
> One day I was returning from a working place and on crossing a log bridge, I slipped and fell into a deep chasm about 100 feet deep. I felt that my whole body was aching. I tried to rise up but my legs gave way. Luckily a bullock-cart passed along a beaten track close to the log bridge. The driver was a Burmese and he noticed me and saved me. He loaded me into his cart and brought me to his house where he gave me food and shelter. Later he tattooed me as he said that was is custom in attending the sick and wounded. I still now have the tattoo marks on my left arm.

After staying here for nearly a year, then I heard of the Japanese surrender. I was not able to walk and I was kindly sent by the Burmese on an elephant to a Railway Station by the name of Hua Hin, thence I travelled to Nakon and stayed here for nearly eight months. There were many Malays here and they subscribed and gave me 50 but [Baht] (Siamese money) — equivalent to $10/-. With this money, I proceeded to Padang Besar and thence to my home in Ipoh and reached there on 23rd May 1946.[7]

The experience of Lance Corporal Ismail Haji Zainal Abidin was even more gruelling. He described what happened after following the Fall of Singapore:

Two months later I was released and after so much difficulties managed to reach my home in KUALA LUMPUR. For months I lived a HOBO'S life and then was employed as a Telegraph Operator in K.L. Telegraph Office. In 1943, I was compelled to go to Siam with the Labourers. Two weeks after my arrival in KANCHANABURI I was sent to THAMBYUZAT the last station on the Death Railway lines about 35 kilometres from Moulmein (BURMA). Here I experienced a very hard life, I suffered very badly from Malaria, dysentery and Beri-beri. The food given was bad and as for vegetables they gave pumpkins and other rotten stuffs — B 29 and fighters of the Allied Forces raided the spot daily and at nights...[8]

Ismail escaped with an Indian labourer. After the Japanese surrender, he contacted his former officers from the Malay Regiment in the British POW camp near Kanchanaburi, and they helped him return to Singapore.

The Burma-Thailand Railway was not the only place which proved deadly. Eight members of the Malay Regiment were sent as forced labour to New Guinea.[9] The eight men were among a group of almost 300 survivors from several thousand Malays shipped there. A group of Malays in the *Heiho* was also taken to New Guinea. After the war, they called themselves the "Lost Legion".[10]

Malays from the former colonial volunteer forces were among those who were taken captive, and sent as forced labour to work on the Burma-Thailand Railway. After the war, British authorities identified 34 Malay members of the volunteer forces who had died there.[11] Historians Abu Talib Ahmad, Mat Zin Mat Kib, and Nakahara Michiko have used oral testimony from Malays who survived.[12] This oral history of the 1980s–1990s reflects terrible suffering. It was not, however, the first

Plate 8.1 Malay workers on the Burma-Thailand Railway

Plate 8.2 Women unloading petrol from trains at Thambyuzat, Burma, on the Burma-Thailand Railway

time such personal narratives were told. Documented testimony also appears in appeals to the colonial state for help, which were written in the immediate postwar period.

The UMNO leadership was acutely aware of the large numbers of Malays who had been used as forced labour on the Burma-Thailand Railway and elsewhere. It chose, however, to de-emphasise this, in order to stress images which might better strengthen Malay national consciousness, unity, and self-confidence.

That this was a choice, and not inadvertent neglect, is shown by UMNO's response when petitioned over the railway. UMNO was pressured by the families of forced labourers who had died to take up their cause with the colonial government. In response, the Central Executive Committee of UMNO, meeting in Kuala Lumpur on 23 November 1951, resolved to ask the Chief Secretary "for statistics of the Malay victims, who lost their lives when they were transported to do forced labour on the "Death Railway" in Siam, and of those transported to countries outside Malaya ..." The Colonial Secretary was Vincent del Tufo, who had himself had been held as a POW by the Japanese at Changi Prison. The purpose of the enquiry was to ascertain "the amounts paid as compensation to the heirs of each of the Malay war victims".[13]

The colonial records on Malay victims of the Occupation were so poor that it was almost a year before a reply was forthcoming. When it did come, in a letter dated 8 August 1952, the Chief Secretary's office could only list the dependents of the 34 Malays from the FMS Volunteers who had died on the railway, along with the combat casualty figures for the volunteers and Malay Regiment. They could not ascertain how many Malay labourers had died on the railway.[14] Zulkifli bin Mohd Hashim, Acting Secretary-General of UMNO, replied, apparently willing to accept that there were no records for forced labourers.[15] It seems that while the UMNO leadership wanted to put on record its response to families' enquiries, it was not particularly eager to press the issue.

Unfortunately for the colonial authorities and UMNO, the issue would not go away. Some families wanted to secure the return to Malaya of forced labourers who still remained in Thailand. Such families sometimes appealed to their sultan, or to the colonial government, though rarely to UMNO.[16] Unfortunately for the families, the colonial authorities proved better at filing these requests than it did at taking action.

In 1947, the State Public Relations Officer of the Malay State of Kelantan, "on his own initiative", meticulously recorded the names of 218 Malay forced labourers who had died on the railway, and their family members in Kelantan, as well as the names of 275 missing Malay forced labourers and their family members. This information was forwarded to the Chief Secretary's Office in Kuala Lumpur.[17] It seems that his report was not acted on in any significant way.

Some forced labourers thus remained in Thailand, unaware that the Malayan government might assist their passage home. Abdulla bin Talif from Pasir Puteh, Kelantan, for instance, explained in 1947 why he had not been repatriated earlier. He told British officials how he "was taken from Kelantan to Kanchanaburi in Siam three years ago by the Japanese in a forced labour in the Siam-Burma railroad" where he was "given food and 1 tical a day and the treatment was so hard that after three months" he "escaped and found his way to Paknampoh" where hiding from the Japanese, he "eked out a living as a boatman".[18] It was only when he arrived in Bangkok in March 1947 that he became aware of the Malaya Refugee Camp. Until September 1946, that camp had repatriated Malayan labourers for free.

As late as 1950, there were still Malay forced labourers in Thailand appealing for repatriation. Nai Sori Ari told how he had in 1943 been "captured by the Japanese and ordered to work as a coolie in the province of Kanchanaburi" but "escaped from the Japanese camp with the intention to return and live with his father" in Batu Pahat, Johor.[19] Ayub Kasim from Telok Anson, told the British authorities that:

> It is now a year that I have been in Bangkok and I feel very homesick. I wish to return home to see my father and mother. It is very difficult for me to live in Siam as I have to lodge with other people. As I possess very little money and most of the time I am totally broke, I feel most miserable and yearn to see the faces of my father, mother and relatives.[20]

The issue of displaced persons is found after many wars, but it was not the only one. Another issue was compensation, and here Asian victims — rightly or wrongly — came to feel discriminated against. In 1956, POWs were each paid £3 compensation from the sale of the Burma-Thailand Railway to Thailand.[21] In effect, the Thai Government purchased the fruits of the POWs and civilian labourers work and suffering. Yet the civilian labourers were, at first, eligible only for assistance when in dire need, not for compensation as of right. The compensation of the mainly Western POWs therefore provoked civilian labourers to make further representations. They agitated strongly for compensation. This struggle would, in turn, come to be about more than mere money, transforming also into a struggle for recognition of their place in the national war memory of the Malay community.

Malay forced labourers and their families initially wanted to know if they were entitled to the payment of £3 per person that the POWs were to receive. In 1956, the Colonial government planned to pay POWs, including members of the Malay Regiment and Malay volunteers.[22]

In October and November 1954, meanwhile, UMNO had received letters on the behalf of the Malay victims requesting that the political party represent them in their quest for compensation and recognition. Basir Bin Saire from Kampong Sungei Bunyi of Pontian in Johor wrote to the executive committee that, "I shall therefore be very obliged if the UMNO could take up my case further with the Government ..." After receiving no reply, he wrote that, "Further proof of my having forcibly recruited by the Japanese as above can be produced by me from the Ketua Kampong if necessary".[23] The leader of UMNO, Tunku Abdul Rahman, responded, saying to the Malay victims that "any hope of assistance would require patience", adding that "the government cannot afford" to compensate the victims.[24] Finally, in March 1955, Tunku Abdul Rahman simply restated the Colonial government's line that $45,102 had been paid out in the 1940s to the widows and dependants of those Malay labourers who had died on the Burma-Thailand Railway, and that was the extent of the Colonial government's obligations. The 1940s payments had, of course, been means-tested assistance to those without a job, or to dependents without means of support, not compensation.[25]

Frustration with UMNO now led the Malay railway victims to form their own group, in June 1958. This was the the "Association of Former Siam-Burma Death Railway Workers".* Its first official meeting commenced on 11 July 1958 in Kota Bharu, Kelantan. 200 attended.[26] Kota Bahru became the association's headquarters, despite most forced labourers being Indian plantation workers. The Malay victims of Kelantan took the lead because there were many of them in touch and in close proximity. After more than a decade of mounting frustration with

---

* Its full name was the "All Malaya Association of Forced Labourers and Families of Forced Labourers of the Siam-Thailand Death Railway 1942–1946".

UMNO and the colonial government, some 2,000 members joined in the first year.[27] It was November 1963 before another branch was established, in Seremban, covering the states of Selangor, Negeri Sembilan, and Malacca.[28]

The secretary of the association was Mohamed Yusoff Yasin and its president Sulaiman bin Hassan.[29] In 1959, these two Malay leaders began by writing to Malay political parties that were in opposition to the UMNO-dominated government. Hence, they wrote to Ahmad Boestamam, Chairman of the Socialist Front; to Dr Burhanuddin Al-Helmy as President of the Malayan Islamic Party; and to Dato Onn bin Ja'afar, who had now left UMNO and was President of Party Negara.[30]

Another letter was sent to Prime Minister Tunku Abdul Rahman, requesting a revision of the peace treaty with Japan (which had voided any subsequent private claims versus the Japanese Government). The letter received press publicity, but was ignored by the government.[31] The pleas of the Association of Former Siam-Burma Death Railway Workers to Malay Left parties fell on deaf ears for rather different reasons. Both Boestamam and Burhanuddin were former members of the KMM, and therefore unlikely to take up the cause of Malay forced labourers that their organisations had helped deliver into the hands of the Japanese, however indirectly.

Two Indian Opposition members of parliament did take up the issue, and pressed Tunku Abdul Rahman during parliamentary questions. V. David and V. Veerappen, of the non-communal Malayan Labour Party, took up the cause not just of Malay forced labourers, but also of Indian forced labourers who were joining the Malay-led association. The Prime Minister told them that "the Government has no intention of paying compensation to the relatives of those who died in the 'Death Railway' for the simple reason that we have no money for this purpose". He added that despite the lists that had been compiled since the 1940s, "we have no record of those who had worked in the 'Death Railway' or of those who had died".[32]

With the rise of the Chinese "Blood Debt" claim against the Japanese government in 1962, the Association of Former Siam-Burma Death Railway Workers again took up the issue. Its secretary-general demanded that Prime Minister Tunku Abdul Rahman set up a commission, whose findings should then be conveyed to the Japanese government. His association now asked for $2,000 for the family of each Malayan who died on the railway, and $1,500 compensation for each survivor.[33] This claim, according to the association, would have cost between $70 million to $101 million to settle, on behalf of the victims on the association's register.[34]

The Japanese government made it clear it was not going to pay compensation to individuals.[35] When Singapore, Sarawak, and Sabah merged with the Federation to form Malaysia in September 1963, Tunku Abdul Rahman as Malaysian Prime Minister took over the handling of the "Blood Debt" issue with Japan on behalf of all Malaysians. This included taking over what was now called "the "blood debt" claim put up by the Siamese Death Railway Labourers' Association".[36] Tan Siew Sin, the Malaysian Minister for Finance, speaking on behalf of the prime minister in the Malaysian Senate in October 1964, fully acknowledged government responsibility for handling claims to Japan as part of an overall "blood debt" issue.[37]

The Malaysian Government finally settled the "Blood Debt" claims with Japan by accepting in 1967 compensation to the value of $25 million. This did not please the victims of the Burma-Thailand Railway. Prime Minister Tunku Abdul Rahman nevertheless made it clear that this compensation as he referred to it was the end of the matter, and that he would not take up further claims with the Japanese government.

This determination was tested when, in 1967, a delegation of the Penang Patriotic Youth Association claimed to represent 10,000 victims of forced labour on the railway. Of these, just 3,000 had registered with the Association. Led by Ismail bin Ibrahim, this body announced that, "We will ask the Prime Minister to take up this matter of compensation during his visit to Japan".[38] Prime Minister Tunku Abdul Rahman did nothing of the sort. For him, the compensation claims were an unwanted complication in trade and investment relations. Thus, after 1967, the Malay victims of forced labour on the railway were pushed even further out of public memory.

The campaign for "Blood Debt" compensation of the mid 1960s had seen membership for the "Association of Former Siam-Burma Death Railway Workers" peak. With the possibility of compensation in the air, many victims and their families had joined up. The association's membership roll rose and fell as follows:

1958 — 1,771
1960 — 1,259
1961 — 1,840
1962 — 1,950
1963 — 15,376
1973 — 841[39]

Failure to secure compensation in 1967 saw numbers plummet. It also marked the end of its efforts to bring the stories of its members into public memory. By 1973, the organisation had been wound up. In 1985, one of the Chinese forced labourers on the railway, Soong Yit Koi, from Kluang in Johor, did briefly revive agitation for compensation. 300 family members of victims formed an association. This centred on Soong and a small group of 19 railway survivors. That was all that was left out of 49 who had returned in 1946, from the group of 780 Chinese, Indians, and Malays who Soong had laboured on the railway with. The group was unable to get any support from the government, and claims Soong submitted to the Japanese government on an August 1991 visit were ignored.[40]

Conclusion

The marginality of the victims of the Burma-Thailand Railway has persisted, though the issue has been raised from time to time. In 2009, James Gonzales wrote to the Malaysian national newspaper, the *New Straits Times*, requesting that on *Hari Pahlawan* (Warriors or Heroes Day), Malaysia should "honour death railway victims, too".[41] His request was not taken up, and it did not ignite any debate. As in Singapore with its *sook ching* victims, so in Malaysia there is no national monument which actually names the civilian dead, whether from the railway or massacres.

By the 1970s, it was clear that Malay victims would remain marginalised in state-sponsored public memory and commemoration, and that their compensation claims would continue to be regarded by the state as "settled". With even Malay victims thus marginalised in public memory, there was relatively little likelihood that Indian victims (of the railway) and Chinese victims (of the *sook ching*) would be incorporated into national remembrance. The war continued to be remembered in public, but with a heavy emphasis on the individuals, organisations and stories whose history best assisted a Malay-dominated project of nation-building, within a plural society.

NATIONS AND STATES

CHAPTER 9

Memory and Nation-Building in Malaysia

THIS CHAPTER DEALS WITH WAR COMMEMORATION IN Malaysia from 1967. This was the first year when the state no longer relied on massive British military assistance for its survival, following Indonesia's formal ending of its 1963–1966 Confrontation of Malaysia, in August 1966.[1] It was also the first full year for the state's new National Monument, the *Tugu Negara*, which opened on 8 February 1966. The date for commemorating the country's fallen in all previous conflicts had also changed by now, from Remembrance Day in November, to *Hari Pahlawan* (Warriors or Heroes Day) on the first Sunday of August. It would eventually settle upon 31 July, this being the anniversary of the official end of the Malayan Emergency.

Every year on *Hari Pahlawan*, dignitaries and members of the security forces would gather around the *Tugu Negara*, with its statue of five Malay warriors standing over two slain communist fighters. The front page of the *Straits Times* described the ceremony held at the *Tugu Negara* on Sunday 4 August 1968. At 0900 hours, the Malaysian flag was lowered. Eight buglers, from the 3rd Malaysian Rangers and the Royal Malaysian Police, sounded the last post. For 15 minutes, wreaths were laid for various units, and then a poem of peace or *Doa Selamat* was read out. Finally, the flag was raised again, and the parade marched off. In that year, ceremonies elsewhere — in Penang, Ipoh and Teluk Anson (today's Teluk Intan) — still used the old, colonial-era cenotaphs, but with the new date. The *Straits Times'* front page ran the story alongside a photograph, in which a Malay Regiment soldier stands in front of the national monument, head bowed, as a wreath is laid.[2] The period around Heroes Day also became the new focus for raising funds to assist veterans (in succession to 11 November as "poppy day"),[3] and for related activities by the Ex-Services Association of Malaysia (now known as *Persatuan Bekas Tentera Malaysia*, PBTM). While the PBTM represented all ethnicities, it excluded anyone who had fought under communist leadership, whether as anti-Japanese guerrillas in 1942–1945, or in the Malayan Emergency.[4]

So a new postcolonial form of national monument, a new date, and a new form of commemoration had emerged. This was matched by the expansion of Malaya (independent on 31 August 1957) to Malaysia (formed 16 September 1963 by the addition of Singapore, Sabah and Sarawak). With Singapore's separation on 9 August 1965, Malaysia settled into its final form, as 13 states and settlements.

By 1967, then, Malaysia had settled into its enduring postcolonial form, and into an equally entrenched mode of politics. Cheah Boon Kheng has argued that the latter revolved around a core "Malay nation-state". The state was taken to embody and represent *ketuanan Melayu* (Malay political primacy), with subordinate accommodation of other communities' interests.[5] This primacy was entrenched in the political force which held uninterrupted power from independence. That force was the Alliance of three communal parties (Malay, Chinese and Indian), reinvented in 1973 as the broader *Barisan Nasional*.

The Alliance/*Barisan* was a combination of one predominant Malay party — the United Malays National Organisation (UMNO) — with multiple parties representing other communal groups. The constitution and various political pacts, as well as electoral logic, ensured that UMNO remained dominant, and Malay rights as the *Bumiputra* or sons of the soil remained legally entrenched. In return, other communities were able to secure concessions by elite accommodation within the Alliance/*Barisan*. They also gained from the nature of the political pact, which assumed that Malaysia was, and would continue to be, a plural society. That is, a society where different groups meet in the marketplace but do not "mingle", but rather retain their distinct cultures and ethnicities. That assumption meant that, while Malay — as *Bahasa Melayu* — remained the National Language, and Malay culture the predominant flavouring for national institutions, other communities continued to be left spaces for their own cultures and languages. Independence did not result in homogenisation. Hence, Chinese- and Tamil-language primary schools continued, alongside Malay-language national schools. More importantly, for us, it meant that separate Chinese and Indian deathscapes and commemoration continued, alongside Malay-dominated national remembrance.

National War Memory in a Malay-Dominated Plural Society

War memory in Malaysia continued to reflect the plural society of the nation-state, in which the different Malay, Chinese, and Indian communities essentially lived separate lives. The terrible events of May 1969 — the May 13 Incident — further cemented these divisions. Following a major fall in the UMNO vote in General Elections, opposition rallies in Kuala Lumpur sparked off several nights of racial killings. The official death toll was 196. Tunku Abdul Rahman resigned in favour of a National Operations Council. By 1971, democracy had been restored, but a "New Economic Plan" or NEP was also instituted, which increased Malay rights and aspired to gradually secure 30 per cent of all capital to Malays. Discussion of sensitive areas of Malay rights was forbidden, and the Internal Security Act — allowing for preventive detention without trial — was made available to enforce the new policies. The post-colonial state had chosen to further entrench the plural society inherited from colonial times.

Leaders of Malaysian public opinion remained open about how they continued to view their country as a plural society, despite decades of "nation-building". As late as 2007, Abdul Rahman Arshad, a former Director-General of Education, concluded that "Malaysia has become a plural society divided by many races, religions and cultures".[6] He even referred back to how much Malaysia resembled J.S. Furnivall's textbook concept of a colonial plural society, rather than a nation-state.[7] Syed Husin Ali, the Deputy President of the People's Justice Party (*Parti Keadilan Rakyat*, PKR) opposition, noted the same thing in 2008. He wrote that "most Malays do not know Chinese values very well and most Chinese are quite ignorant of Malay values, despite the fact that they have been living side by side for so long".[8]

So Malaysia retained "a Malay-dominated plural society".[9] The Malay-dominated state sought to ensure that national level history and culture was, and is, dominated by the idea of *ketuanan Melayu*.[10] Malaysian history textbooks also assert the concept of *ketuanan Melayu* in public life.[11] Other ethnic groups are left to themselves, without the sponsorship of the state, to write their own histories, to nurture their own cultures, and to commemorate their own wartime past.

Chinese War Memories in a Malay-Dominated Plural Society

The remembrance of the largest group of war dead — Chinese civilians killed in the *sook ching* massacres — had developed quite separately from the colonial state. It now remained outside of national commemoration. Remembrance of this group continued to be managed by Chinese families, clans and chambers of commerce, with the latter two maintaining monuments to Chinese *sook ching* victims. Those deathscapes are a special reflection of Chinese identity, with their ornate Chinese inscriptions and imagery reflecting the closeness of the Chinese to their homeland in the 1940s, when most such monuments were created. Most reside in Chinese cemeteries, or on community land, with dedications mostly in Chinese characters.

Under the idea of "Malay primacy", the wartime massacres of the Chinese cannot easily be integrated into the national narrative of the war. It is worthwhile comparing Malaysia's war commemorative sites associated with the *sook ching* to Singapore's Civilian War Memorial. The latter was not precisely what Singapore's Chinese had sought. They had wanted a specifically Chinese monument, for the overwhelmingly Chinese victims of the *sook ching* of February 1942. Instead, the state remoulded their project in a memorial which was opened in 1967, and dedicated to all civilian war dead. Where the Malaysian Government left the Chinese to themselves, the Singapore Government part "nationalised" Chinese commemoration. The Singapore state also placed the nationalised war monument at the very heart of the city.

During the 1960s, by contrast, Chinese deathscapes in Malaysia remained in specifically Chinese spaces, almost sealed off from non-Chinese Malaysia. Chinese communities continued to look after their communally based monuments, and to organise ceremonies at *sook ching* war memorials which originated in the 1940s.

The late 1960s saw Malaysia's Chinese continue previous commemorative practices, albeit with a decreasing desire to use them to assert a connection with China. The cementing of Chinese communist rule, and various anti-landlord campaigns and then the Cultural Revolution, lessened the sense of physical connection. The ongoing Cold War also reduced trade and family contact between Malaysia and communist China. By the 1970s, Malaysian Chinese commemorative practices seemed to have settled down. The signing of the 1967 "Goodwill Payment Agreement" between Malaysia and Japan had "settled" the "blood debt" issue. The Kuala Lumpur edition of the *Straits Times* expressed its belief afterwards that "the admiration of Japan's economic achievements, together with the good deportment of the Japanese Government and the passage of time, has healed the scars of the Pacific War". That, at least, was the hope of the government.[12]

With Prime Minister Tunku Abdul Rahman having made it clear that he would brook no more compensation demands, and some Japanese investment, it seemed as if wartime wounds might be healing. The state felt confident enough to allow Prince Akihito of Japan to visit Malaysia in 1970. He was welcomed by large crowds. The *Straits Times* reported children waving rising sun flags at him. Whether many Chinese were included amongst these onlookers, the *Straits Times* did not say.[13] Not since the Occupation had so many Japanese flags been in Malaysia. The reasons for his warm welcome were clear. Prince Akihito was thanked by Malaysian representatives, notably in the underdeveloped states of Kedah and Perlis, for Japan's investments.[14]

The state's desire to court Japan intensified over the 1970s and 1980s. In December 1981, Dr Mahathir Mohamad, the new Prime Minister (July 1981 to 2003), adopted a "Look East Policy". This emphasised the need to learn from Japan, and to secure Japanese investment and knowhow. Within two years, Mahathir had secured Mitsubishi participation in the establishment of a national car venture: Proton.[15]

In the face of this courting of Japan, resentment amongst Chinese of the wartime generation remained largely unvoiced. In October 1982, the Malaysian Chinese Association (MCA)-owned English language newspaper, the *Star*, did highlight the issue, albeit gently. It printed a letter in which Robert Tan of Malacca wrote: "By all means 'Look East', but for goodness sake not at the expense of re-opening the wounds of the Japanese Occupation. A great number of Malaysians still remember that they lost their loved ones for no rhyme nor reason between 1942–1945".[16] The strong sense of victimhood that the Singapore editions of the *Nanyang Siang Pau* and *Sin Chew Jit Poh* expressed were, in addition, echoed by their Malaysian counterparts of the same name.

That sense of victimhood might have continued merely to simmer, but events in the 1980s and early 1990s dictated otherwise. Singapore's rapid development had seen most *sook ching* mass graves there excavated in the 1960s. In Malaysia, many of these mass graves went undisturbed until the 1980s. Then, in 1982, exhumations began on a large scale in Negeri Sembilan. Within a short time, the mass graves of thousands of

Chinese *sook ching* victims were being exhumed. These exhumations, and the emotions they stirred, would continue for some years.

One of the most dramatic exhumations was at Titi near Jelebu. The mass graves of 1,474 Chinese villagers killed at Joo Loong Loong in Jelebu, and 600 from Kuala Pilah, were uncovered. Their remains were reburied under large memorials in Chinese cemeteries.[17] These exhumations received wide coverage in the main Malaysian Chinese newspapers, the *Nanyang Siang Pau*, the *China Press*, and the *Sin Chew Jit Poh*, and in the MCA-owned, English-language *Star*. Many of these articles were accompanied by gruesome pictures of skulls and bones being dug up, sometimes with relatives looking on. Grief was resurrected in the most vivid and awful way.[18]

The continuing exhumation of Negeri Sembilan victims contributed to a resurfacing of Chinese feelings that blood debt had still not been inadequately requited. When the 50th anniversary of the Fall of Singapore came round in February 1992, a group of Malaysian Chinese organisations lodged a new compensation claim with the Japanese Ambassador. They asked for $320 million as payment for the 5,000 people of Negeri Sembilan massacred by the Japanese.

The Malay state was indifferent to such claims. In August 1994, Prime Minister Mahathir even urged his Japanese counterpart Murayama Tomiichi to "stop apologising for wartime crimes committed about 50 years ago".[19] Mahathir's view was very much in accord with the opinion — held by many Malays — that the Occupation was a time of heightened political consciousness and developing Malay nationalism. That, in the words of the KMM's Mustapha Hussain:

> the Japanese Occupation ... left something positive, a sweet fruit to be plucked and enjoyed only after the surrender ...[20]

In this context, the state showed no interest in supporting Chinese memory work. In 1995, it was the representatives of the Chinese organisations of Malaysia, alone, without the government, who marked the civilians who had died in the war. They did so at ceremonies in the Chinese cemeteries where, in the late 1940s, Chinese community groups had constructed their memorials to massacre victims.[21]

National War Memory under Mahathir

Under Mahathir's Prime Ministership (1981–2003), there was no attempt to reincorporate the memories of the other ethnic groups into a national war memory. Mahathir's book on the need to boost Malay performance, *The Malay Dilemma* (1970), had been deemed so sensitive that it remained banned until the first months of his premiership, and he was temporarily excluded from UMNO. It assumed that "hereditary and environmental factors" — including inbreeding in rural Malays — had been "so debilitating" that Malays required intensified "constructive protection" to improve them.[22]

Mahathir was committed to accelerating Malay progress under the NEP. In addition, he reasoned that it was easier to redistribute national wealth towards Malays if economic development accelerated. In his search for sources of higher economic growth, he had developed a deep admiration of Japan. This resulted in him instituting a "Look East Policy" early in his premiership. This tendency to see Japan as a positive example would inhibit any development of the sentiment that Malaysians had endured common suffering under the Japanese.[23] According to Malaysian historian Abu Talib Ahmad: "Between 1981–2002 the policy of the Mahathir administration was to downplay the negative aspects of a Japanese occupation ... the question of a Japanese apology for what happened during 1942–1945 was never an issue".[24]

The rise of key former *pemuda* within the ranks of UMNO, who might be expected to have more positive opinions about the war's legacy, also coloured views of the war. Several such figures, who had quietly been absorbed by UMNO in the late 1940s–1950s, were rising to prominence. Ghafar Baba, a former member both of the KMM and MNP, had become a Minister as early as 1970. Under Mahathir, he became Deputy Prime Minister from 1987–1993.[25] Ghafar encouraged the Malaysian press to write about wartime experiences.[26]

This greater receptiveness to accounts of wartime cooperation with Japan reflected a broader shift in attitudes. Mahathir's contrast to his more Anglophile predecessors could scarcely have been starker. He was critical of Western countries (especially Britain) for their past (and present) colonial tendencies, while praising Japan as an Asian friend.[27] Mahathir's predecessors as Malaysia's prime minister — Tunku Abdul Rahman, Abdul Razak, and Hussein Onn — had remained friendly towards Britain, if not Anglophile. Under them, Malays who had experienced the Occupation as a time of national awakening had mostly kept quiet.

Mahathir, by contrast, confronted Britain head-on. On 7 September 1981, the Malaysian Government bought out a colonial-era firm, Guthrie, in a "dawn raid" on the London Stock Exchange. Such buyouts helped the Government's policy of ensuring that *bumiputras* acquired at least 30 per cent of country's capital. The British Government viewed the method of takeover as a breach of the spirit of the rules, which they then changed. Mahathir in turn interpreted this as an attempt to make more takeovers difficult. He was also incensed at hikes in university fees which affected Malaysian students in the UK. In October 1981, Mahathir responded, announcing that, all else being equal, the Malaysian Government would prefer to buy non-British goods. This "Buy British Last" policy lasted from 1981 to April 1983. There was a thawing of relations afterwards, until another spat in 1994, over complicated aid and trade deals linked to the Pergau Dam. Taken as a whole, these actions made it abundantly clear that Malaysia really had "looked East".[28]

With government attitudes to Britain and Japan changed so radically, it is scarcely surprising that those who had cooperated with Japan in the war now received a more sympathetic hearing. Some felt encouraged enough to publish memoirs.[29] Senior UMNO politicians now openly endorsed ideas the Malay nationalists had held about the Occupation. The views of people such as Abdullah Ahmad, born in 1933, were given prominence in the state-run media. In 2001, in a piece marking 60 years since the beginning of the Occupation, Abdullah Ahmad argued that the Japanese "were Asian, like us ... they induced the germ of an aspiration" that meant "for my generation the ending of the Occupation was the beginning of nascent Malay nationalism".[30] He gave voice to such sentiments as a member of UMNO and editor-in-chief of the major English-language daily, the *New Straits Times* (2001–2003).

The change in tone reached into education. Malaysian history textbooks were rewritten in 1990 by its Ministry of Education. In discussing the Occupation, the new textbooks airbrushed the *sook ching* massacres of Chinese out of their narrative.[31] The textbooks, as revised again in 2004, carried accounts of how the Occupation strengthened Malay nationalism through encouraging the KMM and Ibrahim Yaacob, with policies of "Asia for Asians". Alongside Ibrahim Yaacob were stories of Lieutenant Adnan and the Malay Regiment, who were also portrayed as representing Malay nationalism, in their case through emphasising Malay martial qualities.[32]

The textbooks now presented national history as starting with the 15th-century Malacca Sultanate. The Sultanate was presented as a golden age of Malay culture and achievement. Malay power is then interrupted by European colonisation. The Occupation is, in this scheme, seen mainly as interrupting British control, accelerating the awakening Malay nationalism, and leading towards greater Malay unity under UMNO. The Occupation becomes a major stepping stone on the road to independence, and towards a new, postcolonial golden age for Malays. There is little or no space in this for any examination of collaboration and nuances, or for victims, whether Malays and Indians sent to labour on the Burma-Thailand Railway, or Chinese villagers massacred in the *sook ching*.[33]

The changes were making it more difficult to reconcile Malay and non-Malay memories. They were, however, allowing the KMM and more conservative Malay memories of the war to be partly reconciled. The personnel of KMM and the Malay Regiment could now be presented as both contributing to the growth of nationalism in the war, though they had been on opposite sides in 1942.

This reconciliation was given prominence in 1996, when Malaysia's new *Muzium Sejarah Nasional* (National Museum of History) was opened in Kuala Lumpur. This made both the KMM's Ibrahim Yaacob and the Malay Regiment's Lieutenant Adnan nationalists fighting for Malaysia. Of the two, Lieutenant Adnan was given the greater prominence. He featured in an exhibit of "*Tokoh Pejuang*: Patriots", which comprised portraits of seven Malay warriors presented as "catalysts towards the rise of the spirit of nationalism". The exhibit claimed that "the spirit of nationalism or national struggle" was "pioneered by the[se] Malay patriots". A large photograph of Lieutenant Adnan sat among a gallery of figures who had rebelled against the British in Pahang from 1891–1895: Tok Gajah, Tok Janggut, Mat Kilau, and Dato' Bahaman. One of the other portraits was of Rosli Dhobi, an anti-colonialist rebel who assassinated the colonial governor of Sarawak in 1949. Then there was Sergeant Jamil bin Mohd Shah, the Malay police officer in command of Bukit Kepong police station which fought to the last man and woman against an attack from a large force of communist guerrillas in 1950, during the Malayan Emergency.

The oddness of placing Lieutenant Adnan among rebels was noticed by some Malaysian historians. Abu Talib Ahmad attributed Lieutenant Adnan's inclusion in this collection of Malay patriots as due to the influence the Ministry of Defence.[34] All the patriots shown were warriors, rather than political leaders. This exhibit placed these patriots in the tradition of Hang Tuah, whose larger than life form, cast on a massive bronze panel, greeted you as you entered the museum.

Plate 9.1 National Museum of History (1996–2007), Kuala Lumpur

With the casting was his famous slogan: *"Ta' Melayu Hilang Di Dunia* (Never shall the Malay race vanish from the face of the earth)".

The Museum of National History also had an Occupation exhibit. This portrayed both Lieutenant Adnan and Ibrahim Yaacob as Malay heroes. Large portraits of them dominated the museum's panel on Malay nationalism during the Occupation. Images of members of the Malay Regiment and the KMM also featured on this panel, which proclaimed that:

> The rise of nationalism among the Malays was inspired indirectly by the Japanese. The mere fact that the Japanese, an Asian force, managed to overthrow the likes of Russia and the British, two major superpowers at the time, incited the Malays' spirit of nationalism. Meanwhile the opportunities given by the Japanese for the Malays to get involved in administration matters made them realise in fact that they were capable of governing their own nation.

The Museum of National History at Merdeka Square (1996–2007) was moved into the National Museum in November 2007, providing some material for the national history gallery there.[35]

The Museum of National History's displays had been creative with the history of both the loyalist Malay Regiment and the KMM. Yet the Malaysian Ministry of Defence was to take this attempt to reconcile opposites further still. It commissioned a film about *Leftenan Adnan*, which was released in August 2000. In this, Lieutenant Adnan is portrayed as a strident Malay nationalist. The script is laden with references to Malay nationalism and martial tradition. The young Adnan is told by Tok Sunat, the circumcision doctor, that "Once you've grown up, may you become a national warrior, carry on the legacy of our forefathers, and continue fighting to defend our religion, race and motherland. Do not take it lightly, this duty is laid down upon you".

The celluloid Adnan (played by Malay actor Hairie Othman), tells his brother that he is fighting not for the British Empire, but for Malay nationalism, which he dates back to the independent Malay kingdoms of the past: "All this while, we have allowed outsiders to be custodians to our motherland. We allowed the whites to defend it without questioning their underlying motives for doing so. This is the land our forefathers bled and died for. I should be the one to preserve it, defend it. That is why I decided to join the army". Later, Adnan tells his troops that:

> Our history has shown that we once invaded the archipelago. We were capable of building huge empires, building big ships, bigger than those made by the Portuguese. That's before we were occupied. People had started to see our potential, our strength. That is why they were afraid when we demanded what is rightfully ours. With great difficulty did the Sultan of Perak, the Yang di-Pertuan Besar of Negeri Sembilan, Raja Chulan and the Undang Lauk Rembau struggle to establish the Malay Regiment because they knew that the Malay race was capable of shaking the world. Remember, the Malay race is free and sovereign. And the Malay race was also the one which invented the idiom *biar putih tulang, jangan putih mata* ['better white bones than white eyes' meaning 'death before dishonour'].

In this way, a young Lieutenant Adnan, serving under British officers, in a Regiment where several officers were executed in 1942 for refusing to denounce their loyalty, is given forthright anti-colonial speeches.

Plate 9.4   *Paloh* poster

Embun was the first film to be produced under the Malaysia's government film financing programme that had been established in 2001. *Paloh*, the second film under this scheme, also dealt with the Occupation. It was released on 10 July 2003, in the lead up to national day.[49] *Paloh* was set in the Johor town of the same name in the last few months of the Occupation, when there was incessant conflict between the Japanese and the MPAJA.

Paloh was made by director Adman Salleh, with Malaysian historian Cheah Boon Kheng as a historical consultant. Adman was explicit that "Paloh to me is a nation building effort. It is not just a movie ..."[50] Mohammed Shariff Ahmad, Director General of the National Development Film Corporation, argued that "it is important for the Government to give people well-crafted movies with strong messages — especially patriotism — at the forefront".[51]

The film represented a brave — if not audacious — attempt to tackle one of the most divisive aspects of the war, namely, the intercommunal clashes that occurred towards its end. In 1986, Mahathir had insisted that Japanese rule had "only widened" the already entrenched "gap between one community and another".[52] In so doing, he had vividly recalled the last days of the Occupation, when:

> The defeat of the Japanese and the delay on the part of the British in sending troops to take power in the Malay States gave the opportunity to communists guerrillas, who were almost 100 percent Chinese, to commit atrocities against people of various communities. For the Malays, these atrocities deepened their hatred of the Chinese. The Chinese felt the same towards the Malays. Several bloody incidents took place between Malays and Chinese. The Indians, in the meantime, were so absorbed in the struggle for independence in India that they remained outside the political movement in Malaya, as if they were not there at all.[53]

By 2003, however, Mahathir was approaching retirement. He would hand the premiership over to Abdullah bin Ahmad Badawi in October 2003. *Paloh*, meanwhile, attempted to reframe and detoxify the inter-communal violence of the late war period. *Paloh* tried to do this by showing personal connections cutting across ethnic and political divides and tragedies.[54]

The film's plot centres on what is said to be a "real life" romance between a female Chinese member of the resistance, Siew Lan, and Ahmad, a Malay soldier from the volunteer army working at the Paloh Police Station. Siew Lan's father Ah Meng is portrayed as a leader of the MPAJA around Paloh.[55]

The film focuses on events in the lives of Ahmad and the Malay members of the Japanese volunteer army billeted at Paloh Police Station.

At the beginning, Japanese and Korean commanders tell their Malay subordinates to kill a Chinese family suspected of aiding the resistance. When they find the father, the bloodthirsty Captain Kim Jung tells his Malay soldiers: "I want you to kill that Chinese with your bayonet ... what are you waiting for?" For the first time, a major Malay film is dealing with anti-Chinese atrocities, and portrays Malay volunteers as horrified by Japanese actions. Ahmad finds the Chinese man's wife and her children hiding in a concealed underground compartment. Hushing them — "Be quiet! The Japanese will kill you" — Ahmad tells his comrade, "We don't have to tell the captain about them, Sergeant".

The film nevertheless shies away from a simplistic presentation. A Japanese soldier finds the mother and children and kills them. The Malay soldiers then reluctantly bayonet to death the father.

As the movie progresses, it reveals that the Malay soldiers have joined the volunteer army to get extra rations. They line up for parade half asleep, and secretly cooperate with the MPAJA, mostly due to personal connections. Thus, Siew Lan is sent by her MPAJA father to spy on Ahmad and his comrades, but instead falls in love with Ahmad. Overwhelmed with guilt, she attempts suicide by drinking acid, but is found by Malay soldiers, and saved by traditional Malay medicine.

In explaining how Malays and Chinese came to clash in the last months of the war, *Paloh* addresses the Japanese massacre of Chinese civilians. Osman, a Malay intellectual, is made to explain the orgy of communal violence in 1945 by reference to the earlier massacre of Chinese:

> The Japanese vented their vengeance on the Chinese Malaya. Almost 60,000 Chinese were murdered during the *sook ching* massacre of 1941 [sic, 1942]. The time has come for the Chinese to get even. When Force 136 began to support their guerrilla movement chaos reigned. Those suspected of working for the Japanese were ruthlessly murdered in the September of 1945. The people of Malaya were forced to live in hardship and poverty as a result of the power struggle between the Japanese and British Empires.

The script thus blames the Japanese and British for this violence, not the Chinese or Malays. This shifting of blame becomes the nation-building theme of the movie. Ahmad's father gives a similar view of developing events in 1945:

> If the Japanese surrender, the British will return, but the communists will still be here. If the Japanese don't kill the communists,

the British will. If the communists don't kill the Japanese they will kill the British. Either way it is the same thing all over again. What difference does it make?

Thus, older members of the Malay and Chinese communities are made to blame circumstance, not Malays and Chinese, for the violence.

The film also suggests the need for Malays and Chinese to reunite. Ahmad and some of his comrades attend a meeting with Malay community leaders. After prayers are said, one Nur Ariffin says to Ahmad: "Do you realise the Japanese are no better than the British?" Ahmad replies that he and his friends are "not serious" and joined for extra rations. Nur Ariffin then criticises KMM leader Ibrahim Yaacob for not objecting to the Japanese ban on the KMM, and for accepting the rank of Lieutenant Colonel in the *Giyugun*. He adds: "We must fight for independence". Later, Puteh, one of the Malay soldiers at the Paloh Police Station, is killed. Nur Ariffin muses that: "Puteh died for a lost cause ... far better to be a communist. At least the communists are fighting for our country against the Japanese and the British". After the war ends, he himself joins the communists, in order to fight for independence.

In *Paloh*, there is a determined attempt to show personal connections between Malays and Chinese overcoming politics, despite strains. Siew Lan's father, Ah Meng, tells Ahmad that he owes Ahmad two lives. One life because Ahmad saved the life of his daughter, and a second because Ahmad saved the life of his son. Ahmad extracts an agreement that Ah Meng will not harm the Malay soldiers at the Paloh Police Station. The MPAJA, however, are desperate to get hold of the guns stored there because the British have not dropped weapons as promised. They attack the Paloh Police Station and kill several men, including Ahmad's best friend, Puteh. Ahmad then confronts the MPAJA leaders. He heads towards Siew Lan's father, Ah Meng. Seeing Ahmad go off with the gun, Nur Ariffin sighs and says: "Now we begin killing each other. This is the result of the power struggle between the British and the Japanese".

Ahmad duly confronts the MPAJA. Lying in hospital after the fight, he muses that, "We're all victims caught ... Ah Meng was just fighting for his oppressed people's rights. We would do the same if it happened to our people". The horrors of the communist-led MPAJA reign of terror are played out at the end of the film with mass executions by the communists.

The film also extends to the postwar Emergency. After the war, Ahmad joins the communist 10th Regiment of Malays, in order to search for Siew Lan. She is now in the jungles along the Malaya-Thailand border, having been forced to recant her affair with Ahmad. The film ends with Ahmad and Siew Lan finally united in the jungle, under attack from the British.

Paloh was perhaps too daring for Malay audiences bred on stories of the communists as the main enemy. When *Paloh* was released in July 2003, the film confused audiences, and for some only seemed to reinforce perceptions of the race-based violence of the time. The film had cost the Malaysian government 4 million ringgit, but raked in just 140,000 ringgit at the cinemas that year. The recurrent use of flash-backs made the storyline difficult to follow. "*Paloh* is a very heavy movie and many viewers were furious — they walked out of the cinemas," observed Janet Abishegam, a teacher. Malaysian film critics were more receptive. "It is the first thinking Malay movie — it is deep and com-plex, but viewers did not have the patience or depth to understand *Paloh*," said Bismee S., writing for the *Sun*. Bismee added that *Paloh* "asked questions about Chinese-Malay race relations that no movie had asked before ... sensitive questions about contemporary history and has helped to bring better understanding between the races that make up this multicultural nation ... for the first time, a mainstream movie questioned the accepted view of the historical conflict between Malays and Chinese and gave credit to the role of the communists in the inde-pendence struggle and highlighted the atrocities committed by the Japa-nese soldiers". [56]

As a piece of nation-building, *Paloh* had failed, because it did not win a big enough audience, or win over enough of those who did see it. On a more positive note, the Malaysian film finance corporation noted that it was the first movie to have 40 per cent of the cast as non-Malay.

The Changing Context for Commemoration: *Reformasi*

By 2003, the political context for commemoration was shifting, raising the issue of "Malay unity" versus the need for *Reformasi*. *Reformasi* arose from 1998, when Deputy Prime Minister and heir apparent for the top post, Anwar Ibrahim, was ousted by Premier Mahathir. He was then tried and jailed for alleged abuse of power. Anwar was a poster boy for moderate Islam, and for reform of the corruption and nepotism that sometimes attached to licensing, contracts, and government management of "Malay rights". In the wake of the Asian financial crisis of 1997, many were ready for a challenge to UMNO's primacy, and Anwar's arrest provided a figurehead and impetus.

Anwar's arrest sparked the formation of *Parti Keadilan Nasional* (PKN, the National Justice Party), which then tried to cement a new, cross-communal coalition to rival the *Barisan Nasional*. It united with *Parti Islam Se-Malaysia*, a traditionalist Islamic party representing Malays, and the Democratic Action Party (DAP), a party which competed with the MCA for Chinese votes.

The coalition was an unsteady mixture, and until Anwar's release from prison in 2004 lacked a political maestro to direct it. Anwar's wife, Wan Azizah, acted more as an emotional lightning rod for protest votes, than as the sort of skilled operator the coalition needed. Consequently, the coalition's fortunes rose and fell in waves. In the wake of the Asian financial crisis, PKN took several seats in the 1999 General Elections, reducing UMNO to less than 50 per cent of the Malay vote for the first time. But Mahathir's retirement in October 2003, in favour of the Abdullah bin Ahmad Badawi, briefly reignited hopes that the *Barisan* could reform itself, and reunify the core Malay vote. Abdullah Ahmad Badawi's father was a religious teacher and founder-member of UMNO, and he himself had a reputation as an honest administrator. In the 2004 elections, PKN, rebranded as PKR (*Parti Keadilan Rakyat*, People's Justice Party), took just one seat, that of Wan Azizah. Briefly, Abdullah Badawi appeared to revive UMNO's fortunes.

Paloh was thus issued in the midst of a tussle over the political future of the country, over the Malay vote, and over how far the nation could be adjusted to better accommodate non-Malay views.

In addition, Abdullah Ahmad Badawi's premiership did not flow smoothly. Within a couple of years Anwar was free and working his magic again, and the hoped for reforms were proving non-existent or disappointing. The 2008 General Elections confirmed the worst fears of UMNO. The opposition PKR took 31 seats, the *Barisan Nasional* lost its two-thirds' majority (necessary to make changes to the constitution). From now on, Anwar tried to raise the spectre of an eventual constitutional overthrow of the *Barisan*, in order to leverage more votes and supporters. It was in this context, of a heightened competition for the Malay vote, and roller-coaster politics, that Chinese made a concerted attempt to increase national-level recognition of the MPAJA from 2003.

The additional context for this attempt was the ending of insurgency by communists who had lingered on at the border since 1960, and the end of the global Cold War. The insurgency was formally ended by a peace agreement of December 1989, and by 1990, the international Cold War was over. Communist Party leader Chin Peng, operating from Thailand, China and Hong Kong, now gave speeches, engaged academics, and wrote his memoirs, all the while developing the case that the communists were anti-Japanese heroes, who according to him also accelerated independence. It is notable that one of the — unsuccessful — communist requests in 1989 negotiations had been that the monument they had tried to blow up on 27 August 1975[57] — the *Tugu Negara* — should be replaced.[58] In the "Peace Villages" in southern Thailand, where many communists settled after 1989, the *Tugu* was for some an object of hatred. 80-year-old Malay communist veteran Shukor Ismail saw it as epitomising the government

> living that lie. In the history books, it's in their national monument
> look at *Tugu Negara*. What do you see? You see British soldiers
> [sic: figures garbed as Malay security force personnel] kicking local
> fighters. That does not reflect the correct historical fact.[59]

Nilai: Chinese Attempts to Reintegrate their "Heroes" into National Commemoration

The ideas that the MCP had accelerated independence, and that Chinese had contributed both as anti-Japanese heroes and as fighters for decolonisation, had a wider purchase amongst Malaysia's Chinese. Members of the Chinese community were soon making their own efforts to increase recognition for the MPAJA in particular. These would lead to the erection of two monuments, at Nilai Memorial Park, just outside Kuala Lumpur in the state of Negeri Sembilan.

The first of these was a new monument for the "September Martyrs". This was a replacement for the *Jiu Yi Lieshi Jinianbei* (September 1st Martyrs' Memorial) unveiled on 1 September 1946 (see pp. 119–20). That first monument had commemorated 18 communists — including leaders and bodyguards — killed in a Japanese ambush on 1 September 1942. In communist parlance, this was also known as the "9-1 Incident". 1 September had become the most emotionally charged date in the communist calendar, involving as it did mass martyrdom, and yet also heroic resistance, as surrounded comrades fought to escape multiple encirclement.

As Chapter 3 showed, 9-1 became the communist equivalent of the colonial Remembrance Day, or the Malaysian *Hari Pahlawan*. In June 1949, the MCP's Central Committee had fixed it as "Revolutionary Martyrs Day". Henceforth, it was celebrated every year by fighters in the jungle, with recitations of the heroic story and the names of the martyrs, silence for the dead, and invocation for all present fighters to show the same heroic determination, even against apparently hopeless odds.

The difference, of course, was that hunted communist guerrillas could no longer, after June 1948, access the September Martyrs monument they had erected in 1946. Worse still, in the 1990s, the site was redeveloped, and the monument put into storage. So at the dawn of the 21st century, the 9-1 martyrs had no monument.

Now that the Cold War was over, the Chinese Assembly Halls of Kuala Lumpur and Selangor favoured making MPAJA commemoration more public, and significant numbers of MNLA veterans had returned to Malaysia under the terms of the 1989 agreements. Where the communists had control, in Princess Chulaporn Village No. 10 in Southern Thailand, they had already erected a memorial column bearing the inscription "Eternal Glory to the Martyrs" in four languages. The column stood on a three-tiered plinth, and was topped by a single five-pointed star.[60]

In Malaysia itself, the pattern of culturally distinct commemoration of the war repeated itself. A new September Martyrs monument was erected in 2003. The granite monument bore the same inscription as the original September 1st Martyrs' Memorial, except with 2003 replacing the original date of 1946. The new memorial was created at Nilai's Xiao En Yuan Memorial Park, close to Kuala Lumpur. Nilai Memorial Park is a traditional Chinese burial ground, albeit one created from 1991. The monument's setting could, therefore, almost be a metaphor for plural society. The park features artificial hills, fronted by a stream, so creating an appropriate *feng shui*.

The monument enjoyed a culturally Chinese unveiling on 7 December 2003. The opening featured speeches, and poetry recitation, almost entirely in Chinese. The ceremony was not only conducted in Chinese, but with echoes of traditional Chinese celebrations. Imitation firecrackers were set off, and incense and fruit offered by ex-fighters. The event was completed by retiring to a nearby Chinese temple for a banquet, and old-comrade's songs. This was a linguistically and culturally Chinese event, at which a non-Chinese speaker would have felt almost entirely excluded. Arguably, such a celebration was acceptable precisely because it was happening in a specifically Chinese setting, relatively

Plate 9.5 September Martyrs Memorial, Nilai, 2003

isolated from the mainstream Malay and English-language world and press. The only obviously Malay "participant" was a Malay with a camera, who participants presumed was from the Internal Security Department, carefully monitoring and filming the event without joining in.

To some extent, however, the ceremony did mark a slightly wider acceptance of the argument that the MPAJA — if not later insurgents — should be endorsed as national heroes. On hand to officiate was Datuk Donald Lim, MCA Central Committee Member and Deputy Information Minister. No overt MPAJA symbols or paraphernalia were displayed, only traditional Chinese offerings of food and joss sticks, alongside unmarked wreaths. The Minister was the first to pay his respects by offering cakes, oranges, and praying with joss sticks. Given that in the Malayan Emergency, the MCP and MCA were on opposite sides, and many MCA were targeted, the keeping of a distance between the 9-1 Martyrs and idea of the Emergency was important.[61]

The opening ceremony and reunion afterwards were attended by about 60 MPAJA veterans, many of whom had been deported or fled to China around 1948–1951. Relatively few MPAJA veterans who now lived in Malaysia and Singapore were present. The daughter of one of the Malaysian MPAJA veterans explained why. Jade Wong, daughter of Zhou Gong Yin, aged 83 (he had been involved in propaganda and newsletter production in the MPAJA Third Regiment in Negeri Sembilan and Northern Johor), described how her father had kept his wartime MPAJA experiences secret. He had not spoken of them until just before the visit. After the war, he was scared, especially when he worked as a teacher and a principal, that he would be tainted as a communist. He only saw two members of his former MPAJA Regiment after the war. Only in recent years did he feel able to identify himself as an MPAJA veteran, and try and find former comrades. Her father being too ill to attend, Jade had come from Seremban on his behalf.[62]

In the days following the 7 December 2003 ceremony, there were fundraising dinners and performances of old MPAJA songs. At these, 1,000 ringgit tables were completely sold out. These events were intended to raise funds to finance a building for the Nilai Peace Garden, and another, future monument for the MPAJA dead.

The attendance of an MCA Government minister, the successful filling of expensive fundraising events, and commentary in the Chinese press, all confirmed a widely held Chinese desire for the MPAJA to be more widely recognised as national heroes. The Chinese press commentary on 8 December 2003 affirmed that the time had now come to honour the MPAJA generation as individuals who sacrificed themselves for the future of their country.[63] Dr Ong Seng Huat, from the Nilai Memorial Park, put this sentiment elegantly, when he said of the MPAJA fighters that, "Simply, people need legends, people need legends".

The Nilai monument could not, however, achieve the desired impact on national commemoration. It was transparently a monument to communist-led fighters, honouring September 1942 martyrs who were entirely Chinese. It stood no chance of being embraced by many Malays, let alone UMNO members. Some Chinese commentators, such as James Wong (ex-opposition Democratic Action Party parliamentarian and by then Malaysiakini.com journalist and analyst), wanted more. They wanted the MCP to be acknowledged as part of the nation's overall history, and as a critical force in accelerating independence. In 2004–2005, James Wong interviewed several veterans of the Emergency, produced a book of communist memoirs, and ran in-depth interviews on *Malaysiakini.com*. He stated that "Like it or not, many in Malaysia and Singapore, like Rashid Maidin and Abdullah C.D [Malays who rose to senior positions within the communist party], still share … justified and justifiable pride of being true partisans in the heroic struggle against the then British colonialism, Japanese militarism and their indigenous quislings and surrogates ..."[64]

The reference to "indigenous quislings and surrogates" could suggest those MCA officials who had helped contain the Emergency. In September 2005, the tensions between DAP and others parties' versions of history exploded into online jousting. DAP International Secretary Mr Ronnie Liu Tian Khiew posted an article on the DAP Youth site entitled "The Real Fighters for Merdeka". This stated that UMNO leaders had been "servants of the British government", textbooks were skewed, and the role of communist insurgents — the real heroes of independence — underplayed. By 9 September, an enraged UMNO Youth had struck back, posting the cover of Chin Peng's book, *Alias Chin Peng*, online, but with a crucial difference. Onto it were superimposed the heads of Mr Ronnie Liu, Karpal Singh, Anwar Ibrahim and other opposition leaders, with the legend "*Komunis selamanya* (Forever Communists)". Legal challenges were mounted by both sides, accusing Mr Liu of sedition and UMNO Youth of defamation, before both sides backed down.[65] Such rigorous exchanges are of course not unusual in the hurly burly of Malaysian politics. A cursory internet search in 2010 could reveal half a dozen such images.[66]

The question for the MPAJA and MNLA veterans, and others wanting the MCP "contribution" acknowledged was: could they force the dominant Malay politicians and academics to relent? The solution that Chinese leaders resorted to was to build another monument, also at Nilai. This was constructed in 2005–2006, and officially unveiled on the anniversary of 9-1, on 1 September 2007.

This time, the organisers were very careful to construct a monument that was *not* specifically for communist fighters. This was the "Monument in Memory of Malayan Heroes in the Resistant [sic] Movement against Japanese Invasion". After this "Peace Monument" officially opened in September 2007, the Nilai Memorial webpages explained that:

> This Monument is the centerpiece [the site uses American spelling] of the Peace Memorial Gardens. It pays homage to the people from many different countries that rose to combat the Japanese occupation. The war was the frontline of World War Two and also marked the first modern jungle war. This was the first time that the Asian, working together with the westerner, including the former Colonial army and even some foreign anti Japanese fought for the justice, peace and freedom of the world. The resistance and guerrilla warfare consisted of a diverse array of cultural groups, both Malaysians and foreigners.

Plate 9.6 "Monument in Memory of Malayan Heroes in the Resistant Movement against Japanese Invasion", Nilai

The monument is dedicated to all groups and individuals that resisted and fought the Japanese army. The monument is comprised of a center obelisk, rising from a reflective pool of water and encircled by hard pavement for gathering and contemplation. The footprint of the obelisk is borrowed from a peace mandala, and is extruded upwards into the form of a traditional four sided obelisk. The base of the obelisk will be made of black granite panels and have dedication inscriptions in different languages on each of its faces. The upper portion of the obelisk is comprised of small panels of differing shades and textures of grey granite, that are revealed only when close up to symbolise the many different individuals that came together to form a strong resistance that fought for peace and justice.[67]

How well did this work? The Malay press ran critical articles, the tenor of which was this was still a monument to communists, and to those who had later fought the state. The Chinese-owned press, whether in English or Chinese, was as a result defensive.[68] Besides which, the monument, rooted as it was in a specifically Chinese cultural and linguistic context, still could not serve the wider purposes its adherents desired.

Indeed, reintegration into national memory was probably only possible in two scenarios. First, if the *Barisan Nasional* lost power. Second, if the *Barisan's* dominant component, UMNO, was persuaded to listen. The spat between DAP Youth and UMNO Youth of 2005 showed how unlikely the latter was.[69] In late 2006 to early 2007, the response to the "Peace Memorial" was outrage from some Malay security force veterans and politicians. Datuk Seri Zainnudin Maidin, Information Minister, denounced the two Nilai monuments as regrettable in December 2006, given that the government had fought communism.[70] Mohamed Hassan, the *Mentri Besar* (Chief Minister) of Negeri Sembilan, called for their demolition, before Chinese community leaders persuaded him to relent.[71] Chinese leaders in the government disagreed with UMNO's hardline stance. Deputy Home Minister Tan Chai Ho, and Dr Chua Soi Lek (Vice-President of the MCA), protested that not all anti-Japanese fighters had been communists. Datuk Liow Tiong Lai of the MCA's youth wing added, "We are honouring them for fighting the Japanese. Whether they were members of the Malayan Communist Party (MCP) is a separate issue".[72]

Malay army veterans, such as Lieutenant Colonel (Retired) Mohd Idris Hassan thought otherwise. He asked, "How do you justify building monuments to commemorate those who fought the Japanese when there is proof that a large number of them actually committed all kinds of atrocities against the people of this country under the communist banner?"[73] Malaysian Premier Dato Abdullah Ahmad Badawi confirmed this broad approach in a forward to a pictorial history of the Emergency published in 2006. In the foreword he stated that:

> this [the Emergency] attack on Malaysia's legitimate right to govern and to determine its own future democratically is an important fact that should not be forgotten; for we cannot allow extremism and intolerance to take root in our nation.
>
> The Malayan Communist Party launched its struggle to purportedly rid British Imperialism from within our shores. However, their core belief and methods were not at all acceptable to the people of Malaya … they were also opponents of all others who did not subscribe to their ideology. They used terror as a weapon to achieve their goals.[74]

He emphasised it showed terrorists could be from any race, and that society must continue to be vigilant against threats to the peace.

It was clear that multiple forces still worked against the acceptance of the MPAJA, let alone of post-1948 insurgents, into national commemoration. They had been communist-led, while the *Tugu Negara* identified communism as the evil that had to be defeated in favour of democracy. Malay memories also identified their own community's growth in martial strength and confidence in the Emergency as a major step towards the *ketuanan Melayu*. Many security force veterans — mostly Malay — had painful memories of comrades lost or injured during the MCP/CPM's post-independence campaign of 1968–1989. Many MCA veterans, and their families, carried memories of the way the MCP had targeted civilian MCA organisers, sometimes by lobbing grenades at leaders or into their shops. Finally, in the context of the struggle between the *Barisan* (including UMNO and the MCA) and the opposition (including the PKR and the DAP), the issue was politically charged. Within the ruling coalition, the MCA could now do little more than manoeuvre for recognition of the wartime MPAJA, while trying to limit how far it was tainted by association with later insurgency. In this context, the old plural society and plural commemoration model offered a safety valve. Chinese war memory could not be "nationalised", but could be celebrated within Chinese community space, in Chinese-language papers, and at Nilai.

Indian Attempts to Revive the Veneration of their Heroes in National Memory

Indians were to have no more success than the Chinese in reintegrating their memories into the Malay-dominated national story. Indian war memory had faded from view, until by the 1980s it was scarcely visible at national level. By that time, the Association which had sought compensation for Burma-Thailand Railway labourers had (in 1973) dissolved without success. Key memory activists for the INA were, however, determined that its memory would not be allowed to die. It had a body which acted as its "memory activist". This was the Netaji Centre, established in Kuala Lumpur in 1977 as a non-profit, charitable organisation. In addition to encouraging research and publications on the INA, and raising money for scholarships for veterans' descendants, this acted as a loose association for the latter. In 1983, it sent a memorandum to the Indian Government. They requested that the Indian Government should intercede with Singapore to facilitate the re-erection of the INA Memorial, and requested that some of Bose's ashes be sent to Kuala Lumpur, to be scattered there. None of this was secured. Instead, the Singapore Government marked the INA memorial site with a large historical plaque, as one of many it installed in 1995, on the 50th anniversary of the end of the war.

As it emerged into the 21st century, the Netaji Centre claimed that there were more than 2,000 surviving IIL and INA members in Malaysia and Singapore, and more than 700 INA veterans registered with it.[75]

The Netaji Centre's Secretary by 2003 was Kalyan Ram Das (K.R. Das). Das had experienced the INA as a liberation from the humiliating feeling of being a paid mercenary to the British, and strongly believed that Bose had helped to restore pride to Indians as a whole, including plantation labourers. Indian-born Das had stayed on in India after INA service, and played a modest part in the early years of the Malayan (later Malaysian) Indian Congress (MIC), whose President (Samy P. Vellu) endorsed the Netaji Centre. Das believed that without the INA, there would have been no MIC.

In 2003, the year the 9-1 monument was unveiled at Nilai, the Netaji Centre therefore sought to increase national recognition for the INA's wartime role. It made arrangements for a major reunion of veterans. When the event kicked off on 21 October 2003, veterans gathered at Plantation House to mark the 60th anniversary of the

formation of the *Azad Hind* (Free India) Government, which had occurred on 21 October 1943. The event was mainly funded by INA
veteran Tan Sri Dato' Dr K.R. Somasundram. He was also the main
patron of the Netaji Centre, and Chairman of the National Land
Finance Cooperative Society.[76]

Plantation House provided a fitting venue. Its walls were adorned
with intricate mosaics, which pictured Indian labourers working on
rubber plantations. In this setting, Rani of Jhansi veteran Mrs P. Meena-
chee (vice-chairmen of the Netaji Centre), gave an address peppered
with Hindi INA freedom songs. She ended her speech by singing
Subramanya Bharati's Tamil poem, *Song of Freedom*:

> Let us dance in joy
> And sing of victory
> For our new found freedom
>
> Gone are the days
> When we bowed to Brahmins
> As men of virtue;
> When Aliens white
> We served as masters;
> When beggars were deemed
> Worth of our regard;
> When we in subjection
> Served the deceitful.
>
> Human voices everywhere
> Hail our freedom
> And the realisation
> That all men are equal:
> Blow the conches loud
> And proclaim this fact
> To all the world:
> The day has finally dawned
> We are all one family.[77]

The INA's claim to be the main focus of Indian community war
memories was affirmed by the attendance of: senior MIC members,
representatives from the Indian High Commission, and a delegation
from the INA organisations in India. Just a year before, on 21 April
2002, the INA and Rani of Jhansi veterans from the Netaji Centre had
visited New Delhi for a reunion there.[78] At the Malaysian INA veterans'
reunion on 21 October 2003, Dato' S. Subramanian, Deputy Minister,

Ministry of Domestic Trade and Consumer Affairs and Deputy President of the MIC, endorsed the view that "the torch of freedom movement lit by Netaji during the 2nd world war years burned brighter and stronger after the war ended and led to the freedom struggle in postwar Malaya".[79] Subramanian added how John A. Thivy, a former member of the *Azad Hind* Government, "founded the MIC to continue the Malaysian Indian struggle for independence". Subramanian suggested the MIC continued the legacy of the INA and transmitted its lessons for the younger generations. This legacy was a politically conscious and educated Indian community asserting its rights and working out, in partnership with other ethnic groups, the postcolonial destiny of the country.

At Plantation House, members of the generation who had grown up hearing the tales of the INA also spoke. Malaysian Managing Director of an environmental engineering firm, R.M. Subbiah, told how he had heard stories of the INA from his parents' generation. "I always wanted to see the elderly people who fought for independence … You all fought, ready to sacrifice your lives. You all participated in the independence movement for the future generations …"

The only problem with this stirring oratory was that there were very few younger Indians at the event, and rows of empty seats. Less than a hundred people attended, including veterans. The marginality of the INA veterans was commented upon. Some veterans suggested making a film to get younger people more interested in Bose and the INA. Subramanian, the MIC Minister, told them that the "Netaji Centre could do a lot more to make its work known to the community". At the event's dinner, Somasundram insisted that, "The history of Malaysia in the school textbooks will not be complete until the story of the INA is included".

The 2003 INA reunion reflected the nature of commemoration in a Malay-dominated plural society. The lack of support by the Malay-dominated state means that it is up to the Indian community itself to keep alive its war memory. Yet the 2003 reunion is an example of how — without integration into a state narrative and textbooks — they have to some extent slipped out of the public eye, even within their own ethnic group.

Fissures in State-Sponsored Commemoration

Malay-shaped narratives of the war remained firmly in control at state level in the early 21st century, though successive war films seemed to have less and less purchase on the public. This main narrative also became slightly more nuanced as it tried to integrate both the Malay Regiment and other loyalist anti-Japanese fighters on the one hand, and the KMM on the other, into textbooks, pronouncements and museum displays.

There were by this point two indications that this model might be vulnerable to further shifts, however slight. First, the publication of the memoirs of Malay communists complicated the simplistic Cold War era paradigm, which portrayed Malaysian communists almost solely as Chinese. Communist fighters such as Rashid Maidin told their stories as those of Malay nationalism. They talked of being inspired by 19th-century Malay rebels — such as Maharaja Lela, who killed the first British Resident J.W. Birch in 1875. They also talked of joining the postwar MNP, and fighting alongside the MPAJA and its successors as anti-British patriots. They had distinctly Malay cultural references and even forms. Hence, Rashid Maidin's memoirs began with references to early Malay nationalism, and ended not with a conclusion or return "home" (he remained in Thailand), but with his haj. That was commenced from Kuala Lumpur and undertaken with encouragement of the Malaysian administration. Again, press criticism suggested that UMNO and veterans were still not ready to absorb even Malay communist narratives openly, but the government's private behaviour nevertheless indicated a greater willingness to accept that these Malays were motivated primarily by nationalism.[80]

There was also, by 2010, a suggestion that the creeping Islamisation of the national stage had fatally undermined *Tugu Negara*'s position as the main, national commemorative monument. There had been rumblings for years that the *Tugu* was un-Islamic. Islamic monuments avoid the human form, and before the Tunku's intervention, initial plans for the *Tugu* had been more abstract. But the Tunku, who had not thought the occasional sip of whisky or bet on a horse unforgivable, had set his heart on a monument modelled on the United States Marine Corps Memorial.[81]

There had been suggestions that the laying of wreaths at such a memorial was un-Islamic, and these had already been replaced with garlands. But a Fatwa against the practices surrounding *Hari Pahlawan* stretching back to 1987 had not produced significant change.[82] These religious bans pointed out that it was un-Islamic for Muslims to pay homage "before human-like statues".[83] The National Fatwa Council and Islamic Development Department of Malaysia had indicated that "such a celebration should not be held at the site of statues of human like sculptures".[84]

Malaysia's National Fatwa Council therefore chose to reiterate that the *Tugu Negara* was an "unsuitable" venue in the wake of Najib Abdul Razak (Dato' Sri Mohd Najib bin Tun Abdul Razak) becoming Prime Minister on 3 April 2009. That same month, it recommended that celebrations be held elsewhere. By 2010, the Government was ready to act. On 25 June 2010, the Malaysian Cabinet under Prime Minister Najib agreed that Dataran Merdeka (Merdeka Square) would be used until a Dataran Pahlawan might be completed, in three years' time, at the nearby administrative centre of Putrajaya. Explaining the decision, Defence Minister Datuk Seri Dr Ahmad Zahid Hamidi said, "This shows that the prime minister (Datuk Seri Najib Razak) is sensitive to the views of the ulama, the National Fatwa Council and the study by the National Fatwa Committee. We take into account the views that holding the celebrations at the monument could lead to syiirk (polytheism, associating others with Allah) even though our intention is not to worship the National Monument".[85] It was suggested this new venue could be between 0.8–1.2 hectares (2–3 acres), and follow guidelines set by the Islamic Development Department (Jakim) and endorsed by the National Fatwa Council.[86]

Whatever the motives, the Government now seemed keen to comply with the religious rulings. For 31 July 2010, the Warriors' Day ceremony was for the first time moved to Dataran Merdeka. This includes a *padang* (green space), the colonial Secretariat Buildings, and the Selangor Club, and is the old colonial heart of the city. The main focus of *Hari Pahlawan* at Merdeka Square in 2010 was a re-enactment by the army of the Malay Regiment in the Battle of Pasir Panjang on 13–14 February 1942. The press reported that in the re-enactment, centre-stage was "a heavily outnumbered Malay platoon led by Lt Adnan Saidi" which "held off Japanese soldiers for two days until they were eventually overpowered". The audience saw an actor playing Adnan captured, "tied to a tree and bayoneted to death".[87]

This moved many spectators, one of whom, W.M. Ramli, wrote of his admiration in a letter to the *News Straits Times*: "Enacting historical scenes for public viewing would go a long way in instilling a love of country, and remind the younger generation that the peace and economic stability that we enjoy today must not be taken for granted. We owe it to the sacrifices made by members of the security forces". Ramli, despite the recent war movie flops, requested: "... more war movies".[88]

As this book was finished, it remained to be seen whether Islam could do what communism could not, and force a significant change in the form of the national monument, and whether any new monument (and ceremonies) would be any more unifying than their predecessor.[89] One thing was certain: whatever emerged was likely to bear very little relation to that of their colonial predecessor.

Conclusion

In the plural society of Malaysia, with Malay dominance in social and cultural life, and with each ethnic group essentially living separately from the others, the other ethnic groups are left to themselves to mark their own history. In Singapore, there is a strong focus on making the experiences of the different ethnic groups part of the Singapore national identity through including them in the national historical narrative, and thus domesticating them.

In contrast, the Malay-dominated state of Malaysia, driven by the idea of *ketuanan Melayu*, has striven to make Malay war memory the national war memory. In 2003, Malaysia introduced its own three- to six-month national service to bind the youths of the different ethnic groups together, and to further patriotic unity. Not surprisingly, the programme has included the screening of the movie *Leftenan Adnan* as obligatory for the 80–90,000 18-year-olds who are randomly selected each year to participate.[90] Thus, Malaysian war memory has Lieutenant Adnan and the Malay wartime nationalism firmly in the centre, with the war memories of the other ethnic groups in the periphery. This is also borne out by the failure of the film *Paloh* in 2003, with its attempt to portray personal relationships as bridging the MPAJA and Malay groups. It is also borne out by the bitter divisiveness of the debate over the Nilai Chinese monuments respectively to the MPAJA (2003), and to all anti-Japanese fighters (2007), and the marginality of the memory of the INA and the Rani of Jhansi. The key forces behind the shaping and reshaping of national commemoration were, and remain, UMNO, and mainly Malay veterans, while more recently Islamic authorities have also made interventions.

CHAPTER 10

Memory and Nation-Building in Singapore

IN THE MID-1960S, SINGAPORE'S PAP GOVERNMENT had successfully struggled to harness the war grievances of the island's Chinese, who constituted more than 77 per cent of its population.[*1] The central focus of these was the Japanese massacre of up to 25,000 Chinese on the island in 1942, in the *sook ching*.[2] To harness Chinese emotions, the PAP had had to manage two burning issues: first, how to settle what the Chinese saw as a Japanese "blood debt"; and second, how to rebury the thousands of victims exhumed in the 1960s.

Chinese had felt that postwar trials and executions of Japanese perpetrators of the *sook ching* involved such small numbers that they scarcely constituted a down payment on Japan's "blood debt". Hence, they had resolved to demand that Japan pay $50 million compensation. The Japanese insisted all claims had been settled with the postwar British administration. Prime Minister Lee Kuan Yew nevertheless secured a compromise in October 1966, by which Japan would provide $50 million, but only as a gesture. Of this, $25 million was an outright grant, and $25 million a loan. Lee insisted the money go to the state for general development, for the sake of all citizens, rather than directly to victims' families. He also insisted that Chinese organisations accept the matter was forever closed, so as not to impede Japanese investment.

The fate of the *sook ching* victims, meanwhile, had become an urgent issue from 1962, as victims began to be exhumed from more

---

[*] By 1968, slightly less than 15 per cent were Malay, and around seven per cent Indian.

292

than a hundred sites around the island. The initial demands for a specifically Chinese monument for these victims had alarmed the government. The PAP had not dared to allow opposition politicians or communal organisations to make capital out of the issue. But it had also been acutely aware that the frictions produced by brief membership of Malaysia (16 September 1963 to exit on 9 August 1965) had produced race riots in 1964, and left some tension between ethnic groups. Singapore's exit from Malaysia — whose communal politics the PAP could not reconcile with — meant that the PAP also had to construct an entirely novel, unheard of species: the Singaporean.[3]

Previous to 9 August 1965, people had thought of themselves as belonging to an ethnic or linguistic community, or as "Malayans".[4] PAP politicians had previously accepted Malay as the national language, and sought to encourage the island's residents to think of themselves as "Malayans". The PAP itself had never believed that independence was desirable, and yet now needed to build a cross-communal, united idea of what a "Singaporean" was. In this context, they had no intention of allowing major monuments or commemorative events to become divisive. They were going to control public space, and what happened in it.

Hence, the PAP had harnessed the original Chinese Chambers of Commerce proposal for a Chinese-style memorial park or monument to *sook ching* victims. It had gently shaped planning, until the end result was the Civilian War Memorial at Beach Road. With its pillars — colloquially known as the "four chopsticks" — said to represent the four main "races" or cultural streams of Singapore — Chinese, Malay, Indian and Eurasian or "other" — this was suitably abstract. Indeed, its very abstractness suited the technocratic, modernising, quasi-socialist temperament of the early PAP.

Lee Kuan Yew presented the new monument's four columns as symbolising "common suffering", and the press followed suit. In opening the monument on 15 February 1967, Lee also suggested the Fall of Singapore as the moment people had thrown off illusions of white superiority, and begun to desire independence. This now provided a satisfying date for annual services at the site, below which resided the bones of thousands of *sook ching* victims. So by the end of 1967, the war debt issue had been addressed, and the thousands of exhumed *sook ching* victims given a decent reburial, while the resulting monument had become a national, rather than a community, one.

At this point, a British announcement, made on 16 January 1968, redoubled the Government's determination to put wartime issues to sleep. Britain's Labour Government announced that it would accelerate its planned withdrawal from Singapore bases, from the mid-1970s to 1971. Thousands of Singaporeans would have to be found new jobs. The economy would lose millions of pounds, and large-scale National Service (legislated for in March 1967) became more urgent than ever.[5]

The impending challenge was all the more formidable because Singapore had high population growth, and significant unemployment. The Government also feared that newly independent neighbours might erode Singapore's position as a regional hub for trade and services. In response, the PAP planned for rapid industrialisation, and aimed to attract large-scale Foreign Direct Investment. The state introduced draconian labour laws in 1968–1971 to reassure foreign investors, and expanded education with a heavy emphasis on languages, science, mathematics and technical training. During the pragmatic 1970s, the modern history of Singapore and Malaya scarcely figured in the school syllabus, and with it any real discussion of the war and its legacy. A PAP in a blinding hurry to escape from the past   with its overcrowding, colonialism and divisions — had little time for history.

At this point, it seemed as if war memories might slowly fade. But this chapter also traces a change in PAP attitudes to remembrance from the 1980s. As the wartime generation started to retire and die, the PAP worried that younger generations would reject the discipline that had underpinned early nation-building and development.[6] They feared that people who had not known war and race riots would not appreciate what the PAP saw as the continuing need for restraint, and for limits to democracy and press freedom. Just after the war, in the 1947 census, Singapore's population had been less than one million. By 1970, it was just over two million, and by 2000, it would be more than 3.2 million excluding foreign workers. The majority of Singapore residents were increasingly postcolonial babies, detached from the "crisis years" of war, communism, Malaysia entry and exit, and British withdrawal.

The result, from the late 1980s, was that the PAP began to re-invigorate war commemoration, albeit more firmly harnessed to state agendas than ever before. This PAP desire would coincide with big anniversaries — of the beginning and end of the war in 1992, 1995, 2002 and 2005 — and with some members of the wartime generation writing memoirs. The PAP, state bodies, and a government-controlled media, also dusted off those the British had selected as heroes in the 1940s–1950s, including Lim Bo Seng and Elizabeth Choy, and looked

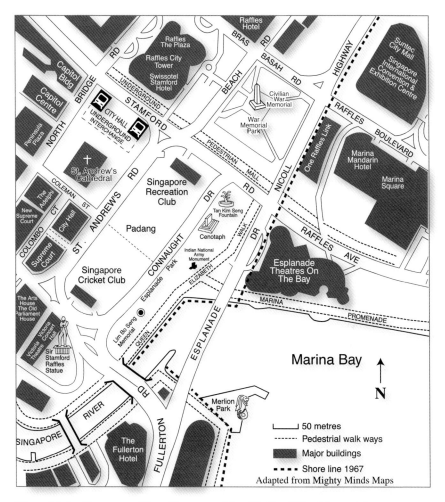

Plate 10.1   Singapore Civic Centre and its Civilian War Memorial

again to Dalforce. Like the British, the PAP looked askance at commemorating the MPAJA, but other wartime figures started to appear in
prime-time television serials. The PAP also re-emphasised history in the
school curriculum, giving it a heavy focus on the war and early postwar
years. The war years were also given special attention through infusing
"National Education" messages into teaching in schools from 1997
onwards.

Ironically, then, the same Singapore whose Government sought to
dampen and control war memory in the 1960s, would enter the 21st

century with a proliferation of museums, plaques, memoirs, and media productions about the war. It would also enter the 21st century with 15 February (from May 1997 rebranded "Total Defence Day" as part of the new "National Education" policy) as one of its main commemorative dates.[7]

Relations with Japan

One of Prime Minister Lee Kuan Yew's motives for harnessing wartime emotions had been to avoid interference with investment. While Malaysia had lasted, the PAP had hoped to achieve development through Import Substitution Industrialisation. That is, through exporting manufactures to a Malaysian free trade area, where their manufactures might push out foreign goods. Following 9 August 1965, they adapted to an Export-Oriented Industrialisation strategy, which required massive direct investment by foreign multinationals. With the Economic Development Board (EDB) working overtime to attract such companies, nothing must be allowed to disturb relations with major industrial powerhouses, such as Japan.

When Sato Eisaku, Japanese Prime Minister (1964–1972), arrived in Singapore on 25 September 1967, Lee therefore greeted him warmly. Sato was told that the people of Singapore had "no inhibitions" from their experiences during the Occupation and "that chapter is closed although not forgotten".[8] Lee stressed that, "Japanese nationals participating in Singapore's plans to industrialise had been welcomed".[9]

State visits from Japanese leaders increased. In 1970, the Japanese Crown Prince Akihito and his wife visited Singapore. This was the first time that a Japanese Crown Prince had come to Singapore since Prince Hirohito's visit in 1921.[10] At the airport, Lee greeted Prince Akihito and told Singaporeans that "Japanese and Singaporeans have got to know each other and work together".[11]

High on Akihito's schedule was a visit to the Jurong area, in the previously underdeveloped far west of Singapore. Prior to the 1960s, this area had more in common with rural Malaysia than with the urban core of the island. Now an industrial park was being carved out of wasteland and jungle. Notwithstanding the island's taming of the unions, critics feared Jurong could become a white elephant.[12] It was vital that this massive project succeed. A prominent government source had revealed that the 12,000-acre project "was to turn the West end of Jurong into a 'Little Japan' bustling with shipbuilding and repairing activities".[13] The government projected that with the help of Japanese investment, by 1980, Jurong would have 500 factories with a population of 70,000, instead of the 24,000 of 1970. Offshore islands would be joined to Jurong "to make them part of 'Little Japan' complex".[14]

Singapore was, however, looking for more than mere capital. By the 1970s, the PAP was scouring the globe for models of industrial and economic policy, and for the patterns of behaviour that made such policies work. What differentiated Singapore from other countries was not this willingness to look at Japanese models, but rather the state's ability to rapidly alter its own society and economy to accommodate them. At this time, Japanese exports, quite dramatically so in the case of motorbikes and later cars, were starting to take on western companies in their home markets. Western countries had started to ask: why is Japan so successful?

Ezra F. Vogel capitalised on this trend by publishing his influential book, *Japan as Number One: Lessons for America*, in 1979. This extracted "lessons" on the Japanese "model", for emulation. In Singapore, it was made required reading for civil servants. By 1980, Goh Keng Swee, Singapore's First Deputy Prime Minister, was extolling the book's lessons.[15] The government adopted a "Learn From Japan Campaign" to encourage workers to identify more with their company. In November 1981, Lee Kuan Yew told Tsuruta Takuhiko, executive director of the leading Japanese daily, *Nihon Keizai Shimbun*, that "I am keen to discover which parts of the Japanese system can be adapted to suit Singapore circumstances. I believe a team spirit is crucial for group success".[16]

"The Learn From Japan Campaign" was, however, disturbing for some members of the wartime generation.[17] In August 1982, PAP parliamentarian Dr Ow Chin Hock acknowledged this when speaking to a constituency audience, noting that:

> In Singapore too, there are people among the older generation who will not forgive or at least not forget. I can sense that some of them do not feel comfortable about our frequent talks of learning from Japan. They however remain silent because they accept the realities that our economic relationship with Japan has benefited Singapore.[18]

Silence implied resentment still simmered. The cloak of silence was to slowly lift, as controversies would reveal Japan unrepentant about past atrocities. The first of these was the "textbook" issue. In July 1982,

China and South Korea protested against the Japanese Ministry of Education's attempt to expunge Japanese aggression in East Asia from history textbooks. The Japanese Ministry had requested that the term "aggression" (*shinryaku*) be replaced with "advancement" (*shinshutsu*), when referring to 1937–1945. By September 1982, the issue had whipped up a press furore across much of East and Southeast Asia.[19]

Singapore and Malaysia's Chinese newspaper editorials became vociferous in the period stretching from July to September 1982. At this time, the *Nanyang Siang Pau* and *Sin Chew Jit Poh* circulated in both Singapore and Malaysia. The *Nanyang Siang Pau* editor was shocked by Japan's attitude: "On one hand, it tries by every means to vindicate itself from the crimes it had committed in the war, but on the other hand, it only makes known to its younger generation the tragedies of Hiroshima and Nagasaki, as if Japan was the greatest victim in World War II…"[20]

The *Sin Chew Jit Poh* noted there had been a lack of criticism of Japanese wartime aggression and cruelties in Singapore during the 1970s. Noting also the link between that and the need for Japanese investment, it added that:

> Despite the current trend among the Asian countries to learn from Japan, none of them has ever 'endorsed' the towering crimes committed by Japan during the Second World War. On the contrary, this part of history has left deep wounds in the minds of Asian peoples, an excruciating lesson they will never forget for generations to come. Hence the swift and vehement responses from various Asian countries to the re-writing of textbooks by Japan to distort historical facts.[21]

By August 1982, the old "blood debt" campaign's call for an apology from Japan was resurfacing. *Sin Chew Jit Poh* argued that:

> Japanese war crimes and atrocities in Asia are modern historical facts, well documented and substantiated. If the Japanese would only show their sincerity to repent the past, assure that they have turned over a new leaf and will never take the well-trodden path again, and back up their words with deeds, no-one would, three decades after the war, dig up the past. Hence, the problem is, in a way, also quite simple — all that is required to bury the past once and for all is a demonstration of genuine sincerity.[22]

This feeling that the Japanese had not openly and sincerely repented wartime actions, was aggravated by Japanese prime ministers' visits to the Yasukuni shrine in Tokyo. This was a shrine for all Japan's war dead. The problem was that from October 1978, Japan's Class "A" war criminals were enshrined there, immortalised, and designated as "martyrs of Showa" (the reign of Hirohito). Successive ministerial visits to Yasukuni hardened opinion in Singapore.

Even the country's principal English-language newspaper, the state-controlled *Straits Times*, responded. The *Straits Times* was particularly strident when Okuno Seisuke, Japan's National Land Agency Director General and a former cabinet minister, visited the Yasukuni shrine in April 1988, and denied that Japan had committed any aggression. It had, he said, gone to war to liberate the countries of Asia from European colonialism. The *Straits Times* editorial, entitled "Selective Amnesia", reported that "the countries that had suffered Japanese occupation are not interested in saddling Japan with a permanent war guilt. What they expect is that it not rewrite the verdict on the war and pretend that it was the victim and not the aggressor".[23]

Japanese media and diplomats reported that the Singapore state was beginning to incorporate the Chinese sense of victimhood into official Singapore history textbooks. Tatsuto Nagaya, a senior journalist, appeared puzzled that years of economic aid and investment had not resulted in a more favourable view of Japan: "They say they admire Japan and want to look east to Japan. But their history books come down hard on Japan".[24]

History was making a comeback in Singapore schools in the 1980s, having been largely neglected and cut back in the curriculum during the 1970s. The first official Singapore history textbooks were introduced by the Ministry of Education in 1984.[25] Teachers were instructed that students should "learn of the different forms of ill-treatment that the people of Singapore were subjected to under Japanese rule" and "understand why the people had to suffer great hardships".[26] Students were asked in workbooks to ponder statements such as, "The Japanese treated everyone cruelly".[27] The Japanese school in Singapore, which catered to the 20,000 Japanese expatriates, translated the Singapore textbook for use in its classes. It wished to show that the Japanese community in Singapore understood local sensitivities, even if the Japanese Government did not.[28]

Japanese politicians now practised the art of seeming to apologise, without quite making an apology. Prime Minister Kaifu Toshiki (1989–1991) visited Singapore in May 1991. On 3 May, he expressed "sincere contrition" before a crowd which included Singapore's then Deputy Prime Minister, Ong Teng Cheong.[29] The term Kaifu used was *kibishii hansei*. This could mean "self-examination", though the Japanese ambassador to Singapore insisted that it "expressed severe remorse".[30]

The Chinese-language, state-run newspaper *Lianhe Zaobao* was not convinced. It felt Kaifu's "sincere contrition" was "falling short of a direct apology".[31] The newspaper tore into Japan's policy of telling its schoolchildren about Hiroshima and Nagasaki, but not atrocities committed by the Japanese army. Lee Kuan Yew, shortly after stepping down as Prime Minister in 1990, noted that "the Japanese conscience is yet to be purified".[32] Lee stated that Kaifu's statement of "sincere contrition" was "a good beginning for a catharsis, a purification by purging her guilt ... However, young Japanese in schools must be part of this catharsis through their teachers and textbooks".[33]

As ever, Lee was trying to harness Chinese war memory, and direct it to achievable goals. He told the *Asahi Shimbun* in December 1994 that "unlike Germany, where the Allies completed their 'denazification' programme, in Japan they never completed their demilitarisation programme before China became communist ... and entered the Korean War in 1950 ..." In 1995, remarking on earlier private apologies by Prime Ministers Murayama Tomiichi (1994–1996) in 1994 and Hosokawa Morihiro (1993–1994) in 1993, he noted that "if the mainstream leaders will join Hosokawa and Murayama in taking the same position (admitting its war of aggression) and the schools and press begin openly to admit these facts and teach them as a part of history, all these doubts (about Japan acknowledging them) will disappear".[34]

The issue of remorse resurfaced in 1995. On the 50th anniversary of the surrender of Japan, Japanese Prime Minister Murayama Tomiichi (1994–1996) spoke of his "feelings of deep remorse" and offered "my heartfelt apology".[35] The same day, George Yeo, Singapore Minister for Information and the Arts, opened an exhibition on the Second World War at the Singapore National Museum. Accompanied by Singapore Chinese heroine and torture victim Elizabeth Choy, Yeo "welcomed" Murayama's apology. But he also noted that Murayama "said it on his own behalf, and not on behalf of the Japanese Government or people". Yeo wanted Murayama to specify acts of aggression. He also desired that Japanese leaders, like Germany's, teach younger Japanese what happened.[36] A *Straits Times* editorial decried the "absence of a German-style de-Nazification programme to cleanse the political system", and the "persistence of a brand of Japanese nationalism that looks back to the martial glories of the past".[37]

Feeling was intensified by the 50th anniversary commemorations of the Second World War, from 1992–1995. The Singapore government, in the face of an unrepentant Japan, eased up on suppressing the sense of Chinese victimhood. By the 1990s, Singapore had a mixture of foreign investment and was no longer heavily dependent on Japanese capital, as in the 1970s. Besides which, there was no serious suggestion that the issue would affect economic relations, especially as Singapore was if anything more moderate in its stance than the People's Republic of China.

The government was by now openly seeking both to intensify memory of the war in terms of victimhood, and to broaden this out to make it into a truly national "collective memory" of the war. This was illustrated when Singapore again revised history textbooks in 1994, with the message from the Occupation being that all "the people suffered and lived in constant fear of the Japanese — the price that a country has to pay when it is occupied by another country".[38]

Students and War Memory I

From the 1990s, the government sought to intensify the "collective memory", or consensus on the war, as a period of shared hardship. It aimed to use this to emphasise shared identity, and also to buttress demands for greater sacrifices in the service and defence of the nation. This suited a country in which all males had to complete two years of national service. To deter any potential future enemy, Singapore claimed that it could bring 300,000 well-trained men under arms in 24 hours. The Social Studies textbook for secondary schools introduced in 1994 explicitly made the connection between the failure of the British in defending Singapore in 1942, and the need for National Service in contemporary Singapore. The textbook said that "from the British defeat we learn" that "a country must always be well-prepared for any attacks from enemies" and that "it must not depend on others to protect its people". It drew the lesson from life during the Occupation that "the people must be trained to defend their own country". Thus, "in 1967, the government started National Service" in order "to enable all young men to be trained to defend Singapore in case of war".[39]

Media Images of Common Suffering I

The new Singapore History and Social Studies textbooks of 1994 arrived just in time for the commemoration of the 50th anniversary of the end of the Second World War, in 1995.

The wider 50th anniversary commemorations, which stretched from 1992–1995, also saw the proliferation of media images of "common suffering". On 11 February 1992, *Between Empires* went to air in time for the 50th anniversary of the fall of Singapore. This was the first Singapore television documentary to graphically depict wartime atrocities.[40] It ran on English- and Chinese-language channels.[41] Its focus was on Chinese as victims. In its most memorable scene, a young Japanese soldier throws a one-month-old Chinese baby girl high into the air. The Japanese soldier raises his gun to point his bayonet skywards, where the camera shows the baby silhouetted against the sun. Then he impales the child as it falls to earth. As the baby is thrust onto his bayonet, the soldier's face is covered in blood. The camera captures him wiping the blood off his cheek, to reveal a smirk. The father of the baby is also shown, as he faints. The documentary drives home the message that this is re-enactment based on testimony. The baby's father, Neo Thian Hock, actually narrates the story of what he saw.[42]

A re-enactment, based on the oral testimony of Tan Ah Seng describes how the Japanese soldiers came calling for girls. The February and March 1942 *sook ching* massacres are also depicted, with streams of blood running from the bodies of machined gunned victims, through the wet sand, onto the beaches. Chua Tai Chian recalls his torture by the *kempeitai*. In the accompanying re-enactment, a Japanese officer fills Chua's body with water, then jumps on his stomach, before burning a cigarette into his eye and cheek: the infamous water torture. These images cumulatively portray the Japanese as brutal, and the Chinese as passive victims. The mixture of oral testimony and dramatisation secured an unprecedented audience for a documentary. The two-part series soon went to video to capitalise on its success.

The next television blockbuster came in 1997. Singapore's Chinese-language channel produced *Heping De Dai Jia* (*The Price of Peace*). This was based on a Chinese-language history book of the same name, which had been published on 5 September 1995 by the Singapore Chinese Chamber of Commerce and Industry (SCCCI) to mark the 50th anniversary of the end of the Occupation. Its editor, Foong Choon Hon, was director of culture and community affairs at the SCCCI. He remarked at its launch that "I read many accounts of the war by foreigners but did not always agree with their perspective. It is time for us to look at our history from our own point of view ... the book is targeted at young Singaporeans ..." Chew Heng Ching, guest of honour and Member of Parliament, expressed the government's hope that "the book would instil in young Singaporeans a sense of loyalty, patriotism, pride, and the need to maintain a strong national defence".[43]

To extend the book's circulation, it was translated into English. On 21 June 1997, George Yeo launched the English-language version of *Heping De Dai Jia*, called *The Price of Peace*. In doing so, he described how it gave Singaporeans the heroes they needed to inspire them, such as Lim Bo Seng and Elizabeth Choy, with their strength in the face of brutal torture by the Japanese:

> If we do not remember our heroes, we will produce no heroes. If we do not record their sacrifices, their sacrifices would have been in vain ...
>
> The greatest strength we have as a people is our common memories of the past and our common hopes for the future ... For without those memories the next generation will not have the fighting spirit to carry on.

On 24 July 1997, state-run television began its dramatisation of the Chinese-language version of the book on TCS 8 (now MediaCorp Channel 8), retaining the title *Heping De Dai Jia*.[44] This $2 million, 32-part Chinese-language television series showed at prime time (9pm). It followed Lim Bo Seng's story, but also traced the lives of figures such as Tan Kah Kee and Elizabeth Choy. It featured a galaxy of local Singapore television stars. James Lye, then a Singapore heartthrob, played one of Lim Bo Seng's comrades. He said that the series was "... to remind our generation what we have forgotten — the pain and the suffering of the war times".[45] The television series was launched to go with the patriotic build up to Singapore's National Day, on 9 August 1997.

Commentators on the first few episodes, on Tan Kah Kee and Lim Bo Seng's fundraising for China in the 1930s, noted that "patriotism is the prevailing motif".[46] *Heping De Dai Jia* had a peak of 714,000 viewers: a ratings record for Chinese-language dramas in Singapore.[47] An English-dubbed version would later be shown on the English-language TCS 5 (now MediaCorp Channel 5) in 1999 as *The Price of Peace*. The drama would be repeated on Channel 8 in 2007.

Heping De Dai Jia featured scenes of Chinese being butchered by Japanese soldiers. Yet its core was Lim Bo Seng, portrayed as both a hero for his sacrifices and as a victim of torture. Even before the war, Lim Bo Seng is shown enduring beatings from Japanese iron ore miners in the Malay state of Terengganu, as he sought in 1938 to get Chinese miners there to strike.[48] The last episode showed Lim Bo Seng, now in Malaya as part of Force 136, being captured. The episode plays on his brutal torture by Onishi Satoru, who had also been the *kempetai* officer responsible for the largest *sook ching* massacre in Singapore (at Siglap).[49] The actor who portrayed Lim Bo Seng, Rayson Tan, noted that "during filming, I found myself becoming Lim Bo Seng; I developed his hatred for the Japanese".[50]

Some Singapore students were so moved by the television portrayal of Lim Bo Seng that there followed more artistic re-enactments of his life in classroom plays.[51]

Students and War Memory II

The context behind school students performing plays on Lim Bo Seng's life was the state's upgrading of 15 February as an anniversary. In 1992, it was designated Heritage Day. The *Straits Times'* Chua Mui Hoong wrote that the "real heritage that we want to preserve is not the memory of one day, February 15, 1942 ... [but] ... the legacy of the entire war, which saw the beginning of an attachment to this land as different peoples on the island banded together ... [who] forgot their differences and fought to defend the land from the intruder".[52] She quoted Lee Kuan Yew's speech at the opening of the Civilian War Memorial back in 1967:

> [It] commemorates an experience which, in spite of its horrors, served as a catalyst in building a nation out of the young and unestablished community of diverse immigrants.[53]

In the wake of the anniversaries of 1992–1995, the state went further. By 15 February 1998, the state had redesignated the anniversary as "Total Defence Day". Total Defence is an imported concept, in which five components — Civil, Military, Economic, Social and Psychological — are interrelated. Since an enemy might undermine security by attacks on any of these, citizens are regularly reminded of the need to remain vigilant in all five. The concept of Total Defence was first introduced in 1984.

From 1998, schools were encouraged to run total defence related events in the week around 15 February, whether through plays, or imposing hardships such as limiting water or turning off fans. One regular activity was having students only eat a small portion of tapioca for recess, aimed "at helping students understand" what life was like "when food supplies were limited during the Japanese Occupation years".[54] In some cases, relatives were invited in to talk to students about the war. Hence, for instance, Hong Kah Secondary students re-enacted the Fall of Singapore on 18 February 1998, "to illustrate and demonstrate Singapore's vulnerability and the need for Total Defence".[55] Most dramatically, some schools invited actors, or even older students or older cadets to perform the roles of attackers or Japanese.

In 1999, schools seemed to be competing, on their own initiative, to show they could respond most successfully to government desires that they should bring the war to life. In one case, things became too real. At Jin Tai Secondary, a mock attack was planned. At about 3.10pm on 26 February 1999, an alarm went off. Secondary 1 and 2 students were ordered into a hall, and onto their knees. Some were brought onto stage, tied, dragged into new positions, or kicked. Eight cadets who had been invited to the school to play the attackers used ski masks and camouflage. Then the "attackers" left, leaving many pupils looking at the floor, others crying. Four of the children were sent to hospital.[56]

The Ministry of Education was quick to reassure the public that people would be properly briefed in future. But they also reassured schools that they should carry on being innovative, as heads had not rolled after the Jin Tai mistake.[57] Hundreds if not thousands of events followed without incident. The penchant for re-enactment also surfaced elsewhere, with actors hired to play "Japanese".

Fort Siloso on Sentosa Island — a museum which acted as an artillery park for old coastal guns from 1975 — held an event called *Fort Siloso Live!*. In November 2001, participating students were invited to imagine they were British recruits, and given a codeword to keep secret. They were then being sedately shown the life of a gunner, when amid explosions and smoke "Japanese" guards appeared, and bundled them into a darkened fortification room. In early versions, the guards — hired actors — were enthusiastic enough to reduce the more timid to tears, so their shouting and demands for the codeword were toned down by the time the authors joined a party in November 2001. Everything ended happily, as it was announced that the atomic bombs were dropped and the war ended. The students could then talk to a veteran. *Fort Siloso Live!* was stopped after a few years because, according to curators (and like the Jin Tai event), "the re-enactment traumatised some students".[58]

Total Defence Day continued to be accompanied by such events, particularly in schools, and by Ministry of Defence run advertising, in

Dear Principal, Head of Social Studies Department and Teachers,

A RARE OPPORTUNITY TO EXPERIENCE

FORT SILOSO LIVE!

WHERE HISTORY COMES ALIVE

Load... Aim... Fire!
Sgt. Maj. Cooper and his platoon
invite your students to experience history as it
unravels at Singapore's only remaining coastal fortification.
Take part in an exciting interactive programme
as the fort literally turns into a living classroom!

Date : **7 - 10 (Wed - Sat) &**
12 - 13 (Mon - Tue) Nov 2001

Show times : 9 am and 2.30 pm daily

Duration : **Approx. 2 hours**

Venue : **Fort Siloso, Sentosa**

FORT SILOSO

Programme Highlights:

- Symbolic role play as Recruits
- Orientation Procedures: fall-in/ fall-out routine of flag-raising ceremony, see barracks and living quarters & receive briefing on daily tasks
- Air Raid Drill: experience the tension of an attack & shelter in tunnels
- See the 64-pounder & 25-pounder Guns that were once used
- Mass Drill: feel unity & cooperation in the mass march
- Drink & biscuits provided
- Worksheet to reinforce the content

Built in the 1880s as part of the British's coastal artillery defence of Singapore, Fort Siloso stands today as a significant historical landmark. *Fort Siloso Live!* re-enacts its role during WWII in authentic surroundings. Actors play host to students participating in a range of educational activities which reflect life as it was before and during the fall of Singapore. The programme also reinforces concepts taught in schools' social studies syllabus.

Contents of this programme are based on the social studies syllabus for Primary 4 students.

Plate 10.1 *Fort Siloso Live!* 2001 flyer

Plate 10.2 *Fort Siloso Live!* 2001 — schoolchildren see "Japanese soldiers" take their teacher "prisoner"

order to make students and adults alike contemplate the full range of "Total Defence".

Media Images of Common Suffering II

The media sector, meanwhile, continued to produce war-related performances after the 1997 success of *Heping De Dai Jia*. In 1998, Lim Bo Seng's life was turned into a Chinese opera for schools, called *The Flames of War*, and sung in Mandarin.[59] In May 1999, Prime Minister Goh Chok Tong declared Lim Bo Seng a "national hero", stating that "a country needs national heroes" in order to create what he called "a Singapore tribe", in the sense of "an extended Singapore family with distinct core values and social characteristics and sharing a common destiny".[60]

Heping De Dai Jia (*The Price of Peace*) included a significant section on Chinese victim and war heroine Elizabeth Choy.[61] The television series faithfully showed Elizabeth Choy and her husband running a canteen at Woodbridge hospital, where civilian internees and POWs were

Plate 10.3   *Price of Peace* opening title

brought for medical treatment. Elizabeth and her husband were tortured
when the Japanese suspected civilian internees of plotting espionage
and using their canteen to pass messages to saboteurs.[62] Elizabeth Choy
had continued to be held up as an example, and by the 1990s, was the
living embodiment of the Chinese victim. She had survived torture to
become a successful public figure, regularly attending events which commemorated the experiences of the civilian population. The television
series *Heping De Dai Jia* (and its English-dubbed version of 1999, *The
Price of Peace*) enhanced her image. She seemed to embody the nobility
of the Chinese victim who, like Lim Bo Seng, is able to endure anything meted out, without betraying friends, helpers or principles.[63]

On 9 March 2001, Singapore's Chinese-language channel launched
yet another war production: a 10-part drama called *In Pursuit of Peace*.[64]
This time, however, the series was purely fictional. It followed two
Chinese families, the Lins and the Huangs, and how family members
became war victims. Samuel Lee, a television critic, noted that it "aspires
to be more than the average wartime serial, surpassing its 1997 predecessor, *The Price of Peace*, in terms of guts and glorified gore ... what
surprises about *Pursuit* thus far is the body count".[65] The last episode,

Plate 10.4 *A War Dairy* opening title

on 11 May 2001, transmitted the message that young national service-men of today are serving to protect Singapore from again suffering such a fate, and should mould themselves after wartime heroes. In the last scene, the anti-Japanese resistance fighter and former member of Dalforce Lin Fan,[66] is shown as an old man in the heart of contemporary Singapore. As he gazes on young National Servicemen in their uniforms, he observes "The same youthfulness but different faces. They're much more fortunate".[67]

In the same year as *In Pursuit of Peace*, the first major English-language drama series on the Occupation was screened. Called *A War Diary*, it cost a record $1.5 million, and ran in the prime slot of 8pm.[68] It concerned the wartime experiences of the Lim family, who were English-speaking Peranakan or Straits Chinese. This series showed the broadest range of Chinese victims, all present in one Chinese family.[69]

The series focused on the grief of the mother of the family, Lim Swee Neo.[70] She has to watch as, one by one, most of her family become victims. Of her four sons, two are taken away in February 1942 after they have been screened. Her second oldest son, the 22-year-old Lim Teck Meng,[71] survives the massacre at Changi Beach and returns home to go into hiding. The younger son, Alex Lim,[72] is taken from the screening centre and imprisoned at Outram Prison, and not heard from again for the duration of the war. Lim Swee Neo's teenage daughter, Rita Lim,[73] is taken from her mother's arms, outside of their family home, by a Japanese soldier, and confined to a brothel as a "comfort woman".[74] Lim Swee Neo's daughter-in-law, Gan Bee Lan,[75] is raped by a Japanese soldier and becomes pregnant.

Lim Swee Neo also discovers that her young neighbour, Susan Wong, has slit her wrists after seeing her missing husband's head on a plank, with the heads of others the Japanese are displaying to deter looting.

On top of all this, Lim Swee Neo's husband, George, cannot find work for months, because he was previously a clerk in a British business. He therefore considers working as a clerk in a Japanese firm. Lim Swee Neo is horrified, saying, "But why would you want to work for the Japanese after all they have done to us?" George replies, "If it will put food on the table, why not?" Lim Swee Neo is having none of it: "I would rather die than eat food bought by Japanese money".[76]

By the end of 2001, the wartime suffering of the Chinese had been represented so many times on Singapore television since 1992 that one critic, Suzanne Sng, was moved to comment that "history repeats itself. I learnt that during those painful lessons which seemed to drone on forever ... The latest wartime drama from MediaCorp, *A War Diary* ... follows in pretty much the same weary footsteps as the Mandarin serial *The Price of Peace* and *In Pursuit of Peace* earlier this year".[77]

The theme that a common collective memory of wartime suffering unites Singaporeans and teaches them that they must be prepared to defend themselves has been repeated not just on television, but in Singapore government-sponsored commemorative events. To mark the 60th anniversary of the end of the Second World War, there was an event on 12 September 2005, at the Kranji War Cemetery. There, Lee Boon Yang, then Minister for Information, Communications and the Arts, hammered home the now familiar "National Education" messages:

> When Singapore gained its full independence, our first generation leaders knew that this independence must be defended ...
>
> They established the Singapore Armed Forces and introduced National Service to defend Singapore. For if Singaporeans are not prepared to defend Singapore, then we may well lose the claim to independent existence. To remind Singaporeans, we mark February 15 every year, the day on which Singapore fell to the Japanese

Imperial Army, as our Total Defence Day. This annual commemoration reminds all Singaporeans of the tragedy that could befall us if we cannot or will not defend ourselves. To remain free and to preserve our sovereignty, despite being a small city-state constrained by history and geography, we must be prepared to defend ourselves in the first instance.

Only a few months later, on 16 February 2006, yet another Second World War site was opened. This was an exhibition gallery and repository called "Memories at Old Ford Factory", created by the National Archives.[78] It was here, on 15 February 1942, that General Percival had surrendered Singapore. The event was already represented at the "Battlebox" at Fort Canning, which had housed Percival's wartime control room, and had before that been marked by mannequin dioramas at Sentosa's waxwork "Images of Singapore" (1981–2005).[†79] Reworking the "Fall of Singapore" as a heritage, nation-making and tourist site, and creating new representations of it, seem to have been almost an obsession for the island Republic.

Now, on 16 February 2006, Defence Minister Teo Chee Hean spoke at yet another representation of "The Fall" at "Memories at Old Ford Factory". This site's claim to the event was that it boasted the boardroom where Percival had surrendered to Yamashita.[80] At the opening, Admiral Teo reiterated the "lessons" of the war.

> The day after the British surrendered, exactly 64 years ago today, Singapore was renamed *Syonan-to*, or light of the South, by the Japanese people. But for the people of Singapore it marked the beginning of dark times, which would last three years and six months.
>
> Singapore and Singaporeans went through extreme hardship and suffering as an occupied people. Conditions were desperate. There was not enough food. There was no health care. Worse than the physical hardship was having to live in constant fear.
>
> The walls of this gallery tell the stories of tortures and massacres. Many families lost loved ones and suffered grievously. The gallery here at the old Ford Motor Factory is a powerful poignant reminder to all Singaporeans that we once paid a terrible price because we could not defend ourselves. We must learn from this most painful lesson of what could be taken away from us if we are not able to defend ourselves.

---

† The Surrender Chambers waxworks were moved to Fort Siloso in 2005.

The need to learn from our past cannot be overstated … Anyone who may be tempted to think our small island would be an easy target, like it was in 1942, must be left in no doubt of the resolve of Singaporeans and our commitment to defend our nation, and that the Singapore Armed Forces can, and will, repel any aggressor and defend Singapore …

"Memories at Old Ford Factory" was constructed to appeal to school groups, with an outside, life-sized "board-game" called the "Syonan Race" (a "Snakes and Ladders" of the Occupation), first-hand accounts, and some hands-on exhibits. It promised that "As you walk through the gallery, you will find important lessons of creativity, adaptability and entrepreneurship from the annals of history, displayed by those who lived through the Occupation years". Beyond that, it also reflected a more recent development in war memory, the branching out to include more about everyday life. A "Syonan Garden" features wartime food substitutes such as tapioca, and in 2009, a book called *Wartime Kitchen* followed, complete with recipes.[81] The site still covers the *sook ching*, but is also inclusive. Optional videos include those on the "Malay Regiment", "Tapioca Days: The Lives of Singapore Malays during the Japanese Occupation", and "*Chalo Dhili* (On To Delhi)".

The National Archives of Singapore, which by now was running both "Reflections at Bukit Chandu" (opened in 2002) and "Memories at Old Ford Factory", also made the Second World War the main focus of its online provision. The war was covered under the title "Singapore's Period of Darkness: Battlefield 1942". Anyone, anywhere, could now access a wider range of materials. These included Lim Bo Seng's and others' diaries, and assorted documents. They could also play the "Syonan Race" online, choosing as their marker one of three iconic figures: of "Resistance" (a loyal patriot who had raised funds for the China war); "Assistance" (an Asian who helped European captives); or "Resident" (who had "persevered relentlessly and adapted creatively"). The memory of the war, suitably channelled, had by now become the fulcrum and beating heart both of Singapore collective memory, and of National Education.[82]

Malay Memory

Chinese images of the war were understandably prominent, in a country which was more than three-quarters Chinese. Nevertheless, the state's policy was to have "a multi-racial Singapore", and the PAP was careful to remain multiracial, and that its top politicians should be able to make select speeches in two, three or more languages.[83] Lee Kuan Yew, although a Straits Chinese and not originally a fluent Chinese speaker, polished his Mandarin and Malay, and added a little Hokkien too.

By the 1970s–1980s, this multiracial balance had, however, resulted only in a token Malay representation in state-supported commemoration. In the 1992 documentary *Between Empires*, there was a short segment on the Malay Regiment. In this, Datuk Abbas Abd. Manan recalled how he had assisted Lieutenant Adnan in heroic but vain attempts to hold back the Japanese, at the Battle of Pasir Panjang of 13–14 February 1942. There was no mention of the INA, nor any other Indian experience. Nor was the removal of Asian labourers to the Burma-Thailand Railway covered. Manan's token inclusion was used to suggest that other ethnic groups also suffered under the Japanese: reinforcing the theme of "common suffering".[84] The memories of Vernon Palmer, a Eurasian, were used in a similar way. In a short segment, his ill-treatment at a Japanese roadblock was re-enacted.

The Ministry of Education's new history textbook of 1994 also took care to include examples of other ethnic groups' suffering, though not avoiding the obvious point that "it was the Chinese who suffered the most".[85]

The approach of both *Between Empires* and the Ministry of Education's 1994 History textbook was to put Chinese victimhood at the centre of war memory, and select those aspects of other ethnic groups' experiences which best reinforced the Chinese pattern. What they did not do is seek to tell each group's experiences on their own terms, including what was unique to each group.

In the 1997 Chinese-language serial *Heping De Dai Jia* (*The Price of Peace*) the only significant non-Chinese character is Sybil Kathigasu, the Eurasian doctor[86] who helped Chinese from the MPAJA. She fits well into the main Chinese themes, since she is arrested for helping the guerrillas, and tortured. The infamous incident where her daughter was suspended over a fire (see p. 77) is shown.[87]

In the follow-up, and now fictional *In Pursuit of Peace*, non-Chinese also appear insofar as they integrate into the main spine of the narrative, about the two Chinese families, the Lins and Huangs. The Malay policeman Ali is shown as a family friend, who rather implausibly joins the Malay Regiment just as the Japanese are about to attack. He is the only significant Malay to appear in the series.[88]

In the English-language drama of 2001, *A War Diary*, there is the same brief inclusion of the Malay Regiment. This time, the Malay soldiers are shown helping Chinese Dalforce fighters, though in fact the two units had no significant contact.[89]

The yearly 15 February ceremony at the Civilian War Memorial has also retained its mainly Chinese character. It has traditionally been organised by the SCCCI. It has become a notable national event, especially since the date became Total Defence Day from 1998, though it is not a public holiday.[90] Other than the events put on by schools, the main focus on Total Defence Day is the ceremony at the Civilian War Memorial, which is meant to mark the national suffering of all, in common. In reality, for most years almost virtually no Malays or Indians attend, nor representatives from their organisations. Nevertheless, a minister from the Singapore government is the guest of honour and diplomatic representatives are invited. The Japanese ambassador shows up. The Singapore Armed Forces Veterans' League lays a wreath. Prayers are said and a wreath laid jointly by the religious leaders of the Inter-Religious Organisation of Singapore, representing the Muslim, Buddhist, Christian, Hindu, Jewish, Sikh, and Zoroastrian faiths. The National Cadet Corps then lay a wreath, followed by students from selected schools. So the format stresses the national and all-inclusive nature of the ceremony, while public attendance is largely by elderly Chinese, who make food offerings and burn joss sticks to the spirits in traditional Chinese style.

What this shows is that the 1967 attempt to flatten everyone's experience into one model — of common suffering — has not entirely worked. It dampened the affective force for Chinese of commemoration of the *sook ching*. At the same time, it limited the space for non-Chinese to express their distinctive war memories in public.

The use of the image of the Malay Regiment in television serials, however, touched a chord. The state-run, Malay-language newspaper, *Berita Harian* picked up on the need to recognise the Malay perspective on the war. On 6 September 1995, at the time of marking of the site of the 1942 Battle of Pasir Panjang, the newspaper suggested that the war heroes of the Chinese and Malays were not the same. It tried to explain "why Singaporeans have different sentiments when they commemorate Singapore's war heroes, such as Lieutenant Adnan, who was killed at Pasir Panjang, and Lim Bo Seng. This point reminds us of the diversity of life in Singapore and our diverse origins. This aspect of our existence cannot be destroyed. In fact, it will endure. However despite its diversity, Singapore has been able to develop in its people the quality of give-and-take and mutual respect".[91] The paper added that, "The war experience shows that danger does not discriminate between race, language, and culture. Singaporeans should face any misfortune and challenge together ... they should continue to develop the fighting spirit as one people and a common identity which shows that there is unity in diversity".[92]

The *Berita Harian* began to champion this line of "unity in diversity", by enthusiastically taking up the commemoration of the Malay Regiment and Lieutenant Adnan in September 1995. It gave extensive coverage to Malay Regiment veterans and relatives who came down to Singapore from Malaysia on 10 September 1995. They came to witness the dedication of a commemorative plaque to the Pasir Panjang battle site at Kent Ridge Park: one of many such plaques about the war installed around Singapore that year.[93] Malay organisations, such the Malay Youth Library Association, suggested that the *Berita Harian* "spearhead" efforts to give greater prominence to Lieutenant Adnan and the Malay Regiment.[94] The paper then endorsed a suggestion by a Malay member of the public to commemorate Lieutenant Adnan by naming a road or park after him. *Berita Harian* reported that the man making the suggestion, Haji Mohd Hamdam Shafil Abdul Rahman, had said that "Lieutenant Adnan was an excellent example because he was willing to defend Singapore with his life".[95]

One of *Berita Harian*'s columnists, Pak Oteh, gave vent to the growing feeling that Lieutenant Adnan might provide a "Malay Singaporean" hero, writing that, "When a plaque was erected at Kent Ridge Park in Pasir ... tears flowed down my face".[96] Mohd Raman Daud in his column argued that "every community should produce a hero" and that for the Malays, "Lieutenant Adnan is our hero ... as a soldier, Lieutenant Adnan was a shining example of bravery, determination, and loyalty".[97]

Berita Harian published a letter in its Readers Forum entitled: "Recognition of Lieutenant Adnan Still Inadequate" by Sa'don bin Anwar.[98] Haji Borhan Muslim, who had lived in Pasir Panjang area all his life pointed out that the site of the 1995 plaque did not even mark the exact location where Lieutenant Adnan was killed, which was one kilometre further down the hill at Bukit Chandu, around several colonial bungalows at Pepys Road. Borhan expressed his hope that this site be preserved and turn into a memorial.[99]

The government took up the idea of raising Lieutenant Adnan's stature, albeit a few years later. In May 1999, Prime Minister Goh Chok Tong identified Lieutenant Adnan as a national hero, alongside Lim Bo Seng.[100] In 2000, Lieutenant Adnan featured in new school history textbooks as a major Singapore hero. These noted that Lieutenant Adnan "defended Singapore bravely", and "although he was caught and tortured, noble he remained till the end". Primary school children were asked to: "Write a poem or a few sentences below to express your respect or admiration for Adnan bin Saidi".[101] Lieutenant Adnan and Lim Bo Seng as "heroes fighting for Singapore" became intertwined with the concept of Total Defence. A Ministry of Defence announcement for the first Total Defence Day, in 1998, proclaimed that "Psychological Defence is probably the most important element of Total Defence. It is the heart of nation building":

> It's about being Singaporean, thinking Singaporean and acting Singaporean. It is about remembering our roots and the sacrifices made by our forefathers and having the resolve to continue their legacy and strengthen the Singaporean identity …
>
> In past years, heroes from the war years like Lim Bo Seng and Lieutenant Adnan have been used as examples of Psychological Defence. But everyone can contribute to building that foundation, making it solid and secure.
>
> We can all do so through the mindset and belief in nationhood which we all share.[102]

To provide a new focus for remembering the wartime heroes used in Total Defence propaganda and to create a place for school history fieldtrips, the National Archives built a new war museum. Called "Reflections at Bukit Chandu", this used multimedia exhibits to depict the Battle of Pasir Panjang at Bukit Chandu, and was dedicated to Lieutenant Adnan and the Malay Regiment's stand there. On 15 February 2002, Reflections at Bukit Chandu was opened by Tony Tan, then Deputy Prime Minister. It had cost $4.8 million, and was described as the "brainchild" of George Yeo, then Minister of Trade and Industry.[103] George Yeo's views on the need for heroes, which he already had uttered at the launch of the English-language edition of the book *Heping De Dai Jia: The Price of Peace*, were engraved into a plaque next to a bronze statue depicting a Malay Regiment mortar team in action. Its key sentiment was that "If we do not remember our heroes, we will produce no heroes".

Malay Regiment soldiers had of course been taught to regard themselves as a test of the martial qualities of the Malay race, and in Malaysia were portrayed as an integral part of developing Malay nationalism. They were recruited mainly from Malay kampongs and towns. But Singapore overcame this Malay, and Malaysian, background by focusing on the site of heroism, and the qualities shown in battle. There were other signs of war memory being pressed into government-sponsored nation-building. One of the multimedia exhibits told the story of the Battle of Pasir Panjang through the eyes of a fictional character, an old Malay man who as a young child lived near the area. The last words of this character's scripted lines were:

> Ahh, that was 60 years ago.
> My family has since moved out of Pasir Panjang, and I now live in a comfortable HDB [government housing estate] flat. I still hear the laughter of the children coming from the playground, but I find it hard to forget how the hill which was once my playground was turned into a battlefield; and I will never forget those brave Malay soldiers who fought and died for the peace that we now enjoy; and looking at these children, I cannot hope but think that we must never let history repeat itself.

The Singapore government found that not all visitors were coming away from Reflections at Bukit Chandu with the "right understanding". Inscribed in the visitor's book for 23 November 2002 was a comment from "Ramli", which simply read: "*Tidak Melayu hilang di dunia*". For Ramli, the site was an affirmation of Hang Tuah's words which meant that the Malay race, language, culture, and tradition will never be lost while there are Malay warriors, such as those in the Malay Regiment. Other Malay visitors reflected on the meaning that it had for them as Malays.[104] This is not exactly what George Yeo had hoped for. He expressed his consternation in 2002 when he presented prizes at a Malay community function:

> Earlier this year, Deputy Prime Minister and Defence Minister Tony Tan opened the World War II museum at Bukit Chandu in honour of Lieutenant Adnan Saidi and the Malay soldiers of C Company.
> I took my wife and children there during the June holidays. I was told the museum has become a cultural shrine to many Malay Singaporeans. Lt Adnan and the men of Company C sacrificed themselves not for the Malay race, but as soldiers of the British Army fighting brutal invaders.

Like volunteers of other races who fought the Japanese, including pro-communists operating in the Malayan Jungle these Malay heroes helped to create modern Singapore.[105]

Indian War Memory

Indian war memories have proved more difficult to integrate into a national story, not least because the INA and IIL involved people who fought on the same side as the Japanese who slaughtered Chinese in the *sook ching*. Partly also because the INA had looked outwards, to India.

Above all, it is hard to integrate the Indian communities' chosen main thread of memory — the INA as a heroic nationalist movement and vehicle for uplifting Indian status — into a core narrative of common suffering. Images of the INA leader Bose with Hitler, or on the steps of the Municipal Building (City Hall) with Japanese Premier Tojo, jar with a Chinese story centred on massacre and suffering.

At the 50th anniversary of the end of the war, a monumental plaque was put up at the site of the old INA memorial. But this was just one of many plaques erected at the time. In 2003, another anniversary came round, the 60th since the Government of *Azad Hind* was proclaimed in Singapore, on 21 October 1943. This was the anniversary which had been marked in the immediate postwar years with processions to what was then the ruins of the INA memorial. These anniversaries had, however, slipped into disuse by the mid-1950s, and Indians had concentrated either on the MIC and its role in the Alliance in Malaya, or on local politics and parties in Singapore.

Singapore did mark the 60th anniversary of *Azad Hind*, but with limited results. There were few surviving veterans in Singapore, compared to the hundred or so INA and seven Rani of Jhansi veterans in Malaysia. A small exhibition was mounted at Singapore's Asian Civilisations Museum, but on 15 August 2003. This was called the *"Chalo Dhili* (On to Delhi) Historical Journey of the Indian National Army". It was timed to coincide with the anniversary of India's 1947 independence, rather than the 1943 formation of the *Azad Hind* government. It was organised by the National Archives of Singapore in cooperation with the National Archives of India and local community groups. Exhibits were loaned mainly by Malaysian INA veterans.

The event opened with the playing of India's "national song", *Vande Mataram*. Encik Yatiman Yusof, Senior Parliamentary Secretary in the Ministry of Information, Communications and the Arts, then told the audience that, "Although the Indian National Army did not succeed ... just like the Indian Mutiny in 1857, we remember these freedom fighters for their fervour and love for their motherland. I admire them for the unwavering faith and sacrifice for the cause of freedom".

Edwin Thumboo, meanwhile, had been asked to compose a poem. Thumboo was born in Singapore to a Tamil father and Chinese mother, in 1933. He described how deeply affected his generation had been by INA fighters because, as he told the audience, "my generation was born into a colony, part of the Straits Settlements, part of the Empire". By contrast, he commented sarcastically on "that lovely period called liberation. You look back and ask yourself was it a liberation or a return to British administration?" Then he read his poem, "Cry Freedom — Chalo Dhili", beginning with a swipe at British colonialists:

> They came; they saw; they stayed. Took by trade and
> Treaty; divide and rule; quick marching regiments;
> Subterfuge; relentless fervour; cunning in high places.
> Imperially, their power installed a Raja here, a Nawab
> There, re-arranged the fate of kingdoms. Thus they stole
> Our history, our sky from Kanniyakumari to Kailas,
> Bay to Sea, leaving disdain, oppression, pain, indignity,
> Till great ancestral voices heaved and rose thundering
> In fifty-seven as Rani and compatriots shook their power,
> As Cobras stuck in Meerut, and Lucknow lay besieged.

Thumboo then eulogised Gandhi, Bose, and the INA in the so-called Second War of Independence:

> Later, a man of destiny spun cloth, made tax-free salt
> And fasted. His spirit, creed and path, quietly firm
> Disobedience, pure non-violence, blunted brutish force.
> Mustered and led peoples into unity. No call to arms but
> A nation's blood, brighter than red coats, tempered by
> The sun's fire, blessed ash and singing bones, pushed
> The cry of freedom in temple, village, town and city,
> Stirred sons and daughters in these eastern lands. Soldiers
> Who fought for King and Empire in Burmah, Hong Kong,
> Malaya, Singapore, dreamt of green fields, simple waters.
> Mohan Singh ... the INA ... Netaji Subhas Chandra Bose ...
>   Cathay Cinema ...
>   Proclamation: October 21st '43 ...

> Provisional Government … Azad Hind …
>   Chalo Dhili
>
>   Remember India.
> Give me blood and I will give you freedom.

He then conjured images of the INA and Rani of Jhansi marching from Singapore to liberate India in 1943–1944:

> Down the road from here, the Padang shone with bayonets.
> Women stood equal to battalions ready to do or die. Steeled
> By faith, hope, love, determined bravery, they travelled north
> Across Arakan hill, ravine, river, jungle, battling hard into
> The motherland, to Imphal and Kohima, capturing cantonment
> And fort; beating the enemy into April, May. Then the rains
> Came, grey skies turning courage into fever, earth into mud.
> And the bite of leeches as the roads became rivers in flood.
> Death for the birth of nation. The last stand at Mount Poppa
> Where overwhelming odds and comradeship gave peace.
> To the air my last breathe; to the earth my last touch;
> To my beloved, and you our children, my last prayer.

After Thumboo's praise of the heroism of the INA, he glorified its legacy:

> Lest we forget what the passing years willingly sanctify:
> Deeds rendered on that sacred road to freedom at midnight

Thumboo's "Cry Freedom — Chalo Dhili" summed up the way many would like to remember the Indian part in the war, as linking them to a wider nationalist story, and providing a time of heroism and increased status. It gave them comfort that although their memory of the war appeared marginal, the Singapore state, with its multiracial goals, had not entirely forgotten them. It could endorse the heroism of Indian actions, even if it abhorred the INA's choice of allies. It could provide an add-on video about the INA at "Memories at Old Ford Factory". Still, at the ceremony, several Chinese members of the audience privately expressed reservations. They saw the exhibition as celebrating Bose — someone who had sided with Hitler, Mussolini, and Tojo — while the Chinese had been slaughtered by Japanese troops, and while the Chinese of the MPAJA were even now relatively neglected, due to their communist links. There was an awkwardness even in the formula of praising INA heroism, rather than their tactics and allies. Images of the Burma-Thailand Railway, meanwhile, remained closely associated with white POWs, with the Indian part in that suffering shunted into a siding. Neither state nor Indian community leaders, nor its young historians, had much motivation to dredge up that story (see pp. 176, 206).

Eurasian War Memory: The Years 2602–2605 (1942–1945)

The sheer variety of Singapore war experiences is also reflected in the memories of Singapore's small Eurasian community, which by 2006 had declined to around 17,000. Like the Indian community, their experience was peripheral to the national story. In terms of possible war heroes, the state held the Chinese empire-loyalist Elizabeth Choy up as a "Singaporean" hero, while the Indian-Eurasian Kathigasu who helped the MPAJA in Perak, tended to fall into the shadows. Dalforce now won some recognition in revised school texts and in television series, while the Eurasian role in the local volunteers went mostly unremarked.

In many ways, Eurasians could fall easily into a narrative about "common suffering". Nevertheless, Eurasians also had distinct nuances to their experience, and sufficient community organisation to push for these to be represented. Eurasians had occupied a particularly invidious position in the war. European blood marked them as potentially anti-Japanese, while Asian blood made them appear to Japan almost as traitorous "Asians". Eurasians were summoned to the Singapore Recreation Club (alongside the Padang) on 3 March 1942. With the spectre of the Chinese *sook ching* behind them, they were told that they must prove their loyalties. The Eurasians thus found themselves neither massacred in numbers like the Chinese, nor left alone as with most Malays, nor courted as with many Indians POWs.

Instead, they found themselves under pressure to make their commitment to Asian-ness and the new Japanese order visibly manifest. Community leaders such as Dr Charles Paglar felt duty bound to answer Japan's demands, in his case to become President of the Syonan Eurasian Association. But they knew that helping their communities placed them on a knife's edge, between being saviours, and collaborators. Dr Charles Paglar was one of several imprisoned after the war, accused of making pro-Japanese speeches and of cooperating in ventures such as sending people to Bahau Resettlement Camp, in Negeri Sembilan.

Bahau was called *Fuji-Go* by the Japanese, meaning beautiful village. The first batch of settlers left from in front of the Cathedral of the Good Shepherd on 28 December 2603 (1943), by the Japanese calendar. This was followed by a second batch on 17 January 2604 and six more up to March. A census taken on 5 April 2604 revealed 839 Eurasians at Bahau. Thanks to a poor location, the camp proved as disastrous — devastated by hunger and disease (mainly malaria) — as the Chinese settlement at Endau proved successful. A July 2605 "Fuji-Go Reclamation Area" report recorded the population for the whole area as 5,167 colonists.[106] But that figure included Chinese settlers in the Bahau area as well. Over 400 Eurasians who went to Bahau died, mainly children.[107] Bishop Devals, their leader, died on 17 January 2605.

Paglar was soon released after the war, but never definitively cleared of the charges. This left relatives such as his son, Eric, with a searing and enduring sense of injustice. The British had left them in Japan's clutches, and then dared to accuse their leaders of treachery for guarding their community. In 2010, Eurasian author Rex Shelley righted the perceived wrong in his *Dr Paglar: Everyman's Hero* (Singapore: Eurasian Association, 2010). In this, Dr Paglar's wartime actions become a part of a wider, prewar and postwar, story of community service. Another Eurasian, F.A.C. Oehlers, also published his memoirs, in his case in 2008. He was a boy in the war, but recalled the angst of his father, George Oehlers, being dragooned to be Vice-President of the Association, and to turn his medical skills to Japanese advantage. He also recalled his father's struggle against the "malaria ... pallagria [pellagra], beri-beri, intractable maggot-laden ulcers" and dysentery which stalked Bahau. After the war, his father was put on trial by the MPAJA for being "pro-Japanese" — a nonsense as gaining medical supplies meant you had to play the game — and acquitted.[108]

The Eurasians organised a 2006 exhibition, called: "World War II: The Eurasian Story", at the headquarters of the Eurasian Association in Ceylon Road: The Eurasian Community House.[‡] This was pervaded by a sense that Eurasian experiences merited some wider acknowledgement. Half of the cost was met by the local town council. Prime Minister Lee Hsien Loong opened the exhibition on 21 February 2006. In his address, Lee noted "a revival of the Eurasian spirit", contrasting this to the then 25,000 Eurasian community's attachment to the colonial administration before independence. He dropped hints that the PAP might field more Eurasian candidates in the upcoming election.[109]

---

‡ Ceylon Road is in the strongly Eurasian area of Katong.

Robert Conceicao, a Eurasian 51-year-old businessman, commented that "It's been quite a long time. Although we're all Singaporeans, we would still like a voice from the community… so that we don't feel left out".[110]

As with Chinese Malaysians, so too with Eurasians, an emphasis on community memories aimed *at the community* — however therapeutic and entertaining — was not seen as enough. Groups tend to seek wider recognition of their story, and its integration or mention in national narratives and performances. This is seen as having political importance, with war commemoration often strongly related to issues of citizenship and identity. It is also seen as cementing a kind of wider immortality for past victims as part of a quasi-immortality of the nation. Integration into national narratives performs both political and commemorative (and almost quasi-religious) functions.

The "World War II: The Eurasian Story" exhibition therefore did more than try and tell a standalone Eurasian story. It integrated the Eurasian experience into the theme of the Singapore national war memory of victimhood and suffering. The introduction of the exhibition told the visitor that:

> This exhibition is dedicated to the memory of the women and men who lived through the Japanese Occupation, many of whom paid the ultimate price. This small community endured much suffering as our fate, like other communities here, was left in the hands of the new colonial master.
>
> Most learned to survive and adapted quickly to the harsh realities. From various testing and searing experience, the community developed bonds which brought us closer together in spirit and in love. Along these corridors and rooms are exhibits and artefacts that sketch our experience. This is our story.

The reference to closeness in "spirit and love" reflected the strong Catholic strand within the community, itself stretching back to Portuguese colonialism in the region. But the strongest thread of this introduction was the attempt to integrate the Eurasian community, by showing the wider public that their community had partaken of "common suffering", if not perhaps at the elevated level of the Chinese. Hence, it blended the wider picture with the community-specific. The exhibition centrepiece was an altar-like structure, called "Reflections" that listed all the Eurasians from the Straits Settlements Volunteer Corps who had fought in the war. Details of the deaths of the Eurasians who had died on the Burma-Thailand Railway were also highlighted.

Many of the displays mirrored the wider national narrative about the everyday hardships of Occupation, with titles such as "Black Market and Barter", and "Food". The Bahau Camp fitted well into the theme of suffering. A large-scale model of the camp and oral history testimony highlighted the suffering in Negeri Sembilan. There Eurasians with a mainly urban background had struggled to come to grips with farming ill-prepared, poor soil. Charles Paglar was depicted as a hero for trying to get the Japanese Welfare Officer in Singapore, Shinozaki Mamoru, to give Bahau more assistance. Aloysius "Lofty" Conceicao was quoted: "Thank God Dr Paglar brought Shinozaki. If not we would have died". The allegations of collaboration against Paglar and others were, not unnaturally, conspicuous for their absence.

Incorporating Eurasian war memory with the Singapore national war memory was emphasised in the captions too. In a summary called "The Resilience of the Human Spirit", Eurasians' suffering was repeatedly depicted as part of the overall "Singaporean" experience, though Eurasian faith in colonial masters slipped in too:

> Despite the bleak times, our spirit remained resilient. Many believed that the British would return one day, and life would become normal again. This belief, coupled with deep faith in higher powers, sustained Singaporeans though the darkest days of their lives.

It remains to be seen if this revival and broadcasting of Eurasian memories is gradually incorporated into the margins of national commemorative displays, as things such as food issues and Malay heroism have, or whether they sink to virtually unseen corners again, as the issue of Asians on the Burma-Thailand Railway has done.

Battlefield Tourism and Schoolchildren Come Together

> "Experience the sounds of battle, the pangs of defeat and the cries of victory, all in one day ..."

> (Singapore Tourism Board brochure, "Uniquely Historical Singapore: World War II Self-Guided Trails, October 2004 edition).[111]

We have already talked of the proliferation of war sites, and their use for what has sometimes been called "learning journeys" by students. Hence students were subjected to "capture" by "Japanese" soldiers at *Fort Siloso Live!* around 2001. This reflects another element of heritage in Singapore: the way some places have become "transational deathscapes". In Australia and Britain, memories of the fall of Singapore and the horrors of POW experiences were transmitted to postwar generations. As these new generations started to visit Singapore, the trickle of veterans and their families grew into a stream of tourists. They visited places, such as Changi Prison Chapel and the Kranji War Memorial, that had their origins in colonial times, but which had also flourished in the postcolonial world.

The foreign tourists were often oblivious to the contrasting views of the historical sites they visited that were held by the local population. In 1997, Joan Henderson, when working with the Singapore Tourist Promotion Board,[§] observed that "interest in the subject appears greatest amongst people of the former colonial power, the UK, and its old allies". By contrast, the local population initially perceived these sites as part of a colonial history they were getting rid of, rather than as part of their own Asian story.[112] Thus, when Singapore's tourism officials initially created sites such as the Changi Chapel and Museum (1988), they did so specifically with foreign tourists in mind.

From 1998, however, the shift in name for 15 February to Total Defence Day, and increased prominence of war history in local schools, meant these sites were also written into school texts and packaged as school trips. By the early 21st century, with the introduction of National Education into Singapore schools, historic war sites were firmly integrated into the narrative of national history presented in schools. Indeed, when the Johore Battery site was opened in February 2002 — where some old 15-inch gun tunnels had stood — both school-children and tourists were anticipated as primary users. A battlefield poster and storyboards that described tactics and strategy were balanced by a mockup 15-inch gun, and a lever system which allowed children to lift a replica of the gun's one-ton shells.

There was poignancy, meanwhile, to the tourist visits, or sometimes "pilgrimages", that swelled over the 1950s–1970s. This is illustrated by the arrival in October 1972, of a group of British relatives of POWs, travelling on the "Memory Lane" tour of Singapore and the Burma-Thailand Railway. Journalist Nancy Bramji described meeting them at the airport:

> They walked out of the arrival hall of the Singapore airport and looked around rather cautiously, unlike other groups of tourists. Then tears filled their eyes …

[§] In 1997 renamed the Singapore Tourism Board.

'We're here! We made it!' some of them whispered to their relatives and colleagues among the group of 40, including 22 former
prisoners-of-war who were held here during the Japanese Occupation.

One of the group members, Alice Kerry, aged 76 and from
Norwich, tearfully described how her eldest son, Leslie, had died as a
POW under the Japanese. But she had never been able to visit his grave:

> Oh I've waited 30 years for this … My biggest wish was to see where
> he was buried.
>   This pilgrimage was burning at the back of my mind all these
> years, and I can't believe I've finally made it. I have got to see where
> my eldest son had been resting for 30 years. My nine brothers and
> sisters and three other sons pooled some money, while I sold a lot of
> my belongings which fetched me about £140 ($1250) to come out
> on this trip.[113]

A focus of these "pilgrimages" would usually be a visit to Changi
Prison. The POWs had been concentrated in and around the prison,
from the surrounding Changi POW camp in 1944. Since the colonial
period, it had been the practice among the prison officials to allow
veterans and their families to pay their respects at the Changi Prison
Chapel (see pp. 87–8).[114]

The publicity surrounding some of these pilgrimages alerted the
Singapore government to the value of battlefield tourism at a time when
they were trying to promote tourism, in turn as part of general development efforts.[115] In November 1986, the Singapore government approved
a one billion dollar Tourism Product Development Plan, which among
many other tourism development projects, featured enhancements to
Singapore as a destination for battlefield tourism.[116] The Tourism Product Development Plan noted that "Singapore's rich colonial past
and history hold special appeal to visitors from the United Kingdom,
Australia and New Zealand, which are among our top 10 visitors
generating markets". It suggested restoring and recreating historic sites
"to highlight this nostalgic link with the colonial past".[117] In September
1986, the Singapore Tourist Promotion Board's consultants specifically
recommended sprucing up the wartime attractions at Changi.[118]

This was timely, since in 1986, security worries also meant the end
of veterans and tourists visiting the chapel inside Changi Prison. Singapore tourism officials meticulously planned a new "Changi Chapel" and
an accompanying museum to target Australian and British tourists' eye
for rustic simplicity, and desire for close historical "authenticity" in sites
and relics.[119] They built a new "chapel" just outside the prison.

This new "Changi Chapel" was an open-air structure made from rough wooden planks, erected with a simple high "A"-shaped frame roof. It was covered in attap palm leaves, with tropical flowers on creeping vines. The structure was consecrated and opened on 15 February 1988.[120] Pamelia Lee, the project coordinator, deliberately had the new chapel built in the shadow of Changi Prison. That way tourists could see Changi Prison's "gurkha guards on duty at their turret towers" in the background. She reasoned: "If I could not preserve the real thing, I wanted to make sure that tourists at least had a real glimpse of prison activity".[121]

The 1988 Changi Prison Chapel and Museum, according to one of its creators, consultant Robertson Collins, was crafted to emotionally engage British and Australian visitors.[122] It was designed to be evocative of the outdoor chapels of the Changi POW Camp in general, rather than a reproduction of any one of them. The tourism officials also created inside the chapel a large notice board, and supplied small paper cards, each with an image of the chapel. Visitors were invited to write their thoughts on these, rather than in the more formal format of a visitors' book. The embedding of comments as part of the visible structure of the site created deep emotional resonance. Initial visitors wrote about relatives who had served in Singapore, and about their emotions. Others were moved by this, creating a deepening spiral of reflection and emotion.

On 17 February 1997, Adam Berwick, describing himself as the "grandson of Clyde Berwick, Australia" wrote:

> To my grandfather who survived but told no-one of the horrors he faced here. Yet he did tell his young grandson stories of the mateship and comradeship that allowed those fortunate ones to endure.

Close to Clyde's card, on 31 August 1997, "Luke" wrote:

> It's so pleasing to see many messages from younger generations like myself. These visits and messages are testament that the bravery and efforts of the older generation, like my grandfather, Mike Huntley, will not be forgotten.
>
> May God bless them all.

Singapore Tourist Promotion Board studies revealed that large numbers of schoolchildren also began to be bussed to these locations. These children's notices began appearing in the Chapel.[123] On 12 September 1997, a student from Dunman High School commented, "God

Plate 10.5   Singapore schoolchildren commemorating the war dead at the Kranji War Memorial on the Battlefield Tour, 1997

Bless those that died for Singapore. Do Rest in Peace". Michelle Ho, another student around the same time, left the message: "This trip has taught us a lot. The pain they [POWs] suffered can be felt when I see what that is left behind. Here I pray that it never will happen again".

In 1997, with the launch of National Education in the Singapore school system, the fall of Singapore and Occupation were now used to highlight the message: "we ourselves must defend Singapore".[124] What had once been considered the history of the colonial powers now became crucial to the history of Singapore too, as 15 February was rebranded "Total Defence Day" from 1998.

Tourism officials were already aware of this trend when they realised they would have to move the Changi Chapel, because of new prison building. In their plans for a new Changi Chapel and Museum, to be built slightly further from the prison, tourism officials wanted both the POW experience for the foreign tourists, and the story of local suffering for school students.

When the new Changi Chapel and Museum was opened on 15 February 2001, the predominant story was still the POW experience, but as part of a larger one about suffering during the Occupation.

This was reflected in a major quotation from Lee Kuan Yew placed near the museum entrance, recalling that he and his contemporaries in the struggle for Singapore's independence were from "that generation of young men who went through the Second World War and emerged determined that no one — neither the Japanese nor the British — had the right to push and kick us around".

During 2000, deciding what narrative should be used in the proposed Changi Chapel and Museum had caused problems, partly because of the perception that there should be some history of the local experience as well as that of POWs. Tourism officials were not keen on having just the story of the POWs. At one point, there were proposals to tell the facts through personal narratives, which would view events through the eyes of a fictional wartime Singapore child, Lin Mei, and an equally fictional teenage Australian POW, Nicholas. The purpose of these fictional characters was to engage the young school children.

On 21 July 2000, "feedback and guidance from a wide group of people, such as historians, teachers, children, tourist guides, POWs and their families as well as the average Singaporean ..." were invited. In this invitation, tourism officials stated: "The New Changi Chapel & Museum is a development that should belong to all Singaporeans, especially young Singaporeans. Another target group is former POWs and their descendants". Inviting Singaporeans to a preview of the new Changi Chapel and Museum was not for assistance on historical accuracy:

> Instead we need you, as a caring and informed Singaporean:
> To tell us what you personally would like to see in the Museum.
> To tell us what message about WWII you want conveyed to young Singaporeans.[125]

Debates between the tourism board, academics and consultants resulted in a late change. The idea of telling the story through fictional characters proved too controversial for the historians and heritage specialists on the project. With only limited time left to devise and execute an alternative, the decision was made to use simple storyboards. These would present small artefacts and quotations, each explaining events in a Spartan way. Some of the storyboards covered the POW experience, with reproductions of the Changi Murals also providing powerful visual imagery. Other storyboards and artefacts focussed more on the local population's experience. The panels had names such as "The Experience Lingers", "Darkest Days", "Living in Fear", and

"Suffering under Japanese Hands". Many quotations were used, with little context. This lightly mediated use of sources and items turned out to provide a peculiarly direct, and so powerful, impression of events.

Hence Changi, once mainly a site for Europeans who were ex-POWs and internees, had become a truly transnational commemorative space, in much the same way as Kranji had become a transnational deathscape, read and used by different nationalities in different ways (see pp. 67–70).

By the early 21st century, other sites were also developed with a careful eye both for tourists and for the local population, especially the key category of student visits. Indeed, some war sites now seemed to be targeted more at students and National Education than tourists. Consider the Labrador tunnels (near the southern coast and where successive coastal artillery guns had been located). Their opening in 2005 was supplemented by a heavily illustrated book — *Labrador Park: The Adventure Begins* — which featured National Education messages for children, with bullet points, pop quizzes and reconstructions of events through the eyes of those who had experienced them.[126] These sites tended to repeat to some extent, with the Fall of Singapore featuring at the Battlebox at Fort Canning, Fort Siloso, Changi Chapel and Museum, and the old Ford Factory. But there was no denying that they covered an increasing range of traumatic and "everyday" experiences, and in many cases were "transnational", being either deliberately layered for different audiences, or read in different ways on the initiative of those audiences and their tour guides.

Conclusion

The Singapore state has proved adept and creative in adapting war memory to the purpose of nation-building, and so harnessing potentially divisive war memories. It has taken an integrating approach, in contrast to Malaysia's "plural commemoration". Themes of common suffering have been designed to create a sense of unity. With increasing integration of sub-stories, including those of everyday suffering, into sites, this has become increasingly sophisticated and inclusive. That inclusivity has become easier to achieve, as the state's adoption of the war as a key moment in Singapore history has resulted in the production of more and more plaques and war heritage sites from 1992 onwards.

There have, nevertheless, been limits. There are still significant experiences shunted to neglected sidings of national war memory, such as those Eurasians and of non-INA Indians, and of Asian labourers on the Burma-Thailand Railway. In addition, there is a lack of "democratisation" of commemoration. There has been little attempt to have individual civilian (as opposed to just military) victims accurately logged, and named in stone at the mass level. That honour has been kept for the dead of the British Empire forces, as named at the Kranji Memorial and cemetery, and to a select, and selected few, who are elevated to the status of individual "hero" or martyr.

The state has, nevertheless, tried to broaden out national war memory beyond that of the Chinese sense of victimhood. This is reflected in television dramas such as *A War Diary*. The Chinese story almost inevitably remains central in these — given the population balance and the scale of their losses — but others are given supporting roles in the theme of suffering. Dramas typically include non-Chinese stock characters and images, including the Malay Regiment, even the occasional "good Japanese".

The wartime experiences of the Chinese are thus still central to the national war memory fostered by the Singapore government, but in a way which mutes the emotional intensity of Chinese memories. The state's preference for nation-building, for the abstract, and for avoidance of potentially separating cultural forms, has a downside for Chinese community memory. It lessens the immediacy and authenticity of the connection between commemorative sites and the events that originated them. It strips them of much of the cultural repertoire that would allow families to feel victims were being symbolically reintegrated into the living community, and so weakens the therapeutic value of commemoration for survivors.

Hence, for instance, the evolution of a proposed site for Chinese massacre victims into the more abstract Civilian War Memorial, and of Pan Shou's emotive evocation of the ghosts of *sook ching* victims floating on the tides into a dry, terse, epitaph. Hence, the Civilian War Memorial — essentially a burial site for thousands of massacre victims — is scarcely recognisable as such, and indeed by many not really thought of in that way. Instead, it was and is described primarily as a symbol of four cultural streams coming together in common suffering, in a way that seeded and sustains the nation. It is startling that the central nature of the site is muffled in public imagination, though equally impressive is how it has been re-narrated as a symbol of national birth and unity.

By the same token, "Reflections at Bukit Chandu" puts the Malays back into the story, but by subordinating them to the preconceived Singapore war story. That makes Malay Regiment soldiers such as Lieutenant Adnan Saidi into martyrs who died for Singapore, rather than the *kampong* boys they were, who had been by culture and training taught to see themselves as latter-day inheritors of the mantle of Hang Tuah, and of Malay martial honour. By its very existence, "Reflections" suggests a state increasingly at ease with its ability to handle communal difference, but still determined to narrate everyone's experience into a unifying story, to a degree that may distort the image of the past which visitors receive.

"The state" has also become more subtle in accommodating difference in other ways. For the Changi area, it initially saw preservation of old sites, and construction of new ones, almost solely as a part of "Battlefield Tourism", embedded within development strategies. Changi was for European, not Asian, consumption. But over time, and especially after 15 February became "Total Defence Day" from 1998, various state and non-state agencies reconfigured some of these places as transnational commemorative spaces, and as transnational death scapes. Either storyboards were tailored with tourists and Singaporeans both in mind, as at the Changi Chapel and Museum, or texts about sites were produced for different audiences. Where Malaysia had plural sites — different for each community and group — Singapore had plural uses for some commemorative sites.

One caveat here is that "the state", even in Singapore, is not monolithic. The trend towards more schoolchildren visiting war sites, for instance, was driven by particular people and agencies, notably the Ministry of Education with its idea of Learning Journeys, PAP leaders of the wartime generation wanting to renew the founding impulse of the nation, and even the consultancy which won the contract to run the Changi Museum: Singapore History Consultants.[127] Likewise, the re-representation of the war story in the rebranded National Museum of Singapore's History Gallery (opened in 2006). Its combination of central war storyline, and yet artefacts and storyboards that allow different voices and perspectives, was not state-mandated. Rather, the museum was determined to show variety, backed up by external consultants, though also constrained by the need not to transgress core PAP tenets and war memories. This underside of war memory production remains largely hidden.

The final point is that, despite its highly sophisticated balancing act, even Singapore has not, ultimately, felt able to allow the image of MPAJA heroism to take any central or emotive place in its war narrative. Its dramas, texts and sites hold up Lim Bo Seng, Tan Kah Kee, Elizabeth Choy, and to a lesser extent the European POW even. The MPAJA, by contrast, are sometimes airbrushed out, and at other times, given oblique or fleeting mention, as if brave but slightly embarrassing parts of the overall anti-Japanese story.

In this one respect, Singapore's integrationist approach to commemoration has proven almost as inadequate as Malaysia's plural commemoration. Hence, though the postcolonial state has come a long way in commemoration, it still faces many challenges: of increasing authenticity and therefore the therapeutic value and historical accuracy of war commemoration; of accurately listing and naming *sook ching* victims; of how to better integrate "supporting" substories such as those of Asian railway labourers and Eurasians; and of how to manage the balance between state initiative, and that of other actors such as community memory activists, consultancies, and academics. For all these reasons and more, collective memory, and commemoration, will remain challenging and fascinating long after the wartime generation themselves have passed away.

CHAPTER 11

Conclusion

MEMORIES OF THE WAR AND JAPANESE OCCUPATION have played a significant part in the moulding of modern Malaysia and Singapore at the individual, community and national levels. This period encompassed so many traumatic events — from British surrender, through the *sook ching*, to Sino-Malay clashes at the war's close — that it seared itself onto people's memories. It also left a diversity of perspectives and commemorative desires that at first looked irreconcilable.

Some individuals were left with gaping holes in their lives — as Chinese fathers and sons never returned from Japanese "screening" in 1942, and Indian and Malay labourers never returned from the Burma-Thailand Death Railway after 1945. Relatives of the dead sought the commemoration of their loss, and compensation from or even revenge upon the perpetrators and Japan. But others sought the glorification of the INA or KMM (both of which sided with Japan); or of Dalforce, the Malay Regiment, the MPAJA, or Force 136 (which all sided against Japan). Even within individual ethnic groups (most of which had significant subdivisions), people had vastly different memories of the war period.

We have traced how community and state leaders responded by trying to suppress some war memories and shape others, so that they could forge myths (stories with a didactic purpose, however true or false) about the war. One of the themes to emerge from this is the malleability of stories about the past, as states and communities seek to nuance their "collective memory".

Chapter 3 showed how Europeans, faced with their appalling failure in 1941–1942, rewrote the story of the POW and internee experience to emphasise the heroism, stoicism, and imperial characteristics which allegedly demonstrated European superiority, even as captives.

This telling of the story warped, for instance, the presentation of the Changi Murals. It also emphasised that the fall of Singapore had been a necessary, and temporary, sacrifice: something required to facilitate the ultimate victory of the British Empire, and so of good over evil. Indeed, where the story of Breavington's attempt to save his colleagues from execution in 1942 is concerned, it took on chameleon characteristics. The story changed in details and meaning according to the narrator. When told by Reverend Lewis Bryan, he had tried to save three men and died reading the Bible. When narrated in an Australian poem, he had perished after trying to save just one colleague, with a picture of his loved one in one hand, and his opposite arm around his "mate". His story, like so many other wartime events, took on the qualities of a palimpsest: a document where the original is written over, but still exists in some trace form.

At least Europeans could generally agree on who their heroes were. They could even agree to incorporate loyalist Asians and Eurasians, such as Elizabeth Choy and Sybil Kathigasu — into their canon of hero-victims. Chinese were less united. Initially, it is true, the story of Overseas Chinese unity in defence of China and Chinese embraced Dalforce, Force 136 and the MPAJA. But in reality, this unity papered over vastly different visions of the future, as contrasting as communism and *towkay* (rich Chinese businessman) capitalism. These differences surfaced in the Malayan Emergency (1948–1960), which led to years of guerrilla fighting. In this, the communists targeted not just Europeans, but also the capitalist and traditionalist Chinese supporters of the MCA. This struggle replicated itself in the realm of memory, with the MPAJA being gradually downplayed in ceremonies, and their remembrance driven underground. Chinese community leaders instead built up Lim Bo Seng, essentially a pro-Nationalist Overseas Chinese businessman — as a Malayan hero.

In both Malaysia and Singapore, the role of communism was thus de-stressed. The state in both cases had the power to dominate or colour the official level of commemoration. But neither state tried to totally suppress war memory in any part of this period. The degree of trauma (the *sook ching*, the Death Railway, the postwar inter-ethnic clashes) and exhilaration (the INA, the stirring of Malay nationalism, and the embrace by some of the Japanese *seishin* or spirit) made simple suppression impractical.

The two states therefore tried to harness, or at least accommodate, some of the most passionately felt community memories. In the case of Malaysia, this was achieved by a model of plural commemoration, which led to the state favouring the remembrance of select Malay groups at the national level, but leaving space for non-Malay communities to remember the war in separate deathscapes and stories.

By contrast, Singapore, with its more unified and unifying approach to society, tended to limit space for alternative stories. Instead, it sought to harness or co-opt them into a single unifying myth of all races suffering together. This tended to become more sophisticated and inclusive from the 1990s, as witnessed by the establishment of "Reflections at Bukit Chandu" in memory of the Malay Regiment in 2002.

But the mythmaking and unifying of the Singapore approach also had costs. Some groups' stories — such as the MPAJA — could not easily be domesticated to the main thread, and so were shunted slightly to one side. Sometimes, the sanitising of the state story — in order to increase the impression of shared experience — resulted in a divorce between presentation of memory, and the raw emotional force of what had actually happened. Hence, the retelling of the *sook ching* story through the Civilian War Memorial (dedicated in 1967) resulted in that site's core nature (as a burial place for thousands of overwhelmingly Chinese massacre victims) being downplayed. By making it a largely abstract design of four pillars, dedicated to the dead of all communities, its value as an emotional symbol of real and specific massacres was weakened. The therapeutic value and emotional force of sites and ceremonies has thus been lessened in Singapore, even as their unifying utility has been enhanced by state re-narration of events and their meaning.

For Indians, by contrast, the main complaint has not been that the Malaysian and Singaporean states have manipulated their history, but rather that they have largely ignored it. Memory activists for the INA such as Mrs Bhupalan (formerly Ms Navarednam) and K.R. Das wanted their story of the INA as one of national and ethnic empowerment to be widely known. They remembered the war as such, at times almost in a reverie, as if it was still in the present. Indeed, they not only *remembered* the war in this way, but they had attempted to act out their part in the war, during the war, guided by such sentiments.

This version of the Indian experience was to a large degree adopted by the postwar Indian press, at the cost of underplaying the larger numbers of Indians sent to the Burma-Thailand Railway as labourers. Many of the first group experienced empowerment and pride, but most of the second group experienced unparalleled new levels of degradation and humiliation, followed in many if not most cases by death.

The Indian case demonstrates the importance of organisations (such as veterans groups and regiments) and articulate elite members (such as Indian journalists, politicians of the MIC, and even poets) who can act as effective "memory activists". The mainly poor, often illiterate Tamil labourers on the railway were relatively poorly served in this respect, while politicians and journalists instead rallied round the INA as a symbol of Indian nationalism and confidence. Indian labourers only ever received meagre assistance — and most of them not even that — whereas better represented European POWs received compensation.

In all these cases, we also see that collective memory was malleable, changing over time, and subject to contestation within as well as between different communities. Remembering the fall of Singapore and Occupation illustrates that memory is not like recalling a movie camera-like image of the past that always stays the same when replayed. Memory is reconstructed in the context in which it is recalled.

Maurice Halbwachs has also explained how when we recall the past we remember not just as individuals but as part of a community or a group.[1] Hence, the personal narratives of Don Lee, K.R. Das, Choi Siew Hong, and Mohd Anis bin Tairan, as told in their oral history accounts, were constructed in the context of their respective community or ethnic groups. Sometimes these were supportive, as with the Anzac myth for Don Lee, sometimes less so. Our study explores the relationship between the individual's oral history, and the wider collective memory of the groups each individual belonged to. We then chart the interaction between the collective memories of communities and state-fostered national memories. Our examination of personal, community, and national levels represents a layering of memory. It allows us to examine the connections or "bridges of memory" between these different spheres.

Historians Ashplant, Dawson, and Roper have used the phrase, "the politics of war memory and commemoration" to describe the interaction of these spheres, which they expand to: state, civil society, "private" social groups, and individuals.[2] In their view, the "politics of war memory and commemoration" is first and foremost shaped by hegemony of the state or a dominant group. These often establish their memory as central while other memories are marginalised.[3] Though we agree to some extent, we emphasise that such "hegemony" has a cost, and in the case of Malaysia and Singapore, it relied on strategies to harness or tolerate potentially contradictory voices. Hence, in examining the transactions and negotiations that occur between the various agencies involved in producing war memories, it is vital to examine the precise processes and moments by which accommodations occur.

It is in these practical attempts to fix memory, around memorials for instance, that qualified hegemony may emerge. Hence, our concentration on competition over which individuals would emerge as "heroes", what form of monument and commemorative ceremony would emerge, and even how such things would be presented in schools. When we examine these critical moments in collective memory — creative moments in so far as they shape what comes after in new ways — we see that Halbwach's idea of collective memory has limitations.

These limitations come partly from paying inadequate attention to the different layers of memory, and their persistence even when the state gains the semblance of hegemony at the national level. One problem in the study of collective memory has been that there has not been enough research on how the different layers of society, and of memory, interact. Academic study has tended to subdivide too much into specialisms, each focussing on a particular layer of society or type of memory. These then fail to adequately cross-fertilise.[4]

Hence, Alistair Thomson, an oral historian, has remarked that: "Memory studies have tended to lose sight of individual experience and memory, or the relationship between individual and collective memory ... [they] have tended to focus on collective or social memory, and are located in disciplines, such as cultural studies, film studies and literature that are centrally concerned with representation".

Thomson sees oral history as having the opposite tendency, in that it tends to focus on the individual or smaller group. Hence, he writes that, "Oral history originated in a large part through a 'history from below' that focused on groups that were under-represented in history and upon the experience and voice of individual historical actors".[5]

Thomson calls for a greater integration of oral history and collective memory.[6] To some extent, this book attempts such integration. It illustrates this relationship between oral history (especially individual recollections) and collective memory. It shows political leaders attempting to fashion collective memories into something that could bind their emerging postcolonial nations.

At the same time, we emphasise the two-directional flow between community and national levels. While the state may help to reshape community memories, it is also influenced by them in turn. To paraphrase Marx, the state may make its own collective memory and commemoration, but not in circumstances of its own choosing.

The same is shown to be true of communities, and their would-be hegemonic leaders. So-called community or collective memories have not proved entirely dominant in Malaya and Singapore. The "hegemonic" Indian, Malay and Chinese memories have all been contested, as well as leaving many individuals excluded and silent, rather than truly integrated into "hegemonic" accounts.

Hence, collective memories certainly have helped to shape personal memories of individuals. Yet the hegemonic state or group never entirely resolves the relationship between the state-sanctioned "collective" or "public" memory on the one hand, and the individual who does the remembering on the other. Individuals such as Choi Siew Hong of Dalforce, or survivors of the Burma-Thailand Railway, may be pushed into the margins of public memory. But they do still retain their discordant memories, and sense of disjunction between them and the collective memory. That means that the potential for contestation of community and national "collective" memories tends to remain significant. Hence, memory activists have appeared time and again for the MPAJA, despite the Malaysian and Singapore states' reluctance to do more than the minimum to acknowledge its role.

Where the individual dies, however, the "collective" level can sometimes hijack their history. The memory of their actions is now open to much greater reshaping by community and state. Unless a widow or friend is determined to guard their memory, such individuals' stories can be shifted in new directions to fit group needs.

We have already mentioned the way Breavington's story was adapted to suit different narrators. Something similar happened with Lim Bo Seng. The "Overseas Chinese" group Lim Bo Seng belonged to underwent dramatic changes in identity in the postwar decades. In these years, it was changing from Chinese who believed China to be their home, through Chinese who thought of Malaya as home, to Chinese who saw the nation-state of Singapore (or of Malaysia) as home. The group doing the remembering was changing, and as it changed, it re-inscribed Lim Bo Seng from being a China patriot, through Malayan and Malaysian, even to being quasi-Singaporean. Lim Bo Seng's life story was, like the tale of Breavington's death, treated as a palimpsest.

It was not simply that overnight the state or another organisation could just change the memory of the past, in the manner of the "double think" of George Orwell's *1984*. The shifting of Chinese identity and collective memory — as reflected in the retellings of Lim Bo Seng's actions — was gradual and came from a converging of needs and ideas about the future within this community. It could not be over-forced on a community that was not ready. Hence in Malaysia, the state-sponsored, fictional film *Paloh* (2003) failed to resonate with audiences, which were not ready for its intended lessons of inter-ethnic solidarity, as communicated through intense relationships between Malays and Chinese who were on different sides (police and MPAJA) in the war.

By examining war memory in Malaysia and Singapore over a period of seven decades, this process whereby a state or ethnic group reconstructs its memory of the war to fit new contexts can be traced. This memory work was going on in Malaya (later Malaysia) as early as the 1940s–1970s. During this period, the Malaysian state pretended to have amnesia about the history of specific groups, such as the MPAJA and the KMM. But what this really meant was that one level only — that of the state — de-emphasised some groups' war memory in the public arena for much of this period. Underneath that level, as we have shown, Chinese, Indians and to a lesser extent, Malays continued to openly mark their specific memories of the war, in their own communities and ways.

Indeed, in both Malaysia and Singapore, a constant theme has been the state's attempt to find a model for mediating between these disparate individual and community memories, and the national level.

We noted above that in postcolonial Singapore, the focus was on the concept of remembering shared wartime suffering for the purpose of nation-building. To varying degrees, members of the different ethnic groups did suffer during the war, so this feeling has had the potential to unite the people beyond just a focus on the massacre of the Chinese. This was in tune with Singapore seeing itself not as a Chinese state, but as a multiracial society where no ethnic group had dominance over any other. There was an attempt to find "bridges" across the different layers of memory, personal, collective, and national. However, the war memory of the large Chinese population has been at the core of this national memory of common suffering, even if presented in a way that is stripped of most of its culturally specific elements.

For Malaysia, the idea of *ketuanan Melayu* (Malay political primacy) in political life has meant that the wartime experience of the Malay warrior, personified by Lieutenant Adnan, has been enshrined as the preeminent national war memory. After the 1980s, radical groups and leaders who had collaborated with the Japanese were also acknowledged, on the grounds that they had helped to boost Malay nationalism.

War memories of the other ethnic groups, however, have been marginalised even if, following the plural commemoration model, they are allowed to flourish in specifically Indian and Chinese space, languages, and cultural forms.

Interestingly, the idea of common suffering of all ethnic groups has not been embraced in Malaysia, when it could have been, because the Malays and Indians both suffered as labourers on the Burma-Thailand Railway. The Chinese of course suffered mainly through the *sook ching* and Japanese reprisals for MPAJA activity. Suffering can provide a common war memory as most people, from victors and the vanquished, do suffer in war.

On the other hand, it is perhaps not that simple. If suffering was experienced as part of a group, then that may actually entrench a sense of distinct and separate group identity. If the suffering was specifically due to group membership, that sense of separate identity may become acute. In the Chinese case, their experience of suffering was perceived as a continuation of the wider "Great Patriotic" war for China, and as a result of the export of Japanese practices of massacre from China.

There is, anyway, little prospect of the Malaysian state using the theme of common suffering. That would put the suffering of the Chinese at the core of war memory, because of the large *sook ching* massacres. This would hardly be the way the Malay-dominated state would fashion memory. By contrast, the focus on the role of the Malay warrior — for instance, in the Malay Regiment — builds on the idea of unique Malay martial values. This also ties in with the idea that Malay servicemen who fought the communists in the Malayan Emergency, and so ensured the primacy of the Malays in political life in independent Malaya, were emblematic of Malay character as a whole.

Where does this emphasis on postcolonial nation-building leave the memory of European POWs and internees? Contrary to common-sense expectations, the memory of these groups has been well preserved, at least in pragmatic Singapore. The colonial state bequeathed to Singapore in particular iconic war and POW sites, such as the Changi area with its prison, Kranji, and Blakang Mati (Sentosa) with its guns. Singapore has preserved a wide selection of these, and even fabricated new sites from the late 1990s, such as the Changi Museum and Chapel (1988 and 2001 versions), and the Johore Battery at Changi (2002). These have been encouraged partly to foster war tourism, quickly being adopted by tour guides serving tourists and expatriates. As such, they continue to be the sites for "pilgrimages", now for children and grand-children of POWs and veterans even more than for veterans themselves. But Singapore has also integrated the war into the story of its national emergence from a moment of common suffering, and as a justification for national service and the need for "Total Defence" (Chapter 10).

This means that POW sites also have a value in the Singapore state's security, resilience, and nation-building agendas. Schoolchildren can be made to imbibe lessons of patriotism and the need for total de-fence by visiting sites which mark European defeat and imprisonment. This became increasingly common after 1998.

In the case of Singapore, therefore, we witness the emergence of transational, transcultural commemorative places, deathscapes, and monuments. Places such as Kranji are read and used by different groups in very different ways. Take ceremonies at Kranji memorial and war graves. Australians on Anzac Day meet there to remember a time when the British let them down and Australians are supposed to have again manifested the "Anzac spirit", and so their embryonic national character and independence. British can view Kranji as evidence of stoicism and of the captive as hero. Yet Singaporean children on school visits can see the site as a warning against relying on any external power, and a symbol of the beginning of the struggle for independence in the broadest sense of the term. They can also find the names of units and men selected as local heroes, such as Dalforce, and Lieutenant Adnan. All three uses can manifest respect for the "fallen", but within very dif-ferent narratives. Colonial war memory of the POW as both victim and hero can thus continue to be marked alongside postcolonial nationalist war commemoration.

Thus, remembering the fall of Singapore and the Japanese Occu-pation has produced a multitude of commemorative acts from many people with different memories of the same event. In this sense, there never was one common Fall and Occupation to recover and remember. With memory activists still clamouring for greater recognition of the MPAJA role in the war in both Malaysia and Singapore, the politics of these memories will continue to be debated long into the future.

GLOSSARY

AIF	Australian Imperial Force
amah	maid, more particularly those who looked after children
API	*Angkatan Pemuda Insaf* (Generation of Aware Youth)
attap	palm thatch (in Malay)
AWM	Australian War Memorial
BMA	British Military Administration
bin	*bin*, meaning "son of" in Malay
bte	*binte*, meaning "daughter of" in Malay
CPM	Communist Party of Malaya
Dalforce	British name for the Overseas Chinese Volunteer Army, so-called after its British commander, Col. J.D. Dalley (then of the FMS police)
DAP	Democratic Action Party
FMS	Federated Malay States
MNLA	Malayan National Liberation Army
Mohd	Mohammed
Giyugun	Japanese-recruited local volunteer army
Giyutai	Japanese-recruited local volunteer auxiliary corps
Gunseibu	Department of Military Administration
Heiho	auxiliary worker or serviceman
HVS	Hind Volunteer Service
Kempei	military policeman, hence *Kempeitai* is military police
IIL	Indian Independence League
INA	Indian National Army
ISEAS	Institute of Southeast Asian Studies, Singapore
IWM	Imperial War Museum, London
JMBRAS	*Journal of the Malaysian Branch of the Royal Asiatic Society*
JSEAS	*Journal of Southeast Asian Studies*
kampong	village (in Malay)
KMM	*Kesatuan Melayu Muda* (Young Malay Union)

MCA	Malayan/Malaysian Chinese Association
MCP	Malayan Communist Party
MCS	Malayan Civil Service
MICA	Ministry of Information, Communications and the Arts
MNP	Malay Nationalist Party (in Malay, *Partai Kebangsaan Melayu Malaya* or PKMM)
MPAJA	Malayan People's Anti-Japanese Army
MPU	Malayan Planning Unit
MSS	Malayan Security Service, for 1945–1948, during which time Malaya and Singapore Special Branch functions were amalgamated in this body
NAA	National Archives of Australia
NAM	National Archives of Malaysia
NAS	National Archives of Singapore
NEP	New Economic Policy
PAP	People's Action Party
pemuda	youth (in Indonesian and Bahasa Melayu)
PKN	*Parti Keadilan Nasional* (National Justice Party)
PKR	*Parti Keadilan Rakyat* (People's Justice Party)
romusha	labourer, in theory freely recruited, in effect often coerced from their communities
SCCCI	Singapore Chinese Chamber of Commerce and Industry
SEAC	South East Asia Command
SEALF	South East Asia Land Forces
silat	a Malay martial art
SOE	Special Operations Executive
SPH	Singapore Press Holdings
TNA	The National Archives, Kew, London
UMNO	United Malays National Organisation

NOTES

Chapter 1

1. The heritage site, located near the Changi Chapel and Museum, contains a full-sized replica of one gun, storyboards, above-ground markings where the underground tunnels are, and a replica of the original shells which can be lifted by pivot, to illustrate their weight.
2. Karl Hack and Kevin Blackburn, *Did Singapore Have to Fall? Churchill and the Impregnable Fortress* (London: Routledge, 2004, paperback 2005), Chapter 1, "Introduction", and Chapter 6, "After the Battle".
3. Ibid., Chapter 6, "After the Battle'.
4. Diana Wong, "Memory Suppression and Memory Production: The Japanese Occupation of Singapore", in *Perilous Memories: The Asia-Pacific War(s)*, eds. T. Fujitani, Geoffrey M. White and Lisa Yoneyama (Durham, North Carolina: Duke University Press, 2001), p. 222; Diana Wong, "War and Memory in Malaysia and Singapore: An Introduction", in *War and Memory in Malaysia and Singapore*, eds. P. Lim Pui Huen and Diana Wong (Singapore: ISEAS, 2000), pp. 4–6.
5. Wong, "Memory Suppression and Memory Production: The Japanese Occupation of Singapore", p. 222.
6. Diana Wong, "War and Memory in Malaysia and Singapore: An Introduction", in *War and Memory in Malaysia and Singapore*, eds. Lim and Wong, p. 5.
7. Ibid., p. 6.
8. Cheah Boon Kheng, "The 'Black-Out' Syndrome and the Ghosts of World War II: The War as a 'Divisive Issue' in Malaysia", in *Legacies of World War II in South and East Asia*, ed. David Koh Wee Hock (Singapore: Institute of Southeast Asian Studies, 2007), pp. 47–59.
9. Asad-ul Iqbal Latif, "Singapore's Missing War", Chapter 8 of *Legacies of World War II in South and East Asia*, ed. David Koh Wee Hock, pp. 92–103.
10. Abu Talib Ahmad, *Malay Muslims, Islam and the Rising Sun* (Singapore: JMBRAS Monograph no. 34, 2003), pp. 193, 141–9.
11. This commemorated the Battle of Pasir Panjang, Singapore, of 13–14 February 1942.

12. In some cases, leaders of the Malaysian Chinese Association (MCA), a partner in the ruling coalition, attended ceremonies at the new memorials, on the grounds that everyone who had resisted the Japanese should be honoured, regardless of their ideology.

13. The agreement was reached in October 1966.

14. In effect, these multiple accounts were "domesticated" and so made acceptable to the main narrative. "Domestication" here meant re-narrating each group's war stories in a way that fitted the national themes of the war's unifying effect, and the emergence of a loyalty to Singapore. Hence, the Malay Regiment, whose primary loyalties had been to the sultans, their Regiment, and the idea of Malay tradition (particularly Malay martial tradition), were rebranded as dying to defend Singapore. In reality, most people thought of Singapore as destined to be part of a wider "Malayan" state until after 1965. See Karl Hack, "The Malayan Trajectory in Singapore's History", in *Singapore from Temasek to the 21st Century*, eds. Karl Hack and Jean-Louis Margolin, with Karine Delaye (Singapore: NUS Press, 2010), pp. 243–91.

15. *Straits Times*, 9 February 1992.

16. Breen's book includes discussion of the revelation that Emperor Hirohito stopped visiting Yasukuni because Class "A" War Criminals were enshrined there in 1978.

Chapter 2

1. Aruna Gopinath, *Footprints on the Sands of Time, Rasammah Bhupalan: A Life of Purpose* (Kuala Lumpur: Arkib Negara Malaysia, 2007).

2. Sadly, Don Lee died in 2007.

3. Jane Ross, *The Myth of the Digger: The Australian Soldier in Two World Wars* (Sydney: Hale and Iremonger, 1985).

4. The writer who expressed the myth of the Anzac soldier was C.E.W. Bean, *Official History of Australia in the War of 1914–1918: Volume 1: The Story of ANZAC, From The Outbreak of War to the First Phase of the Gallipoli Campaign May 4 1915* (Sydney: Angus and Robertson, 1939), 9th edition, originally published in 1921.

5. See Russel Ward, *Australian Legend* (Melbourne: Oxford University Press, 1958).

6. For the debate over the Australian legend, see the 1978 issue of *Historical Studies* vol. 18 no. 71 called *The Australian Legend Re-Visited* (Melbourne: University of Melbourne, 1978).

7. Lachlan Grant, "Monument and Ceremony: The Australian Ex-Prisoners of War Memorial and the Anzac Legend", in *Forgotten Captives in Japanese Occupied Asia*, eds. Karl Hack and Kevin Blackburn (London: Routledge, 2008), pp. 41–56.

8.   See Karl Hack and Kevin Blackburn, "*The Bridge on the River Kwai* and *King Rat*: Protest and Ex-Prisoner of War Memory in Britain and Australia"; and Sibylla Jane Flower, "Memory and the Prisoner of War Experience in the United Kingdom", in *Forgotten Captives*, eds. Hack and Blackburn, pp. 57–63, 147–71.

9.   Donald Lee, *The Silvered Shovel* (New York: Vantage Press, 1989); and Don Lee, *A Yarn or Two*, 2nd edition (Perth: Hesperian Press, 2000).

10. Rod Beattie, *The Thai-Burma Railway: The True Story of the Bridge on the River Kwai* (Kanchanaburi, Thailand: T.B.R.C., 2007), pp. 30–41; Gavan McCormack and Hank Nelson, eds., *The Burma-Thailand Railway: Memory and History* (Chiang Mai, Thailand: Silkworm Books, 1993), p. 1.

11. Aruna Gopinath, *Footprints on the Sands of Time, Rasammah Bhupalan: A Life of Purpose*, pp. 49–104.

12. Ibid.

13. K.R. Das interview with Kevin Blackburn at the Netaji Service Centre, 49 Leboh Ampang, Kuala Lumpur, 17 December 2004.

14. K.R. Das, "The Bharat Youth Training Centre", in *Netaji Subhas Chandra Bose: A Malaysian Perspective* (Kuala Lumpur: Netaji Centre, 1992), pp. 55–6.

15. Malaya had a central spine of mountains that rose around the Thai border. The roads from southeastern Thai beaches ran to the southwest, skirting this range and hence entering Malaya's west coast road system. By contrast, if you travelled down Malaya's east coast, you would have to use poorer roads, and only be able to cross in the centre or very south of the country.

16. Hack and Blackburn, *Did Singapore Have to Fall?*, p. 66, *passim*.

17. Lionel Wigmore, *The Japanese Thrust* (Canberra: Australian War Memorial, 1957), pp. 160–1.

18. K.D. Bhargava and K.N.V. Sastri, *Official History of the Indian Armed Forces in the Second World War, 1939–1945: Campaigns in South-East Asia, 1941–42*, ed. Bisheshwar Prasad (Calcutta: Combined Inter-Services Historical Section India and Pakistan, 1960), p. 234; cross-checked with Das, "The Bharat Youth Training Centre", p. 47.

19. K.R. Das, "The Bharat Youth Training Centre", p. 49.

20. K.R. Das talk at the "Open Public Forum with Veterans and Members of the Wartime Generation", 4 September 2005, Singapore History Museum; and Das, "The Bharat Youth Training Centre", p. 50.

21. K.R. Das interview with Kevin Blackburn at the Netaji Service Centre, 49 Leboh Ampang, Kuala Lumpur, 17 December 2004.

22. See the extracts reprinted as a supplement to the *Straits Times*, 27 February 1948. For the full report, see Lieutenant General A.E. Percival, "Operations of Malaya Command from 8 December 1941 to 15 February 1942", *Second Supplement to the London Gazette of 20 February 1948*, No. 38215,

26 February 1948, pp. 1245–346. Quotations are from the section on the Battle of Muar.

23. K.R. Das speaking at the "Open Public Forum with Veterans and Members of the Wartime Generation", 4 September 2005, Singapore History Museum; and Das, "The Bharat Youth Training Centre", p. 47.

24. Das, "The Bharat Youth Training Centre", p. 50.

25. Ibid., pp. 47–51.

26. Ibid., p. 51.

27. K.R. Das interview with Kevin Blackburn at the Netaji Service Centre, 49 Leboh Ampang, Kuala Lumpur, 17 December 2004.

28. Das, "The Bharat Youth Training Centre", p. 52.

29. K.R. Das speaking at the "Open Public Forum with Veterans and Members of the Wartime Generation", 4 September 2005, Singapore History Museum.

30. Das, "The Bharat Youth Training Centre", p. 52.

31. Ibid.

32. K.R. Das speaking at the "Open Public Forum with Veterans and Members of the Wartime Generation", 4 September 2005, Singapore History Museum.

33. The six companies trained at the centre were given names such as Nehru, Gandhi, and Bose. Das became commanding officer of Ghaffar Company. The high turnover meant that Das was soon given additional responsibilities, as Quartermaster and camp Adjutant. K.R. Das speaking at the "Open Public Forum with Veterans and Members of the Wartime Generation", 4 September 2005, Singapore History Museum.

34. Das, "The Bharat Youth Training Centre", pp. 59–60.

35. K.R. Das speaking at the "Open Public Forum with Veterans and Members of the Wartime Generation", 4 September 2005, Singapore History Museum.

36. Das, "The Bharat Youth Training Centre", pp. 64–5.

37. K.R. Das interview with Kevin Blackburn at the Netaji Service Centre, 49 Leboh Ampang, Kuala Lumpur, 17 December 2004.

38. Ibid.

39. Rajesway Ampalavanar, *The Indian Minority and Political Change in Malaya, 1945–1957* (Kuala Lumpur, 1981), p. 173; Netaji Centre, "Publisher's Preface", in *Netaji Subhas Chandra Bose: A Malaysian Perspective* (Kuala Lumpur: Netaji Centre, 1992), p. iii; and K.R. Das interview with Kevin Blackburn at the Netaji Service Centre, 49 Leboh Ampang, Kuala Lumpur, 17 December 2004.

40. Joyce Lebra Chapman, *Women Against the Raj: The Rani of Jhansi Regiment* (Singapore: ISEAS, 2008), p. 86. This book is imbued with a hint of hagiography, no doubt inspired by Lebra's interviews and cooperation with the Netaji Research Centre. The wider issue of use of women for

violent nationalism is raised by Karl Hack in a review in *JMBRAS* 82, 2 (December 2009).

41. The Andaman and Nicobar Islands were in the Bay of Bengal, west of Burma, and a part of British India. With the British fleet chased from the Indian Ocean, the Japanese were in a position to hand the islands over to the government of Azad Hind.

42. Compare Joyce Lebra Chapman's scholarly *The Indian National Army and Japan* (Singapore: ISEAS, 2008, [first edition 1971]) to the more personal tone of her *Women Against the Raj: The Rani of Jhansi Regiment*. Lebra's exposure to the Netaji Research Bureau, Kolkatta (http://www.netaji. org/oracle.php) and to veterans is significant, as is her *The Rani of Jhansi: A Study in Female Heroism in India* (Honolulu: University of Hawai'i, 1986). The problems of tracing "female heroism" through almost suicidal Bengali nationalists to the INA (while ignoring metamorphosis into suicide bombers) is discussed by Karl Hack, in *JMBRAS*, 82, 2 (December 2009).

43. Hack and Blackburn, *Forgotten Captives*, p. 9. Some 20,000 Indians defected — about a third — but the Japanese limited the size of the INA to about one division.

44. G.J. Douds, "Indian POWs in the Pacific, 1941–45", in *Forgotten Captives*, eds. Hack and Blackburn, p. 74 suggests far more refused, but Fay concludes that just 5,000 of the 45,000 Indian POWs in Singapore refused in 1942–1943, compared with 40,000 willing. When the INA was officially formed on 1 September 1942, however, the Japanese would only arm 16,000. The Japanese became more generous with the arrival of S.C. Bose in mid-1943. 18,000 Indian civilians in Malaya and Singapore joined the INA after that point. Peter Ward Fay, *The Forgotten Army: India's Armed Struggle for Independence 1942–1945* (Ann Arbor: University Michigan Press, 1993), pp. 525–6.

45. Netaji Centre, *Netaji Subhas Chandra Bose: A Malaysian Perspective* (Kuala Lumpur, Netaji Centre, 1992).

46. Mr Choi Siew Hong held prominent business positions in Malaysia after retiring from public service, and finally died aged 90, in July 2011.

47. Choi Siew Hong interview with Kevin Blackburn in Kuala Lumpur, 24 February 2009.

48. See Lee Kip Lee, *Amber Sands: A Boyhood Memoir* (Singapore: Times, 1999), 2nd edition, p. 73; and Lee Kuan Yew, *The Singapore Story: Memoirs of Lee Kuan Yew* (Singapore: Times, 1998), p. 44.

49. Karl Hack, "Dalforce", in *Singapore: The Encyclopedia* (Singapore: EDM, 2006), 154.

50. Daniel Chew Ju Ern, "Reassessing the Overseas Chinese Legend of Dalforce at the Fall of Singapore", National Institute of Education, 2005, pp. 53–9,

passim. See Kevin Blackburn and Daniel Chew Ju Ern, "Dalforce at the Fall of Singapore in 1942: An Overseas Chinese Heroic Legend", *Journal of the Chinese Overseas* 1, 2 (2005): 233–59.

51. Lee, *The Singapore Story*, p. 44.
52. Lee, *The Singapore Story*, p. 57.
53. Choi Siew Hong's written statement from which he addressed the audience at the "Open Public Forum with Veterans and Members of the Wartime Generation", 4 September 2005, Singapore History Museum. Henceforth this will be referred to as "Wartime Generation Forum".
54. Choi Siew Hong's written statement, 4 September 2005.
55. Ibid.
56. Ibid.
57. Ibid. Choi stated that the officers were "entirely" police, civil service and members of the Chinese Protectorate.
58. Choi Siew Hong interview with Kevin Blackburn in Kuala Lumpur, 16 December 2004
59. Ibid.
60   Foong Choon Hon, ed., *He Ping de Dai Jia: Malai ban dao lun xian qi jian 136 Bu Dui ji qi ta fan qin lue shi li ji shi* [*The Price of Peace: The Record of Force 136 and Other Forms of Resistance during the Japanese Occupation of the Malay Peninsula*] (Singapore: Xinjiapo Zhonghua Zong Shang Hui [Singapore Chinese Chamber of Commerce and Industry], 1995, 1997 in English); and *Eternal Vigilance: the Price of Freedom* (Singapore: Asiapac, 1999, English 2006). For an extended analysis of the "forgotten legend" division around language difference, see Daniel Chew Ju Ern, "Reassessing the Overseas Chinese Legend of Dalforce at the Fall of Singapore", Singapore, National Institute of Education Academic Exercise, 2005; and Blackburn and Chew, "Dalforce at the Fall of Singapore in 1942: An Overseas Chinese Heroic Legend", *Journal of the Chinese Overseas*: 233–59.
61. See Chris Bayly and Tim Harper, *Forgotten Armies: the Fall of British Asia, 1941–1945* (London: Allen Lane, 2004), Preface, p. 136. But even English-language textbooks in Singapore made some mention of Dalforce: you could only consider them "forgotten" from a Europe-based point of view.
62. Victor Grosse discussions with Karl Hack at Changi Prison, Singapore, 17 February 2002; and see the documentary *Remembering Syonan-to*, Singapore, Channel News Asia, 10 September 2005.
63. Don Lee, *A Yarn or Two: The Wool Industry in Australia and Three and a Half Years As a P.O.W. of the Japanese* (Perth: Hesparian Press, 1994), p. 44.
64. Lee, *A Yarn or Two*, p. 79.
65. Anis in the three-disc DVD set, Discovery Channel, *The History of Singapore* (Singapore: Discovery Channel, 2006).

66. Mohd Anis bin Tairan interview with Kevin Blackburn at Kampong Siglap Mosque, Singapore, 15 February 2002.

67. Lee, *A Yarn or Two*, p. 15.

68. Yoji Akashi, "Japanese Policy Towards Malayan Chinese 1941–1945", *Journal of South East Asian Studies* 1, 2 (September 1970): 68.

69. N.I. Low and H.M. Cheng, *This Singapore: Our City of Dreadful Night* (Singapore: City Book Store, 1947), pp. 16–9.

70. Henry Frei, *Guns of February: Ordinary Japanese Soldiers' Views of the Malayan Campaign and the Fall of Singapore* (Singapore: Singapore University Press, 2004), pp. 146ff.

71. Choi Siew Hong interview with Kevin Blackburn in Kuala Lumpur, 16 December 2004.

72. Ibid.

73. Ibid.

74. Mohd Anis bin Tairan interview with Kevin Blackburn at Kampong Siglap Mosque, Singapore, 15 February 2002.

75. Ibid. Chinese witnesses confirm this; see: Chen Su Lan, *Remember Pompong and Oxley Rise* (Singapore: Chen Su Lan Trust, 1969), pp. 198–9, and *Straits Times*, 13 September 1951.

76. *Straits Times*, 24 February 1962.

77. Kevin Blackburn, "The Collective Memory of the *Sook Ching* Massacre and the Creation of the Civilian War Memorial of Singapore", *JMBRAS* 73, 1 (2000): 71–90.

78. See Lee, *Amber Sands*; Onishi Satoru, *Hiroku Shonan Kakyo Shukusei Jiken* [*Secret Record of the Purge of the Chinese of Singapore*] (Tokyo: Kongo Shuppan, 1977); and C.K. Lim, "Letter to the Editor: Telok Kurau Echo", *Straits Times*, 13 June 1946, p. 4.

79. The women's earrings are catalogued at National Museum of Singapore 2008-05895. The Singapore Chinese Chamber of Commerce describes these artefacts in Foong Choon Hon, ed., *Eternal Vigilance: The Price of Freedom*, trans. Yuen Chen Ching (Singapore: AsiaPac Books, 2006), pp. 270–3.

80. C.C. Chin and Karl Hack, eds., *Dialogues with Chin Peng: New Light on the Malayan Communist Party* (Singapore: Singapore University Press, 2004), p. 80.

81. Firdaus Haji Abdullah, *Radical Malay Politics: Its Origin and Early Development* (Petaling Jaya, Selangor: Pelanduk, 1985), pp. 64–7. See also Rustam A. Sani, *Social Roots of the Malay Left: An Analysis of Kesatuan Melayu Muda* (Petaling Jaya, Selangor: SIRD, 2008), pp. 31–6.

82. Another senior KMM leader, Onan Haji Siraj, led the *Giyutai*.

83. For KMM activities at Kampong Tanglin, Singapore, see Ismail bin Zain interviewed by Tan Beng Luan, 5 September 1985, Accession No. A 000601/05, Reel 01 (NAS).

84. Mohd Anis bin Tairan interview with Kevin Blackburn at Kampong Siglap Mosque, Singapore, 30 April 2004; and Mohd Anis bin Tairan's written statement from which Mohd Anis bin Tairan addressed the audience at the "Open Public Forum with Veterans and Members of the Wartime Generation", 4 September 2005, Singapore History Museum.

85. Mohd Anis bin Tairan interview with Kevin Blackburn at Kampong Siglap Mosque, Singapore, 30 April 2004.

86. Rex Shelley, *Dr Paglar: Everyman's Hero* (Singapore: Eurasian Association, 2010).

87. Ismail bin Zain interviewed by Tan Beng Luan on 5 September 1985, Accession Number A 000601/05, Reel 01 (NAS).

88. Mohd Anis bin Tairan interview with Kevin Blackburn at Kampong Siglap Mosque, Singapore, 30 April 2004.

89. Ibid.

90. Mohd Anis bin Tairan interview with Kevin Blackburn at Kampong Siglap Mosque, Singapore, 15 February 2002.

91. Mohd Anis bin Tairan interview with Kevin Blackburn at Kampong Siglap Mosque, Singapore, 30 April 2004.

92. Mohd Anis bin Tairan's written statement from which he addressed the audience at the "Open Public Forum with Veterans and Members of the Wartime Generation", 4 September 2005, Singapore History Museum.

93. Ibid.

94. Mohd Anis bin Tairan interview with Kevin Blackburn at Kampong Siglap Mosque, Singapore, 15 February 2002.

95. Alias Saleh bin Sulaiman.

96. Mohd Anis bin Tairan's written statement from which he addressed the audience at the "Open Public Forum with Veterans and Members of the Wartime Generation", 4 September 2005, Singapore History Museum.

97. Kassim Ahmad and Noriah Mohamed, eds., *Hikayat Hang Tuah* (Kuala Lumpur: Yayasan Karyawan dan Dewan Bahasa dan Pustaka, 1997), p. xxviii.

98. Mohd Anis bin Tairan's written statement from which he addressed the audience at the "Open Public Forum with Veterans and Members of the Wartime Generation", 4 September 2005, Singapore History Museum.

99. Mohd Anis bin Tairan's written statement.

100. Mohd Anis bin Tairan interview with Kevin Blackburn at Kampong Siglap Mosque, Singapore, 30 April 2004.

101. Mohd Anis bin Tairan interview with Kevin Blackburn at Kampong Siglap Mosque, Singapore, 19 February 2009.

102. Kevin Blackburn, "Public Forum With Veterans and the Wartime Generation at Singapore in 2005", *Oral History Association of Australia Journal* 28 (2006): 69–74.

103. Maurice Halbwachs, *On Collective Memory* (Chicago: University of Chicago Press, 1992), pp. 38, 182. In Halbwach's eyes, memory is continually changing according to present day concerns.
104. Stephane Audion-Rouzeau and Annette Becker, *14–18: Understanding the Great War*, trans. Catherine Temerson (New York: Farrar, Straus and Giroux, 2002), p. 182.
105. Alistair Thomson, *Anzac Memories: Living with the Legend* (Melbourne: Oxford University Press, 1994).
106. Paul Connerton, *How Societies Remember* (Cambridge: Cambridge University Press, 1989), pp. 41–71.
107. James V. Wertsch, *Voices of Collective Remembering* (London: Cambridge University Press, 2002), pp. 67–148.
108. Cheah Boon Kheng, "The 'Black-Out' Syndrome and the Ghosts of World War II: The War as a 'Divisive Issue' in Malaysia", in *Legacies of World War II in South and East Asia*, ed. David Koh Wee Hock (Singapore: ISEAS, 2007), pp. 47–59.
109. Alessandro Portelli, "The Peculiarities of Oral History", *History Workshop Journal* 12, 1 (Autumn 1981): 99–100.

Chapter 3

1. We cannot be sure of the 1941 population, as wartime conditions meant the census due that year was not taken. The 1931 census suggested 557,745 and a growth rate of 2.9%, reflecting the depression. The average population growth rate for the previous two decades was about 3%, with this accelerating rapidly postwar. By 1947, the population was 938,144. Allowing 3% a year growth from 1931 would give, in 1941, 720,000 plus. See Saw Swee Hock, "Population Growth and Control", in *A History of Singapore*, eds. Edwin Lee and Ernest Chew (Singapore: Oxford University Press, 1991), p. 221
2. Hack and Blackburn, *Did Singapore Have to Fall?*, pp. 12–26, citation on p. 26 is of Braddon, *The Naked Island* (Edinburgh: Birlinn, 2001 [first published 1951]), pp. 60–1.
3. June Reeve Tucker née Ferguson, at http://www.malayanvolunteersgroup.org.uk/files/image-2111212-0001.pdf [accessed 4 June 2010].
4. Our excuse for using this epithet is that it is the title of a book. See Geoffrey Brooke, *Singapore's Dunkirk* (London: Leo Cooper, 1989).
5. June Reeve Tucker nee Ferguson, at http://www.malayanvolunteersgroup.org.uk/files/image-2111212-0001.pdf [accessed 4 June 2010].
6. O.W. Gilmour, *With Freedom to Singapore* (London: Ernest Benn, 1950), p. 26.
7. McKerron had been a member of the MCS since the 1920s. Turnbull, *A History of Modern Singapore, 1819–2005* (Singapore: NUS Press, 2009), pp. 225–30.

8. For an overview, see Karl Hack, *Defence and Decolonisation in Southeast Asia: Britain, Malaya and Singapore* (Richmond: Curzon, 2001), pp. 35–55.
9. Gilmour, *With Freedom to Singapore*, p. 33, 125.
10. For details on the various surrenders, see Romen Bose, *The End of the War: Singapore's Liberation and the Aftermath of the Second World War* (Singapore: Marshall Cavendish, 2005).
11. Gilmour, *With Freedom to Singapore*, pp. 94, 125.
12. Ibid., pp. 91–3.
13. Ibid., p. 101. See Use of Japanese Troops for Various Work in Singapore, 209/45 Microfilm MSA 10, in Ministry of Social Affairs Records (NAS). Also see Andrew Gilmour, *My Role in the Rehabilitation of Singapore, 1946–1953* (Singapore: ISEAS, 1973).
14. Propaganda: The Ashley Gibson Report, circulated in Malaya in September 1945 after discussion by the Malayan Working Party in London in May 1945, file PR/1/6, British Military Administration (Malaya) (NAM).
15. Some remarks on the Reconquest and Political Reconstruction of Malaya by P. Curtis, discussed by the Malayan Working Party in London during May 1945, in Intelligence: Suggestions and Views on Reconstruction of Malaya, file number 506/27, British Military Administration (NAM).
16. Ibid.
17. In the postwar MCS, Hammett became Acting Deputy Chief Secretary of Malaya (1947–1948), and head the state of Malacca as Resident Commissioner (1952 and 1954–1957). J. Victor Morais, ed., *The Leaders of Malaya and Who's Who, 1957–58* (Kuala Lumpur: Khee Meng Press, 1957), p. 76.
18. Secretariat Propaganda, Increased Propaganda Memorandum, by H.G. Hammett, 1 November 1945 to Colonel M.C. Hay SCAO [Senior Civil Affairs Officer], BMA (M) Johore in file number PR/1/7, British Military Administration (NAM).
19. Secretariat Propaganda, Increased Propaganda Memorandum, by H.G. Hammett.
20. Anthony Stockwell, *Malaya*, Vol. I (London: HMSO, 1995), p. 124 gives text of the eight points.
21. Secretariat Propaganda, Increased Propaganda Memorandum, by H.G. Hammett.
22. Colonel M.C. Hay from BMA Johor Headquarters wanted to target towns where the communists were strong, such as Segamat and Kluang. Secretariat Propaganda, Appreciation of the Publicity Situation in the Malay Peninsula on 16 November 1945 by Major G.S. Walker; and Propaganda by Colonel M.C. Hay SCAO BMA (M) Johore to DCCAO [Deputy Chief Civil Affairs Officer] in Kuala Lumpur, in file PR/1/7, British Military Administration, (NAM).
23. *Who's Who in Malaya, 1939: A Biographical Record of Prominent Members of Malaya's Community in Official, Professional and Commercial Circles* (Singapore: Fishers, 1939), p. 54.

24. Secretariat Propaganda, From SCAO, Publicity and Printing Department to DCCAO in Kuala Lumpur, Subject P.W. Division, 22 October 1945 in PR/1/7, British Military Administration (NAM).

25. Secretariat Propaganda, Headquarters, Supreme Allied Command, South East Asia Directive to Head of Political Warfare Division by Lieutenant General F.A.M. Browning 23 September 1945, in file number PR/1/7, British Military Administration (NAM).

26. *Straits Times*, 24 September 1945.

27. *Desert Victory* (British Ministry of Information, 1943, reissued on VHS in 1999 by DD Video).

28. Stops included the Selangor Chinese Assembly Hall in Kuala Lumpur, where Chinese might easily view it Exhibition of War Pictures SELCA in file SELCA 51/46, British Military Administration (NAM). In Singapore, more than 10,000 a day visited.

29. Chin Peng, *Alias Chin Peng: My Side of History* (Singapore: Media Masters, 2003), pp. 149–55. Henceforth referred to as *My Side of History*.

30. Afterwards, the MPAJA members rather spoilt the effect of their boycott, when they allowed themselves to be browbeaten into signing a letter of apology to the Heads of the British services.

31. *Straits Times*, 8 January 1946.

32. See the full list of the Malayan Contingent Victory published by the *Straits Times*, 25 April, 1946. *Straits Times*, 25 April 1946; and Chin Peng, *My Side of History*, pp. 229, 475.

33. *Straits Times*, 9 June 1946.

34. *Straits Times*, 8 June 1946.

35. *Straits Times*, 26 June 1947. Also among these films was *Theirs is the Glory* (1945). This used British veterans from the Battle of Arnhem, returning to Holland to re-enact that battle one year after the original action of September 1944.

36. Letter to Editor by Choong Kum Swee, "Man in the Street: Chinese Thoughts on Victory Day", *Straits Times*, 10 June 1946.

37. Karl Hack, "Contentious Heritage", in *Understanding Heritage and Memory*, ed. Tim Benton (Manchester: Manchester University Press, 2010), pp. 94–6. See also Tim Benton and Penelope Curtis, "The Heritage of Public Commemoration", in ibid., pp. 56–69.

38. Hack, "Contentious Heritage", pp. 94–65.

39. Combined War Memorials file 81/1945 NA 871 in British Military Administration Records (NAS); Malayan War Memorials, MU 13/1946, Malayan Union Files (NAM).

40. *Straits Times*, 26 September 1947, p. 1, 25 May 1947, p. 3, and 18 June 1947, p. 4.

41. Combined War Memorials file 81/1945 NA 871 in British Military Administration Records (NAS); Malayan War Memorials, MU 13/1946, Malayan Union Files (NAM).

42. *Singapore Free Press*, 24 July 1946.

43. *Singapore Free Press*, 11 November 1946.

44. *Straits Times*, 10 and 11 November 1947.

45. Hack and Blackburn, *Did Singapore Have to Fall?*, p. 150.

46. Details from the official Commonwealth War Graves Commission site, at http://www.cwgc.org.

47. Imperial War Graves Commission, *The War Dead of the British Commonwealth and Empire 1939–1945: The Singapore Memorial Part I*, London, Imperial War Graves Commission, 1959, p. xvii.

48. CO1032/73, War Memorial, General Department, original correspondence, 1950–56 (TNA).

49. Initially, the Colonial Office did not want a member of the royal family to open the monument, fearing that forthcoming constitutional negotiations might raise the political temper in Singapore, and lead to protests. But the Duke of Gloucester, as the Chairman of the Imperial War Graves Commission was the perfect choice, and as it was the Constitutional talks of March 1957 passed off successfully: they paved the way for virtually full self-government in 1959. See War Memorial Singapore, CO 1032/73 (TNA) See also Muzaini Hamzah and Brenda S.A. Yeoh, "Memory-Making 'From Below': Rescaling Remembrance at the Kranji War Memorial and Cemetery, Singapore" *Environment and Planning A* 39, 6 (2007). 1288 -305; and Romen Bose, *Kranji: The Commonwealth War Cemetery and the Politics of the Dead* (Singapore: Marshall Cavendish, 2006).

50. *Malaya Tribune*, 5 September 1946. For the Malayan intelligence's early view of Tan Cheng Lock as "anti-government", see *MSS: Political Intelligence Journal* (30 April 1947): 88 and (15 February 1948): 89–90.

51. Gilmour, *With Freedom to Singapore*, p. 192.

52. Its owners included Tan Cheng Lock, who had long sought to forge a cross-ethnic "Malayan" nationalism. In 1947–1948, Tan was one of the supporters of the Malayan Union and a more inclusive citizenship, against British abandonment of both in the face of Malay anger.

53. For analysis of the British imperial hero, see John M. MacKenzie, *Propaganda and Empire: The Manipulation of British Public Opinion 1880–1960* (Manchester: Manchester University Press, 1984), pp. 173–98; J.A. Mangan, "Noble Specimens of Manhood: School Literature and the Creation of a Colonial Chivalric Code", in *Imperialism and Juvenile Literature*, ed. Jeffrey Richards (Manchester: Manchester University Press, 1989), pp. 173–95; and J.A. Mangan, "The Grit of our Forefathers Invented Traditions, Propaganda and Imperialism", in *Imperialism and Popular Culture*, ed. John M. MacKenzie (Manchester University Press, 1986), pp. 113–39.

54. John M. MacKenzie, "Heroic Myths of Empire", in *Popular Imperialism and The Military, 1850–1950*, ed. John MacKenzie (Manchester University Press, 1992), p. 114.

55. A.E. Percival, "Introduction" in J.N. Lewis Bryan, *The Churches of The Captivity in Malaya* (London: Society For Promoting Christian Knowledge, 1946), p. 7.

56. *Straits Times*, 11 August 1947. This is a letter is from a "H.S. Bull", but the "S." is most likely a typo as the only civilian internee in Malaya with the name of Bull was Harold Robert Bull. The letter writer does suggest he was an internee imprisoned by the Japanese. Harold Robert Bull stayed in Singapore after the liberation — see the *Straits Times*, 2 September 1949. See also the most accessible list of the Changi civilian internee register at http://www.changimuseum.com/civilian.htm.

57. See Hack and Blackburn, *Did Singapore Have to Fall?*, *passim*, for the underlying debate about whether and why Singapore had to fall. Churchill took a gamble that the Japanese either would not attack, or if they did would be blunted by American intervention. Given those calculations, he sent almost all new aircraft and tanks to Russia and North Africa in 1941, thus rendering plans for the forward defence of Malaya ineffective. This means that he gambled rather than sacrificed Singapore, though the resource decision underpins the "sacrifice" position.

58. For an overview, see Joseph Kennedy, *British Civilians and the Japanese War in Malaya and Singapore, 1941–45* (London: Macmillan, 1987), pp. 147–51, 157–8.

59. Colin Sleeman and S.C. Silkin, eds., *Trial Sumida Haruzo and Twenty Others (the "Double Tenth" Trial)* (London: W. Hodge, 1951), p. xxx.

60. Sleeman and Silkin, *Trial Sumida Haruzo and Twenty Others*, pp. 594–5.

61. Roy McKay, *Leonard Wilson: Confessor for the Faith* (London: Hodder and Stoughton, 1973), p. 33.

62. Ibid., p. 38.

63. Ibid., pp. 45, 185–6. For the quotation, see pp. 13–4.

64. Lord Montgomery's Reflections on Members of the M.C.S., CO 537/2179 (TNA).

65. *Straits Times*, 5 September 1946. See also *Straits Times*, 20 March 1952.

66. *Straits Times*, 7 July 1946; and a letter dated 19/12/45 from Lam Hong addressed to the C.C.A.O. [Chief Civil Affairs Officer] (the Statue of Sir Stamford Raffles) in Statue of Sir Stamford Raffles, British Military Administration Records 83/45 (NAS).

67. *Malay Mail*, 12 August 1946; *Straits Times*, 18 July 1946; *Straits Times*, 12 August 1946; *Straits Times*, 21 October 1946; and *Malay Mail*, 15, 16, and 17 November 1946.

68. Hack and Blackburn, *Did Singapore Have to Fall?*, pp. 149–50.

69. *Straits Times*, 13 September 1945. See James Bradley, *The Tall Man Who Never Slept: A Tribute to Cyril Wild* (London: Woodfield Publishing, 1991), pp. 88–9, 176–83.

70. Brian Montgomery, *Shenton of Singapore: Governor and Prisoner of War* (Singapore: Times Books International, 1984), pp. 175–6.
71. Reverend Hobart Amstutz of the Methodist Church, Reverend Thomas Gibson and Mr Harold Cheeseman of the Presbyterian Church, and Reverend Sorby Adams of the Church of England, were all ex-internees. See Bobby E.K. Sng, *In His Good Time* (Singapore: Graduates' Christian Fellowship, 1980), p. 206; and Robert Hunt, Lee Kam Hing, and John Roxborogh, *Christianity In Malaysia: A Denominational History* (Petaling Jaya, Selangor: Pelanduk, 1992).
72. Venerable David Rosenthall, Archdeacon of Singapore, to J. Morley, Under Secretary, Singapore, 29 July 1946, in Anniversary of the Signing of the Japanese Surrender in Singapore on September 12th to be declared a public holiday, 2890/46, Social Affairs Ministry (NAS).
73. See Sng, *In His Good Time*, pp. 193–201.
74. *Straits Times*, 15 February 1946.
75. Victory Day Celebration 12.9.46 by Colonial Secretary's Office, Singapore, 4 September 1946, in Anniversary of the Signing of the Japanese Surrender in Singapore on September 12th to be declared a public holiday, 2890/46, Social Affairs Ministry (NAS).
76. *Straits Times*, 13 September 1946.
77. See a copy of his speech in the file, Anniversary of the Signing of the Japanese Surrender in Singapore on September 12th to be declared a public holiday, 2890/46, Social Affairs Ministry (NAS).
78. Proposed arrangements for the celebrations of September 12 1946, 2 September 1946, CGT/GFL, in Anniversary of the Signing of the Japanese Surrender in Singapore on September 12th to be declared a public holiday, 2890/46, Social Affairs Ministry (NAS).
79. Minute by H.E. The Governor, 13 September 1946, in Anniversary of the Signing of the Japanese Surrender in Singapore on September 12th to be declared a public holiday, 2890/46, Social Affairs Ministry, (NAS).
80. *Malaya Tribune*, 5 September 1946.
81. For an example of this view from other Europeans, see Margaret Shennan, *Out in the Midday Sun: The British in Malaya 1880–1960* (London: John Murray, 2000), pp 301–2.
82. *Straits Times*, 13 September 1946; and *Malaya Tribune*, 13 September 1946.
83. *Malaya Tribune*, 6 December 1950.
84. *Straits Times*, 13 September 1952 and 4 February 1952. See also John Hayter, *Priest in Prison: Four Years of Life in Japanese-Occupied Singapore* (London: Tynron Press, 1991), p. 233; and Lee Geok Boi, *The Religious Monuments of Singapore: Faiths of our Forefathers* (Singapore: Landmark Books, 2002), p. 53.
85. Ann and Cyril Parkinson, *Heroes of Malaya* (Singapore: Donald Moore, 1956), p. 104.

86. Sybil Kathigasu, *No Dram of Mercy* (London: Neville Spearman, 1954), p. 10.

87. Ann and Cyril Parkinson, *Heroes of Malaya* (Singapore: Donald Moore, 1956), p. 106.

88. *Straits Times*, 20 February 1946.

89. *Straits Times*, 22 February 1946.

90. Sybil Kathigasu, *No Dram of Mercy*, p. 237.

91. Zhou Mei, *Elizabeth Choy: More Than a War Heroine* (Singapore: Landmark Books, 1995), p. 86. Those she helped included Lady Shenton, the wife of the prewar Governor.

92. *Sunday Times* (Singapore), 16 June 1946. On 25 July 1946, she was escorted to Buckingham Palace by Sir Shenton Thomas and Lady Shenton Thomas. On 30 July 1946, she visited Princess Elizabeth, this time as a representative of the nurses of Singapore. Zhou Mei, *Elizabeth Choy*, pp. 86–7, 90–1.

93. Zhou Mei, *Elizabeth Choy*, p. 58.

94. *Straits Times*, 23 December 1949.

95. *Sunday Times* (Singapore), 7 November 1954.

96. Sybil Kathigasu, Norma Miraflor and Ian Ward, *Faces of Courage: A Revealing Historical Appreciation of Colonial Malaya's Legendary Kathigasu Family* (Singapore: Media Masters, 2006), p. 231.

97. *Straits Times*, 9 and 10 January 1948; and *Malaya Tribune*, 10 January 1948.

98. *Morning Tribune*, 10 January 1948.

99. See the affidavit of Major F.A.H. Magee on page 137 in Defendant Fukuei Shimpei: Place of Trial: Singapore: 1946 February 15–946 June 9, WO 235/825 (TNA). See the Australian collection of testimony which also suggests that there were different escapes and that Breavington could not have ordered at least Fletcher and Waters to escape in Correspondence concerning Cpl R E Breavington VX63100 and Pte L Gale VX62289, B3856 144/14/65 (NAA, Melbourne).

100. Affidavit of Lieutenant-Colonel Archer Edward Tawney who witnessed the execution, p. 124 in Defendant Fukuei Shimpei: Place of Trial: Singapore: 1946, WO 235/825 (TNA).

101. *Straits Times*, 7 September 1945, and 19 August 1957. David Nelson, *The Story of Changi, Singapore* (Perth: Changi Publications, 1974), pp. 10, 210–1. According to Lewis Bryan's *Churches of the Captivity in Malaya*, 809 POWs were buried in Changi's cemeteries from 1942 to 1945. See also R.P.W. Havers, *Reassessing the Japanese Prisoner of War Experience: The Changi POW Camp, Singapore, 1942–5* (London: RoutledgeCurzon, 2003).

102. H.A. Probert, *History of Changi* (Singapore: Prison Industries, 1965), p. 47.

103. "F.E. P.O.W. Claims Against the Japanese, Progress Report No. 10", *Malaya* (formerly called *British Malaya*) (May 1952): 27.

104. J.N. Lewis Bryan, "The Churches of Captivity in Malaya", *British Malaya* (March 1947): 166.

105. Probert, *History of Changi* (Singapore: Changi Museum, 2006), pp. 36–7. Probert does not name the author.

106. See testimony for the war crimes trial in Defendant Fukuei Shimpei: Place of Trial: Singapore: 1946 February 15–1946 June 9, WO 235/825 (TNA); and Correspondence concerning Cpl R E Breavington VX63100 and Pte L Gale VX62289, B3856 144/14/65 (NAA, Melbourne).

107. *Sunday Times* (Singapore), 28 March 1946.

108. See his tombstone marker at Kranji War Cemetery cited in *The War Dead of the Commonwealth (and non World War and Foreign Nationals Burials): Kranji War Cemetery Singapore* (London: Commonwealth War Graves Commission, reprinted, September 2001) p. 30. The tombstone is row 3A, number 2. His military records at the Australian War Memorial indicate that he was a private, but he is recorded as a corporal on panel 90 of the Australian War Memorial's roll of honour. See http://www.awm.gov.au/find/index.asp. The defence record file indicates this as well, Posthumous MIDs [Mention-in-Dispatches], AWM 119, 112.

109. Breavington, Rodney Edward Service Number VX63100, B883, VX63100 (NAA, Canberra).

110. Defendant Fukuei Shimpei: Place of Trial: Singapore: 1946 February 15–1946 June 9, WO 235/825 (TNA); and Correspondence concerning Cpl R E Breavington VX63100 and Pte L Gale VX62289, B3856 144/14/65 (NAA, Melbourne).

111. Eric Lambert, *MacDougal's Farm* (London: Muller, 1965), pp. 152, 155.

112. "Malayan Affairs", *Malaya* (January 1953): 20; John Hattendorf, *The Two Beginnings: A History of St. George's Church, Tanglin* (Singapore: St George's Church, 1984), pp. 47–52; and Lee, *The Religious Monuments of Singapore: Faiths of Our Forefathers*, p. 58. The sermon on the day was preached by an ex-POW, Reverend G.M.R. Bennett.

113. James Boyle, *Railroad to Burma* (Sydney: Allen & Unwin, 1990), p. xiii.

114. Kevin Blackburn, "Changi: A Place of Personal Pilgrimages and Collective Histories", *Australian Historical Studies* 30, 112 (April 1999): 153–73.

115. *Annual Report of Singapore Prisons, 1954* (Singapore: Singapore Prisons Department, 1954), p. 10; Religious Services in the Prisons, Records of Singapore Prisons, C Pris 173/47 (NAS); and Changi Prison Chapel, in The Battle for Singapore, Changi Prison Chapel & Museum, serial number 58, file reference number PD/PRJ/45/87, vol. 2, Singapore Tourist Promotion Board (NAS).

116. Reverend Henry Khoo, Changi Prison Chaplain since 1967 and son of the first Singapore Prisons Chaplain Reverend Khoo Siaw Hua, interview with Kevin Blackburn on 2 October 1997.

117. *The Memorial Changi Prison Chapel Visitors Book* is kept in the Heritage Room of Changi Prison.

118. Shortly after his release from captivity, Goode had become Principal Assistant Secretary in Singapore, then Deputy Economic Secretary in Malaya.

119. See his entry in *The Memorial Changi Prison Chapel Visitors Book*; *Straits Times*, 19 August 1957; and *Annual Report of Singapore Prisons, 1957* (Singapore: Singapore Prisons Department, 1957), p. 26. For details on William A.C. Goode, see Lee Kuan Yew, *The Singapore Story* (Singapore: Times, 1998), p. 197; and J. Victor Morais, ed., *Leaders of Malaya and Who's Who, 1956* (Kuala Lumpur: Economy Printers, 1956), p. 53.

120. After release in 1946, Black had been was appointed Deputy Chief Secretary of North Borneo (now the Malaysian state of Sabah). Morais, *Leaders of Malaya and Who's Who, 1956*, p. 3; and *Straits Times*, 23 November 1957.

121. Joseph Kennedy, *British Civilians and the Japanese War in Malaya and Singapore, 1941–1945* (London: Macmillan, 1987), p. 148. For Scott's trial and imprisonment in Outram Road as a "spy", see Obituary, Sir Robert H. Scott, "Inspiring Influence in Occupied Singapore", *Times*, 2 March 1982. Scott was a witness at the postwar trials, but also arranged meetings with some former gaolers.

122. In March 1946, Scott had become political adviser to Special Commissioner Lord Killearn, at the time the senior British official in Southeast Asia, and in 1947, he had transferred to the Foreign Office. *Straits Times*, 18 November 1959. Transmission from National Library of Scotland, Edinburgh, Accession 8181, R.H. Scott papers, Box 4, "Transmission after the Liberation of Singapore, 1945".

123. "Far East Bookshelf, Escape to Captivity by Peter Hartley, Reviewed by Revd. A.J. Bennitt", *Malaya* (October 1952): 47. This was the journal of the British Association of Malaya.

124. Blackburn, "Changi: A Place of Personal Pilgrimages and Collective Histories", pp. 153–73.

125. Changi Prison Chapel in The Battle for Singapore, Changi Prison Chapel & Museum, serial number 58, file reference number PD/PRJ/45/87, vol. 2; and Changi East Coast Tour, in The Battle for Singapore, Changi Prison Chapel & Museum, serial number 61, file reference number PD/PRJ/45/87, vol. 8, Singapore Tourism Promotion Board Records (NAS).

126. See the model of St David's, which also received versions of the murals in 1945, in Peter W. Stubbs' *The Changi Murals: The Story of Stanley Warren's War* (Singapore: Landmark: 2003), p. 42.

127. "The Story of St. Luke's Chapel, Singapore and the Stanley Warren Murals: A Personal Viewpoint By Wally Hammond, ex-197 Field Ambulance, RAMC In Memory of Those've Left Behind", revised version dated March 1995. Provided to the authors courtesy of the Singapore Ministry of

Defence. Wally Hammond was at the hospital, and also played the organ in St Luke's.

128. Warren, *The Changi Murals*, pp. 54–67, for quotation of Warrren on the frangipani.
129. "The Story of St. Luke's Chapel, Singapore and the Stanely Warren Murals: A Personal Viewpoint by Wally Hammond". The author called this "one of the most memorable services".
130. Blackburn, "Changi: A Place of Personal Pilgrimages and Collective Histories", pp. 153–73. Stubbs, *The Changi Murals*, pp. 49–69.
131. Letter from James Lowe, Lumb Rossendale, 31 March 1998 (billeted at Changi 1948–1949).
132. Stubbs, *The Changi Murals*, pp. 83–8.
133. Stubbs, *The Changi Murals*, p. 92.
134. *The Changi Murals* (Singapore: Kok Wah Press, 1966?) — a copy sent in correspondence with John Gimblett, a guide to the Changi Murals for the Church of England in Singapore at Changi military base (1967 to 1970), 14 August 1999.
135. Blackburn, "Changi: A Place of Personal Pilgrimages and Collective Histories", pp. 153–73.
136. See, for instance, *Daily Mirror*, 23 October 1968, p. 12.
137. "The Story of St. Luke's Chapel, Singapore and the Stanley Warren Murals: A Personal Viewpoint by Wally Hammond". The complete quotation is "as a memorial chapel as it is so close to the war graves of the POW camp. I believe it would be a great comfort for relatives of the fallen to be able to visit the place in which so many of their men found comfort and peace in God".

Chapter 4

1. The "best of times, worst of times" formulation may appear Anglo-centric — coming from Charles Dickens, *A Tale of Two Cities*. But it is also used by Chinese-speaking ex-DAP assemblyman and Malaysiakini contributor James Wong Wing On, in his book on (in his words) "the heroes and heroines" of the MPAJA and MCP, *From Pacific War to Merdeka: Reminiscences of Abdullah CD, Rashid Maidin, Suriani Abdullah and Abu Samah* (Petaling Jaya, Selangor: SIRD, 2005: being articles and interviews from Malaysiakini.com).
2. Chin Peng clearly identified pre-1939 as an era when speakers talked of Overseas Chinese, with gradual shifts from around 1939 to 1945 through these terms to "Malayans" and "Malayan Chinese". Chin and Hack, *Dialogues*, pp. 67–8.
3. "The Price of Peace" was the title of a work that first appeared in Chinese in 1995. The English-language version is Foong Choon Hon, ed., *The

Price of Peace: True Accounts of the Japanese Occupation, trans. Clara Show (Singapore: Asiapac, 1997). The term was further popularised as the title of a 32-part Chinese-language dramatisation of 1997 (TCS 8, rerun on MediaCorp Channel 8 in 2007) and dubbed in English in 1999 (TCS 5). It featured semi-fictionalised portrayals of Lim Bo Seng and Tan Kah Kee as heroes, but marginalised the MCP and MPAJA.

4. For Chan Peng Kun @ Chan Ah Kai, see MCP, *Freedom News*, 4, 15 April 1949, in Ramakrishna, *Freedom News*, pp. 43–4. He joined the MPAJA aged around 19, and supposedly told his wife and girlfriend just before death that "It is a glory for a man to die with a meaning".

5. Li Fuk is discussed in Wong, *From Pacific to Merdeka*, p. 97. He also recruited Suriani Abdullah (@ Eng Ming Ching) and future MCP Malay leader Rashid Maidin. For biographical details, see Hara Fujio, "Leaders of the Malayan Communist Party during the Anti-Japanese War", in *New Perspectives on the Japanese Occupation in Malaya and Singapore, 1941–1945*, eds. Akashi Yoji and Yoshimura Mako, pp. 91–2, 103–4n138. Nagayasu was sentenced to death for his war crimes.

6. The larger MPAJA number comes from a Malaysian Chinese admirer of MPAJA "heroes and heroines, who had also been a DAP Parliamentarian, and Malaysiakini.com writer. See *From Pacific War to Merdeka*, pp. 74–5.

7. See Hack, *Defence and Decolonisation*, pp. 114, 152n30; Saw Swee-Hock, "Population Growth and Control", in *A History of Singapore*, eds. Edwin Lee and Ernest Chew (Singapore: Oxford University Press, 1991), p. 221. Singapore's 1931 population had only been 557,745.

8. At its extreme, a popular 1998 cartoon version — which ran through several reprints — managed to not mention the MCP or MPAJA even once, so that Lim Bo Seng appears to launch an independent mission, with only British help. See Clara Show, *Lim Bo Seng: Singapore's Best-Known War Hero* (Singapore: Asiapac, 1998 and 2009 editions).

9. Shan Ru-hong, *The War in the South: The Story of Negeri Sembilan's Guer-rillas* (Bangkok: Mental Health Publishing, 2003, originally in Chinese in 1995). The original was written to mark the 50th, 1995, anniversary "of the world's victory over Japanese imperialism", p. 10.

10. Hack and Blackburn, *Did Singapore Have to Fall?*, p. 172.

11. Lara Hein and Mark Seldon, "Learning Citizenship from the Past: Textbook Nationalism, Global Context and Social Change", *Bulletin of Concerned Asian Scholars* 30, 2 (1998): 8.

12. James, C. Hsiung, "The War and After: World Politics in Historical Con-text", in *China's Bitter Victory: The War with Japan, 1937–1945*, eds. James C. Hsiung and Stephen I. Levine (New York: M.E. Sharpe, 1992), pp. 295–7.

13. Lucien Bianco, *Origins of the Chinese Revolution, 1915–1949*, trans. Muriel Bell (Stanford, California: Stanford University Press, 1971), pp. 148–59.

Chalmers A. Johnson, *Peasant Nationalism and Communist Power: The Emergence of Revolutionary China 1937–1945* (London: Stanford University Press, 1963), p. 2.

14. Wang Gungwu, "Memories of War: World War II in Asia" in *War and Memory in Malaysia and Singapore*, eds. P. Lim Pui Huen and Diana Wong (Singapore: ISEAS, 2000), p. 17.

15. See the Singapore Chinese Chamber of Commerce and Industry publication by Foong Choon Hon, *The Price of Peace*, pp. 249–94. This was an English translation of a Chinese-language publication of the same name. Lee Kuan Yew, *The Singapore Story: Memoirs of Lee Kuan Yew* (Singapore: Times, 1998), p. 57.

16. Singapore Overseas Chinese Anti-Japanese Volunteer Army, Mah Khong Chairman of the Dalforce, S.V.C. Drill Hall, Singapore, 20 December 1946, to Secretary for Chinese Affairs in Dalforce file 76/1945 NA 878 in the British Military Administration Records (NAS).

17. Ibid.

18. Stephen Fitzgerald, *China and the Overseas Chinese: A Study of Peking's Changing Policy, 1949–1970* (Cambridge: Cambridge University Press, 1972), p. x

19. Li Tie Min, ed., *Da Zhan Yu Nan Qiao: Maluiya Zhi Bu* [*The Great War and the Overseas Chinese: Malayan Branch*] (Singapore: Singapore Overseas Chinese Publishing Company, 1947), pp. 58–9.

20. Hu Tie Jun, ed., *Xing Hua Yi Yong Jun Zhan Dou Shi: 1942 Xing Zhou Bao Wei Zhang* [*Singapore Chinese Volunteer Army: The Battle of Singapore, 1942*] (Singapore: Sin Ching Hwa Publishing, 1945), p. 13.

21. See Tan Kah Kee, *The Memoirs of Tan Kah Kee*, trans. A.H.C. Ward, Raymond W. Chu, and Janet Salaff (Singapore: Singapore University Press, 1994) pp. 153–8 and Note on the Singapore Chinese Anti-Japanese Mobilisation Council, and J.D. Dalley to H.P. Bryson, Ag. Colonial Secretary of Singapore, 30 September 1946, in Dalforce file 76/1945 NA 878 in British Military Administration Records (NAS). Ng Yeh Lu's case (also @ Huang Ya Lu) is complicated. He seems to have avoided giving names after surrender to the Japanese, tried to alert the MCP to Lai Tek's treachery after the war, and as Wee Mong Chen became a businessman and later Singapore Ambassador to Japan (1973–1980) before settling in Hong Kong. See Hara Fujio, "Leaders of the Malayan Communist Party", pp. 83–6.

22. See Tan Kah Kee, *The Memoirs of Tan Kah Kee*, pp. 153–8; and Note on the Singapore Chinese Anti-Japanese Mobilisation Council in Dalforce file 76/1945 NA 878, British Military Administration Records (NAS).

23. J.D. Dalley to H.P. Bryson, Ag. Colonial Secretary of Singapore, 30 September 1946 in Dalforce file 76/1945 NA 878 in British Military Administration Records (NAS).

24. Dalforce by E.C.S. Adkins, Ag. Secretary for Chinese Affairs, 24 June 1946, in Dalforce file 76/1945 NA 878 in British Military Administration Records (NAS). See also Dal Force Status in file number MLF/261B, British Military Administration (NAM); and Ian Alexander MacDonald Papers, 01/10/1, (IWM), London.

25. Ian Morrison, *Malayan Postscript* (London: Faber and Faber, 1946), p. 171.

26. Kevin Blackburn and Daniel Chew Jun Ern, "Dalforce at the Fall of Singapore in 1942: An Overseas Chinese Heroic Legend", *Journal of the Chinese Overseas* 1, 2 (2005): 233–59.

27. See Mah Khong's gripping account in Singapore Oversea Chinese Anti-Japanese Volunteer Army, Mah Khong, Chairman of the Dalforce, S.V.C. Drill Hall, Singapore, 20 December 1946, to Secretary for Chinese Affairs in Dalforce file 76/1945 NA 878 in British Military Administration Records (NAS).

28. Singapore Overseas Chinese Anti-Japanese Volunteer Army, Mah Khong, Chairman of the Dalforce, S.V.C. Drill Hall, Singapore, 20 December 1946, to Secretary for Chinese Affairs in Dalforce file 76/1945 NA 878 in British Military Administration Records (NAS).

29. He Wei Bo, "I Joined the Volunteer Army", in *The Price of Peace*, ed. Foong, pp. 291–2.

30. For the issue of Dalforce "myths" versus battlefield performance, see Kevin Blackburn and Daniel Chew Ju Erm, "Dalforce and the Fall of Singapore in 1942: An Overseas Chinese Heroic Legend", *Journal of Chinese Overseas* 1, 2 (November 2005): 233–52.

31. Dalforce by E.C.S. Adkins, Ag. Secretary for Chinese Affairs, 24 June 1946, in Dalforce file 76/1945 NA 878 in British Military Administration Records (NAS).

32. Lieutenant General A.E. Percival, "Operations of Malaya Command from 8 December 1941 to 15 February 1942", *Second Supplement to the London Gazette of 20 February 1948*, No. 38215, 26 February 1948, pp. 1245–346. Quotes are from "Section X Civil Defence" paragraphs 82, 86, 87, and 90; and "Section XXVII Scorched Earth Policy", paragraph 235.

33. *Nan Chiao Jit Pau*, 27 and 29 February 1948. See also *Straits Times*, 1 March 1948; and *Malaya Tribune*, 28 February 1948.

34. For the full text of the letter by Tan Kah Kee to Secretary of War, London, 3 March 1948 is in General Percival's Despatch on the Malayan Campaign: Protest Against Certain References to the Chinese, SCA 8 133/48, in the Singapore Chinese Affairs Files (NAS). See excerpts in the *Morning Tribune*, 5 March 1948.

35. *Morning Tribune*, 27 February 1948.

36. *Morning Tribune*, 17 March 1948; *Straits Times*, 24 March 1948; and 448 *H.C. DEB.*, 5 s., 17 March 1948 col. 248.

37. E.C.S. Adkins' minute of 2 September 1946 and in Dalforce file 76/1945 NA 878 in the British Military Administration Records (NAS).

38. *Straits Times*, 6 and 7 January 1946.

39. See letter from Colonel R.N. Broome, 15 January 1946, Clothing for Representative of Dalforce to be Present at the Parade to Receive Campaign Ribbons File 16/46 NA 878 in British Military Administration Records (NAS).

40. E.C.S. Adkins, Ag. Secretary for Chinese Affairs, Singapore, to the Colonial Secretary, Singapore, 19 July 1946 in Combined War Memorials file 81/1945 NA 871 in British Military Administration Records (NAS); and see Singapore War Memorials Committees in the Singapore Improvement Trust Files (25 October 1946) HDB 1086 (NAS); and Re-Burial of Chinese Volunteers Who Died during the Japanese Invasion of Singapore, SCA 7 387/47, in Singapore Chinese Affairs Files (NAS).

41. *Straits Times*, 6 February 1946. Tan Kah Kee, the Chairman of the Singapore China Relief Committee, and Chew Hean Swee of the same Committee had visited the site and found it suitable.

42. E.C.S. Adkins, Ag. Secretary for Chinese Affairs, Singapore to H.P. Bryson, M.C.S., Under Secretary, Singapore 30 August 1946; and H.T. Pagden, War Memorial, 2 April 1946 in Combined War Memorials file 81/1945 NA 871 in British Military Administration Records (NAS).

43. H.T. Pagden, War Memorial, 2 April 1946 in Combined War Memorials file 81/1945 NA 871 in British Military Administration (NAS).

44. *Sunday Times* (Singapore), 26 September 1948.

45. *Straits Times*, 19 December 1946; *Malaya Tribune*, 19 December 1946; *Sunday Tribune*, 22 December 1946; *Straits Times*, 29 March 1947; and *Singapore Free Press*, 13 December 1947.

46. Dalley's assurance was supposed to have been given at the Dalforce headquarters in the Nanyang Normal School. Mah Khong to J.D. Dalley, 16 March 1947, in Dalforce file 76/1945 NA 878 in the British Military Administration Records (NAS).

47. *Straits Times*, 10 February 1947; Dalco in file MLF/377, British Military Administration (NAM).

48. Singapore Overseas Chinese Anti-Japanese Volunteer Army, Mah Khong Chairman of the Dalforce, S.V.C. Drill Hall, Singapore, 20 December 1946, to Secretary for Chinese Affairs in Dalforce file 76/1945 NA 878 in the British Military Administration Records (NAS).

49. Madam Cheng and her husband appear to have had Cantonese names. Her name as reported in the Singapore press is consistently Cheng Seang Ho, which is close to the Cantonese pronunciation of the Chinese characters. The Wade-Giles Romanization of the Chinese characters in her name is Cheng Shuang-hao.

50. *Straits Times*, 25 July 1948. Imperial War Graves Commission, *The War Dead of the British Commonwealth and Empire: The Register of the Names of Those Who Fell in the 1939–1945 War and Have no Known Grave: The Singapore Memorial* (London: Her Majesty's Stationery Office, 1956), p. 837.

51. Hu Tie Jun, *Xing Hua Yi Yong Jun Zhan Dou Shi: 1942 Xing Zhou Boa Wei Zhang*, Preface.

52. See enclosures regarding Cheong Sang Hoo in Dalforce file 76/1945 NA 878 in the British Military Administration Records (NAS). In internal correspondence, meanwhile, the colonial authorities referred to Madam Cheng as "the Passionaria of Malaya in Dalforce", after Doleres Ibarruri, the female Communist fighter known as the *Pasionaria* in the Spanish Civil War; see E.C.S. Adkins, minute on translated request from Cheong Seng Hoo, 21 December 1949 in Dalforce file 76/1945 NA 878 in the British Military Administration Records (NAS).

53. *Sunday Times* (Singapore), 3 March 1957; *Singapore Standard*, 1 March 1957; and *Straits Times*, 8 March 1957.

54. *Sunday Times* (Singapore), 4 July 1948.

55. Ibid. Another Dalforce veteran, Robert Lim was "willing to help the British in the present emergency". He explained that "whether or not members of the force wish to fight again is for each individual member to decide".

56. Poh Guan Huat, "Lim Bo Seng: Nanyang Chinese Patriot", University of Singapore, unpublished diss., 1972, p. 17. What is interesting here is that Poh is writing of Lim Bo Seng as the main hero, but recycles the "Dalforce Legend".

57. Gene Z. Hanrahan, *The Communist Struggle in Malaya* (Kuala Lumpur: University of Malaya Press, 1971, originally published 1954), p. 115.

58. *Straits Times*, 24 July 1948.

59. P. Lim Pui Huen, "War and Ambivalence: Monuments: Monuments and Memorials in Johor", in *War and Memory in Malaysia and Singapore*, eds. P. Lim Pui Huen and Diana Wong (Singapore: ISEAS, 2000), pp. 153–4.

60. "Xue Bei Zeng Bu Ben Bianji Weiyuanhui [Xue Bei Revised Edition Editorial Committee]", in *Xue Bei: Zeng Bu Ben* (Hong Kong: Xue Bei Zeng Bu Ben Bianji Weiyuanhui, 1997), pp. 1–2.

61. "Xing Zhou Kangri Tongzhi Lian Yi Hui [Singapore Branch of the MPAJA Ex-Comrades Association]", in *Xue Bei* (Singapore: Sin Min Chu Service, 1945), p. 32.

62. Hai Shang Ou, *Malaiya Renmin Kangri Jun* [*Malayan People's Anti-Japanese Army*] (Singapore: Sin Min Chu Cultural Service, 1945). For the strength of Overseas Chinese nationalism, see Hara Fujio, "The Japanese Occupation and the Chinese Community", in *Malaya and Singapore During the Japanese Occupation*, ed. Paul. H. Kratoska (Singapore: Singapore University Press, 1995), p. 45; and Fujio Hara, *Malayan Chinese and China*, p. 13.

63. Tzu Szu, *Kangri Yingxiong Zai Rou Nan* (Singapore: Sin Min Chu Cultural Service, 1945), p. 23.
64. *Nanyang Siang Pau*, 9 September to 17 October, 1945. The story appears to be a romanticisation of MPAJA female guerrilla Cheah Swee Seng. She was active in communist-inspired student protests while at school. Cheah left Chung Hwa Girls School in Kuala Lumpur to join the MPAJA, was arrested in 1942 and spent the rest of the war in Pudu Gaol, making an unsuccessful attempt to escape. After the war, she recommenced communist activities. For the latter, see "Malayan Security Service Who's Who: Supplement No. 3 to Political Intelligence Journal No. 1 of 1948", *Malayan Security Service: Political Intelligence Journal* (15 January 1948).
65. Handling of Resistance Movements in Malaya CO 537/1570 (TNA).
66. J.L.H. Davis, Labour Office Bentong, Pahang to Major General Admiral General, Headquarters Far East Land Forces, Singapore, 14 January 1948, in CO 537/4245 (TNA).
67. *Straits Times*, 4 December 1945.
68. For Adam from Mountbatten, SAC 936, 2 December 1945 in WO 172/1794 (TNA). *Straits Times*, 3 and 4 December 1945.
69. *Sunday Times* (Singapore), 6 January 1946; and *Straits Times*, 7 January 1946.
70. Lieutenant Colonel George Thomas, Department of Publicity and Printing to Chief Secretary, BMA (M) HQ, Kuala Lumpur, 20 February 1946 in Victory Parade Contingent in PRI/31 MU 2682/46, British Military Administration (NAM).
71. See details on these MPAJA heroes in Chin Peng, *My Side of History*, pp. 151–2, 229; and Edgar O'Balance, *Malaya: The Communist Insurgent War, 1948–60* (London: Faber and Faber, 1966), p. 86. See also Hanrahan, *The Communist Struggle*, pp. 230–1.
72. Liew Yao is sometimes rendered Lau Yew.
73. The Third Regiment (northern Johor) was represented by its commander, Lin Chang (Lin Tien), and the Fourth Regiment by Chuan Seng (Chuang Ching). Chen Tien, representing the Fourth Regiment (Johor), was another trainee of the British 101 STS school, who infiltrated into the Kota Tinggi area in 1942. In the 1960s, Chen moved to China, where he died in the late 1980s.
74. Chin Peng, *My Side of History*, pp. 153–4. The boycott was partly a protest against the treatment of MCP member Soon Kwong, charged with having extorted money from a man between 4–10 September. The MCP regarded revenge against extortioneers (this man was so accused) and collaborators as right. Chin Peng's memoirs, p. 143, accept that Soon Kwang did extort money, but also claims that the "extortioner" was thereby treated lightly.

75. FARELF to War Office, 22 July 1948 in Guerrilla organisations: rewards, 1948 CO 537/4245 (TNA).

76. Ho Thean Fook, *Tainted Glory* (Kuala Lumpur: University of Malaya Press, 2000), p. x and for the reference to "tainted glory", see p. 256.

77. Cheah Boon Kheng, *Red Star Over Malaya: Resistance and Social Conflict During and After the Japanese Occupation, 1941–1946*, 2nd edition (Singapore: Singapore University Press, 1987), p. 260; Anthony Short, *In Pursuit of Mountain Rats: The Communist Insurrection in Malaya* (Singapore: Cultured Lotus, 2000, originally published in 1975), p. 96; O'Balance, *Malaya: The Communist Insurgent War, 1948–60*, p. 66; and Fujio Hara, *Malayan Chinese and China* (Singapore: Singapore University Press, 2003), p. 16.

78. J.L.H. Davis, Labour Office Bentong, Pahang to Major General Admiral General, Headquarters for Far East Land Forces, Singapore, 14 January 1948, in Guerrilla organisations: rewards, 1948 CO 537/4245 (TNA).

79. Chin Peng, *My Side of History*, p. 145.

80. *Combatant's Friend*, 25 February 1946. See Press Summaries: Chinese Press Summaries, 23/1/46-22/3/46 in File Number PR/3/2 P.III in British Military Administration (NAM).

81. *New Democracy* (*Xin Min Zhu Bao*), 14 February 1946.

82. *Straits Times*, 26 August 1947.

83. Chin Peng, *My Side of History*, p. 159. *Combatant's Friend*, 25 February 1946; and see Press Summaries: Chinese Press Summaries, 23/1/46–22/3/46 in File Number PR/3/2 P.III in British Military Administration, NAM.

84. For Weld from Browning, S.A.C.S.E.A. to Cabinet Offices, 18 February 1946, in Strikes and Demonstrations CO 537/1579 (TNA). Another objective of the event was dissemination of communist propaganda.

85. Mountbatten to British Chiefs of Staff, 11 February 1946, in Strikes and Demonstrations CO 537/1579 (TNA).

86. G.H. Hall to P. Piratin, Secretary of State, House of Commons, 23 April 1946, in Strikes and Demonstrations CO 537/1579 (TNA).

87. Victor Purcell, *The Chinese in Malaya* (Kuala Lumpur: Oxford University Press, 1967, originally published 1948), p. 273.

88. *Straits Times*, 18 February 1946.

89. BMA (M) to War Office 13 March 1946, in Strikes and Demonstrations CO 537/1579 (TNA).

90. HQ BMA (M) to War Office, 9 March 1946 and For Weld from Browning, S.A.C.S.E.A. to Cabinet Offices, 18 February 1946, in Strikes and Demonstrations CO 537/1579 (TNA).

91. F.S.V. Donnison, *British Military Administration in the Far East, 1943–1946* (London: Her Majesty's Stationery Office, 1956), p. 393.

92. *New Democracy*, 20 February 1946.

93. *New Democracy*, 19 February 1946.

94. *Nanyang Siang Pau*, 16 February 1946.

95. *Sin Chew Jit Poh*, 11 February 1946.

96. *New Democracy*, 22 February 1946.

97. *Combatant's Friend*, 23 February 1946; and see Press Summaries: Chinese Press Summaries, 23/1/46–22/3/46 in File Number PR/3/2 P.III in British Military Administration (NAM).

98. Li Ye Lin, ed., *Tai Ping Yang Zhan Zheng Shi Liao Hui Ban: Selected Historical Materials of the Pacific War: Sumber Sejarah Peperangan Pasifik* (Kuala Lumpur: Huazi Enterprise, 1996), pp. 370, 373–4. See also Chen Ya Cai, ed., *Malaiya Kangri Jinianbei Tupianji* [*Malaysian Anti-Japanese Memorials: A Pictorial*] (Kuala Lumpur: Selangor Chinese Assembly Hall, 1999), pp. 30–5.

99. C.A.S. Williams, *Chinese Symbolism & Art Motifs* (Boston: Tuttle, 1988, originally published in 1941), pp. 111–3; and Henry Dore, *Chinese Customs*, trans. M. Kennelly (Singapore: Graham Brash Publishers, 1987, originally published in 1911), pp. 74–84, 150–7.

100. Chin Kee Onn, *Ma-Rai-Ee* (Singapore: Eastern Universities Press, 1981), p. 276.

101. Hugh T. Pagden, Unrest in Malaya, Appendix I, page 62 in Political Developments: Chinese Affairs and Correspondence with Mr. H.T. Pagden CO 537/3757 (TNA).

102. These banned books are: *Xinma Qiaoyou Hui*, ed., *Malaiya Renmin Kangri Jun* [*Malayan People's Anti-Japanese Army*] (Hong Kong: Witness Publishing, 1992); and *Xinma Qiaoyou Hui*, ed., *Malaiya Renmin Kangri Douzheng Shiliao Xianji* [*Selected Historical Materials of the Malayan People's Anti-Japanese Struggle*] (Hong Kong: Witness Publishing, 1992).

103. See *Freedom News* no. 7, 1 September 1949, articles 1, 3 and 4, and no. 8, 1 October 1949, article 3. in Ramakrishna, *Freedom News*, attached CD.

104. "History of 'September 1st' Revolutionary Martyrs Day", *Freedom News*, 29, 15 September 1952, in Ramakrishna, *Freedom News*, pp. 76–80 and (for 1955), pp. 236–8. For an editorial on "Commemoration of the 35th Anniversary of the Great October Revolution [given as 7 November]", see *Freedom News*, 31, 15 November 1952, in ibid., pp. 99–100. For commemoration of the founding day of the MCP (which the MCP of the time wrongly dated to 1 July 1931), see *Freedom News*, 34, 15 February 1953, in ibid., p. 117.

105. *Freedom News*, no. 77, September 1956, in Ramakrishna, ed., *Freedom News*, CD.

106. The British more overtly chose a symbolic form, the Cenotaph or empty tomb. The Martyrs Memorial established in September 1946 did not claim to be a cenotaph in this way, but in reality probably was. The Japanese had removed the heads if not the bodies, and when the site was later dug up for reinterral, no remains were found.

107. *Freedom News* has a solid enough selection of proud boasts of running dog eliminations by these means to make recourse to British "propaganda"

unnecessary. See, for example, Ramakrishna, ed., *Freedom News*, CD, no. 22, 15 February 1951, "Punish One to Deter a Hundred", p. 7. This particular case at least involved an informant, others included MCA organisers involved in civil actions.

108. See the serialisation of Lim Bo Seng's diary in *New Nation*, 24 May 1971; and details recorded by Lim Bo Seng's friend N.I. Low, in N.I. Low and H.M. Cheng, *This Singapore (Our City of Dreadful Night)* (Singapore: City Book Store, 1947), p. 55.

109. C.F. Yong and R.B. McKenna, *The Kuomintang Movement in British Malaya 1912–1949* (Singapore: Singapore University Press, 1990), pp. 98, 188–9.

110. Poh Guan Huat, "Lim Bo Seng: Nanyang Chinese Patriot", University of Singapore, unpublished diss., 1972, pp. 15, 39, citing N.I. Low and H. Cheng, p. 54, for close relations with police intelligence officer Frederick Tremlett.

111. Yoji Akashi, *The Nanyang Chinese National Salvation Movement, 1937–1941* (Lawrence, KS: Centre for East Asian Studies, The University of Kansas, 1970), p. 159.

112. Tan Kah Kee, *Memoirs of Tan Kah Kee*, p. 158.

113. Excerpts from Lim Bo Seng's diary in the CD-ROM *Attacked!: The Japanese Occupation of Singapore 1942–1945* (Singapore: Daiichi Media and National Archives of Singapore, 1999). The full manuscript was deposited at the National Archives of Singapore by Lim Bo Seng's son Lim Leong Geok in 1992. See One Diary of Lim Bo Seng, NA 1738 (NAS).

114. Poh Guan Huat, "Lim Bo Seng: Nanyang Chinese Patriot", University of Singapore, unpublished diss., 1972, p. 23.

115. The Story of Lim Boh Seng, A Broadcast Talk by Col R.N. Broome of the Dept of Chinese Affairs, Singapore, on Dec 5/45 in The Lim Bo Seng Memorial manuscript collection file (National University of Singapore). Poh claims that, but for Lim's intervention, the European SOE officers might never have found suitable Malayan Chinese, putting the whole Malayan operation in doubt. Poh Guan Huat, "Lim Bo Seng: Nanyang Chinese Patriot", University of Singapore, unpublished diss., 1972, p. 25.

116. See the serialisation of Lim Bo Seng's diary in *New Nation*, 26 May 1971.

117. Tan Chong Tee, *Force 136: Story of a WWII Resistance Fighter*, trans. Lee Watt Sim and Clara Show (Singapore: Asiapac, 1995), p. 26. Tan Chong Tee, Singapore History Museum talk and interview afterwards on 14 February 2004.

118. Poh Guan Huat, "Lim Bo Seng: Nanyang Chinese Patriot", University of Singapore, unpublished diss., 1972, pp. 26–9.

119. Tan, *Force 136: Story of a WWII Resistance Fighter*, p. 26. Tan Chong Tee, Singapore History Museum talk and interview afterwards on 14 February 2004.

120. Show, *Lim Bo Seng*. The edition the authors' used was the 7th print in the first year of publication.
121. Poh Guan Huat, "Lim Bo Seng: Nanyang Chinese Patriot", University of Singapore, unpublished diss., 1972, p. 35.
122. Chin Peng, *My Side of the Story*, here shows its defects. The level of detail is all but implausible, and the text appears to be deft storytelling by collaborators Ian Ward and Norma Miraflor, with details woven in from other accounts, such as the submarine number. Contrast this, pp. 97–100, with Poh.
123. The Story of Lim Boh Seng A Broadcast Talk by Col R.N. Broome of the Dept of Chinese Affairs, Singapore, on Dec 5/45 in The Lim Bo Seng Memorial manuscript collection file (National University of Singapore). Poh Guan Huat, "Lim Bo Seng", diss., pp. 36–41.
124. Tan Chong Tee, *Force 136* (Singapore: Asiapac, 1995, Chinese edition 1994), pp. 227–52.
125. Lim Bo Seng, Special Operations Executive Personnel Files, HS 9/1341/6 (TNA).
126. Hugh T. Pagden, Unrest in Malaya, paragraph 50, p. 36 in Political Developments: Chinese Affairs and Correspondence with Mr. H.T. Pagden CO 537/3757 (TNA).
127. *Straits Times*, 4 and 7 December 1945.
128. *Straits Times*, 4, 7, and 8 December 1945.
129. *Straits Times*, 20 December 1945 and 14 January 1946.
130. *Straits Times*, 15 February 1946.
131. *Straits Times*, 4 January 1951.
132. *Straits Times*, 10 July 1952, 18 September 1952, and 3 November 1953.
133. *Straits Times*, 6 November 1952; and *Singapore Free Press*, 23 January 1953.
134. *Straits Times*, 26 September 1951.
135. *Singapore Free Press*, 5 November 1952.
136. *Singapore Free Press*, 27 June 1951.
137. Wang Gungwu, *Only Connect! Sino-Malay Encounters* (Singapore: Times Academic Press, 2001), pp. 127–9.
138. Fujio Hara, *Malayan Chinese and China*, pp. 98–104.
139. Speech by his Excellency The Commissioner-General at the Foundation Stone Ceremony of the Lim Bo Seng Memorial: November 3rd 1953 in the Lim Bo Seng Memorial manuscript collection file (National University of Singapore, 1971).
140. Text of Speech by Mr Lim Keng Lian, Chairman of the Lim Bo Seng Memorial Committee at the Foundation Stone Laying Ceremony at the Esplanade at 5.30 p.m. on November 3, 1953 in the Lim Bo Seng Memorial manuscript collection file (National University of Singapore, 1971). The three million figure for Chinese reflected the general growth of population locally, such that Malaya's five million of 1947 was now closer to six million, and Singapore's 938,144 of 1947 was heading towards the

1,445,929 it would reach in the 1957 census. See also Saw, "Population and Growth", p. 221.

141. *Nanfang Evening Post*, 30 June 1954.
142. *Singapore Standard*, 30 June 1954.
143. Ann and Cyril Parkinson, *Heroes of Malaya* (Singapore: Donald Moore, 1956), p. 107. See also "Heroes of Malaya". Publication of a book by Professor C.N. Parkinson, PRO 270/55 (PRO 20) in Public Relations Department Records (NAS).
144. *Straits Times*, 20 June 1959.
145. *Straits Times*, 19 January 1956.
146. *Straits Times*, 26 July 1965.
147. *Singapore Standard*, 7 October 1955; *Straits Times*, 6 and 27 October 1955; *Sunday Times* (Singapore), 9 and 16 October 1955.
148. Poh Guan Huat, "Lim Bo Seng", diss., pp. 39–40. Chin Peng has, to the contrary, made it clear that he got on extremely well with Davis, while he regarded Lim Bo Seng as a shortlived and ineffectual failure. See Chin Peng, *My Side of History*, pp. 15–6, 98–9.
149. National Archives of Singapore, Lim Bo Seng war diary, pp. 5–7, at http://www.s1942.org.sg/s1942/images/lim_bo_seng/Lim_Bo_Seng.djvu.
150. Clara Show, *Lim Bo Seng*, p. 118. The classic emotion shot of Lim as Confucian-patriotic hero is of him saying goodbye to his family in February 1942, when each "stupefied" child kissed him goodbye, and where he wrestles with his conscience over leaving "My dear Neo". It was used to great effect the Singapore television dramatisation, *The Price of Peace*. The "parting words", however, do not appear in his diary, nor anything like them (see the previous endnote for the citation). In that, he focuses on the unbearable parting from his children, and ends by discussing where his wife should stay, before adding, "I could not bear the strain any longer, and left hurriedly in order not to prolong the agony of separation".
151. In fact, his diary suggests that Gan Choo Neo, not Lim, may have been the main impetus behind the family staying. It reads: "Choo Neo chose to remain behind with the children and advised me to arrange for my own getaway". So it seems the "heroic" version might overemphasise the patriarchal and male heroic role in decision-making, in order to heighten the focus on Lim and his sacrifice. See National Archives of Singapore, Lim Bo Seng war diary, p. 5, at http://www.s1942.org.sg/s1942/images/lim_bo_seng/Lim_Bo_Seng.djvu. As this requires downloading a reader, it may be necessary to access first via http://www.s1942.org.sg/s1942/home/.

Chapter 5

1. Fuji-Go simply means Fuji Village.
2. Chin Kee Onn, *Malaya Upside Down* (Kuala Lumpur: Federal Publishers, 1976, first published 1946).

3. Goh Sin Tub, "A Victory of Spirit", *Intersect Japan-Asia*, 26–31 September 1995.

4. WO 235/1004, Defendants: Nishimura Takoma, Kawamura Saburo, Oishi Masayuki, Yokota Yoshitaka, Jyo Tomotatsu, Onishi Satoru, and Hisahatsu Haruji, Place of Trial: Singapore, pp. 265–6 and p. 621 (TNA).

5. Hayashi Hirofumi, "Japanese Treatment of Chinese Prisoners, 1931–1945", *Nature-People-Society: Science and Humanities* 26 (1999): 39–52.

6. Edward L. Dreyer, *China at War, 1901–1949* (Harlow, Essex: Longman, 1995), p. 237; and Henry Frei, *Guns of February: Ordinary Japanese Soldiers' Views of the Malayan Campaign and the Fall of Singapore, 1941–42* (Singapore: Singapore University Press, 2004), pp. 27–36. Iris Chang, *The Rape of Nanking* (New York: Penguin, 1997), p. 55; and Ienaga Saburo, *The Pacific War: World War II and the Japanese, 1931–1945* (New York: Pantheon, 1978), pp. 166–8.

7. Lincoln Li, *The Japanese Army in North China, 1937–1941: Problems of Political and Economic Control* (Tokyo: Oxford University Press, 1975), pp. 187–216; Edgar Snow, *The Battle for Asia* (New York: World Publishing Company, 1942) pp. 349–56; and Chalmers A. Johnson, *Peasant Nationalism and Communist Power: The Emergence of Revolutionary China 1937–1945* (London: Stanford University Press, 1963), pp. 55–6, 207.

8. Dr Chen Su Lan, *British Military Administration, Malaya, Singapore Advisory Council, Report of Proceedings, Volume 1*, 23 January 1946, pp. 101–4.

9. See the war diaries of the coastal batteries, as held in WO172/176; WO172/180; and the affidavit of Mr R.G Bruce in WO235/1004 (all TNA). This is also discussed in Hack and Blackburn, *Did Singapore Have to Fall?*, pp. 94, 238–9n153. These documents suggest 138 bodies on one stretch of shore alone, and more than 500 overall, for Blakang Mati alone.

10. The quotation is cited in Paul Kratoska, *The Japanese Occupation of Malaya, 1941–1945* (London: Allen and Unwin, 1998), pp. 97–8.

11. Singapore's 1942 population, swollen by refugees, had reportedly risen from the prewar estimate of 720,000 to a wartime peak of nearly a million. Take a million as the upper limit, and assume that around 75 per cent of that million was Chinese. That leaves an absolute maximum of 750,000 in February 1942. Assume a third of that were 14 or below, so leaving about 500,000 Chinese adults. The male-to-female sex ratio was changing, from far more males in 1931 to not far off even in 1947. However, in the 15–29 bracket, men still outnumbered women more than 2:1 at the latter date. We can assume, therefore, somewhere between 300,000 (assuming 60% of adult Chinese were male) and 350,000 (assuming 75% of adults were male) Chinese adult males in Singapore in early 1942. For the swollen population, see C.M. Turnbull, *A History of Modern Singapore, 1819–2005* (Singapore: NUS Press, 2009), p. 184. For the sex and juvenile ratios used for the rough calculations above, see Saw Swee-Hock, *The Population of Singapore* (Singapore: ISEAS, 2007 edition), pp. 10–35.

12. See Sugita's testimony on p. 54 of WO 235/1004 (TNA).

13. Exhibit "S" pp. 574–5 of WO 235/1004, Defendants Nishimura Takoma, Kawamura Saburo, Oishi Masayuki, Yokota Yoshitaka, Jyo Tomotatsu, Onishi Satoru, and Hisamatsu Haruji, Place of Trial: Singapore (TNA).

14. Dr Chen Su Lan, *British Military Administration, Malaya. Singapore Advisory Council, Report of Proceedings, Volume 1*, 23 January 1946, p. 129.

15. Chen, *Remember Pompong and Oxley Rise*, pp. 213–7.

16. WO 325/85 Malacca, Malaya: Killing and Ill Treatment of Asians (TNA).

17. WO 235/1096, Defendant: Yokokoji Kyomi: Kuala Lumpur (TNA). Quotations from *Malay Mail*, 17 December 1947, p. 5.

18. George Hicks, *The Comfort Women: Sex Slaves of the Japanese Imperial Forces* (Singapore: Heinemann Asia, 1995), pp. vii–viii, xii–xiii. Hicks only gives the name as "Madam X", and states he was introduced to her by Haji Mustapha Yaakub of UMNO Youth. See also pp. 89–93, 197–8. The majority of comfort women across the Japanese possessions were Korean.

19. WO 235/931 — Defendant: Higashigawa Yoshinoru: Place of Trial Penang, pp. 383–93 (TNA).

20. WO 235/1070, Defendant: Hashimoto Tadashi: (TNA). *Straits Times*, 23 October 1947, p. 1.

21. Mohd Anis bin Tairan interview with Kevin Blackburn, Kampong Siglap Mosque, 15 February 2002.

22. Kevin Blackburn and Daniel Chew Jun Ern, "Dalforce at the Fall of Singapore in 1942: An Overseas Chinese Heroic Legend", *Journal of the Chinese Overseas* 1, 2 (2005): 233–59.

23. *Straits Times*, 28 May 1947.

24. *The Star*, 15 August 1984; and Chen Ya Cai, ed., *Malaiya kang ri ji nian bei tu pian ji* [*Malaysian Anti-Japanese Memorials: A Pictorial*] (Kuala Lumpur: Selangor Chinese Assembly Hall, 1999). See the records from the Chinese press kept on file at the Centre for Malaysian Chinese Studies at the Selangor Chinese Assembly Hall in Kuala Lumpur.

25. *Malay Mail*, 17 October 1947.

26. Wolfgang Franke and Chen Tieh Fan, *Chinese Epigraphic Materials in Malaysia*, Volume II (Kuala Lumpur: University of Malaya Press, 1985), p. 493.

27. Li Tie Min, ed., *Da Zhan Yu Nan Qiao: Malaiya Zhi Bu* [*The Great War and the Overseas Chinese: Malayan Branch*] (Singapore: Singapore Overseas Chinese Publishing Company, 1947)

28. Ong Hean-Tatt, *Scientific Statistical Evidence for Feng Shui* (Subang Jaya, Malaysia: Gui Management Centre, 2006), p. 116; and Wan Meng Hao, Executive Secretary of The Preservation of Monuments Board, personal communication, 2006.

29. Lowell Dittmer and Samuel S. Kim, eds., *China's Quest for National Identity* (Ithaca, NY: Cornell University Press, 1993), p. 26.

30. *Singapore Free Press*, 5 February 1948.
31. See Hack and Blackburn, *Did Singapore Have to Fall?*, p. 172. For brief explanations of Singapore views of the festivals mentioned in this section, see Singapore Federation of Chinese Clan Associations, *Chinese Customs and Festivals in Singapore* (Singapore: Landmark, 1989).
32. *Straits Times*, 3 February 1947.
33. *Chung Nan Daily*, 24 February 1947.
34. *Sunday Times* (Singapore), 25 July 1948. See also Hack and Blackburn, *Did Singapore Have to Fall?*, p. 174. The date of the ceremony is not entirely clear. The article says the event culminated on Tung-chek, which implies December 1947 (Tung-chek/Dong Zhi or the Winter Solstice and family reunion falls in December). But then it wrongly identifies Tung-chek as after Chinese New Year. This looks like an article that has reused earlier research more fully to fill a Sunday slot. See, for example, *Straits Times*, 23 December 1947, p. 7 which either describes the same event, or a near-identical one.
35. See Wu Jingrong and the Beijing Foreign Languages Institute, *The Pinyin Chinese-English Dictionary* (Hong Kong: Commercial Press, 1979).
36. Chen Su Lan, *Remember Pompong and Oxley Rise* (Singapore: Chen Su Lan Trust, 1969), p. 221.
37. Extract from letter dated 26 February 1946 in WO 311/541 Miscellaneous Correspondence (TNA).
38. War Criminals: Proceedings of Trial of Military Court of Major Mizuno Keiji WO 235/1110 (TNA).
39. *Straits Times*, 19 May 1947.
40. *Straits Times*, 5 April 1947.
41. *Nan Chiau Jit Pao*, 4 April 1947.
42. *Straits Times*, 14 June 1947. See Chinese outrage at verdicts in *Kong Pao*, 3, 5, and 8 April 1947.
43. *Straits Times*, 20 June 1947.
44. *Straits Times*, 24 June 1947.
45. *Straits Times*, 27 June 1947.
46. *Straits Times*, 24 June 1947. See similar sentiments expressed in letters to the editor in *Straits Times*, 25 and 26 June 1947.
47. *New Democracy*, 13 April 1946.
48. Si Ma Chun Ying, *Chan Tong De Huiyi* [*Memories of Painful Grievances*] (Singapore: Guo Lian Publication Company, 1946).
49. Treatment of People in Malaya During the Japanese Military Occupation, Memorandum compiled by the General Affairs Section of the KMT, Selangor Branch, Kuala Lumpur, September 1945, in Chinese Affairs Review of Occupation, file ADM8/1, British Military Administration, (NAM).

50. N.I. Low and H.M. Cheng, *This Singapore (Our City of Dreadful Night)* (Singapore: City Book Store, 1947), pp. 12–3.

51. *Malaya Tribune*, 12, 13, and 14 September 1946.

52. *Sin Chew Jit Poh*, 26 November 1952; and *Nanyang Siang Pau*, 26 and 29 November 1952.

53. Japanese War Criminals, 14 May 1955 p. 45 in Draft Submission on Granting Clemency to Japanese War Criminals FJ 1661/36 in FO 371/115292 (TNA).

54. J.C.O. Dywer, 24 January 1956, in Publicity of Releases of Japanese War Criminals FJ 1663/1 in FO 371/121085, British Foreign Office Files (TNA).

55. Japanese Minor War Criminal, NOPAR Commission recommendation for parole for Onishi Satoru FJ 1661/35 in FO 371/105435; J.C.O. Dywer, 31 January 1956, Singapore Massacre Case p. 84 in Clemency for Yokota, Jyo, Hisamatsu and Mizuno FJ1161/5 in FO 371/121081; and Alphabetical List and Chronological Order of Releases of Thirty War Criminals who will be due to have their sentences terminated in September, October, and November 1955 Owing to reduction of original terms of life imprisonment and 20 years imprisonment to 15 years p. 174 in Release of Minor War Criminals FJ 1661/46 in FO 371/115292 in British Foreign Office Files (TNA).

56. Lee Kuan Yew, *The Singapore Story*, pp. 223–7.

57. W.D. Allen, Foreign Office, 8 May 1956, p. 139 in Clemency for Japanese War Criminals, FJ 1161/14 in FO 371/121082, (TNA). For background, see Hack, *Defence and Decolonisation in Southeast Asia*, pp. 235–8.

58. C.T. Crowe, Clemency for "C" and "B" Class War Criminals, 22 February 1956, in Clemency for Yokota, Jyo, Hisamatsu and Mizuno FJ 1161/5 in FO 371/121081, (TNA).

59. Clemency for Class "B" and "C" War Criminals, pp. 92–3 in Clemency for Yokota, Jyo, Hisamatsu and Mizuno FJ 1161/5 in FO 371/121081, (TNA).

60. Clemency for Yoshitaka Yokota — recommends release on parole FJ 1661/4, and Medical Reports on War Criminals FJ 1661/1, in FO 371/121081, British Foreign Office Files (TNA); and Request to the Ministry of Foreign Affairs, Tokyo, for the date on which Yokota is released from medical parole and Hisamatsu FJ 1661/28 in FO 371/121083 (TNA).

61. Note 139 to Ministry of Foreign Affairs giving new date of release for Ito and dates of release for Mizuno and Jyo Japanese Accepted there should be no publicity for these releases FJ 1161/33 in FO 371/121083 (TNA).

62. Foreign Office Confidential by His Excellency Esler Dening, 21 August 1956, p. 21, in Clemency for Class "B" and "C" Japanese War Criminals Yokota, Jyo, Hisamatsu and Mizuno FJ 1161/24 in FO 371/121083 (TNA).

63. Ken Ninomiya, Japanese Consul General, to W.A.C. Goode, Colonial Secretary, Singapore, 10 October 1953 in War Graves in Southeast Asia FJ 1851/1 pp. 2–5, in FO 371/110523 (TNA).

64. War Graves in Southeast Asia FJ 1851/1 pp. 2–5, in FO 371/110523 (TNA).

65. Chaen Yoshio, *BC-Kyu Senpan Eigun Saiban Shiryo, Volume 2* [*An Historical Record of British War Crimes Trials*] (Tokyo: Fuji Shuppan, 1989), p. 228.

66. Public Relations Department: Exhumation and Removal to Japan of Remains of Japanese War Criminals, PRD186/55, microfilm PRO 19 (NAS); and *Nanyang Siang Pau*, 16 March 1955 and *Straits Times*, 16 March 1955.

67. *Straits Times*, 19 November 1957.

68. Visit of Japanese Prime Minister to Kuala Lumpur, FJ 16234/18 in FO 371/12754 (TNA); and R.H. Scott to Foreign Office, London, 30 November, 1957, in Mr Kishi's Visit to Singapore and Malaya, FJ 1634/20 in FO 371/127574 (TNA).

69. *Singapore Standard*, 26 November 1958.

70. *Singapore Standard*, 17 May 1958.

71. Junko Tomaru, *The Postwar Rapprochement of Malaya and Japan, 1945–1961: The Roles of Britain and Japan in South East Asia* (New York: St. Martin's Press, 2000).

72. *Singapore Free Press*, 9 June 1958.

73. *Singapore Standard*, 6 August 1958.

74. *Straits Times*, 11 December 1958.

75. *Sin Chew Jit Poh*, 6 August 1958.

76. *Nanfang Evening Post*, 5 August 1958.

77. *Straits Times*, 5 August 1958.

78. *Straits Times*, 24 February 1962. In fact, there had been earlier finds of mass graves, there as well, in 1951, when the press dubbed it "the valley of death". See *Straits Times*, 13 September 1951, p. 7.

79. Fong Choon Hon, ed., *Eternal Vigilance: The Price of Freedom* (Singapore: Singapore Chinese Chamber of Commerce and Industry, 1999), pp. 308–9. See also *Nanyang Siang Pau* and *Sin Chew Jit Poh*, 26 June 1966. For a 1946 description from an eyewitness of the Siglap massacre, see Chen Su Lan, *Remember Pompong and Oxley Rise*, pp. 198–9.

80. *Nanyang Siang Pau*, 18 October 1966; and *Sin Chew Jit Poh*, 13 June 1966.

81. *Sin Chew Jit Poh*, 1 March 1962.

82. *Straits Times*, 8 September 1947, p. 5. The other committee members were Tay Koh Yat and Yang Sing-hua.

83. *Singapore Free Press*, 4 February 1955, p. 7.

84. *Nanyang Siang Pau*, 2 March 1962.

85. *Sin Chew Jit Poh*, 31 March 1963.
86. *Nanyang Siang Pau*, 9 April 1963.
87. *Sin Chew Jit Poh*, 1 July 1962.
88. N.C.C. Trench, British Embassy, Tokyo, to A.J. de la Mare, Foreign Office, London, 19 April 1962 in Reparations for Singapore: Views about the Terms of Compensation to be offered by the Japanese FJ 1492/12 in FO 371/165018, British Foreign Office Files (TNA).
89. *Legislative Assembly Debates of State of Singapore*, Vol. 18, 29 June 1962, columns 285–8.
90. *Nanyang Siang Pau*, 2 March 1962.
91. *Straits Times*, 5 April 1962.
92. *Straits Times*, 26 March 1962.
93. *Sin Chew Jit Poh*, 27 February 1962.
94. *Sin Chew Jit Poh*, 1 March 1962.
95. Alex Josey, *Lee Kuan Yew: The Crucial Years* (Singapore: Times, 1980), p. 179.
96. *Legislative Assembly Debates of State of Singapore*, Vol. 17, 14 March 1962, column 13.
97. Paul Kratoska, *The Japanese Occupation of Malaya, 1941–1945* (Sydney: Allen & Unwin, 1998), pp. 347–61.
98. *Sin Chew Jit Poh*, 27 July 1962.
99. *Nanyang Siang Pau*, 6 April 1962.
100. *Nanyang Siang Pau*, 22 April 1962; and English Version of Text Of Speech by the Prime Minister, Mr. Lee Kuan Yew, at a Meeting of the Memorial Fund Committee at the Victoria Theatre on Sunday, April 21, 1963, at 10 A.M., in Republic of Singapore: *Prime Minister's Speeches, Press Conferences, Interviews, Statements, Etc: 1962–1963*, National University of Singapore.
101. Josey, *Lee Kuan Yew: The Crucial Years*, pp. 172–3. For the full text of the speech, see English Version of Text Of Speech by the Prime Minister, Mr. Lee Kuan Yew, at a Meeting of the Memorial Fund Committee at the Victoria Theatre on Sunday, April 21, 1963, at 10 A.M., in Republic of Singapore: *Prime Minister's Speeches, Press Conferences, Interviews, Statements, Etc: 1962–1963*, National University of Singapore.
102. *Sin Chew Jit Poh*, 27 July 1962.
103. *Straits Times*, 28 July 1962, p. 4. *Straits Times*, 1 August 1962, p. 4.
104. *Sin Chew Jit Poh*, 1 March 1963; and *Sin Chew Jit Poh*, 14 March 1963.
105. The PAP were defeated by ex-PAP member and populist Ong Eng Guan, but this was also seen as leaving the PAP vulnerable to left-wing attack from within and outside the party.
106. Karl Hack, "The Malayan Trajectory in Singapore's History", in *Singapore from Temasek to the 21st Century*, eds. Hack and Margolin with Delaye, p. 266.
107. *Utusan Melayu*, 28 August 1963.

108. *Sin Chew Jit Poh*, 22 April 1963.
109. Prime Minister's Speech at "Breaking of the Sod" for the Memorial to Civilian Victims During the Japanese Occupation, on 15 June, 1963 in Republic of Singapore: Prime Minster's Speeches, Press Conferences, Interviews, Statements, Etc: 1962–1963 (National University of Singapore).
110. Lee Kuan Yew, *The Singapore Story: Memoirs of Lee Kuan Yew* (Singapore: Times, 1998), p. 473.
111. *Straits Times*, 26 August 1963.
112. *Sin Chew Jit Poh*, 16 August 1963.
113. *Sin Chew Jit Poh*, 23 and 25 August 1963.
114. See examples in Shu Yun-Tsiao and Chua Ser-Koon, eds., *Malayan Chinese Resistance to Japan 1937–1945: Selected Source Materials Based on Colonel Chuang Hui-Tsuan's Collection* (Singapore: Cultural and Historical Publishing House, 1984), pp. 788–89.
115. Text of Speech by the Prime Minister, Mr. Lee Kuan Yew, at a Mass Rally on the Padang on Sunday, August 25, 1963 in Republic of Singapore: *Prime Minister's Speeches, Press Conferences, Interviews, Statements, Etc: 1962–1963*, National University of Singapore.
116. *Sin Chew Jit Poh*, 25 August 1963.
117. Josey, *Lee Kuan Yew: The Crucial Years*, p. 180.
118. Record of Conversation with Mr Anwar Ibrahim, Secretary for External Affairs in the Prime Minister's Office, 3rd September 1963, by P.J. Curtis, First Secretary, to the Secretary of External Affairs, Australian Commission, Singapore, A1838/333 3006/10/4 Part 3, Federation of Malaya Relations with Singapore, in the Records of the Australian Department of External Affairs (NAA).
119. UK Commissioner Telegram no. M258, Memo 1503 to Secretary of Department of External Affairs, 20 September 1963 by Peter J. Curtis, First Secretary, A1838/1303/11/109 Part 1, Japan — Relations with Singapore, in the Records of the Australian Department of External Affairs (NAA).
120. *Sin Chew Jit Poh*, 27 August 1963.
121. *Nanyang Siang Pau*, 28 August 1963. *Sin Chew Jit Poh*, 19 September 1963 and 29 September 1963.
122. *Nanyang Siang Pau*, 28 September 1963.
123. *Kerala Bandu*, 16 October 1963.
124. *Nanyang Siang Pau*, 11 and 13 February 1965.
125. See the entry in *Japan: An Illustrated Encyclopedia Volume 1 A-L* (Tokyo: Kodansha, 1993), p. 111 for the Japanese characters of the phrase.
126. Transcript of a speech by the Prime Minister, Lee Kuan Yew at the Chinese Chamber of Commerce on 4th July 1966 and W.B. Pritchett, Australian Commission to Secretary, Department of External Affairs, 19 July 1966, A1838/280 3024/2/1 Part 15, Singapore — Political — General, in the

Records of the Australian Department of External Affairs (NAA); *Straits Times*, 26 October 1966; and *Straits Times*, 1 November 1966.

127. Singapore press reports in 1966–1967 variously say 10,000 (*Straits Times*, 11 June 1966, p. 1, estimate for remains uncovered at that point) or 20,000 remains (*Eastern Sun*, 20 October 1966) were reburied in 600 plus urns (at 30 per urn) in November 1966. Yet the Chairman of the Remains Disposal Committee for 1965–1966 (Chew Teng How — who is quoted in an *Eastern Sun* article of 2 November which says 20,000 victims) has subsequently given a breakdown. This lists 605 urns. See Chew Teng How, "Rest in Peace: Our Martyrs", in *Eternal Vigilance: The Price of Peace*, ed Foong Choon Hon (Singapore: Asiapac, 2005), p. 270. It seems reasonable to accept his later, considered 605 figure (and thus dismiss the 665 in *Eastern Sun*, 20 October 1966, p. 2 as a typo). The problem is that his detailed breakdown suggests that two-thirds of the urns (428 out of 605) interred were from Jalan Puipoon (this corresponds to the Siglap area). Since most accounts only suggest remains in the low thousands for Siglap, that would suggest a much lower overall figure, and a lower figure for remains per urn. To get to 20,000, the remaining, non-Siglap one-third of urns would have had to contain implausible numbers per urn, far above 30. Yet this seems not to be the case. The largest number of urns from any other site was for 37 urns only (for two sites: Changi 10½ miles, and King's Road). For these sites, only hundreds not thousands were believed killed. In other words, it seems extremely unlikely that the non-Siglap other urns had more than 20 remains each on average. There is at least a suspicion that the average per urn was much lower than 30 (perhaps a fraction of that figure). Thus, we can only say with certainty that the total remains interred under the Civilian War Memorial is over 5,000, and under 20,000. 20,000 just does not work unless there were more urns, as 605 times 30 is only 18,000. Whatever the number interred, many more bodies must have been lost.

128. *Straits Times*, 16 February 1967.

129. English Version of A Text of Speech by Prime Minister, Mr Lee Kuan Yew, at a Meeting of the Memorial Fund Committee at the Victoria Theatre on Sunday, April 21, 1963, at 10 A.M. in Republic of Singapore: Prime Minister's Speeches, Press Conferences, Interviews, Statements, etc. 1962–63 (National University of Singapore).

130. Li Ye Lin, ed., *Tai Ping Yang Zhan Zheng Shi Liao Hui Ban: Selected Historical Materials of the Pacific War: Sumber Sejarah Peperangan Pasifik* (Kuala Lumpur: Huazi, 1996), pp. 360–93.

131. *Sraits Times*, 31 May 1963, p. 4, "Top Design for a Memorial".

132. Assessors Report, "Competition for a Memorial to Civilian Victims of the Japanese Occupation", *Journal of the Singapore Institute of Architects* 6 (December 1963): 7–22. See also the discussion of this in Karl Hack,

"Contentious Heritage", in *Understanding Heritage and Memory*, ed. Tim Benton (Manchester: Manchester University Press, 2010), pp. 102–5.

133. *Straits Times*, 31 May 1963, p. 4, "Top Design for a Memorial".
134. Ibid. *Straits Times*, 15 June 1963, p. 22, "Lee to Break the Sod Today".
135. *Nanyang Siang Pau* and *Sin Chew Jit Poh*, 1 October 1965. For details on the troubled design of the monument, see Ministry of Culture, Publicity Division of Designs for Memorial of Victims of Japanese Occupation, 29 May 1963 to 3 October 1963 AR 66 (NAS).
136. *Eastern Sun*, 20 October 1966.
137. Pan Shou's rollercoaster fortunes in terms of national fame and relations with the government is traced by Huang Jianli in Hong Lysa and Huang Jianli, *The Scripting of A National History: Singapore and its Pasts* (Singapore: NUS Press, 2008), pp. 178–80.
138. *Straits Times*, 25 July 1948, p. 2.
139. *The Straits Times*, 9 July 1985, p. 27.
140. Verses taken from the Civilian War Memorial itself. See also National Archives of Singapore, *The Japanese Occupation 1942–1945* (Singapore: Times, 1996), pp. 185–6.
141. Shu and Chua, *Malayan Chinese Resistance to Japan 1937–1945*, p. 85.
142. *Nanyang Siang Pau*, 28 May 1962; and *Sin Chew Jit Poh*, 31 March 1963.
143. Prime Minister's Speech at the Unveiling Ceremony of Memorial to Civilian Victims of Japanese Occupation on 15th February, 1967, in Republic of Singapore Prime Minister's Speeches. Press Conferences, Interviews, Statements, Etc (National University of Singapore).
144. *Eastern Sun*, 6 February 1967, p. 8.
145. *Straits Times*, 16 February 1968; *Eastern Sun*, 16 February 1969; *Straits Times*, 16 February 1970.
146. *Sin Chew Jit Poh*, 11 December 1966.
147. *Sin Chew Jit Poh*, 29 December 1966.
148. *Nanyang Siang Pau*, 31 December 1966.
149. *Eastern Sun*, 23 September 1967.
150. *Sin Chew Jit Poh*, 11 January 1967.
151. *Straits Times* (Malaysian Edition), 19 January 1967.
152. *Eastern Sun*, 18, 19, 21 August 1967.
153. *Eastern Sun*, 22 September 1967. See also Shu and Chua, *Malayan Chinese Resistance to Japan 1937–1945*, p. 87.

Chapter 6

1. Joyce Chapman Lebra, *The Indian National Army* (Singapore: ISEAS, 2008, first published 1971), pp. 102–27. For his desire to secure outside help and fight with the Axis, see Leonard A Gordon, *Brothers Against the Raj: A Biography of Indian Nationalists Sarat and Subhas Chandra Bose* (New York: Columbia University Press, 1990), p. 428.

2. See, for example, Gordon, *Brothers Against the Raj*, pp. 520–1.
3. Das, "The Bharat Youth Training Centre", p. 52.
4. K.R. Das speaking at the "Open Public Forum with Veterans and Members of the Wartime Generation", 4 September 2005, Singapore History Museum.
5. See pp. 348–9. For the almost hagiographical view of the Rani of Jhansi Regiment that some of its leaders fostered after the war, and the wider context of Bengali terrorism in which they rooted their significance, see Joyce Lebra Chapman, *Women Against the Raj: The Rani of Jhansi Regiment* (Singapore: ISEAS, 2008).
6. Romen Bose, *A Will for Freedom: Netaji and the Indian Independence Movement in Singapore and Southeast Asia, 1942–1945* (Singapore: VJ Times, 1993), p. 3.
7. Romen Bose, *A Will for Freedom*, p. 56.
8. G.J. Douds, "Indian POWs in the Pacific, 1941–45", in *Forgotten Captives in Japanese Occupied Asia*, eds. Karl Hack and Kevin Blackburn (London: Routledge, 2008), pp. 94–110.
9. Nakahara Michiko, "Malayan Labor on the Thailand-Burma Railway", in *Asian Labor in the Wartime Japanese Empire*, ed. Paul Kratoska (Singapore: NUS Press, 2006), p. 255. The number given on p. 252 of the same book as a postwar estimate is 78,204, of whom the British estimated 40,000 or 51 per cent had died. Part of the explanation for the higher figures is that the true picture only emerged over time. By contrast, Charles Gamba *The Origins of Trade Unionism in Malaya* (Singapore: Eastern Universities Press, 1962), p. 14 (drawing on a Malayan Union *Annual Report* of The Department of Labour for 1946, Kuala Lumpur, 1947, p. 1), has 73,502 from Malaya and 24,490 dying. There is Major Arbutnott and Major Chamie's report that says the Japanese Labour Department told them there were 76,600 from Malaya with 24,770 deaths — CO 537/1571 Malayans in Thailand. Nakahara's essay in K.S. Jomo, ed., *Rethinking Malaysia: Malaysian Studies* 1 (Kuala Lumpur: Malaysian Social Science Association, 1999) has the 41.3 percent death rate from the first batch, p. 225 and justifies.
10. The *kirani* were frequently Ceylonese and Malayalees, so the perception by mainly Tamil labourers that some had been overzealous in meeting Japanese requests, or had abused power, possibly helped to set the scene for increased postwar unionism and militancy. See P. Ramasamy, "Indian War Memory in Malaysia", in *War and Memory in Malaysia and Singapore*, eds. P. Lim Pui Huen and Diana Wong (Singapore: ISEAS, 2000), pp. 92–4.
11. Nakahara Michiko, "Malayan Labor on the Thailand-Burma Railway", p. 257.
12. Arthur Lane, *Lesser Gods, Greater Devils* (Stockport: Lane, 1993), pp. 163, 171–7, 216–7. As cited in E. Bruce Reynolds, "History, Memory, Compensation, and Reconciliation: The Abuse of Labor along the Thailand-

Burma Railway", in *Asian Labor in the Wartime Japanese Empire*, ed. Kratoska, pp. 330–1.

13. Maurice Halbwachs, *On Collective Memory*, trans. Lewis A. Coser (Chicago: University of Chicago Press, 1992), pp. 182–3.

14. Hack and Blackburn, *Forgotten Captives*, p. 9. Alan Warren, *Singapore 1942: Britain's Greatest Defeat* (Singapore: Talisman, 2002), pp. 301–2.

15. Fujiwara Iwaichi, *F. Kikan: Japanese Army Intelligence Operations in Southeast Asia During World War II*, trans. Yoji Akashi (Hong Kong: Heinemann Asia, 1983), pp. 78–89. 178–88. Leonard A. Gordon, *Brothers Against the Raj: A Biography of Indian Nationalists Sarat and Subhas Chandra Bose*, pp. 466–7.

16. Mohan Singh, *Soldiers' Contribution to Indian Independence* (New Delhi: Army Educational Stores, 1974), pp. 108–9.

17. Peter Ward Fay, *The Forgotten Army: India's Armed Struggle for Independence 1942–1945* (Ann Arbor: University Michigan Press, 1993), pp. 525–6.

18. Interview with Lieutenant K.R. Das at the Netaji Centre in Kuala Lumpur, 17 December 2004.

19. *Syonan Sinbun*, 3 July 1943.

20. Hugh Toye, *The Springing Tiger: A Study of a Revolutionary* (London: Cassell, 1959), p. 73.

21. Fay, *Forgotten Army*, p. 236. See M.R. Vyas' 1982 book, *Passage Through a Turbulent Era* cited in Leonard A. Gordon, *Brothers Against the Raj: A Biography of Sarat & Subhas Chandra Bose* (New Delhi: Viking, 1990), p. 460.

22. *Syonan Sinbun*, 5 July 1943.

23. *Syonan Sinbun*, 9 July 1943. For a full text of the speech, see Fred Saito and Tatsuo Hayashida, "To Delhi! To Delhi! 1943–1945", in *A Beacon Across Asia: A Biography of Subhas Chandra Bose*, eds. Sisir K. Bose, Alexander Werth and S.A. Ayer (New Delhi: Longman, 1973), pp. 177–9.

24. *Young India*, 18 July 1943.

25. *Young India*, 18 July 1943.

26. Fay, *Forgotten Army*, pp. 215–6, and Carol Hills and Daniel C. Silverman, "Nationalism and Feminism in Late Colonial India: The Rani of Jhansi Regiment, 1943–1945", *Modern Asian Studies* 27, 4 (1993): 741–60. See the commander of the Rani of Jhansi Regiment's remarks about the regiment being mainly Malayan Indian women who had never seen India, and did not fight but were at the Burma front with the INA nursing casualties, in *Indian Daily Mail*, 7 March 1946. See also Lebra, *Women Against the Raj*, pp. 82–4.

27. *Young India*, 21 November 1943.

28. Jitendra Nath Ghosh, *Netaji Subhas Chandra Bose: Political Philosophy of Netaji History of the Azad Hind Government I.N.A. and International Law* (Calcutta: Orient Book Company, 1946), p. 128.

29. *Young India*, 21 November 1943.

30. The events covered in the Japanese propaganda newspaper of Singapore, *Syonan Shimbun*, 22 January 1944, 22 February 1944, and 23 March 1944.

31. *Syonan Shimbun*, 22 February 1944.

32. *Syonan Sinbun*, 2 October 1943.

33. Toye, *The Springing Tiger*, p. 138.

34. *Syonan Shimbun*, 24 January 1945.

35. *Syonan Shimbun*, 3 July 1944.

36. *Syonan Shimbun*, 4, 5, 6, and 7 July 1945.

37. Toye, *The Springing Tiger*, p. 190.

38. *Syonan Shimbun*, 24 August 1945.

39. *Syonan Shimbun*, 25 and 28 August 1945.

40. *Straits Times*, 8 September 1945.

41. See various letters by soldiers of the British Indian Army in *The Statesman* (Calcutta) 1945–1946.

42. *Indian Daily Mail*, 17 April 1956.

43. *Straits Times*, 22 February 1946.

44. *Indian Daily Mail*, 20 May 1946.

45. *Indian Daily Mail*, 14 and 21 March 1946. See also The Visit of Pandit Jawaharlal Nehru to Malaya CO 717/149/8 (TNA).

46. *Indian Daily Mail*, 14, 20, and 21 March 1946.

47. *Indian Daily Mail*, 20 and 21 March 1946.

48. *Indian Daily Mail*, 23 March 1946; see commemorative material produced by the Netaji Centre for the 60th anniversary of the establishment of the *Azad Hind* government on 21 October 2003, and the 100th anniversary of the birth of Bose on 23 January 1996.

49. Akhil Bakshi, *The Road To Freedom: Travels Through Singapore, Malaysia, Burma and India in the Footsteps of the Indian National Army* (New Delhi: Odyssey, 1998), pp. 33–4.

50. Michael Stenson, *Class, Race and Colonialism in West Malaysia: The Indian Case* (St Lucia: University of Queensland, 1980), pp. 144–6. See Arrests and Detention of Suspected Collaborators and War Criminals, BMA CSO 151/45 Box 11, Ministry of Social Affairs BMA List 1945–9, (NAS).

51. S.K. Chettur, *Malayan Adventure* (Mangalore: Basel Mission Press, 1948), p. 68.

52. *Indian Daily Mail*, 18 March 1946. For confirmation of this point, see G.P. Ramachandra, "The Indian Independence Movement in Malaya, 1942–1975", MA thesis, University of Malaya, 1970; and Shahilla K. Balakrishnan, "Political Attitudes of Indians in Post-War Malaya 1945–1955", BA Honours thesis, National University of Singapore, 1991.

53. *Indian Daily Mail*, 18 March 1946.

54. *Indian Daily Mail*, 22 April 1946.

55. *Indian Daily Mail*, 24 June 1946. For the establishment of the Indian Relief Committee, see *Indian Daily Mail*, 5 April 1946.
56. For an account of the formation of the Malayan Indian Congress, see S. Subramanian, "Politics of the Indians in Malaya, 1945–1955", MA thesis, University of Malaya, 1973.
57. *Indian Daily Mail*, 6 July 1946. See the documents relating to the working of the constitution of the MIC in the John Thivy papers (University of Malaya, Kuala Lumpur).
58. *Indian Daily Mail*, 10 September 1946.
59. *Indian Daily Mail*, 23 July 1946.
60. *Indian Daily Mail*, 11 July 1946.
61. *Indian Daily Mail*, 23 August 1946.
62. *Indian Daily Mail*, 23 August 1946.
63. *Indian Daily Mail*, 23 September 1946.
64. *Indian Daily Mail*, 21 October 1946.
65. *Indian Daily Mail*, 26 October 1946.
66. *Indian Daily Mail*, 22 October 1946.
67. *Indian Daily Mail*, 21 October 1946.
68. *Indian Daily Mail*, 25 October 1946.
69. *Indian Daily Mail*, 23 October 1946.
70. Use of the Term "Cooly", MU 5353/46, Malayan Union Files (NAM).
71. *Indian Daily Mail*, 22 January 1947. See the origins of the term "cooly" or "coolie" in Henry Yule and A.C. Burnell, *Hobson-Jobson: The Anglo-Indian Dictionary*, first published in 1886 (Ware, Hertfordshire, Wordsworth Editions, 1996), pp. 249–51.
72. *Indian Daily Mail*, 22 January 1947. See also *Indian Daily Mail*, 30 January 1947. For celebrations of Bose's birthday, see *Indian Daily Mail*, 25 January 1947.
73. *Indian Daily Mail*, 9 June 1947.
74. *Indian Daily Mail*, 19 April 1947.
75. J.A. Gagan, War Prisoners (Singapore) Association to Colonial Secretary, 7 July 1947, in Establishment of Memorials to Indian National Army in the Land Office Records, Box 16, Serial number 1912, file reference LO832/47R, microfilm number LO 160 (NAS).
76. *Malaya Tribune*, 9 June 1947.
77. P.A.B. McKerron, 19 July 1947 in Establishment of Memorials to Indian National Army in the Land Office Records, Box 16, Serial number 1912, file reference LO832/47R, microfilm number LO 160 (NAS).
78. Colonial Secretary to J.A. Gagan, 21 July 1947, in Establishment of Memorials to Indian National Army in the Land Office Records, Box 16, Serial number 1912, file reference LO832/47R, microfilm number LO 160 (NAS).
79. *Indian Daily Mail*, 11 July 1947.

80. *Indian Daily Mail*, 9 July 1947.
81. Ibid.
82. G.S. Dillon and his two comrades were the only ones tried for waging war against the King Emperor, and under intense pressure from the Indian National Congress and others their life deportation sentences were eventually commuted by Governor-General Auchinleck. Most INA defendants were ultimately released, though their entry into the Indian Army was barred at independence.
83. *Indian Daily Mail*, 15 March 1947.
84. *Indian Daily Mail*, 18 August 1947.
85. See *MSS: Political Intelligence Journal Political Intelligence Journal*, 15 October 1946, p. 4 and 30 November 1946, p. 5. (Rhodes House, Oxford University).
86. *Indian Daily Mail*, 19 July 1947.
87. *Morning Tribune*, 24 February 1948.
88. *Morning Tribune*, 17 March 1948 and *Malaya Tribune*, 18 March 1948.
89. *Malaya Tribune*, 27 and 29 March 1947.
90. *Indian Daily Mail*, 20, 23, and 26 January, 1949.
91. *Indian Daily Mail*, 23 January 1950; and see commemorative articles to honour Bose's in the lead up to his birthday in *Tamil Murasu*, 13 January 1952.
92. *Indian Daily Mail*, 13 July 1950.
93. *Indian Daily Mail*, 27 March 1956.
94. *Indian Daily Mail*, 26 March 1956.
95. *Indian Daily Mail*, 26 March 1956.
96. *Indian Daily Mail*, 16 April 1956.
97. *Indian Daily Mail*, 17 April 1956.
98. Charles Gamba, *The National Union of Plantation Workers: History of the Plantation Workers of Malaya 1946–1958*, p. 14.
99. *Indian Daily Mail*, 14 February 1953.
100. *Straits Times*, 18 October 1954.
101. Sinnappah Arasaratnam, *Indians in Malaysia and Singapore* (Kuala Lumpur: Oxford University Press, 1970), pp. 121–2, 132.
102. N. Veeriah, "Indian Independence League and Indian National Army: A Calendar of Events and Afterthoughts", in *Netaji Subhas Chandra Bose: A Malaysian Perspective*, p. 9.
103. See Netaji Centre, "Publisher's Preface"; and S. Govindaraj "Indian Independence League and Indian National Army Inspire Birth of Malayan Indian Congress", in *Netaji Subhas Chandra Bose: A Malaysian Perspective*, pp. ii, 6; and Subramanian, "Politics of the Indians in Malaya, 1945–1955" for his entries on people in the MIC on p. 333. See also entries in Ampalvanar, *The Indian Minority and Political Change in Malaya*, p. 215.

104. *Indian Daily Mail*, 10 August 1954.
105. *MSS: Political Intelligence Journal* (31 July 1947): 258 (Rhodes House, Oxford University).
106. Letter to the Editor: Tan Ah Wee, "Mr. Tan Cheng Lock and Chandra Bose", *Straits Times*, 11 July 1940, p. 4.
107. *Straits Times*, 3 August 1946.
108. *Indian Daily Mail*, 20 October 1954.
109. *Indian Daily Mail*, 17 September 1954 and 16 February 1955.
110. *Indian Daily Mail*, 10 March 1955.
111. Interview with Lieutenant K.R. Das at the Netaji Centre in Kuala Lumpur, 17 December 2004. See Rajeswary Ampalavanar, *The Indian Minority and Political Change in Malaya 1945–1957* (Kuala Lumpur: Oxford University Press, 1981), p. 173.
112. *Indian Daily Mail*, 22 and 27 October 1954.
113. *Straits Times*, 20 October and 9 November 1954.
114. Netaji Centre, "Publisher's Preface"; and S. Govindaraj "Indian Independence League and Indian National Army Inspire Birth of Malayan Indian Congress", in *Netaji Subhas Chandra Bose: A Malaysian Perspective*, p. iii; and see *Indian Daily Mail*, 11, 12, 15, 23, 24, and 29 March, 6 and 15 May 1955.
115. *Indian Daily Mail*, 29 March 1955.
116. *Indian Daily Mail*, 2 May 1955.
117. Ummadevi Suppiah, *Tun V.T. Sambanthan: Pemimpin Berjiwa Malaysia* [*Tun V.T. Sambanthan: A Leader who Created Malaysia*] (Kuala: Lumpur: Penerbit Universiti Malaysia, 2004), pp. 15–31; and see *Indian Daily Mail*, 8, 10 and 11 May, and 6 June 1955.
118. *Indian Daily Mail*, 22 April and 1 May 1956.
119. *Indian Daily Mail*, 25 January 1955.
120. *Indian Daily Mail*, 21 January 1955.
121. *Indian Daily Mail*, 21 August 1956.
122. Ibid.
123. *Indian Daily Mail*, 27 January 1951.
124. *Indian Daily Mail*, 20 October 1952.
125. *Indian Daily Mail*, 6 November 1956.
126. Ram Singh Rawal, *I.N.A. Saga* (Allahabad: K.P. Khattri, 1946), pp. 165–6 cited in E. Bruce Reynolds, "The Thailand-Burma Railway: Reflections on a Regional Tragedy", in Symposium on the Japanese Occupation in Southeast Asia, December 14–16 1995 (National University of Singapore).
127. Nakahara Michiko, "Labour Recruitment in Malaya Under the Japanese Occupation: The Case of the Burma-Siam Railway", in *Rethinking Malaysia: Malaysian Studies*, ed. K.S. Jomo (Kuala Lumpur: Malaysian Social Science Association, 2000), pp. 233–4.
128. M. Sivaram, *Road to Delhi* (Tokyo: Charles E. Tuttle, 1966), pp. 104–5, as cited in E. Bruce Reynolds, "History, Memory, Compensation, and

Reconciliation: The Abuse of Labor along the Thailand-Burma Railway", p. 334.

129. M. Sivaram, *Road to Delhi*, p. 101, as cited in E Bruce Reynolds, "History, Memory, Compensation, and Reconciliation", p. 335.

130. Figures are incredibly difficult to be precise with, given the chaotic nature of recruitment and management of labour on the railway. For the 182,000 figure, see Nakahara Michiko, "Malayan Labor on the Thailand-Burma Railway", in *Asian Labor in the Wartime Japanese Empire*, ed. Kratoska, pp. 252, 255. For the maximum of 80,000 at any one time, see Gavin McGormack and Hank Nelson, eds., *The Burma-Thailand Railway* (Singapore: Sikworm, 1993), p. 61.

131. Malayan Union, "Annual Report of the Labour Department 1946" (Kuala Lumpur, 1947), pp. 1, 7 (National University of Singapore Library).

132. British numbers for end of September 1945 can be found in Table 13.1 of Nakahara Michiko, "Malayan Labor on the Thailand-Burma Railway", in *Asian Labor in the Wartime Japanese Empire*, ed. Kratoska, p. 251. This table gives a total of 78,204 Asian labourers, of which 29,634 were dead, 6,456 employed at present, 24,626 deserted, and 17,488 repatriated. Figures originally from WO 325/7 D (TNA). The Japanese total mobilisation of labour for the railway was 62,000 POWs and around 200,000 Asian labourers. A high percentage of the "deserted" probably died, as peak desertions were at the time cholera raged through the camps. That said, a death rate of 40 per cent would be extremely conservative. Later Allied figures, given on p. 252, suggest at least 182,492 Asian labourers, with a minimum of 74,025 deaths (40 per cent). Those later figures give 78,204 for "Malayans", with a minimum of 40,000 dead (51 per cent).

133. Nakahara Michiko, "Malayan Labor on the Thailand-Burma Railway", in *Asian Labor in the Wartime Japanese Empire*, ed. Kratoska, p. 252.

134. Malayan Union, "Annual Report of the Labour Department 1946" (Kuala Lumpur, 1947), pp. 1, 7 (National University of Singapore Library).

135. Bernard Ridgway, "Malaya's Death Railway 'D.P.'S' Come Home", *British Malaya* (July 1946): 42.

136. G.S. Wodeman (Colonial Office, London) to Mr Paskin on the Report by Major Chamier and Major Arbutnott, 19 November 1945, in Malayans in Thailand, 1945–1946, CO 537/1571 (TNA). This recorded the breakdown of the 23,000 Malayans then still known to want to return home as: Malays, 2,000; Chinese 4,000; and Indians 17,000.

137. *Indian Daily Mail*, 27 March 1946.

138. *Indian Daily Mail*, 6 August 1946.

139. *Indian Daily Mail*, 23 April 1946.

140. *Indian Daily Mail*, 30 August 1946.

141. *Indian Daily Mail*, 23 November 1946.

142. *Indian Daily Mail*, 23 December 1947; Malayan Union, "Annual Report of the Labour Department 1946", p. 7; *Indian Daily Mail*, 8 April 1954.

143. *Indian Daily Mail*, 24 December 1947.

144. See M.V. del Tufo, *Malaya: A Report on the 1947 Census of Population* (Kuala Lumpur: Government Printer, Federation of Malaya, 1949); see p. 39 for the quotation and p. 38 for observations on the decline in the Indian population; R.C. Burgess and Laidin bin Alang Musa, *A Report on the State of Health: The Diet and Economic Conditions of Groups of People in the Lower Income Levels in Malaya* (Kuala Lumpur: Division of Nutrition, Institute for Medical Research, 1950), pp. 8–9; and *Indian Daily Mail*, 18 October 1949.

145. Leong Yee Fong, *Labour and Trade Unionism in Colonial Malaya* (Pulau Pinang: Penerbit Universiti Sains Malaysia, 1999), p. 122.

146. *Indian Daily Mail*, 6 November 1954.

147. *Straits Times*, 12 March 1948

148. *Indian Daily Mail*, 8 April 1954.

149. Enemy Property: Claims Against Siam: Burma-Siam Railway CO 537/3014 (TNA); *Straits Times*, 21 November 1947; and *Sunday Times* (Singapore), 23 November 1947.

150. *Straits Times*, 4 December 1947.

151. *Straits Times*, 26 April 1961.

152. *Proceedings of the Legislative Council of the Federation of Malaya For The Period (Seventh Session) March 1954 to January 1955* (Kuala Lumpur: Government Press, 1955), column 1240; *Proceedings of the Legislative Council of the Federation of Malaya For The Period (Eighth Session) March 1955 to June 1955* (Kuala Lumpur: Government Press, 1956), columns 533–4; and *Malaya Federal Legislative Council Debates: Official Report of the Second Legislative Council (First Session) 30th August 1956 to 13th September 1956* (Kuala Lumpur: Government Press, 1958), column 944.

153. *Straits Times*, 3 August 1961.

154. For an account of the organisation, see Mat Zin Mat Kib, "Persatuan Bekas Buruh Paksa dan Keluarga Buruh Jalan Keretapi Maut Siam-Burma 1942–1946 Persekutuan Tanah Melayu 1958–1973: Satu Tinjauan Sejarah Perkembangannya [The All Malaya Association of Forced Labourers and Families of Forced Labourers of the Burma-Siam Death Railway, 1958–1973: A Survey of its Development]", BA thesis, School of Humanities, Universiti Sains Malaysia, 1988. See also his book, Mat Zin Mat Kib, *Persatuan Buruh Keretapi Maut Siam-Burma* [*The Association of Labourers on the Burma-Siam Death Railway*] (Kuala Lumpur: UPENA, 2005).

155. Ravindra K. Jain, *South Indians on the Plantation Frontier in Malaya* (New Haven: Yale University Press, 1970), p. 302.

156. Raphael Samuel and Paul Thompson, eds., *The Myths We Live By* (London: Routledge, 1990), p. 7.

157. Lt-Col. Mahmood Khan Durrani tells a story of aiding the western POWs, and then trying to set up a separate nationalist military and espionage organisation. His attitude is one of deep suspicion of the INA as Hindu-biased (he writes of the "Hindu dream of Congress rule over India"), compared with his support for distinctive Muslim identity. See his *The Sixth Column: The Heroic Personal Story of Lt-Col. Mahmood Khan Durrani* (London: Cassell, 1955), pp. 5–6, 28–9, 30, 44–5, 77–8.

158. Cholera victims on the railway, already weakened by inadequate diet, might expect to suffer intense cramps, white stools, devastating diarrhoea, and dehydration, followed by death within a few days.

159. Goh Chor Boon, *Living Hell: Story of a WWII Survivor at the Death Railway* (Singapore: Asiapac, 1999), pp. 80–3. Tan is describing events at "Nieke", close to the Burma-Thai border, in mid-1944.

Chapter 7

1. Abu Talib Ahmad, "The Malay Community and Memory of the Japanese Occupation", in *War and Memory in Malaysia and Singapore*, eds. P. Lim Pui Huen and Diana Wong (Singapore: ISEAS, 2000), pp. 47–8.

2. Abu Talib Ahmad, *Malay Muslims, Islam and the Rising Sun: 1941–45* (Selangor: JMBRAS Monograph no. 34, 2003), p. 41.

3. Abu Talib Ahmad, "The Malay Community and Memory of the Japanese Occupation", pp. 47–54.

4. This evolved into today's *Universiti Pendidikan Sultan Idris*.

5. Mohd Anis bin Tairan interview with Kevin Blackburn at Kampong Siglap Mosque, Singapore, 15 February 2002.

6. Alias Saleh bin Sulaiman.

7. Mohd Anis bin Tairan interview with Kevin Blackburn at Kampong Siglap Mosque, Singapore, 19 February 2009.

8. Karl Hack, "Imperialism and Decolonisation in Southeast Asia: Colonial Forces and British World Power", *Colonial Armies*, eds. Hack and Rettig, pp. 239–65 (especially pp. 254–9).

9. Dol Ramli, "History of the Malay Regiment 1933–1942", *Journal of the Malaysian Branch of the Royal Asiatic Society* 38 (1965): 200.

10. T. Iskander, "Some Historical Sources Used by the Author of *Hikayat Hang Tuah*", *Journal of the Malaysian Branch of the Royal Asiatic Society* 43 (1970): 45–6.

11. Kassim Bin Ahmad, *Characterisation in Hikayat Hang Tuah* (Kuala Lumpur: Dewan Bahasa dan Pustaka, 1966).

12. See A.C. Milner, *Kerajaan: Malay Political Culture on the Eve of Colonial Rule* (Tucson, AZ: University of Arizona Press, 1982), pp. 38–9, 112–3. Shaharuddin b. Maaruf, *Concept of A Hero in Malay Society* (Singapore: Eastern Universities Press, 1984).

392	*Notes to pp. 212–4*

13. See the Malaysian Ministry of Defence's "official" history of the Malay Regiment by Tan Sri Datuk Abdul Samad Idris, *Askar Melayu: 50 Tahun* [*The Malay Regiment: 50 Years*] (Kuala Lumpur: Pustaka Budiman, 1983), pp. 1, xvi; and Kassim Ahmad and Noriah Mohamed, eds., *Hikayat Hang Tuah* (Kuala Lumpur: Yayasan Karyawan dan Dewan Bahasa dan Pustaka, 1997), p. xxviii.

14. See Ismail Noor and Muhammed Azaham, *Takkan Melayu Hilang Di Dunia* (Subang Jaya, Selangor: Pelanduk, 2000), p. 31.

15. See the Malaysian Ministry of Defence's "official" history of the Malay Regiment by Tan Sri Datuk Abdul Samad Idris, *Askar Melayu: 50 Tahun* [*The Malay Regiment: 50 Years*] (Kuala Lumpur: Pustaka Budiman, 1983), pp. 18–23; and Major-General Dato Nordin Yusof and Abdul Razak Abdullah Baginda, *Honour and Sacrifice: The Malaysian Armed Forces* (Kuala Lumpur: Ministry of Defence, 1994), pp. 1–2.

16. A Malay, Johore Bahru, Letter to the Editor, "Malay Soldiers: First Suggestion to Form Regiment", *Straits Times*, 4 March 1941.

17. M.C. ff Sheppard, *The Malay Regiment: 1933–1947* (Kuala Lumpur: Department of Public Relations, 1947), p. 5.

18. *Straits Times*, 31 March 1941.

19. See Abu Talib Ahmad, *Malay Muslims, Islam and the Rising Sun*, pp. 91–2.

20. Sheppard, *Malay Regiment*, p. 6. The Crown could conceivably symbolise the link both to the local Rulers, and to the British Crown.

21. M.C. ff. Sheppard, "The Malay Soldier", *The Straits Times Annual, 1939*, p. 29.

22. Professor Dr. Syed Muhammad Naquib al-Attas interviewed in Mohamed Abid, *Reflections of Pre-Independence Malaya* (Subang Jaya, Selangor: Pelanduk, 2003), p. 74. See G.F.F.G. to A.E. Cooper, 29 May 1940, in CO 717/141/51515/13 (TNA).

23. Karl Hack, *Defence and Decolonisation in Southeast Asia*, pp. 111–2.

24. Trafford Smith and J.D. Higham, 26 March 1949, Colonial Office London, in King's Commissions — Malay's 1949 CO 537/4657 and J.C. Morgan, Colonial Office, London, to Lt. Col. Grist, 16 February 1949 in Re-Constitution of Malay Regiment, 1949 CO 537/4656 (TNA).

25. See Milner, *Kerajaan*, and Ariffin Omar, *Bangsa Melayu: Malay Concepts of Democracy and Community, 1945–1950* (Kuala Lumpur: Oxford University Press, 1993).

26. Sir Henry Gurney to Colonial Office, 31 December 1948 in CO 537/3576 (TNA).

27. M.C. ff. Sheppard, "The Malay Soldier", *The Straits Times Annual, 1939*, pp. 26–36.

28. *Malaya Tribune*, 15 February 1941.

29. *Singapore Free Press*, 22 March 1941.

30. Sheppard, *The Malay Regiment*, p. 12.
31. Sheppard, *The Malay Regiment*, p. 18. See also commentary on why the Malay Regiment performed doggedly — compared to British and Australian failings — in Karl Hack, "Imperialism and Decolonisation in Southeast Asia: Colonial Forces and British World Power", in *Colonial Armies in Southeast Asia*, eds. Karl Hack and Tobias Rettig (London: Routledge, 2006), pp. 256–7.
32. Conversation with Abu Talib Ahmad in September 2002 about his 1950s–1960s boyhood, and see his reflections on this topic in Abu Talib Ahmad, *Malay Muslims, Islam and the Rising Sun*, p. 88.
33. *Malay Mail*, 14 February 1952 and *Singapore Standard*, 15 February 1958.
34. A.E. Percival, *The War in Malaya* (London: Eyre and Spottiswoode, 1949), p. 291.
35. Sheppard, *Malay Regiment*, p. 3.
36. See the use of the quote in the official history of the Malaysian Armed Forces, by Major-General Dato Nordin Yusof and Abdul Razak Abdullah Baginda, *Honour and Sacrifice*, p. 6; and also in Ismail Noor and Muhammed Azaham, *Takkan Melayu Hilang Di Dunia* (Subang Jaya, Selangor: Pelanduk, 2000), p. 31.
37. Wan Meng Hao, "Malay Soldiering in Singapore, 1910–1942", in *Malays/ Muslims in Singapore: Selected Readings in History, 1819–1965*, eds. Khoo Kay Kim, Elinah Abdullah and Wan Meng Hao (Subang Jaya, Selangor: Pelanduk, 2006), p. 194.
38. Wan Meng Hao, "Malay Soldiering in Singapore, 1910–1942", p. 207.
39. *Straits Times*, 11 November 1957 and 10 November 1958.
40. See Tan Sri Dato Mubin Sheppard, *Taman Budiman: Memoirs of an Unorthodox Civil Servant* (Kuala Lumpur: Heinemann Educational Books Asia, 1979), pp. 246–251; and Haji Mubin Sheppard, "The Massacre on Bedok Hill", in *Straits Times* (Malaysian edition), 3 March 1966, p. 6; and Haji Mubin Sheppard, "A Paragon of Loyalty", *Straits Times* (Malaysian edition), 28 February 1967, p. 8.
41. He served in the Perak and Negeri Sembilan battalions of the FMS Volunteer Service. Haji Mubin Sheppard, "A Paragon of Loyalty", *Straits Times* (Malaysian edition), 28 February 1967, p. 8.
42. See their entries in Imperial War Graves Commission, *The War Dead of the British Commonwealth and Empire: The Register of the Names of Those Who Fell in the 1939–1945 War and Have No Known Grave: The Singapore Memorial* (London: Her Majesty's Stationery Office, 1956). There were three other Malay volunteer officers.
43. Mustapha Hussain, *Malay Nationalism Before UMNO*, p. 229.
44. Haji Mubin Sheppard, "A Paragon of Loyalty", *Straits Times* (Malaysian edition), 28 February 1967, p. 8.

394 *Notes to pp. 218–20*

45. Haji Mubin Sheppard, "The Massacre on Bedok Hill", in *Straits Times* (Malaysian edition), 3 March 1966, p. 6.
46. Mustapha Hussain, *Malay Nationalism Before UMNO*, pp. 229, 235.
47. Mustapha Hussain, *Malay Nationalism Before UMNO*, Introduction, which claims he "saved thousands". Imprisoned by the British in 1945–1946, he later advised MNP, and then joined UMNO, running Tunku Abdul Rahman close for the Presidency in June 1951. He was released by the British in 1946 following petitions from Malay Regiment men he had helped, pp. 241, 322.
48. Mubin Sheppard, *Tunku: A Pictorial Biography: 1903–1957*, Vol. 1 (Petaling Jaya, Selangor: Pelanduk, 1988), p. 80; and *Reminiscences of Tunku Abdul Rahman on the Japanese Occupation 1941–1945* (Penang: Perpustakaan Universiti Sains Malaysia, 1989) pp. 3–4, 17.
49. See "Perilous Search Mass Graves Yield Awful Secret of Terrible Massacre", from *The Star*, 15 September 1975, in Tunku Abdul Rahman Putra Al-Haj, *Looking Back: Monday Musings and Memories* (Kuala Lumpur: Pustaka Antara, 1977), pp. 143–9.
50. This had been formed as a private regular force by the Sultan of Johor in 1885. In the First World War, it helped the British put down the German inspired sepoy Mutiny in Singapore.
51. The independent Malayan government after 1957 continued the arrangement for the sultan's bodyguards. Tunku Shahriman bin Tunku Sulaiman, "The Johore Military Forces", BA thesis, University of Malaya, 1958; and Tunku Shahriman bin Tunku Sulaiman, "The Johore Military Forces: The Oldest Army of Malay Regulars in the Peninsula", *Journal of the Malaysian Branch of the Royal Asiatic Society* 77, 2 (2004): 95–105.
52. Those who joined the Malay Regiment later included the future Malaysian General Ibrahim Bin Ismail; Ibrahim Bin Ismail, *Have You Met Mariam?* (Johor Bahru: Westlight, 1984), pp. 140–1.
53. *Straits Times*, 1 July 1962.
54. Wan Hashim Wan Teh, *Perang Dunia Kedua: Peranan Gerila Melayu Force 136* [*World War II: The Role of the Malay Guerrilla Force 136*] (Kuala Lumpur: Dewan Bahasa dan Pustaka Kementerian Pendidikan Malaysia, 1993), pp. 64, 128.
55. Wan Hashim Wan Teh, *Peranan Gerila Melayu Force 136*, p. 168.
56. William Shaw, *Tun Razak: His Life and Times* (London: Longman, 1976), p. 50.
57. Sheppard, *Tunku: A Pictorial Biography: 1903–1957*, Vol. 1, p. 91.
58. Abdul Aziz bin Zahariah, *Leftenan Nor: Pahlawan Gerila* [*Lieutenant Nor: Guerrilla Fighter*] (Kuala Lumpur: Dewan Bahasa dan Pustaka, 1959), pp. 12–6.
59. Halinah Bamadhaj, "The Impact of the Japanese Occupation of Malaya on Malay Society and Politics (1941–1945)", MA thesis, University of Auckland, 1975, pp. 128–9.

60. *Fajar Asia* (Singapore), December 1942, cited and translated by Cheah Boon Kheng, "The Japanese Occupation of Malaya, 1942–45: Ibrahim Yaacob and the Struggle for Indonesia Raya", *Indonesia*, 28 (1979): 107.
61. Mustapha Hussain, *Malay Nationalism Before UMNO*, ed. K.S. Jomo, trans. Insun Sony Mustapha (Kuala Lumpur: Utusan Publications & Distributors, 2005), pp. 193, 257.
62. Cheah Boon Kheng, *Red Star Over Malaya: Resistance and Social Conflict During and After the Japanese Occupation, 1941–1946*, 2nd edition (Singapore University Press, 1987), p. 36.
63. Cheah, *Red Star Over Malaya*, p. 34.
64. Cheah, "The Japanese Occupation of Malaya, 1942–45: Ibrahim Yaacob and the Struggle for Indonesia Raya", *Indonesia*, pp. 103, 109.
65. Mastura Abdul Rahman, "The Japanese Occupation Through Malay Fiction", in *Malays/Muslims in Singapore: Selected Readings in History, 1819–1965*, eds. Khoo Kay Kim, Elinah Abdullah and Wan Meng Hao (Subang Jaya, Selangor: Pelanduk, 2006), p. 228.
66. See the articles in Arena Wati, eds., *Cherpen Zaman Jepun* [*Short Stories from the Japanese Period*] (Kuala Lumpur: Pustaka Antara, 1968), pp. 146–57.
67. Mastura Abdul Rahman, "The Japanese Occupation Through Malay Fiction", p. 240.
68. Mustapha Hussain, *Malay Nationalism Before UMNO*, pp. 313–4.
69. Halinah Bamadhaj, *The Impact of the Japanese Occupation of Malaya on Malay Society and Politics*, pp. 122–7.
70. Mustapha Hussain, *Malay Nationalism Before UMNO*, pp. 269–70.
71. Ibid., p. 282.
72. See the account of KRIS given in Cheah Boon Kheng, *Red Star Over Malaya*, pp. 113–23.
73. *MSS: Political Intelligence Journal* (30 April 1946): 5 (Rhodes House, Oxford University). Some former Malay Regiment members also went over to fight the Dutch alongside the Indonesian Republicans.
74. J.J. Raj Jr, *The War Years and After*, rev. ed. (Subang Jaya, Selangor: Pelanduk, 2000), p. 59.
75. *MSS: Political Intelligence Journal* (31 December 1947): 539 (Rhodes House, Oxford University).
76. Firdaus Haji Abdullah, *Radical Malay Politics: Its Origins and Early Development* (Petaling Jaya, Selangor: Pelanduk, 1985), p. 145.
77. Mustapha Hussain, *Malay Nationalism Before UMNO*, p. 368; and Senator Datuk Ahmad Zahid Hamidi, *UMNO Youth: Leadership and Struggle* (Kuala Lumpur: Yayasan Gerakbati Kebangsaan, 2005), pp. 12–3.
78. Ahmad Zahid Hamidi, *UMNO Youth*, pp. 12–3; and Cecilia Tan, *Tun Sardon Jubir: His Life and Times* (Petaling Jaya, Selangor: Pelanduk, 1986), p. 18.
79. Alias Mohamed, *Ghafar: A Biography* (Petaling Jeya, Selangor: Pelanduk, 1993), pp. 33–6.

80. Ahmad Boestamam, *Memoir Ahmad Boestamam: Merdeka dengan Darah dalam Api [Ahmad Boestamam's Memoirs: Independence through blood and inside API]* (Bangi: Penerbit Universiti Kebangsaan Malaysia, 2004), p. 136. This volume is a reprinting of his three previous memoirs into one. In these memoirs, Ahmad Boestamam admits that many members of the KMM and KRIS joined the Malay Nationalist Party.

81. Firdaus Haji Abdullah, *Radical Malay Politics*, p. 79.

82. Letter to the Editor: A Member of the MNP, "The MNP in Malaya: A Reply", *Straits Times*, 25 November 1946.

83. Ahmad Boestamam, *Carving the Path to the Summit*, trans. William R. Roff (Athens, OH: Ohio University Press, 1979), p. 34.

84. Boestamam, *Carving the Path to the Summit*, pp. 34–9.

85. *MSS: Political Intelligence Journal* (31 October 1946): 1 (Rhodes House, Oxford University).

86. *MSS: Political Intelligence Journal* (28 February 1947): 10–15 (Rhodes House, Oxford University).

87. *MSS: Political Intelligence Journal* (15 August 1946): 7 (Rhodes House, Oxford University).

88. *MSS: Political Intelligence Journal* (31 August 1946): 1 (Rhodes House, Oxford University).

89. *MSS: Political Intelligence Journal* (31 August 1946): 2 (Rhodes House, Oxford University).

90. *MSS: Political Intelligence Journal* (31 May 1947): 138–9; and MSS Supplement to Political Intelligence Journal No.10/1947, dated 30/6/1947: Indonesian Influences in Malaya p. 22 (Rhodes House, Oxford University).

91. *MSS: Political Intelligence Journal* (15 July 1948): 522 (Rhodes House, Oxford University).

92. *MSS: Political Intelligence Journal* (15 March 1947): 32 (Rhodes House, Oxford University).

93. *MSS: Political Intelligence Journal* (15 April 1947): 204 (Rhodes House, Oxford University).

94. See A.J. Stockwell, *British Policy and Malay Politics During the Malayan Union Experiment, 1942–1948* (Kuala Lumpur: MBRAS, 1979), p. 136.

95. Karl Hack, "The Origins of the Cold War: Malaya", *Journal of Southeast Asian Studies* 40, 3 (October 2009): 471–96.

96. See Handling of Resistance Movements in Malaya, 1946 CO 537/1570; Guerrilla Organisations: Rewards, 1948 CO 537/4245; and see Trafford Smith, 4 April 1949, Colonial Office, London, 1946, in King's Commissions — Malays CO 537/4657 (TNA).

97. Mustapha Hussain, *Malay Nationalism Before UMNO*, p. 367.

98. Mohd Anis bin Tairan interview with Kevin Blackburn at Kampong Siglap Mosque, Singapore, 19 February 2009.

99. *MSS: Political Intelligence Journal* (30 June 1947): 185 (Rhodes House, Oxford University).

100. Tan Liok Ee, *The Rhetoric of Bangsa and Minzu: Community and Nation in Tension, The Malay Peninsula, 1900–1955* (Melbourne: Monash University, 1988), p. 14. See also A.J. Stockwell, *British Policy and Malay Politics During the Malay Union Experiment, 1942–1948* (Kuala Lumpur: MBRAS, 1979), pp. 69–70.

101. Karl Hack, "The Malayan Emergency's Counter-Insurgency Paradigm", *Journal of Strategic Studies* 32, 3 (June 2009): 383–414.

102. *Straits Times*, 13 February 1952, *Singapore Standard*, 14 February 1952, *Sunday Times* (Singapore), 1 March 1953, and *Malay Mail*, 1 March 1953.

103. Secretary for Defence (contribution to Federal Annual Report 1953) 5114/1954 in the files of the Federal Secretariat (NAM).

104. Hack, *Defence and Decolonisation*, pp. 145–6. The quotation is from Templer to Colonial Secretary, 17 November 1952, CO968/341, (TNA). Britain abandoned the idea of making the Malay Regiment itself mixed-race — as a part of multicommunal nation building — in 1946.

105. "Editorial: Malay Regiment", *Utusan Melayu*, 5 December 1952.

106. Trafford Smith, Colonial Office, 4 April 1949 in CO 537/4657, (TNA).

107. *Sunday Times* (Singapore), 1 March 1953.

108. Ramlee adapted a story by Englishman Ralph Modder for *Sergeant Hassan*; see Ahmad Sarji, *P. Ramlee Erti Yang Sakti* [*The Magic of P. Ramlee*] (Subang Jaya, Selangor: Pelanduk, 1999), pp. 353–6, James Harding and Ahmad Sarji, *P. Ramlee: The Bright Star* (Subang Jaya, Selangor: Pelanduk, 2002), pp. 125–8, *Singapore Free Press*, 31 August 1958, and *Malay Mail*, 21 August 1958.

109. See *Straits Times*, 30 August 1958 and *Singapore Free Press*, 31 August 1958. Shaw Brothers' Malay Film Productions obtained the permission of the Regiment to make the film.

110. *Malay Mail*, 21 August 1958.

111. See *Singapore Standard*, 28 August 1958, and credits in *Sergeant Hassan* (Singapore: Shaw Brothers, Malay Film Productions, 1958). The British were Captains John Gray and David Downe.

112. The 1,500 movie tickets of the premiere had not only been on sale at the movie theatre, the Capitol, but at the Headquarters of the Armed Forces.

113. *Malay Mail*, 21 August 1958.

114. *Malay Mail*, 27 August 1958.

115. *Sergeant Hassan* (Singapore: Shaw Brothers, Malay Film Productions, 1958).

116. See Ariffin Omar, *Bangsa Melayu*.

117. *Utusan Melayu*, 19 September 1962.

118. Ahmad Murad Bin Nasruddin, *Nyawa Di-Hujong Pedang* (Kuala Lumpur: Kee Meng Press, 1967).

119. Sahlan Mohd Saman, *A Comparative Study of the Malaysian and Philippines War Novels* (Bangi, Malaysia, Penerbit Universiti Kebangsaan Malaysia, 1984), p. 23.
120. The novel had been reprinted seven times by 1967.
121. Abu Talib Ahmad *Malay Muslims, Islam and the Rising Sun*, pp. 193, 141–9.
122. Sheppard, *The Malay Regiment: 1933–1947*.
123. Bandman Omar Attached "C" Company 1st Battalion, statement 18 in History of the Malay Regiment, 2nd Battalion in the Mubin Sheppard Papers (NAM).
124. 39 R.S.M. Ismail Babu, HQ Company — 1st Battalion in History of the Malay Regiment, 2nd Battalion in the Mubin Sheppard Papers (NAM). See also War Diary of 1535 Pte Sulong Ahmad bin Hamzah in History of the Malay Regiment, 2nd Battalion in the Mubin Sheppard Papers (NAM), for Private Sulong Ahmad bin Hamzah. He also told Sheppard that he too "was forced to join the Gyutai as the Japanese Kempei were playing havoc". See also Lieut. Ibrahim bin Alla Ditta (Malay Officer) "D" Company 2nd Battalion The Malay Regiment", statement number 22 in History of the Malay Regiment, 2nd Battalion in the Mubin Sheppard Papers (NAM), for another claim of being forced to join.
125. Sheppard, *The Malay Regiment: 1933–1947*, p. 25.
126. *Malay Mail*, 1 and 3 March 1958.
127. *Straits Times*, 29 and 30 August 1958.
128. *Malay Mail*, 1 March 1958 and *Sunday Times* (Singapore), 27 April 1958.
129. *Singapore Standard*, 21 November 1957 and *Sunday Times* (Singapore), 27 April 1958.
130. *Singapore Free Press*, 15 August 1959 and *Straits Times*, 9 July 1968.
131. Rehabilitation of Ex-Servicemen in Malaya BANS 14/55 in Mubin Sheppard Papers (NAM).
132. *Berita Harian*, 13 February 1967 and *Straits Times*, 13 February 1967.
133. Film Production "Hang Tuah" in Mubin Sheppard Papers (NAM).
134. See M.C. ff Sheppard, *The Adventures of Hang Tuah* (Singapore: Donald Moore, 1949) and *Hang Tuah* (Singapore: Shaw Brothers, Malay Film Productions, 1956).
135. M.C. ff. Sheppard, "The Malay Warrior", *The Straits Times Annual for 1957*, p. 12. The article begins with several pages on historical Malay warriors, juxtaposing photographs of the modern Malay Regiment. It then relates the Regiment's history, finishing with the words: "The spirit of Hang Tuah is still very much alive today …"
136. *Hang Jebat* (Singapore: Cathay Keris, 1961, reissued as a VCD in 2003).
137. He mixed with its leaders, such as vice-chairmen Yahya bin Ahmad, from Negeri Sembilan, Yazid bin Ja'afar from Perak, secretary Abdul Ghani bin Saman from Selangor, and treasurer, and Raja Saidin from Selangor.
138. *Malay Mail*, 7 November 1955.

139. *Singapore Free Press*, 15 August 1959.
140. *Straits Times*, 9 July, 5 August 1968, 31 July 1969, and 1 August 1976.
141. *Straits Times*, 9 November 1959, 14 November 1960, and 13 November, 1961.
142. *Straits Times*, 11 November 1957 and 10 November, 1958.
143. Mubin Sheppard, *Tunku: A Pictorial Biography: 1903–1957*, Vol. 1 (Petaling Jaya, Selangor: Pelanduk, 1988), p. 80; and *Reminiscences of Tunku Abdul Rahman on the Japanese Occupation 1941–1945* (Penang: Perpustakaan Universiti Sains Malaysia, 1989), pp. 3–4, 17.
144. *Straits Times*, 16 November, 1958. The greater focus on paying respects to the Malay war dead also raised delicate issues. On Remembrance Day 1958 at Ipoh, the Sultan of Perak and his Mentri Besar did not attend "on advice of the Religious Affairs Department" which said "that it is against Islam to pay obeisance to a stone monument and this was being followed since Islam is now the state religion".
145. Sheppard, *Tunku: A Pictorial Biography: 1957–1987*, Vol. 2, p. 31.
146. The photograph by Joseph Rosenthal possibly showed the raising of a second, larger flag on the mountain, the day after a first was raised.
147. *Straits Times*, 31 July 1961.
148. *Straits Times*, 1 August 1961.
149. Lai Chee Kien, *Building Merdeka: Independence Architecture in Kuala Lumpur, 1957–1966* (Kuala Lumpur: Petronas, 2007), Image 10.8 on p. 123, compared to 10.14 on p. 129, and p. 127.
150. Karl Hack, "Contentious Heritage", in *Understanding Heritage and Memory*, ed. Tim Benton (Manchester: Manchester University Press, 2010), pp. 114–8. Lee Chai Kien, *Building Merdeka*, pp. 121–31.
151. *Straits Times*, 11 November 1961; *Straits Times*, 12 November 1962; *and Straits Times* (Kuala Lumpur edition), 8 February, 1966.
152. *Straits Times*, 9 September 1963.
153. *Straits Times*, 28 July 1965; and *Straits Times* (Kuala Lumpur edition), 9 February 1966.
154. *Straits Times* (Kuala Lumpur edition), 9 February 1966.
155. *Eastern Sun*, 19 October 1966, 23 October, 1966, and 24 September 1967. Dr Zakir Husain, India's Vice-President, also laid a wreath on the colonial memorial in October 1966.

Chapter 8

1. Sheppard, *The Malay Regiment*, p. 25.
2. Such memories are minimised in the realm of *state sanctioned commemoration*, but retain a significant presence in *both private memory and in fiction*. Abu Talib Ahmad, *The Malay Muslims, Islam, and the Rising Sun*, pp. 49–53 (Japanese atrocities), and pp. 65–76 (forced labour).

3. British numbers for end of September 1945 can be found in Table 13.1 of Nakahara Michiko, "Malayan Labor on the Thailand-Burma Railway", in *Asian Labor in the Wartime Japanese Empire*, ed. Kratoska, p. 251. This table gives a total of 78,204 Asian labourers, of which 29,634 were dead, 6,456 employed at present, 24,626 deserted, and 17,488 repatriated. Figures originally from WO 325/7 D (TNA). The Japanese total mobilisation of labour for the railway was 62,000 POWs and around 200,000 Asian labourers. A high percentage of the "deserted" probably died, as peak desertions were at the time cholera raged through the camps. That said, a death rate of 40 per cent would be extremely conservative. Later Allied figures, given on p. 252, suggest at least 182,492 Asian labourers, with a minimum of 74,025 deaths (40 per cent). Those later figures give 78,204 for "Malayans", with a minimum of 40,000 dead (51 per cent).

4. Nakahara Michiko, "Malayan Labor on the Thailand-Burma Railway", in *Asian Labor in the Japanese Empire*, ed. Kratoska, p. 252.

5. G.S. Wodeman (Colonial Office, London) to Mr Paskin on the Report by Major Chamier and Major Arbutnott, 19 November 1945, in Malayans in Thailand, 1945–1946, CO 537/1571: (TNA).

6. 278 L/CPL 'Ian "A" Coy 1st BN. The Malay Regiment, in 2nd Battalion in the Mubin Sheppard Papers (NAM).

7. 1286 Pte Mohd Yunus Bin Jamal "C" Coy 1st Battalion, statement 28, in 2nd Battalion in the Mubin Sheppard Papers (NAM).

8. Personal History of 823 CPL Ismail, The Malay Regiment, in 2nd Battalion in the Mubin Sheppard Papers (NAM).

9. Repatriation of Malays (MALF) From New Guinea, 3192/46, in the files of the Malayan Union (NAM).

10. Alleged ill-treatment of Malays Repatriated from New Guinea, 1054/1947, in the files of the Malayan Union (NAM).

11. Compensation to heirs of Malay War Victims, 12535/1951, in the files of the Federal Secretariat (NAM).

12. Abu Talib Ahmad, *Malay Muslims, Islam and the Rising Sun*, pp. 65–74; Mat Zin Mat Kib, *Persatuan Buruh Kerata Api Maut Siam-Burma* [*The Association of Labourers on the Burma-Thailand Railway*] (Shah Alam, Malaysia: Pusat Penerbitan Universiti, UPENA, UiTM, 2005); and Nakahara Michiko, "Labour Recruitment in Malaya Under the Japanese Occupation: The Case of the Burma-Siam Railway", in *Rethinking Malaysia: Malaysian Studies 1*, ed. K.S. Jomo (Kuala Lumpur: Malaysian Social Science Association, 1999), pp. 215–45.

13. Zulkifli bin Mohd Hashim, Acting Secretary-General, UMNO to Chief Secretary, Federation of Malaya, 8 December 1951, in Compensation to heirs of Malay War Victims, 12535/1951, in the files of the Federal Secretariat (NAM).

14. For P.O. Wickens Acting General Chief Secretary to The Secretary-General, U.M.N.O., 8 August 1952 in Compensation to heirs of Malay War Victims, 12535/1951, in the files of the Federal Secretariat (NAM).

15. Zulkifli bin Mohd Hashim, Acting Secretary-General, UMNO to Chief Secretary, Federation of Malaya, 11 August 1952, in Compensation to heirs of Malay War Victims, 12535/1951, in the files of the Federal Secretariat (NAM).

16. Repatriation of Labourers taken to Burma/Siam During Japanese Occupation 13979/1949, in the files of the Federal Secretariat (NAM).

17. List of Missing Persons from Kelantan Taken Away by the Japanese for Forced Labour, 6335/47, in the files of the Malayan Union (NAM).

18. British Embassy, Consular Section to Chief Secretary, Government of Malayan Union, Kuala Lumpur, 7 April 1947 in Repatriation of Certain Malays from Siam to Malaya, 4917/47, in the files of the Malayan Union (NAM).

19. Translation Details of the Domicile of Nai Sori Ari and His Family, in Padang Besar: Report From Siam to Malaya, 12834/1950, files of the Federal Secretariat (NAM).

20. Ayub Kasim to British Embassy Consular Section, 5 September 1950, Translation, in Padang Besar: Report From Siam to Malaya, 12834/1950, in the files of the Federal Secretariat (NAM).

21. The sale had gone ahead in 1954. *Straits Times*, 3 and 19 September 1955; and Lionel De Rosario, *Nippon Slaves* (London: Janus, 1995), pp. 206–7.

22. Burma/Siam Death Railway Payment of Assets, 815/1956, in the files of the Federal Secretariat (NAM); Chief Secretary, *Proceedings of the Legislative Council of the Federation of Malaya*, 19 January 1955, cols. 1239–1240; and Chief Secretary, *Proceedings of the Legislative Council of the Federation of Malaya*, 1 June 1955, col. 533.

23. Basir Bin Saire to State Secretary, Johore UMNO, 18 October 1954 and Basir Bin Saire to President United Malays National Organisation, 28 October 1954, in Forced Labour Siam Burma Railway UMNO YDP 29/54 in UMNO files, (NAM).

24. Tunku Abdul Rahman to Basir bin Saire, 7 November 1954 and Tunku Abdul Rahman to Samion bin Suradi 14 November 1954, in Forced Labour Siam Burma Railway UMNO YDP 29/54 in UMNO files, (NAM).

25. Tunku Abdul Rahman to Ibrahim bin Musa, 8 March 1955, in Forced Labour Siam Burma Railway UMNO YDP 29/54 in UMNO files, (NAM).

26. Mat Zin Mat Kib, *Persatuan Bekas Buruh Paksa dan Keluarga Buruh Jalan Keretapi Maut Siam-Burma 1942–46 Persekutuan Tanah Melayu, 1958–1973: Satu Tinjauan Sejarah Perkembangannya* [*The All Malaya Association of Forced Labourers and Families of Forced Labourers of the Burma-Siam Death Railway, 1958–1973: A Survey of its Development*] (Academic Exercise, School of Humanities, Universit Sains Malaysia, 1988), p. 33.

27. *Straits Times*, 17 March 1959.

28. *Straits Times*, 20 November 1963.

29. *Sunday Times* (Singapore), 11 January 1959 and 8 September 1959.

30. *Sunday Times* (Singapore), 11 January 1959.

31. *Straits Times*, 16 May 1960.

32. Prime Minister, *Parliamentary Debates: Dewan Ra'ayat (House of Representatives) Official Report*, 9 January 1962, column 2422.

33. *Straits Times*, 3 May 1962.

34. *Straits Times*, 1 June and 26 August 1964.

35. *Straits Times*, 14 July 1962.

36. Saidon bin Kechut, *Parliamentary Debates: Dewan Negara (Senate) Official Report* 19 October 1964, column 663.

37. Tan Siew Sin, *Parliamentary Debates: Dewan Negara (Senate) Official Report* 19 October 1964, columns 663–4.

38. *Straits Times*, 15 May 1967.

39. Mat Zin Mat Kib, *Persatuan Bekas Buruh Paksa dan Keluarga Buruh Jalan Keretapi Maut Siam-Burma 1942–46 Persekutuan Tanah Melayu, 1958–1973*, p. 35.

40. See *Japan Times*, 14 August 1991; and Reynolds, "History, Memory, Compensation, and Reconciliation: The Abuse of Labour along the Thailand-Burma Railway", in *Asian Labor in the Wartime Japanese Empire*, ed. Kratoska, p. 331. Association documents were transferred to Chin Gin Lin of Paloh, Malaysia, and accessed via his daughter-in-law, Ann Chin and son Chin Chen Onn.

41. *New Straits Times*, 29 July 2009.

Chapter 9

1. Confrontation, or Konfrontasi (1963 to August 1966) was Indonesia's way of opposing the formation of Malaysia of 16 September 1963. Using techniques that had won it the transfer of Dutch West New Guinea, it combined diplomatic pressure, invocation of the rights of newly decolonising forces against imperialism, and persistent, low-level military pressure. The latter featured incursions across the Indonesian-Malaysian jungle border, small boat and paratroop landings in the south of the Malayan peninsula, and bombs let off in Singapore.

2. *Straits Times*, 9 July 1968, p. 5, and 9 August 1968, p. 7.

3. Hence, on 19 July 2010, the Prime Minister's wife, Datin Seri Rosmah Mansor, presented in excess of 4.51 million ringgit raised by corporations and individuals, when launching the appeal ahead of 2010 Warrior's Day. See *Star Online*, 20 July 2010, at http://thestaronline.com [accessed 24 July 2010]. The appeal period was July 2010 to 30 September 2010, with donors recieving a flower.

4.   In Malay, the Ex-Servicemen's League is Persatuan Bekas Tentera Malaysia or PBTM. Its webpage is at http://www.pbtm.org.my/ [accessed 24 July 2010]. It originated from the mainly expatriate Ex Services Association of Malaya (ESAM) established 1922, changing to PBTM in the 1960s, when Sabah and Sarawak branches were admitted. In 2010, it claimed more than 125,000 members.

5.   Cheah Boon Kheng, *Malaysia: The Making of a Nation* (Singapore: ISEAS, 2002), pp. 5–7.

6.   Abdul Rahman Arshad, *Unity and Education in Malaysia* (Kuala Lumpur: Dewan Bahasa dan Pustaka, 2007), p. 249.

7.   Arshad, *Unity and Education in Malaysia*, p. 65.

8.   Syed Husin Ali, *Malays: Their Problems and Future* (Petaling Jaya: Other Press, 2008), p. 171.

9.   A.B. Shamsul, "Debating About Identity in Malaysia: A Discourse Analysis", in *Cultural Contestations: Mediating Identities in a Changing Malaysian Society*, ed. Zawawi Ibrahim (London: ASEAN Academic Press, 1998), p. 29.

10. Kua Kia Soong, ed., *Malaysian Cultural Policy and Democracy*, 2nd edition (Kuala Lumpur: Selangor Chinese Assembly Hall, 1990); and Ariffin Omar, *Bangsa Melayu: Malay Concepts of Democracy and Community: 1945–1950* (Kuala Lumpur: Oxford University Press, 1999).

11. *The Star*, 11 December 2004; Ramlah binti Adam, Abdul Hakim bin Samuri and Muslimin bin Fadzil, *Sejarah Tingkatan 3: Kurikulum Bersepadu Sekolah Menengah* [*History for Form 3: Secondary School*] (Kuala Lumpur: Dewan Bahasa dan Pustaka, 2004), pp. 22–3.

12. *Straits Times* (Malaysian Edition), 22 September 1967.

13. *Straits Times*, 22 February 1970.

14. *Eastern Sun*, 21 February 1970; and *Straits Times*, 23 February 1970.

15. See K.S. Jomo, ed., *Japan and Malaysian Development: In the Shadow of the Rising Sun* (London: Routledge, 1994); and Lim Hua Sing, *Japan's Role in ASEAN: Issues and Prospects* (Singapore: Times Academic Press, 1994).

16. *The Star*, 1 October 1982.

17. *The Star*, 15 August 1984; and Chen Ya Cai, ed., *Malaiya kang ri ji nian bei tu pian ji* [*Malaysian Anti-Japanese Memorials: A Pictorial*] (Kuala Lumpur: Centre for Malaysian Chinese Studies, 1999). See the records from the Chinese press kept at the Centre for Malaysian Chinese Studies at the Selangor Chinese Assembly Hall in Kuala Lumpur.

18. *Straits Times*, 11 August 1992. Senmeilan Zhonghua da hui tang bian [Negeri Sembilan Chinese Assembly Hall], eds., *Ri Zhi Shi Qi Sen Zhou Hua Zu Meng Nan Shi Liao* [*The Japanese Massacre of Negeri Sembilan Chinese*] (Seremban, Malaysia: Negeri Sembilan Chinese Assembly Hall, 1988).

19. *Straits Times*, 28 August 1994.

20. Mustapha Hussain, *Malay Nationalism Before UMNO*, pp. 313–4.

21. Li Ye Lin, ed., *Tai Ping Yang Zhan Zheng Shi Liao Hui Ban: Selected Historical Materials of the Pacific War* (Kuala Lumpur: Selangor Chinese Assembly Hall, 1996), pp. 396–412.

22. Mahathir was himself a half Indian-half Malay doctor, and in the book implied the Malays were actually genetically inferior, and so needed additional help if not out-breeding. He followed the traditional route of fiery advocacy of Malay rights in UMNO Youth as he rose, followed by some accommodation of non-Malays, and advocacy of a wider "Malaysian" identity on top of Malay primacy, once in power. See Mahathir bin Mohammad, *The Malay Dilemma* (Singapore: Times Books, 1970 [1995 reprint]), pp. 16–31, especially pp. 25, 51–2, 97.

23. Khoo Boo Teik, *Paradoxes of Mahathirism: An Intellectual Biography of Mahathir Mohamad* (Kuala Lumpur: Oxford University Press, 1995), pp. 70–4.

24. Abu Talib Ahmad, "Museums and the Japanese Occupation of Malaya", in *Reflections on Southeast Asian History Since 1945*, eds. Richard Mason and Abu Talib Ahmad (Penang: Penerbit Universiti Sains Malaysia, 2006), pp. 38–9.

25. Alias Mohamed, *Ghafar: A Biography* (Petaling Jaya, Selangor Pelanduk, 1993), pp. 29–30.

26. See Muzaini Hamzah, "Tense Pasts, Present Tensions: Postcolonial Memory-scapes and the Memorialisation of the Second World War in Perak", PhD thesis, University of Durham, 2009, p. 117.

27. Barry Wain, *Malaysian Maverick: Mahathir Mohamad in Turbulent Times* (New York: Palgrave Macmillan, 2009), pp. 255–62.

28. Karl Hack, "Decolonisation and the Pergau Dam Affair", *History Today* 44, 1 (November 1994): 9–15. The Pergau Dam Affair did not stop trade with Britain increasing, but did result in a temporary banning of British firms from Malaysian Government contracts. The problem was that the British press uncovered links between British aid to Pergau — a controversial dam project in Borneo — and British arms sales. Digging around, they then also alleged corruption. The 30 per cent target for capital was enshrined in the New Economic Policy of 1971. See also Michael Leifer, "Anglo-Malaysian Alienation Revisited", *Round Table* 83, 331 (July 1994): 347–59.

29. Abu Talib Ahmad, *Malay Muslims, Islam and the Rising Sun*, p. 149.

30. *New Straits Times*, 18 December 2002.

31. Cheah Boon Kheng, "Memory as History and Moral Judgement" in *War and Memory in Malaysia and Singapore*, eds. P. Lim Pui Huen and Diana Wong (Singapore: ISEAS, 2000), pp. 29–30.

32. Ramlah binti Adam, Abdul Hakim bin Samuri and Muslimin bin Fadzil, *Sejarah Tingkatan 3: Kurikulum Bersepadu Sekolah Menengah* [*History for Form 3: Secondary School*] (Kuala Lumpur: Dewan Bahasa dan Pustaka,

2004), pp. 22–3; Ramlah binti Adam, Abdul Hakim bin Samuri, Shakila Parween binti Yacob and Muslimin bin Fadzil, *Sejarah Tingkatan 5: Kurikulum Bersepadu Sekolah Menengah* [*History for Form 5: Secondary School*] (Kuala Lumpur: Dewan Bahasa dan Pustaka, 2004), pp. 56–9; Sabihah Osman, Muzaffar Tate, and Ishak Ibrahim, *Sejarah Tingkatan 3: Kurikulum Bersepadu Sekolah Menengah* [*History for Form 3: Secondary School*] (Kuala Lumpur: Dewan Bahasa dan Pustaka, 1990), pp. 11–2; and Siti Zurainia Abdul Majid, Muhammad Yusoff Hashim, Abdullah Zakaria Ghazali, Lee Kam Hing, Ahmad Fawzi Basri, and Zainal Abdin Abdul Wahid, *Sejarah Tingkatan 5: Kurikulum Bersepadu Sekolah Menengah* [*History for Form 5: Secondary School*] (Kuala Lumpur: Dewan Bahasa dan Pustaka, 1992), pp. 85–7.

33. Abu Talib Ahmad, "The Malay Community and Memory of the Japanese Occupation", in *War and Memory in Malaysia and Singapore*, eds. P. Lim Pui Huen and Diana Wong (Singapore: ISEAS, 2000), p. 81.

34. Abu Talib Ahmad, "Museums and the Japanese Occupation of Malaya", p. 42.

35. For the National Museum, see http://www.muziumnegara.gov.my/ [accessed October 2010].

36. *Berita Harian*, Malaysia, 1 August 2000.

37. *New Straits Times*, 2 October 2000.

38. *Straits Times*, 3 July 2000.

39. Ibid.

40. For box-office figures, see FINAS: Perbadanen Kemajuan Filem Nasional Malaysia, at http://finas.gov.my/; and the numerous web-based discussion groups set up by young Malaysians.

41. *New Straits Times*, 27 September 2000.

42. Z.A. Penang, "Many Confusing Scenes in the Movie 'Lt Adnan'", *New Straits Times*, 29 August 2000.

43. See Khoo Gaik Cheng, "'You've Come a Long Way, Baby' Erma Fatimah, Film and Politics", *South East Asia Research* 14, 2 (July 2006): 179–209.

44. Umie Aida who starred in *Leftenan Adnan* as Adnan's wife.

45. Played by Hani Moshin.

46. Khoo, "'You've Come a Long Way, Baby'", p. 201.

47. Ibid.

48. *New Straits Times*, 19 December 2002.

49. *New Straits Times*, 14 December 2002.

50. Ibid.

51. Ibid.

52. Mahathir Mohamad, *The Challenge* (Petaling Jaya, Selangor: Pelanduk, 1986), p. 160.

53. Mahathir, *The Challenge*, p. 160.

54. *New Straits Times*, 24 September 2002.

55. The character Siew Lan was played by well-known Malaysian Chinese actress, Janet Khoo. Ahmad was played by the equally well-known Malay actor Nan Ron.

56. Baradan Kuppusamy, "Malaysia's Break from Bollywood a Bust", *Asia Times* online, 21 August 2003, at http://www.atimes.com.

57. *New Straits Times*, 11 July 2010.

58. Mohammad Agus Yusoff and Nik Anuar Nik Mahmud, "Managing Terrorism Through Peaceful Political Negotiations: The Malayan Experience", *Jebat* 29 (2002): 126. Chin Peng, *My Side of History*, pp. 493–4; Dato General Kitti Rattanachaya, *The Communist Party of Malaya, Malaysia and Thailand: Truce Talks Ending The Armed Struggle of The Communist Party of Malaya* (Bangkok: Duangkew, 1996).

59. Malaysiakini.com, K. Kabilan article of 31 August 2009 [accessed April 2010].

60. Chin Peng, *My Side of History*, p. 500.

61. *New Straits Times*, 8 December 2003; *Nanyang Siang Pau*, 8 December 2003; *China Press*, 8 December 2003; and *Sin Chew Daily* (Metro Edition), 9 December 2003.

62. *Sin Chew Daily* (Negeri Sembilan Edition), 20 September 2003; and an interview with Jade Wong at the MPAJA veterans' seminar at the UE3 shopping centre in Kuala Lumpur on 7 December 2003.

63. See in particular, *China Press* and *Nanyang Siang Pau*, 8 December 2003.

64. James Wong, "Chin Peng — Hero or Enemy?", Malaysiakini.com, 11 September 2003 [accessed April 2010]. James Wing On Wong, *From Pacific War to Merdeka: Articles from Malaysiakini.com* (Petaling Jaya, Selangor: SIRD, 2005).

65. *Straits Times*, 20 September 2005, p. 21.

66. Some images were more general attacks on the MCA, for instance, splicing together the MCA symbol, that of Singapore's PAP (from which the DAP originated in the 1960s), and various images of Chin Peng or books on him.

67. http://www.nilaimemorialpark.com/park.phtml [accessed 24 May 2010].

68. There is a summary of the Malaysian press debate at *Straits Times*, 4 October 2003, p. A17.

69. Leadership in UMNO Youth falls to politicians hoping to become tomorrow's leaders. One of the key figures countering Ronnie Liu's September 2005 article was the son-in-law of the Prime Minister at the time, namely Khairy Jamaludin, in his capacity as Deputy UMNO Youth leader.

70. *Straits Times* (Singapore), 19 December 2006.

71. *Straits Times* (Singapore), 22 December 2006.

72. *New Straits Times* (Kuala Lumpur), 23 December 2006.

73. *New Straits Times* (Kuala Lumpur), 28 December 2006.

74. Mohd Azzam bin Mohd Hanif Ghows (Lt. Col., Retd), *The Malayan Emergency Revisited 1948–1960: A Pictorial History* (Petaling Jaya, Selangor: AMR and Yayasan Pelejaran, 2006).

75. There is a brief description of the Kuala Lumpur Centre at http://www.missionnetaji.org/article/the-netaji-centre [accessed 26 July 2010]. For the Netaji Research Bureau in India, see also http://www.netaji.org/ [accessed 24 July 2010]. The KL Netaji Centre sent a memorandum to the Indian High Commissioner on 11 March 1983. This requested:

    (a) That early arrangements be made to bring back the ashes of Netaji from the Renkoji Temple in Japan to India and also for disbursement to Kuala Lumpur;

    (b) To erect a memorial in Imphal for the INA personnel who perished there, for which the Japanese are willing to share expenses under the sponsorship of General Fujiwara;

    (c) To help in re-erecting the memorial of the fallen INA personnel in Singapore which was destroyed by the returning British forces; and to seek cooperation of the Singapore Government in this regard; and to set up a Netaji Foundation which will grant scholarships to Malaysian students of all races to study in Indian institutions of higher learning.

76. This was founded upon the savings of the Indian rubber estate worker.

77. See the translation of the poem in *Mahakavi Subramanya Bharati: A Heroic Hindu Poet and Patriot*, trans. S.M. Ponniah (Kuala Lumpur: UMA Publications, 1988), p. 29. Proceedings of the anniversary day were tape-recorded by Kevin Blackburn.

78. "These INA Veterans made it to Delhi" in Delhi Newsline of the *Indian Express* online at http://cities.expressindia.com/fullstory.php?newsid=15465.

79. *Netaji Service Centre, 60th Anniversary of the establishment of the Arzi Hukumat-e-Azad Hind, 21 October 2003 souvenir programme* (Netaji Centre Records, Kuala Lumpur).

80. See *Utusan Malaysia*, 22 January 2005, J. Tan on reviews of *Memoir Ibrahim Chik*; *Malaysiakini.com*, K. Kabilan, 31 August 2009; K. Kabilan, "Deleted from Victors' History: The Other Freedom Fighters", Malaysiakini.com, 31 August 2009, at http://www.malaysiakini.com/news/111764; Rashid Maidin, *The Memoirs of Rashid Maidin: From Armed Struggle to Peace* (Petaling Jaya, Selangor: SIRD, 2005; Abdullah C.D., *The Memoirs of Abdullah C.D. (Part One: The Movement Until 1948)* (Petaling Jaya, Selangor: SIRD, 2009 [first published in Malay 2005]).

81. Wain, *Malaysian Maverick*, p. 18.

82. See http://www.e-fatwa.gov.my/fatwa-kebangsaan/hari-kenangan-rakan-seperjuangan-di-tugu-negara, for an October 1987 decision of the Fatwa Committee of the National Council for Islamic Affairs. This pronounced

the silence, prayers, Last Post, garlands of flowers, poetry and singing before the monument as contrary to Islam.

83. *New Straits Times*, 27 June 2010.
84. *New Straits Times*, 1 August 2010.
85. *New Straits Times*, 27 June 2010.
86. *The Star Online*, 31 March 2010, http://thestar.com.my [accessed 24 July 2010] suggested that the National Fatwa Council had stated that the "sounding of The Last Post and The Rouse, observing one minute's silence with heads bowed, laying of wreaths, reading of poetry and singing before a sculptured monument are in conflict with Islamic teachings". The original fatwa dated back to 1987, but it seems an April 2009 ruling brought the issue to a head. See http://www.e-fatwa.gov.my/fatwa-kebangsaan/pembinaan-monumen-peringatan-bagi-angkatan-tentera [accessed 26 July 2010].
87. *New Straits Times*, 1 August 2010.
88. *New Straits Times*, 6 August 2010.
89. *New Straits Times*, 27 June 2010.
90. Zedeck Siew, "National Unity Crash Course", formerly posted in Kakiseni. com at http://www.kakiseni.com/articles/features/MDUyNA.html#top.

Chapter 10

1. Saw, "Population Growth and Control", in *A History of Singapore*, eds. Lee And Chew, and Singapore Government Statistics, at http://www.singstat. gov.sg/stats/themes/people/hist/popn.html [accessed 27 July 2010]. 1968: 2.012m. 2010: 4,978m, of which 3.733m resident.
2. For the estimate of 25,000, see also pp. 139, 381n127. A Japanese source suggested as much as half of a 50,000 target were killed in Singapore. This tallies with the, 20,000 exhumed and reburied under the Civilian War Memorial, considering that additional victims were killed at sea (more than 500 washed up on Sentosa), and others will lie undiscovered. The largest single massacre site exhumed in Singapore contained the remains of around 1,500. Given the scale of oral history and written testimony since — including war crimes trials — and the amount of redevelopment in Singapore, the chances of there being further, large undiscovered sites remaining is slim. We can only speculate that from hundreds to the low thousands lie undiscovered. But this *excludes* the thousands of victims on the Malayan peninsula, which would take the total closer to some Chinese estimates of a total of 50,000 Chinese victims. Additional Chinese civilians will have been killed in the fighting in February 1942, which extended to the suburbs of Singapore Town itself, and included bombing.
3. See Karl Hack, "The Malayan Trajectory in Singapore's History", in *Singapore from Temasek to the 21st Century: Reinventing the Global City*, eds. Karl

Hack and Jean-Louis Margolin, with Karine Delaye (Singapore: NUS Press, 2010), pp. 243–91.

4. See Hack, "The Malayan Trajectory". Many had also previously been "British subjects" by dint of birth in a British colony (the Straits Settlements up to 1946, and Colony of Singapore thereafter).

5. Karl Hack, *Defence and Decolonisation*, pp. 280–8.

6. Diana Wong, "Memory Suppression and Memory Production: The Japanese Occupation of Singapore", in *Perilous Memories: The Asia-Pacific War(s)*, eds. T. Fujitani, Geoffrey M. White and Lisa Yoneyama (Durham, NC: Duke University Press, 2001), pp. 225–7.

7. http://www.moe.gov.sg/media/press/1997/pr01797.htm [accessed 22 October 2010].

8. *Straits Times* (Malaysian Edition), 26 September 1967.

9. *Straits Times* (Malaysian Edition), 26 September 1967.

10. *Eastern Sun*, 18 February 1970.

11. *Eastern Sun*, 27 February 1970; and *Straits Times*, 27 February 1970.

12. *Eastern Sun*, 26 February 1970.

13. *Straits Times*, 14 February 1970.

14. *Straits Times*, 15 February 1970.

15. *Straits Times*, 13 September 1980.

16. *Straits Times*, 28 November 1981.

17. *Business Times*, 7 January 1982; and *Straits Times*, 5 May 1983.

18. *Straits Times*, 9 August 1982.

19. See Inokuchi Hiromitsu and Nozaki Yoshiko, "Japanese Education, Nationalism, and Ienaga Saburo's Court Challenges", *Bulletin of Concerned Asian Scholars: Textbook Nationalism, Citizenship, and War Comparative Perspectives* 30, 2 (1998): 43. See also Yue-Him Tam, "To Bury the Unhappy Past: The Problem of Textbook Revision in Japan", *East Asian Library Journal* VII, 1 (Spring, 1994): 7–42; and Irie Yoshimasa, "The History of the Textbook Controversy", *Japan Echo* 24 (August 1997): 34–8.

20. "Editorial: Japan's Military Build-Up and Its Accounting to History", *Nanyang Siang Pau* (Singapore Edition), 26 July 1982. The issue of such "relativisation" of war crimes is elegantly discussed in R.J. Bosworth, *Explaining Auschwitz and Hiroshima* (London: Routledge, 1993).

21. "Editorial: Japan's 'Advance' Conception of History", *Sin Chew Jit Poh* (Singapore Edition), 3 August 1982.

22. "Editorial: Special Envoy Easki's 'Unexpected Accomplishment'", *Sin Chew Jit Poh* (Singapore Edition), 6 August 1982.

23. "Editorial: Selective Amnesia", *Straits Times*, 27 April 1988.

24. *Straits Times*, 17 August 1983.

25. Curriculum Development Institute of Singapore (CDIS), *Social and Economic History of Modern Singapore*, Vol. 2 (Singapore: Longman, 1985), pp. 160–9.

26. CDIS, *Social and Economic History of Modern Singapore, Workbook 2*, p. 39.

27. Ibid., p. 70.

28. Ishiwata Nobuo, Masuo Keizo, eds., *Gaikoku no kyokasho no naka no Nihon to Nihonjin: Nihon no kokosei ga Shingaporu no chugaku kyokasho o hon'yakushite saihakkenshita Nihon kindaishi — Social and Economic History of Modern Singapore* (Singapore: Japanese School, 1988).

29. *Straits Times*, 4 May 1991.

30. *Straits Times*, 30 May 1991.

31. "Editorial: Japan Should Demonstrate its Sincerity of Contrition in Specific Terms", *Lianhe Zaobao*, 6 May 1991.

32. "Editorial", *Lianhe Zaobao*, 6 May 1991.

33. *Straits Times*, 10 May 1991.

34. *Straits Times*, 4 January 1995.

35. For a comparison of self-examination in postwar West Germany and Japan, see Sebastian Conrad, *Auf der Suche nach der verlorenen Nation: Geschictsschreibung in Westdeutschland und Japan 1945–1960* [*In Search of the Lost Nation: Coming to Terms with National History in West Germany and Japan, 1945–1960*] (Gottingen: Vandenhoeck and Ruprecht, 1999).

36. *Straits Times*, 16 August 1995.

37. "Editorial: The Japan Asia Seeks", *Straits Times*, 15 August 1995.

38. *History of Modern Singapore* (Singapore: Curriculum Development Institute of Singapore, 1994), pp. 147–50.

39. Curriculum Development Institute of Singapore, *Social Studies: Secondary 1* (Singapore: Longman, 1994), p. 97. See also Curriculum Development Institute of Singapore, *History of Modern Singapore: Secondary 1* (Singapore: Longman, 1994), pp. 153 and Curriculum Planning and Development Division, Ministry of Education, *Understanding Our Past: Singapore From Colony to Nation* (Singapore: Federal Publications, 1999), p. 103.

40. *Between Empires*, VHS (Singapore Broadcasting Corporation, 1992).

41. *Straits Times*, 10 February 1992.

42. Ibid.

43. *Straits Times*, 6 September 1995.

44. "Dramas", *8 Days*, issue 354 (19–26 July 1997): 98.

45. *Straits Times*, 21 July 1997.

46. *Straits Times*, 29 August 1997.

47. Ibid.

48. Episode 2, aired 25 July 1997, *Heping De Dai Jia: The Price of Peace* (Singapore, MediaCorp).

49. Episode 32, 5 September 1997, *Heping De Dai Jia: The Price of Peace* (Singapore, MediaCorp).

50. *New Straits Times*, 11 January 1998.

51. *Straits Times*, 2 October 1998.

52. *Straits Times*, 9 February 1992.
53. Ibid.
54. School Notification No.19/2010 — National Education (NE): Total Defence Day, 2010, Xingnan Primary School.
55. Ministry of Education, "Five Schools" Programme for Total Defence Day, at http://www.moe.gov.sg/media/press/1998/980209.htm#Annex%20A [accessed 28 July 2010].
56. *Straits Times*, 27 and 28 February 1999, and 2 March 1999.
57. *Straits Times*, 6 September 1999.
58. Personal communication with Peter Seow of the Singapore National Institute of Education, 15 August 2008, who spoke with the staff at Fort Siloso.
59. *Straits Times*, 10 February, 7 March, 24 October, and 22 November 2000.
60. *Straits Times*, 12 May 1999. See Hong Lysa and Huang Jianli, "The Scripting of Singapore's National Heroes: Toying with Singapore's Pandora Box", in *New Terrains in South East Asian History*, eds. Abu Talib Ahmad and Tan Loik Ee (Athens, OH: Ohio University Press, 2003), pp. 219–46.
61. Played by Singapore actress Xiang Yun.
62. Episode 29, aired 2 September 1997, *Heping De Dai Jia* (Singapore, MediaCorp).
63. Zhou Mei, *Elizabeth Choy: More Than a War Heroine* (Singapore: Landmark Books, 1995).
64. *Straits Times*, 5 March 2001.
65. *Straits Times*, 30 March 2001.
66. Played by Jerry Qi Yuwu.
67. Episode 10, 11 May 2001, *In Pursuit of Peace* (Singapore, MediaCorp).
68. *Straits Times*, 24 July 2001.
69. *Straits Times*, 3 September 2001.
70. Played by Tan Kheng Hua.
71. Played by Tay Ping Hui.
72. Played by Samuel He.
73. Played by Fiona Xie.
74. Episode 6: A Flower That Will Never Bloom, 28 September 2001, *A War Diary* (Singapore, MediaCorp).
75. Played by Carole Lin who was also in *Heping De Dai Jia*.
76. Episode 7: And the Meek Shall Not Inherit the Earth, 12 October 2001, *A War Diary* (Singapore, MediaCorp).
77. *Straits Times*, 3 September 2001.
78. The official website is at http://www.s1942.org.sg/s1942/moff/ [accessed 28 July 2010].
79. Hack and Blackburn, *Did Singapore Have to Fall?*, pp. 176–7. The 12 September surrender had been moved to Sentosa from City Hall Chambers in 1976.

80. As with the last surviving outdoor chapel from Changi POW camp, the surrender table had been taken to Australia. There it resides in the Australian War Memorial.

81. Wong Hong Suen, *Wartime Kitchen: Food and Eating in Singapore, 1942–1950* (Singapore: National Museum of Singapore and Editions Didier Millet, 2009).

82. The most stable entry point is that of the archives in general, at http://www.nhb.gov.sg/nas/. The war site in specific is at http://www.s1942.org.sg/s1942/home/ [accessed 22 October 2010]. The latter includes links to the entire Lim Bo Seng diary, and oral history clips including those of Elizabeth Choy.

83. Raj Vasil, *Asianising Singapore: The PAP's Management of Ethnicity* (Singapore: Heinemann Asia, 1995), p. 40.

84. *Between Empires*, VHS (Singapore Broadcasting Corporation, 1992).

85. *History of Modern Singapore* (Singapore: Curriculum Development Institute, 1994), pp. 147–50.

86. Played by Jacintha Abisheganadan.

87. Episode 31, aired 4 September 1997, *Heping De Dai Jia: The Price of Peace* (Singapore, MediaCorp).

88. Episode 2, 16 March 2001, *In Pursuit of Peace* (Singapore, MediaCorp).

89. Episode 3: Dream of the Light of the South, 22 August 2001, *A War Diary* (Singapore, MediaCorp).

90. School Notification No. 19/2010 — National Education (NE): Total Defence Day, 2010, Xingnan Primary School.

91. "Editorial: Lessons from World War Two", *Berita Harian*, 6 September 1995.

92. Ibid.

93. *Berita Harian*, 9 and 11 September 1995.

94. *Berita Harian*, 12 September 1995.

95. *Berita Harian*, 11 September 1995; Wak Cantuk, "A Road in Memory of Lieutenant Adnan", *Berita Minggu*, 10 September 1995.

96. Pak Oteh, "Remembering the Deeds of Past Personalities", *Berita Harian*, 13 September 1995.

97. Mohd Raman Daud, "Why Lieutenant Adnan is our Hero", *Berita Harian*, 14 September 1995.

98. Sa'don Bin Anwar, "Recognition of Lieutenant Adnan is Still Inadequate", *Berita Harian*, 21 September 1995.

99. *Berita Harian*, 12 September 1995.

100. *Straits Times*, 12 May 1999.

101. For the quotation, see Curriculum Planning & Development Division, Ministry of Education, Singapore, *Social Studies: Discovering Our World: The Dark Years: Activity Book, 4B* (Singapore: Federal, 1999), p. 22. See also Curriculum Planning & Development Division Ministry of Education, Singapore, *Social Studies: Discovering Our World: The Dark Years, 4B*

(Singapore: Federal, 1999), p. 21; and Curriculum Planning & Development Division Ministry of Education, Singapore, *Understanding Our Past: Singapore from Colony to Nation* (Singapore: Federal, 1999), p. 78.

102. *Straits Times*, 13 February 1998.
103. *Straits Times*, 8 February 2002.
104. For visitors' reactions, see Donna Brunero, "Archives and Heritage in Singapore: The Development of 'Reflections at Bukit Chandu', a World War II Interpretive Centre", *International Journal of Heritage Studies* 12, 5 (2006): 427–39; Muzaini Hamzah and Brenda S.A. Yeoh, "War Landscapes as 'Battlefields' of Collective Memories: Reading the Reflections at Bukit Chandu, Singapore", *Cultural Geographies* 12, 3 (2005): 345–65; and Hong Lysa and Huang Jianli, "The Scripting of Singapore's National Heroes", in *New Terrains in South East Asian History*, eds. Abu Talib Ahmad and Tan Liok Ee (Athens, OH: Ohio University Press, 2003), pp. 219–46.
105. *Straits Times*, 1 August 2002.
106. Kratoska, *The Japanese Occupation of Malaya*, p. 281.
107. These are the figures of Dr Barry Pereira whose research on Bahau was showcased in the 2006 Exhibition "World War II: The Eurasian Story" at The Eurasian Community House, 139 Ceylon Road, Singapore. Kratoska, *The Japanese Occupation of Malaya, 1941–1945*, p. 281, mentions the Japanese claimed that in July 1945, the population of Bahau was 5,167 colonists.
108. F.AC. Oehlers, *That's How it Goes: Autobiography of a Singapore Eurasian* (Singapore: Select Books, 2008), pp. 75–6, 93–4, 125, 151, *passim*. Hence, warning people of dangers could be a favour, but could also be seen as collaboration (pp. 93–4).
109. *Straits Times*, 22 February 2006.
110. Ibid.
111. There are similar brochures or leaflets for "ethnic" areas such as Chinatown and Little India. This one has six main sections, namely: "A Prelude"; "Of Forts, Guns & Battles — The Southern Trail" (Labrador, Siloso, Bukit Chandu, Alexandra Hospital); "Heroes, Rebels & Leaders — The Central Trail" (Fort Canning and Battle-Box, St Andrews, Civic District Monuments); "Behind Barbed Wire — The Eastern Trail (Changi)"; "In Memoriam — The Northern Trail" (Kranji, Old Ford Factory); and "World War Two Tours in Singapore".
112. Joan C. Henderson, "Singapore's Wartime Heritage Attractions", *Journal of Tourism Studies* 8, 2 (December 1997): 47.
113. *Straits Times*, 24 October 1972.
114. Interview with Reverend Henry Khoo, Changi Prison Chaplain (1968–2006) and son of the first Singapore Prisons Chaplain Reverend Khoo Siaw Hua, on 2 October 1997.
115. *Straits Times*, 15 and 17 February 1967; and *Eastern Sun*, 15 February 1967. See also *Straits Times*, 19 January 1972 and 8 February 1972.

116. Pamelia Lee (Division Director, Product Development) to Mr Quek Shi Li, Director of Prisons, serial 57, PD/PRJ/45/88, vol. 1 (MFL AJ024), Records of Singapore Tourist Promotion Board (NAS).

117. Ministry of Trade and Industry and the Singapore Tourist Promotion Board, *Tourism Product Development Plan* (Singapore: Singapore Tourist Promotion Board, 1986), p. 4.

118. Kerr Foster, *Tourism Development in Singapore* (Singapore: Singapore Tourist Promotion Board, 1986), pp. 27–9.

119. Pamelia Lee, *Singapore, Tourism & Me* (Singapore: Pamelia Lee, 2004), pp. 176–7.

120. Robertson Collins, *A Disorderly Excursion: ASEAN Profiles* (Singapore: Pepper, 2003), p. 47, and Lee, *Singapore, Tourism & Me*, pp. 177–8. For the chapel picture selection, see J.N. Lewis Bryan, *The Churches of the Captivity in Malaya* (London: Society for Promoting Christian Knowledge, 1946), p. 65.

121. Interview with Pamelia Lee, 23 September 1997; and Lee, *Singapore, Tourism & Me*, p. 177.

122. Collins, *A Disorderly Excursion*, pp. 50–1.

123. Kevin Blackburn's notes from the Singapore Tourism Board (Singapore Tourist Promotion Board before November 1997) Meeting on Changi Chapel and Museum, 1 August 2000 convened by Pamelia Lee.

124. Diana Wong, "Memory Suppression and Memory Production: The Japanese Occupation of Singapore", in *Perilous Memories: The Asia-Pacific War(s)*, eds. Fujitani, White and Yoneyama, pp. 225–7.

125. Fax from Pamelia Lee, Changi Chapel & Museum, dated 21 July 2000, in the authors' possession.

126. The tunnels told the story of the guns' part in Singapore's fall, retaining some war damage. The book included cartoon features, "pop quizes", bullet points, photographs, and Total Defence messages, prefaced by the claim that "History Comes Alive! At the tunnels, you smell the 'cordite' from the guns". David Lim and Edmund Chua, *Labrador Park: The Adventure Begins* (Singapore: SNP Pacific, 2005).

127. Singapore History Consultants hold contracts to run key sites such as the Changi Chapel and Museum, and also run tours, programmes for schools and consultancy. See for instance http://www.singaporehistoryconsultants. com/ [accessed 22 October 2010].

Chapter 11

1.   Halbwachs, *On Collective Memory*, pp. 38, 182.

2.   T.G. Ashplant, Michael Dawson and Graham Roper, "Preface", in *The Politics of War Memory and Commemoration*, eds. Ashplant, Dawson and Roper (London: Routledge, 2000), pp. xi–xii.

3. T.G. Ashplant, Michael Dawson and Graham Roper, "The Politics of War Memory and Commemoration: Contexts, Structures and Dynamics", in *The Politics of War Memory and Commemoration*, eds. Ashplant, Dawson and Roper, pp. 3–86.

4. Paula Hamilton and Linda Shopes, "Introduction", in *Oral History and Public Memories*. eds. Paula Hamilton and Linda Shopes (Philadelphia: Temple University Press, 2008), pp. vii, x.

5. Alistair Thomson, "Review of Paula Hamilton and Linda Shopes Oral History and Public Memories", *History Australia* 6, 1 (2009): 21.

6. Alistair Thomson, "Oral History in the 21st Century: International Developments and the Southeast Asian Context" at the Conference on History Fragments in Southeast Asia: At the Interfaces of Oral History, Memory and Heritage, 23–24 June 2010.

BIBLIOGRAPHY

Archives

Australia

Australian War Memorial, Canberra (AWM)
National Archives of Australia, Canberra and Melbourne (NAA)

Malaysia

National Archives of Malaysia, Kuala Lumpur (NAM)
University of Malaya Library, Kuala Lumpur
Centre for Malaysian Chinese Studies, Selangor Chinese Assembly Hall, Kuala Lumpur

Singapore

Institute of Southeast Asian Studies Library
National Archives of Singapore (NAS)
National Archives of Singapore website (http://www.nhb.gov.sg/nas/)
National Archives of Singapore war site (http://www.s1942.org.sg/s1942/home/)
National Museum of Singapore
National University of Singapore Library

United Kingdom

Imperial War Museum, London, United Kingdom (IWM)
National Library of Scotland, Edinburgh
Rhodes House, Oxford University
The National Archives, Kew, United Kingdom (TNA)

Parliamentary Records

Parliamentary Debates: Dewan Ra'ayat (House of Representatives) Official Report
Parliamentary Debates: Dewan Negara (Senate) Official Report
Singapore: Advisory Council
Legislative Assembly Debates of the State of Singapore: Official Report
Parliamentary Debates: Singapore
Proceedings of the Legislative Council of the Federation of Malaya

Published Works (Books, Articles and Chapters)

Abdul Aziz bin Zahariah. *Leftenan Nor: Pahlawan Gerila* [*Lieutenant Nor: Guerrilla Fighter*]. Kuala Lumpur: Dewan Bahasa dan Pustaka, 1959.

Abdul Rahman Arshad. *Unity and Education in Malaysia*. Kuala Lumpur: Dewan Bahasa dan Pustaka, 2007.

Abdul Rahman Putra Al-Haj. *Looking Back: Monday Musings and Memories*. Kuala Lumpur: Pustaka Antara, 1977.

_____. *Reminiscences of Tunku Abdul Rahman on the Japanese Occupation 1941–1945*. Penang: Perpustakaan Universiti Sains Malaysia, 1989.

Abdul Samad Idris, Tan Sri Datuk. *Askar Melayu: 50 Tahun* [*The Malay Regiment: 50 Years*]. Kuala Lumpur: Pustaka Budiman, 1983.

Abdullah C.D. *The Memoirs of Abdullah C.D. (Part One: The Movement Until 1948)*. Petaling Jaya, Selangor: SIRD, 2009 (first published in Malay 2005).

Abu Talib Ahmad. "The Malay Community and Memory of the Japanese Occupation". In *War and Memory in Malaysia and Singapore*, eds. P. Lim Pui Huen and Diana Wong. Singapore: ISEAS, 2000, pp. 45–89.

_____. *The Malay Muslims, Islam and the Rising Sun: 1941–45*. Selangor: MBRAS Monograph no. 34, 2003.

_____. "Museums and the Japanese Occupation of Malaya". In *Reflections on Southeast Asian History Since 1945*, eds. Richard Mason and Abu Talib Ahmad. Penang: Penerbit Universiti Sains Malaysia, 2006, pp. 25–53.

Ahmad Boestamam. *Carving the Path to the Summit*, trans. William R. Roff. Athens, OH: Ohio University Press, 1979.

_____. *Memoir Ahmad Boestamam: Merdeka dengan Darah dalam Api* [*Ahmad Boestamam's Memoirs: Independence Through Blood and Inside API*]. Bangi: Penerbit Universiti Kebangsaan Malaysia, 2004.

Ahmad Murad Bin Nasruddin. *Nyawa Di-Hujong Pedang* [*Life at the Tip of a Sword*]. Kuala Lumpur: Kee Meng Press, 1967.

Ahmad Sarji. *P. Ramlee Erti Yang Sakti* [*The Magic of P. Ramlee*]. Subang Jaya, Selangor: Pelanduk, 1999.

Ahmad Zahid Hamidi, Senator Datuk. *UMNO Youth: Leadership and Struggle*. Kuala Lumpur: Yayasan Gerakbakti Kebangsaan, 2005.

Akashi, Yoji. "Japanese Policy Towards Malayan Chinese 1941–1945". *Journal of Southeast Asian Studies* 1, 2 (September 1970): 61–89.

_____. *The Nanyang Chinese National Salvation Movement, 1937–1941*. Lawrence, KS: Centre for East Asian Studies, The University of Kansas, 1970.

Alias Mohamed. *Ghafar: A Biography*. Petaling Jeya, Selangor: Pelanduk, 1993.

Amir Muhammad. *120 Malay Movies*. Petaling Jaya, Selangor: Matahari Books, 2010.

Ampalavanar, Rajeswary. *The Indian Minority and Political Change in Malaya, 1945–1957*. Kuala Lumpur: Oxford University Press, 1981.

Arasaratnam, Sinnappah. *Indians in Malaysia and Singapore*. Kuala Lumpur: Oxford University Press, 1970.

Arena Wati, ed. *Cherpen Zaman Jepun* [*Short Stories from the Japanese Period*]. Kuala Lumpur: Pustaka Antara, 1968.

Ariffin Omar. *Bangsa Melayu: Malay Concepts of Democracy and Community, 1945–1950*. Kuala Lumpur: Oxford University Press, 1993.

Asad-ul Iqbal Latif. "Singapore's Missing War". In *Legacies of World War II in South and East Asia*, ed. David Koh Wee Hock. Singapore: ISEAS, 2009, pp. 92–103.

Ashplant, T.G., Michael Dawson, and Graham Roper, eds. *The Politics of War Memory and Commemoration*. London: Routledge, 2000.

Assessors Report. "Competition for a Memorial to Civilian Victims of the Japanese Occupation". *Journal of the Singapore Institute of Architects* 6 (December 1963): 7–22.

Audion-Rouzeau, Stephane and Annette Becker. *14–18: Understanding the Great War*, trans. Catherine Temerson. New York: Farrar, Straus and Giroux, 2002.

Australian Historical Studies. *The Australian Legend Re-Visited*. Melbourne: Melbourne University, 1978.

Bakshi, Akhil. *The Road To Freedom: Travels Through Singapore, Malaysia, Burma and India in the Footsteps of the Indian National Army*. New Delhi: Odyssey, 1998.

Bayly, Chris and Tim Harper. *Forgotten Armies: The Fall of British Asia, 1941–1945*. London: Allen Lane, 2004.

Bean, C.E.W. *Official History of Australia in the War of 1914–1918: Volume 1: The Story of ANZAC, From The Outbreak of War to the First Phase of the Gallipoli Campaign May 4 1915*. Sydney: Angus and Robertson, 1939 edition (originally published 1921).

Beattie, Rod. *The Thai-Burma Railway: The True Story of the Bridge on the River Kwai*. Kanchanaburi, Thailand: T.B.R.C., 2007.

Benton, Tim and Penelope Curtis. "The Heritage of Public Commemoration". In *Understanding Heritage and Memory*, ed. Tim Benton. Manchester: Manchester University Press, 2010, pp. 88–125.

Bhargava, K.D. and K.N.V. Sastri. *Official History of the Indian Armed Forces in the Second World War, 1939–1945: Campaigns in South-East Asia, 1941–42*, ed. Bisheshwar Prasad. Calcutta: Combined Inter-Services Historical Section India and Pakistan, 1960.

Bianco, Lucien. *Origins of the Chinese Revolution, 1915–1949*, trans. Muriel Bell. Stanford, CA: Stanford University Press, 1971.

Blackburn, Kevin. "Changi: A Place of Personal Pilgrimages and Collective Histories". *Australian Historical Studies* 30, 112 (1999): 153–73.

_____. "The Collective Memory of the *Sook Ching* Massacre and the Creation of the Civilian War Memorial of Singapore". *Journal of the Malaysian Branch of the Royal Asiatic Society* 73, 2 (2000): 71–90.

————. "Commodifying and Commemorating the Prisoner of War Experience in Southeast Asia: The Creation of Changi Prison Museum". *Journal of the Australian War Memorial* 33 (2000), at http://www.awm.gov.au/journal.

————. "The Historic War Site of the Changi Murals: A Place for Pilgrimages and Tourism". *Journal of the Australian War Memorial* 34 (2001), at http://www.awm.gov.au/journal.

————. "Nation Building and Public Representation of History: The Japanese Occupation as a "Shared Past" in Singapore". *Public History Review* 9 (2001): 8–22.

————. "Reminiscence and War Trauma: Recalling the Japanese Occupation of Singapore, 1942–1945". *Oral History* 33, 2 (2005): 91–8.

————. "Public Forum With Veterans and the Wartime Generation at Singapore in 2005". *Oral History Association of Australia Journal* 28 (2006): 69–74.

————. "Colonial Armies as Postcolonial History: Commemoration and Memory of the Malay Regiment in Modern Singapore and Malaysia". In *Colonial Armies in Southeast Asia*, eds. Karl Hack and Tobias Rettig. London: Routledge, 2006, pp. 302–26.

————. "Heritage Site, War Memorial and Tourist Stop: The Japanese Cemetery of Singapore, 1891–2005". *Journal of the Malaysian Branch of the Royal Asiatic Society* 80, 1 (2007): 17–39.

————. "Nation Building, Identity and War Commemoration Spaces in Malaysia and Singapore". In *Southeast Asian Culture and Heritage in a Globalising World: Diverging Identities in a Dynamic Region*, eds. Rahil Ismail, Ooi Giok Ling, and Brian Shaw. Farnham, Surrey: Ashgate, 2009, pp. 93–114.

————. "Recalling War Trauma of the Pacific War and the Japanese Occupation in the Oral History of Malaysia and Singapore". *Oral History Review* 36, 2 (2009): 231–52.

————. "War Memory and Nation Building in South East Asia". *South East Asia Research* 18, 1 (2010): 5–31.

————. "Oral History as a Product of Malleable and Shifting Memories in Singapore". In *The Makers and Keepers of Singapore History*, eds. Loh Kah Seng and Liew Kai Khiun. Singapore: Ethos, 2010, pp. 205–31.

————. "Mary Turnbull's History Textbook for the Singapore Nation". In *Mary Turnbull*, ed. Nicholas Tarling. Singapore: NUS Press, forthcoming.

Blackburn, Kevin and Daniel Chew Ju Ern. "Dalforce at the Fall of Singapore in 1942: An Overseas Chinese Heroic Legend". *Journal of the Chinese Overseas* 1, 2 (2005): 233–59.

Blackburn, Kevin and Edmund Lim. "The Japanese War Memorials of Singapore: Monuments of Commemoration and Symbols of Japanese Imperial Ideology". *South East Asia Research* 7, 3, (1999): 321–40.

Bose, Romen. *A Will for Freedom: Netaji and the Indian Independence Movement in Singapore and Southeast Asia, 1942–1945*. Singapore: VJ Times, 1993.

_____. *The End of the War: Singapore's Liberation and the Aftermath of the Second World War.* Singapore: Marshall Cavendish, 2005.

_____. *Kranji: The Commonwealth War Cemetery and the Politics of the Dead.* Singapore: Marshall Cavendish, 2006.

Bosworth, R.J. *Explaining Auschwitz and Hiroshima.* London: Routledge, 1993.

Boyle, James. *Railroad to Burma.* Sydney: Allen & Unwin, 1990.

Braddon, Russell. *The Naked Island.* Edinburgh: Birlinn, 2001 (first published 1951).

Bradley, James. *The Tall Man Who Never Slept: A Tribute to Cyril Wild.* London: Woodfield Publishing, 1991.

Breen, John, ed. *Yasukuni: The War Dead and the Struggle for Japan's Past.* Singapore: Horizon Books, 2007.

Brooke, Geoffrey. *Singapore's Dunkirk.* London: Leo Cooper, 1989.

Brunero, Donna. "Archives and Heritage in Singapore: The Development of 'Reflections at Bukit Chandu'. A World War II Interpretive Centre". *International Journal of Heritage Studies* 12, 5 (2006): 427–43.

Bryan, J.N. Lewis. *The Churches of The Captivity in Malaya.* London: Society For Promoting Christian Knowledge, 1946.

_____. "The Churches of the Captivity in Malaya". *British Malaya* (March 1947): 165–70.

Burgess, R.C. and Laidin bin Alang Musa. *A Report on the State of Health: The Diet and Economic Conditions of Groups of People in the Lower Income Levels in Malaya.* Kuala Lumpur: Division of Nutrition, Institute for Medical Research, 1950.

Chaen Yoshio. *BC-Kyu Senpan Eigun Saiban Shiryo, Volume 2 [An Historical Record of British War Crimes Trials].* Tokyo: Fuji Shuppan, 1989.

Chang, Iris. *The Rape of Nanking.* New York, Penguin, 1997.

Cheah Boon Kheng. "The Japanese Occupation of Malaya, 1942–45: Ibrahim Yaacob and the Struggle for Indonesia Raya". *Indonesia* 28 (1979): 85–120.

_____. *Red Star Over Malaya: Resistance and Social Conflict During and After the Japanese Occupation, 1941–1946.* Singapore: Singapore University Press, 1987 edition.

_____. "Memory as History and Moral Judgement". In *War and Memory in Malaysia and Singapore*, eds. P. Lim Pui Huen and Diana Wong. Singapore: ISEAS, 2000, pp. 23–41.

_____. *Malaysia: The Making of a Nation.* Singapore: ISEAS, 2002.

_____. "The "Black-Out" Syndrome and the Ghosts of World War II: The War as a 'Divisive Issue' in Malaysia". In *Legacies of World War II in South and East Asia*, ed. David Koh Wee Hock. Singapore: ISEAS, 2007, pp. 47–59.

Chen Su Lan. *Remember Pompong and Oxley Rise.* Singapore: Chen Su Lan Trust, 1969.

Chen Ya Cai, ed. *Malaiya Kangri Jinianbei Tupianji [Malayan Anti-Japanese Memorials: A Pictorial].* Kuala Lumpur: Selangor Chinese Assembly Hall, 1999.

Chettur, S.K. *Malayan Adventure*. Mangalore: Basel Mission Press, 1948.

Chin, C.C. and Karl Hack, eds. *Dialogues with Chin Peng: New Light on the Malayan Communist Party*. Singapore: Singapore University Press, 2004.

Chin Kee Onn. *Malaya Upside Down*. Kuala Lumpur, Federal Publishers, 1976 (first published 1946).

————. *Ma-Rai-Ee*. Singapore: Eastern Universities Press, 1981.

Chin Peng, with Ian Ward and Norma Miraflor. *Alias Chin Peng: My Side of History*. Singapore: Media Masters, 2003.

Collins, Robertson. *A Disorderly Excursion: ASEAN Profiles*. Singapore: Pepper Publications, 2003.

Commonwealth War Graves Commission. *The War Dead of the Commonwealth (and Non World War and Foreign Nationals Burials): Kranji War Cemetery Singapore*. London: Commonwealth War Graves Commission, reprinted, September 2001.

Connerton, Paul. *How Societies Remember*. Cambridge: Cambridge University Press, 1989.

Conrad, Sebastian. *Auf der Suche nach der verlorenen Nation: Geschictsschreibung in Westdeutschland und Japan 1945–1960* [*In Search of the Lost Nation: Coming to Terms with National History in West Germany and Japan, 1945–1960*]. Gottingen: Vandenhoeck and Ruprecht, 1999.

Das, K.R. "The Bharat Youth Training Centre". In *Netaji Subhas Chandra Bose: A Malaysian Perspective*. Kuala Lumpur: Netaji Centre, 1992, pp. 47–65.

De Rosario, Lionel. *Nippon Slaves*. London: Janus, 1995.

del Tufo, M.V. *Malaya: A Report on the 1947 Census of Population*. Kuala Lumpur: Government Printer, Federation of Malaya, 1949.

Dittmer, Lowell and Samuel S. Kim, eds. *China's Quest for National Identity*. Ithaca, NY: Cornell University Press, 1993.

Dol Ramli. "History of the Malay Regiment 1933–1942". *Journal Malaysian Branch of the Royal Asiatic Society* 38, 1 (1965): 199–243.

Donnison, F.S.V. *British Military Administration in the Far East, 1943–1946*. London: Her Majesty's Stationery Office, 1956.

Dore, Henry. *Chinese Customs*, trans. M. Kennelly. Singapore: Graham Brash Publishers, 1987 (originally published 1911).

Douds, G.J. "Indian POWs in the Pacific, 1941–45". In *Forgotten Captives*, eds. Hack and Blackburn, pp. 73–93.

Dreyer, Edward L. *China at War, 1901–1949*. Harlow, Essex: Longman, 1995.

Durrani, Lt-Col. Mahmood Khan. *The Sixth Column: The Heroic Personal Story of Lt-Col. Mahmood Khan Durrani*. London: Cassell, 1955.

Fay, Peter Ward. *The Forgotten Army: India's Armed Struggle for Independence 1942–1945*. Ann Arbor, MI: University Michigan Press, 1993.

Firdaus Haji Abdullah. *Radical Malay Politics: Its Origin and Early Development*. Petaling Jaya, Selangor: Pelanduk, 1985.

Fitzgerald, Stephen. *China and the Overseas Chinese: A Study of Peking's Changing Policy, 1949–1970*. Cambridge: Cambridge University Press, 1972.

Flower, Sibylla Jane. "Memory and the Prisoner of War Experience in the United Kingdom". In *Forgotten Captives*, eds. Hack and Blackburn, pp. 57–63.

Foong Choon Hon, ed. *The Price of Peace: True Accounts of the Japanese Occupation*, trans. Clara Show. Singapore: Asiapac, 1997.

Foong Choon Hon. *Eternal Vigilance: The Price of Freedom*, trans. Yuen Chen Ching. Singapore: AsiaPac Books, 2006.

Foster, Kerr. *Tourism Development in Singapore*. Singapore: Singapore Tourist Promotion Board, 1986.

Franke, Wolfgang and Chen Tieh Fan. *Chinese Epigraphic Materials in Malaysia*, Volume II. Kuala Lumpur: University of Malaya Press, 1985.

Frei, Henry. *Guns of February: Ordinary Japanese Soldiers' Views of the Malayan Campaign and the Fall of Singapore*. Singapore: Singapore University Press, 2004.

Fujiwara Iwaichi. *F. Kikan: Japanese Army Intelligence Operations in Southeast Asia During World War II*, trans. Yoji Akashi. Hong Kong: Heinemann Asia, 1983.

Gamba, Charles. *The National Union of Plantation Workers: History of the Plantation Workers of Malaya 1946–1958*. Singapore: Eastern Universities Press, 1962.

Ghosh, Jitendra Nath. *Netaji Subhas Chandra Bose: Political Philosophy of Netaji History of the Azad Hind Government I.N.A. and International Law*. Calcutta: Orient Book Company, 1946.

Gilmour, Andrew. *My Role in the Rehabilitation of Singapore, 1946–1953*. Singapore: ISEAS, 1973.

Gilmour, O.W. *With Freedom to Singapore*. London: Ernest Benn, 1950.

Goh Chor Boon. *Living Hell: Story of a WWII Survivor at the Death Railway*. Singapore: Asiapac, 1999.

Goh Sin Tub. *The Ghost Lover of Emerald Hill and Other Stories*. Singapore: Heineman Asia, 1987.

————. "A Victory of Spirit". *Intersect Japan-Asia*, 26–31 September 1995.

————. "Re-Union with Jack". In *Memories and Desires: A Poetic History of Singapore*, ed. Robbie B.H. Goh. Singapore: Unipress NUS, 1998, pp. 23–5.

Gopinath, Aruna. *Footprints on the Sands of Time, Rasammah Bhuplan: A Life of Purpose*. Kuala Lumpur: Arkib Negara Malaysia, 2007.

Gordon, Leonard A. *Brothers Against the Raj: A Biography of Indian Nationalists Sarat and Subhas Chandra Bose*. New York: Columbia University Press, 1990.

Grant, Lachlan. "Monument and Ceremony: The Australian Ex-Prisoners of War Memorial and the Anzac Legend". In *Forgotten Captives in Japanese Occupied Asia,* eds. Hack and Blackburn, pp. 41–56.

Hack, Karl. "Decolonisation and the Pergau Dam Affair". *History Today* 44, 1 (November 1994): 9–15.

_____. *Defence and Decolonisation in Southeast Asia: Britain, Malaya and Singapore*. Richmond, Surrey: Curzon Press, 2001.

_____. "Imperialism and Decolonisation in Southeast Asia: Colonial Forces and British World Power". In *Colonial Armies in Southeast Asia*, eds. Karl Hack and Tobias Rettig London: Routledge, 2006, pp. 239–65.

_____. "Dalforce". In *Singapore: The Encyclopedia*. Singapore: Editions Didier Millet, 2006, p. 154.

_____. "The Malayan Emergency As Counter-Insurgency Paradigm". *Journal of Strategic Studies* 32, 3 (June 2009): 383–414.

_____. "The Origins of the Cold War: Malaya". *Journal of Southeast Asian Studies* 40, 3 (October 2009): 471–96.

_____. "Review of Joyce Lebra, *Women Against the Raj: The Rani of Jhansi Regiment* (Singapore: ISEAS, 2008) and *The Indian National Army* (Singapore: ISEAS edition, 2008)". *Journal of the Malaysian Branch of the Royal Asiatic Society* 82, 2 (December 2009): 195–8.

_____. "Contentious Heritage". In *Understanding Heritage and Memory*, ed. Tim Benton. Manchester: Manchester University Press, 2010, pp. 88–125.

_____. "The Malayan Trajectory in Singapore's History". In *Singapore from Temasek to the 21st Century: Reinventing the Global City*, eds. Karl Hack and Jean-Louis Margolin, with Karine Delaye. Singapore: NUS Press, 2010, pp. 243–91.

Hack, Karl and Kevin Blackburn. *Did Singapore Have to Fall? Churchill and the Impregnable Fortress*. London: Routledge, 2004.

Hack, Karl and Kevin Blackburn, eds. *Forgotten Captives in Japanese Occupied Asia*. London: Routledge, 2008.

Hack, Karl and Jean-Louis Margolin, with Karine Delaye, eds. *Singapore from Temasek to the 21st Century: Reinventing the Global City*. Singapore: NUS Press, 2010.

Hai Shang Ou. *Malaiya Renmin Kangri Jun* [*Malayan People's Anti-Japanese Army*]. Singapore: Sin Min Chu Cultural Service, 1945.

Halbwachs, Maurice. *On Collective Memory*, trans. Lewis A. Coser. Chicago: Chicago University Press, 1992.

Hamilton, Paula and Shopes Linda, eds. *Oral History and Public Memories*. Philadelphia: Temple University Press, 2008.

Hanrahan, Gene Z. *The Communist Struggle in Malaya*. Kuala Lumpur: University of Malaya Press, 1971 (originally published 1954).

Hara Fujio. "The Japanese Occupation and the Chinese Community". In *Malaya and Singapore During the Japanese Occupation*, ed. Paul. H. Kratoska. Singapore: Singapore University Press, 1995, pp. 83–120.

_____. *Malayan Chinese and China: Conversion in Identity Consciousness 1945–1957*. Singapore: Singapore University Press, 2003.

_____. "Leaders of the Malayan Communist Party During the Anti-Japanese War". In *New Perspectives on the Japanese Occupation in Malaya and*

Singapore, 1941–1945, eds. Akashi Yoji and Yoshimura Mako. Singapore: NUS Press, 2008, pp. 65–104.

Harding, James and Ahmad Sarji. *P. Ramlee: The Bright Star*. Subang Jaya, Selangor: Pelanduk, 2002.

Hattendorf, John. *The Two Beginnings: A History of St. George's Church, Tanglin*. Singapore, St George's Church, 1984.

Havers, R.P.W. *Reassessing the Japanese Prisoner of War Experience: The Changi POW Camp, Singapore, 1942–5*. London: RoutledgeCurzon, 2003.

Hayashi Hirofumi. "Japanese Treatment of Chinese Prisoners, 1931–1945". *Nature-People-Society and the Humanities* 26 (January 1999): 39–52.

————. "Massacre of Chinese in Singapore and its Coverage in Postwar Japan". In *New Perspectives on the Japanese Occupation in Malaya and Singapore, 1941–1945*, eds. Akashi Yoji and Yoshimura Mako. Singapore: NUS Press, 2008, pp. 234–49.

Hayter, John. *Priest in Prison: Four Years of Life in Japanese-occupied Singapore*. London: Tynron Press, 1991.

He Wei Bo. "I Joined the Volunteer Army". In *The Price of Peace*, ed. Foong Choon Hon, pp. 289–94.

Hein, Lara and Mark Seldon. "Learning Citizenship From the Past: Textbook Nationalism, Global Context and Social Change". *Bulletin of Concerned Asian Scholars* 30, 2 (1998): 3–15.

Henderson, Joan C. "Singapore's Wartime Heritage Attractions". *Journal of Tourism Studies* 8, 2 (December 1997): 39–49.

Hicks, George. *The Comfort Women: Sex Slaves of the Japanese Imperial Forces*. Singapore: Heinemann Asia, 1995.

Hills, Carol and Daniel C. Silverman. "Nationalism and Feminism in Late Colonial India: The Rani of Jhansi Regiment, 1943–1945". *Modern Asian Studies* 27, 4 (1993): 741–60.

Ho Thean Fook. *Tainted Glory*. Kuala Lumpur: University of Malaya Press, 2000.

Hong Lysa and Huang Jianli. "The Scripting of Singapore's National Heroes: Toying with Singapore's Pandora Box". In *New Terrains in South East Asian History*, eds. Abu Talib Ahmad and Tan Liok Ee. Athens, OH: Ohio University Press, 2003, pp. 219–46.

————. *The Scripting of A National History: Singapore and its Pasts*. Singapore: NUS Press, 2008.

Hsiung, James, C. "The War and After: World Politics in Historical Context". In *China's Bitter Victory: The War with Japan, 1937–1945*, eds. James C. Hsiung and Stephen I. Levine. New York: M.E. Sharpe, 1992.

Hu Tie Jun, ed., *Xing Hua Yi Yong Jun Zhan Dou Shi: 1942 Xing Zhou Bao Wei Zhang* [*Singapore Chinese Volunteer Army: The Battle of Singapore, 1942*]. Singapore: Sin Ching Hwa Publishing, 1945.

Hunt, Robert, Lee Kam Hing and John Roxborogh. *Christianity In Malaysia: A Denominational History*. Petaling Jaya, Selangor: Pelanduk, 1992.

Ibrahim Bin Ismail, General. *Have You Met Mariam?*. Johor Bahru: Westlight, 1984.

Ienaga Saburo. *The Pacific War: World War II and the Japanese, 1931–1945*. New York: Pantheon, 1978.

Imperial War Graves Commission. *The War Dead of the British Commonwealth and Empire: The Register of the Names of Those Who Fell in the 1939–1945 War and Have No Known Grave: The Singapore Memorial*. London: Her Majesty's Stationery Office, 1956.

————. *The War Dead of the British Commonwealth and Empire 1939–1945: The Singapore Memorial Part I*. London: Imperial War Graves Commission, London, 1959.

Inokuchi Hiromitsu and Nozaki Yoshiko. "Japanese Education, Nationalism, and Ienaga Saburo's Court Challenges". *Bulletin of Concerned Asian Scholars* 30, 2 (1998): 37–46.

Irie Yoshimasa. "The History of the Textbook Controversy". *Japan Echo* 24 (August 1997): 34–8.

Iskander, T. "Some Historical Sources Used by the Author of *Hikayat Hang Tuah*". *Journal Malaysian Branch of the Royal Asiatic Society* 43 (1970): 35–47.

Ismail Noor and Muhammed Azaham. *Takkan Melayu Hilang Di Dunia* [*Malays Will Never Disappear off the Face of the Earth*]. Subang Jaya, Selangor: Pelanduk, 2000.

Jain, Ravindra K. *South Indians on the Plantation Frontier in Malaya*. New Haven: Yale University Press, 1970.

Japan: An Illustrated Encyclopedia. Tokyo: Kodansha, 1993.

Johnson, Chalmers A. *Peasant Nationalism and Communist Power: The Emergence of Revolutionary China 1937–1945*. London: Stanford University Press, 1963.

Jomo, K.S., ed. *Japan and Malaysian Development: In the Shadow of the Rising Sun*. London: Routledge, 1994.

Josey, Alex. *Lee Kuan Yew: The Crucial Years*. Singapore: Times, 1980.

Kassim Bin Ahmad. *Characterisation in Hikayat Hang Tuah*. Kuala Lumpur: Dewan Bahasa dan Pustaka, 1966.

Kassim Ahmad and Noriah Mohamed, eds. *Hikayat Hang Tuah*. Kuala Lumpur: Yayasan Karyawan dan Dewan Bahasa dan Pustaka, 1997.

Kathigasu, Sybil. *No Dram of Mercy*. London: Neville Spearman, 1954.

Kathigasu, Sybil, Norma Miraflor and Ian Ward. *Faces of Courage: A Revealing Historical Appreciation of Colonial Malaya's Legendary Kathigasu Family*. Singapore: Media Masters, 2006.

Kennedy, Joseph. *British Civilians and the Japanese War in Malaya and Singapore, 1941–45*. London: Macmillan, 1987.

Khoo Boo Teik. *Paradoxes of Mahathirism: An Intellectual Biography of Mahathir Mohamad*. Kuala Lumpur: Oxford University Press, 1995.

Khoo Gaik Cheng. "'You've Come a Long Way Baby': Erma Fatimah, Film and Politics". *South East Asia Research* 14, 2 (2006): 179–209.

Klein, Donald. *The Other Empire: Literary Views of Japan from the Philippines, Singapore and Malaysia*. Quezon City: University of Philippines Press, 2008.

Kratoska, Paul. *The Japanese Occupation of Malaya, 1941–1945*. Sydney: Allen & Unwin, 1998.

Kratoska, Paul, ed. *Asian Labor in the Japanese Empire*. Singapore: NUS Press, 2006.

Kua Kia Soong, ed. *Malaysian Cultural Policy and Democracy*, 2nd edition. Kuala Lumpur: Selangor Chinese Assembly Hall, 1990.

Lai Chee Kien. *Building Merdeka: Independence Architecture in Kuala Lumpur, 1957–1966*. Kuala Lumpur: Petronas, 2007.

Lambert, Eric. *MacDougal's Farm*. London: Muller, 1965.

Lane, Arthur. *Lesser Gods, Greater Devils*. Stockport: Lane, 1993.

Lebra Chapman, Joyce. *The Indian National Army and Japan*. Singapore, ISEAS, 2008 (first edition 1971).

————. *The Rani of Jhansi: A Study in Female Heroism in India*. Honolulu: University of Hawai'i, 1986.

————. *Women Against the Raj: The Rani of Jhansi Regiment*. Singapore: ISEAS, 2008.

Lee, Donald. *The Silvered Shovel*. New York: Vantage Press, 1989.

————. *A Yarn or Two*, 2nd edition. Perth: Hesperian Press, 2000.

Lee Geok Boi. *The Religious Monuments of Singapore: Faiths of our Forefathers*. Singapore: Landmark Books, 2002.

————. *The Syonan Years*. Singapore: National Archives of Singapore, 2005.

Lee Kip Lee. *Amber Sands: A Boyhood Memoir*. Singapore: Times, 1999 edition.

Lee Kuan Yew. *The Singapore Story: Memoirs of Lee Kuan Yew*. Singapore: Times, 1998.

Lee, Pamelia. *Singapore, Tourism & Me*. Singapore: Pamelia Lee, 2004.

Leifer, Michael. "Anglo-Malaysian Alienation Revisited". *Round Table* 83, 331 (July 1994): 347–59.

Leong Yee Fong. *Labour and Trade Unionism in Colonial Malaya*. Pulau Pinang: Penerbit Universiti Sains Malaysia, 1999.

Li, Lincoln. *The Japanese Army in North China, 1937–1941: Problems of Political and Economic Control*. Tokyo: Oxford University Press, 1975.

Li Tie Min, ed. *Da Zhan Yu Nan Qiao: Malaiya Zhi Bu* [*The Great War and the Overseas Chinese: Malayan Branch*]. Singapore: Singapore Overseas Chinese Publishing Company, 1947.

Li Ye Lin, ed. *Tai Ping Yang Zhan Zheng Shi Liao Hui Ban: Selected Historical Materials of the Pacific War: Sumber Sejarah Peperangan Pasifik*. Kuala Lumpur: Huazi Enterprise, 1996.

Lim, David and Edmund Chua. *Labrador Park: The Adventure Begins*. Singapore: SNP Pacific, 2005.

Lim Hua Sing. *Japan's Role in ASEAN: Issues and Prospects*. Singapore: Times Academic Press, 1994.

Lim Pui Huen. "War and Ambivalence: Monuments and Memorials in Johor". In *War and Memory in Malaysia and Singapore*, eds. P. Lim Pui Huen and Diana Wong. Singapore: ISEAS, 2000, pp. 139–59.

Lim Pui Huen and Diana Wong, eds. *War and Memory in Malaysia and Singapore*. Singapore: ISEAS, 2000.

Low, N.I. and H.M. Cheng. *This Singapore: Our City of Dreadful Night*. Singapore: City Book Store, 1947.

MacKenzie, John M. *Propaganda and Empire: The Manipulation of British Public Opinion 1880–1960*. Manchester: Manchester University Press, 1984.

————. "Heroic Myths of Empire". In *Popular Imperialism and the Military, 1850–1950*, ed. John M. MacKenzie. Manchester: Manchester University Press, 1992, pp. 109–38.

Mahakavi Subramanya Bharati: A Heroic Hindu Poet and Patriot, trans. S.M. Ponniah. Kuala Lumpur: UMA Publications, 1988.

Mahathir bin Mohammad. *The Malay Dilemma*. Singapore: Times Books, 1970, as reprinted in 1995.

————. *The Challenge*. Petaling Jaya, Selangor: Pelanduk, 1986.

Mahmood Khan Durrani. *The Sixth Column: The Heroic Personal Story of Lieutenant Mahmood Khan Durrani*. London: Cassell, 1955.

Mangan, J.A. "The Grit of Our Forefathers Invented Traditions, Propaganda and Imperialism". In *Imperialism and Popular Culture*, ed. John M. MacKenzie. Manchester: Manchester University Press, 1986, pp. 113–39.

————. "Noble Specimens of Manhood: School Literature and the Creation of a Colonial Chivalric Code". In *Imperialism and Juvenile Literature*, ed. Jeffrey Richards. Manchester: Manchester University Press, 1989, pp. 173–95.

Mastura Abdul Rahman, "The Japanese Occupation Through Malay Fiction". In *Malays/Muslims in Singapore: Selected Readings in History, 1819–1965*, eds. Khoo Kay Kim, Elinah Abdullah, and Wan Meng Hao. Subang Jaya, Selangor: Pelanduk, 2006, pp. 223–44.

Mat Zin Mat Kib. *Persatuan Buruh Keretapi Maut Siam-Burma* [*The Association of Labourers on the Burma-Siam Death Railway*]. Kuala Lumpur: UPENA, 2005.

McCormack, Gavan and Hank Nelson, eds. *The Burma-Thailand Railway: Memory and History*. Chiang Mai, Thailand: Silkworm Books, 1993.

McKay, Roy. *Leonard Wilson: Confessor for the Faith*. London: Hodder and Stoughton, 1973.

Milner, A.C. *Kerajaan: Malay Political Culture on the Eve of Colonial Rule*. Tucson, AZ: University of Arizona Press, 1982.

Ministry of Trade and Industry and the Singapore Tourist Promotion Board. *Tourism Product Development Plan*. Singapore: Singapore Tourist Promotion Board, 1986.

Mohamed Abid. *Reflections of Pre-Independence Malaya*. Subang Jaya, Selangor: Pelanduk, 2003.

Mohammad Agus Yusoff and Nik Anuar Nik Mahmud. "Managing Terrorism Through Peaceful Political Negotiations: The Malayan Experience". *Jebat* 29 (2002): 123–33, at http://pkukmweb.ukm.my/jebat/v1/.

Mohan Singh. *Soldiers' Contribution to Indian Independence*. New Delhi: Army Educational Stores, 1974.

Mohd Azzam bin Mohd Hanif Ghows (Lt Col., Retd). *The Malayan Emergency Revisited 1948–1960: A Pictorial History*. Petaling Jaya, Selangor: AMR and Yayasan Pelejaran, 2006.

Montgomery, Brian. *Shenton of Singapore: Governor and Prisoner of War*. Singapore: Times Books International, 1984.

Morais, J. Victor, ed. *The Leaders of Malaya and Who's Who, 1957–58*. Kuala Lumpur: Khee Meng Press, 1957.

Morrison, Ian. *Malayan Postscript*. London: Faber and Faber, 1946.

Mustapha Hussain. *Malay Nationalism Before UMNO*, trans. Insun Sony Mustapha, ed. K.S. Jomo. Kuala Lumpur: Utusan Publications & Distributors, 2005.

Muzaini, Hamzah and Brenda S.A Yeoh. "War Landscapes as 'Battlefields' of Collective Memories: Reading the Reflections at Bukit Chandu, Singapore" *Cultural Geographies* 12, 3 (2005): 345–65.

————. "Memory-Making 'From Below': Rescaling Remembrance at the Kranji War Memorial and Cemetery, Singapore". *Environment and Planning A* 39, 6 (2007): 1288–305.

Nakahara Michiko. "Labour Recruitment in Malaya Under the Japanese Occupation: The Case of the Burma-Siam Railway". In *Malaysian Studies 1: Rethinking Malaysia*, ed. K.S. Jomo. Kuala Lumpur: Malaysian Social Science Association, 2000, pp. 214–45

————. "Malayan Labor on the Thailand-Burma Railway". In *Asian Labor in the Wartime Japanese Empire*, ed. Paul Kratoska. Singapore: NUS Press, 2006, pp. 249–66.

National Archives of Singapore. *The Japanese Occupation 1942–1945*. Singapore: Times, 1996.

Nelson, David. *The Story of Changi, Singapore*. Perth: Changi Publications, 1974.

Netaji Centre. *Netaji Subhas Chandra Bose: A Malaysian Perspective*. Kuala Lumpur, Netaji Centre, 1992.

————. *Netaji Service Centre, 60th Anniversary of the Establishment of the Arzi Hukumat-e-Azad Hind, 21 October 2003 Souvenir Programme*. Kuala Lumpur, Netaji Service Centre, 2003.

Nordin Yusof, Major-General Dato and Abdul Razak Abdullah Baginda. *Honour and Sacrifice: The Malaysian Armed Forces*. Kuala Lumpur: Ministry of Defence, 1994.

Nozaki, Yoshiko. *War Memory, Nationalism and Education in Postwar Japan, 1945–2007: The Japanese History Textbook Controversy and Ienaga Saburo's Court Challenges*. London: Routledge, 2008.

O'Balance, Edgar. *Malaya: The Communist Insurgent War, 1948–60*. London: Faber and Faber, 1966.

Oehlers, F.A.C. *That's How It Goes: Autobiography of a Singapore Eurasian*. Singapore: Select Books, 2008.

Ong Hean-Tatt. *Scientific Statistical Evidence for Feng Shui*. Subang Jaya, Selangor: Gui Management Centre, 2006.

Onishi Satoru. *Hiroku Shonan Kakyo Shukusei Jiken* [*Secret Record of the Purge of the Chinese of Singapore*]. Tokyo: Kongo Shuppan, 1977.

Parkinson, Ann and Cyril Northcote Parkinson. *Heroes of Malaya*. Singapore: Donald Moore, 1956.

Percival, Lieutenant General A.E. "Introduction". In *The Churches of The Captivity in Malaya*, ed. J.N. Lewis Bryan. London: Society For Promoting Christian Knowledge, 1946, p. 7.

————. "Operations of Malaya Command from 8 December 1941 to 15 February 1942". *Second Supplement to the London Gazette of 20 February 1948*, No. 38215, 26 February 1948, pp. 1245–346.

————. *The War in Malaya*. London: Eyre and Spottiswoode, 1949.

Portelli, Alessandro. "The Peculiarities of Oral History". *History Workshop Journal* 12, 1 (Autumn 1981): 96–107.

Prasad, Bisheshwar, ed. *Official History of the Indian Armed Forces in the Second World War 1939–45: Campaigns in South-East Asia 1941–42*. New Delhi: Combined Inter-Services Historical Section India & Pakistan, 1960.

Probert, H.A. *History of Changi*. Singapore: Prison Industries, 1965 (now also a second edition, by Changi University Press of Singapore, 2006).

Purcell, Victor. *The Chinese in Malaya*. Kuala Lumpur: Oxford University Press, 1967 (originally published 1948).

Raj, Dato J.J. *The War Years and After*, rev. ed. Subang Jaya, Selangor: Pelanduk, 2000.

Ramakrishna, Kumar (intro). *Freedom News: The Untold Story of the Communist Underground Publication*. Singapore: S. Rajaratnam School of International Studies, 2008.

Ramasamy, P. "Indian War Memory in Malaysia". In *War and Memory in Malaysia and Singapore*, eds. P. Lim Pui and Diana Wong. Singapore: ISEAS, 2000, pp. 90–105.

Rashid Maidin. *The Memoirs of Rashid Maidin: From Armed Struggle to Peace*. Petaling Jaya, Selangor: SIRD, 2005.

Rattanachaya, Dato General Kitti. *The Communist Party of Malaya, Malaysia and Thailand: Truce Talks Ending The Armed Struggle of The Communist Party of Malaya*. Bangkok: Duangkew, 1996.

Rawal, Ram Singh. *I.N.A. Saga*. Allahabad: K.P. Khattri, 1946.

Republic of Singapore. *Prime Minster's Speeches, Press Conferences, Interviews, Statements, Etc: 1962–1963*. National University of Singapore.

Reynolds, E. Bruce. "History, Memory, Compensation, and Reconciliation: The Abuse of Labor along the Thailand-Burma Railway". In *Asian Labor in the Wartime Japanese Empire*, ed. Kratoska, pp. 326–48.

Ridgway, Bernard. "Malaya's Death Railway 'D.P.'S' Come Home". *British Malaya* (July 1946): 42.

Ross, Jane. *The Myth of the Digger: The Australian Soldier in Two World* Wars. Sydney: Hale and Iremonger, 1985.

Rustam A. Sani. *Social Roots of the Malay Left: An Analysis of Kesatuan Melayu Muda*. Petaling Jaya, Selangor: SIRD, 2008.

Sahlan Mohd Saman. *A Comparative Study of the Malaysian and Philippines War Novels*. Bangi, Malaysia: Penerbit Universiti Kebangsaan Malaysia, 1984.

Saito, Fred and Tatsuo Hayashida. "To Delhi! To Delhi! 1943–1945". In *A Beacon Across Asia: A Biography of Subhas Chandra Bose*, eds. Sisir K. Bose, Alexander Werth and S.A. Ayer. New Delhi: Longman, 1973.

Samuel, Raphael and Paul Thompson, eds. *The Myths We Live By*. London: Routledge, 1990.

Saw Swee Hock. "Population Growth and Control". In *A History of Singapore*, eds. Lee and Chew. Singapore: Oxford University Press, 1991, pp. 219–41.

Seaton, Philip A. *Japan's Contested War Memories: The "Memory Rifts" in Historical Consciousness of World War II*. London: Routledge, 2007.

Senmeilan Zhonghua da hui tang bian [Negeri Sembilan Chinese Assembly Hall], eds. *Ri Zhi Shi Qi Sen Zhou Hua Zu Meng Nan Shi Liao* [*The Japanese Massacre of Negeri Sembilan Chinese*]. Seremban, Malaysia: Negeri Sembilan Chinese Assembly Hall, 1988.

Seraphim, Franziska. *War Memory and Social Politics in Japan, 1945–2005*. Cambridge, Mass.: Harvard University Press, 2006.

Shaharuddin b. Maaruf. *Concept of A Hero in Malay Society*. Singapore: Eastern Universities Press, 1984.

Shahriman bin Tunku Sulaiman, Tunku. "The Johore Military Forces: The Oldest Army of Malay Regulars in the Peninsula". *Journal of the Malaysian Branch of the Royal Asiatic Society* 77, 2 (2004): 95–105.

Shamsul, A.B. "Debating About Identity in Malaysia: A Discourse Analysis". In *Cultural Contestations: Mediating Identities in a Changing Malaysian Society*, ed. Zawawi Ibrahim. London: ASEAN Academic Press, 1998, pp. 17–50.

Shan Ru-hong. *The War in the South: The Story of Negeri Sembilan's Guerrillas*. Bangkok: Mental Health Publishing, 2003 (originally in Chinese in 1995).

Shaw, William. *Tun Razak: His Life and Times*. London: Longman, 1976.

Shelley, Rex. *Dr Paglar: Everyman's Hero*. Singapore: Eurasian Association, 2010.

Shennan, Margaret. *Out in the Midday Sun: The British in Malaya 1880–1960*. London: John Murray, 2000.

Sheppard, M.C. ff, Tan Sri. "The Malay Soldier". *The Straits Times Annual, 1939*, pp. 26–39.

_____. *The Malay Regiment: 1933–1947*. Kuala Lumpur: Department of Public Relations, 1947.

_____. *The Adventures of Hang Tuah*. Singapore: Donald Moore, 1949.

_____. "The Malay Warrior". *The Straits Times Annual for 1957*.

_____. "The Massacre on Bedok Hill". *Straits Times* (Malaysian Edition), 3 March 1966, p. 6

_____. "A Paragon of Loyalty". *Straits Times* (Malaysian Edition), 28 February 1967, p. 8.

_____. *Taman Budiman: Memoirs of an Unorthodox Civil Servant*. Kuala Lumpur: Heinemann Educational Books Asia, 1979.

_____. *Tunku: A Pictorial Biography*, 2 vols. Petaling Jaya, Selangor: Pelanduk, 1988.

Short, Anthony. *In Pursuit of Mountain Rats: The Communist Insurrection in Malaya*. Singapore: Cultured Lotus, 2000 (originally published 1975).

Show, Clara. *Lim Bo Seng: Singapore's Best-Known War Hero*. Singapore: AsiaPacific, 1998 and 2009 editions.

Shu Yun-Tsiao and Chua Ser-Koon, eds. *Malayan Chinese Resistance to Japan 1937–1945: Selected Source Materials Based on Colonel Chuang Hui-Tsuan's Collection*. Singapore: Cultural and Historical Publishing House, 1984.

Si Ma Chun Ying. *Chan Tong De Huiyi* [*Memories of Painful Grievances*]. Singapore: Guo Lian Publication Company, 1946.

Singapore Federation of Chinese Clan Associaitons. *Chinese Customs and Festivals in Singapore*. Singapore: Landmark, 1989.

Singh, Gurchan. *Singa, The Lion of Malaya, being the Memoris of Gurchan Singh*. London: Quality Press, 1949.

Singh, Mohan. *Soldiers' Contribution to Indian Independence*. New Delhi: Army Educational Stores, 1974.

Singapore Ministry of Information and the Arts. *Singapore 1996*. Singapore: Ministry of Information and the Arts, 1996.

Sivaram, M. *Road to Delhi*. Tokyo: Charles E. Tuttle, 1966.

Sleeman, Colin and S.C. Silkin, eds. *Trial Sumida Haruzo and Twenty Others (The 'Double Tenth' Trial)*. London: W. Hodge, 1951.

Sng, Bobby E.K. *In His Good Time*. Singapore: Graduates' Christian Fellowship, 1980.

Snow, Edgar. *The Battle for Asia*. New York: World Publishing Company, 1942.

Stenson, Michael. *Class, Race and Colonialism in West Malaysia: The Indian Case*. St. Lucia: University of Queensland, 1980.

Stockwell, A.J. *British Policy and Malay Politics During the Malayan Union Experiment, 1942–1948*, Malaysian Branch of the Royal Asiatic Society Monograph No. 8. Kuala Lumpur: MBRAS, 1979.

_____. *Malaya*. London: HMSO, 1995, 3 volumes.

Stubbs, Peter W. *The Changi Murals: the Story of Stanley Warren's War*. Singapore: Landmark: 2003.

Syed Husin Ali. *Malays: Their Problems and Future*. Petaling Jaya, Selangor: Other Press, 2008.

Syed Othman Syed Omar. *Rejimen Askar Melayu Diraja, 1933–1968* [*The Royal Malay Regiment, 1933–1968*]. Kuala Lumpur: University of Malaya Press, 2005.

Tan, Cecilia. *Tun Sardon Jubir: His Life and Times*. Petaling Jaya, Selangor: Pelanduk, 1986.

Tan Chong Tee. *Force 136: Story of a WWII Resistance Fighter*, trans. Lee Watt Sim and Clara Show. Singapore: Asiapac, 1995.

Tan Kah Kee. *The Memoirs of Tan Kah Kee* trans A.H.C. Ward, Raymond W. Chu and Janet Salaff. Singapore: Singapore University Press, 1994.

Tan Liok Ee. *The Rhetoric of Bangsa and Minzu: Community and Nation in Tension, The Malay Peninsula, 1900–1955*, Centre of Southeast Asian Studies Working Paper No. 52. Melbourne: Monash University, 1988.

Thomson, Alistair. *Anzac Memories: Living with the Legend*. Melbourne: Oxford University Press, 1994.

————. "Review of Paula Hamilton and Linda Shopes' Oral History and Public Memories". *History Australia* 6, 1 (2009): 211–2.

————. "Oral History in the 21st Century. International Developments and the Southeast Asian Context" at the Conference on History Fragments in Southeast Asia: At the Interfaces of Oral History, Memory and Heritage, 23–24 June 2010, organised by the ISEAS and Singapore Heritage Society.

Tomaru, Junko. *The Postwar Rapprochement of Malaya and Japan, 1945–1961: The Roles of Britain and Japan in South East Asia*. New York: St Martin's Press, 2000.

Toye, Hugh. *The Springing Tiger: A Study of a Revolutionary*. London: Cassell, 1959.

Turnbull, C.M. *A History of Modern Singapore, 1819–2005*. Singapore: NUS Press, 2009.

Tzu Szu. *Kangri Yingxiong Zai Rou Nan* [*Anti-Japanese Heroes in Southern Johor*]. Singapore: Sin Min Chu Cultural Service, 1945.

Ummadevi Suppiah. *Tun V.T. Sambanthan: Pemimpin Berjiwa Malaysia* [*Tun V.T. Sambanthan: A Leader who Created Malaysia*]. Kuala: Lumpur: Penerbit Universiti Malaysia, 2004.

Vasil, Raj. *Asianising Singapore: The PAP's Management of Ethnicity*. Singapore: Heinemann Asia, 1995.

Vyas, M.R. *Passage Through a Turbulent Era: Historical Reminscences of the Fateful Years, 1937–1947*. Bombay: Indo-Foreign Publications & Publicity, 1982.

Wain, Barry. *Malaysian Maverick: Mahathir Mohamad in Turbulent Times*. New York: Palgrave Macmillan, 2009.

Wan Hashim Wan Teh. *Perang Dunia Kedua: Peranan Gerila Melayu Force 136* [*World War II: The Role of the Malay Guerrilla Force 136*]. Kuala Lumpur: Dewan Bahasa dan Pustaka Kementerian Pendidikan Malaysia, 1993.

Wan Meng Hao. "Malay Soldiering in Singapore, 1910–1942". In *Malays/ Muslims in Singapore: Selected Readings in History, 1819–1965*, eds. Khoo Kay Kim, Elinah Abdullah, and Wan Meng Hao. Subang Jaya, Selangor: Pelanduk, 2006, pp. 183–222.

Wang Gungwu. "Memories of War: World War II in Asia". In *War and Memory in Malaysia and Singapore*, eds. P. Lim Pui Huen and Diana Wong. Singapore: ISEAS, 2000, pp. 11–22.

————. *Only Connect! Sino-Malay Encounters*. Singapore: Times Academic Press, 2001.

Ward, Russel. *Australian Legend*. Melbourne: Oxford University Press, 1958.

Warren, Alan. *Singapore 1942: Britain's Greatest Defeat*. Singapore: Talisman, 2002.

Wertsch, James V. *Voices of Collective Remembering*. London: Cambridge University Press, 2002.

Who's Who in Malaya, 1939: A Biographical Record of Prominent Members of Malaya's Community in Official, Professional and Commercial Circles. Singapore: Fishers, 1939.

Wigmore, Lionel. *The Japanese Thrust*. Canberra: Australian War Memorial, 1957.

Williams, C.A.S. *Chinese Symbolism & Art Motifs*. Boston: Tuttle, 1988 (originally published 1941).

Wong, Diana. "Memory Suppression and Memory Production: The Japanese Occupation of Singapore". In *Perilous Memories: The Asia-Pacific War(s)*, eds. T. Fujitani, Geoffrey M. White and Lisa Yoneyama. Durham, NC: Duke University Press, 2001, pp. 218–38.

Wong Hong Suen. *Wartime Kitchen: Food and Eating in Singapore, 1942–1950*. Singapore: National Museum of Singapore and Editions Didier Millet, 2009.

Wong Loke Jame and Low Poh Gek. *Japanese Tourist Market and Singapore*. Singapore: Research Department, Singapore Tourist Promotion Board, March 1971.

Wong Wing On, James. *From Pacific War to Merdeka: Reminiscences of Abdullah CD, Rashid Maidin, Suriani Abdullah and Abu Samah*. Petaling Jaya, Selangor: SIRD, 2005: being articles and interviews from Malaysiakini.com.

Wu Jingrong and the Beijing Foreign Languages Institute. *The Pinyin Chinese-English Dictionary*. Hong Kong: Commercial Press, 1979.

Xing Zhou Kangri Tongzhi Lian Yi Hui [Singapore Branch of the MPAJA Ex-Comrades Association]. *Xue Bei* [*Blood Memorials*]. Singapore: Sin Min Chu Cultural Service, 1945.

Xing Zhou Zhuidao Beinan Geming Zhanshi Weiyuanhui Ban [Singapore Memorial Committee for Dead Revolutionary Warriors], ed. *Xue Chou* [*Blood Enmity*]. Singapore: Sin Min Chu Cultural Service, 1945.

Xinma Qiaoyou Hui [Singapore and Malaysian Returned Chinese Association], ed. *Malaiya Renmin Kangri Douzheng Shiliao Xianji* [*Selected Historical Materials of the Malayan People's Anti-Japanese Struggle*]. Hong Kong: Witness Publishing, 1992.

_____. *Malaiya Renmin Kangri Jun* [*Malayan People's Anti-Japanese Army*]. Hong Kong: Witness Publishing, 1992.

Xue Bei Zeng Bu Ben Bianji Weiyuanhui [Xue Bei Revised Edition Editorial Committee]. *Xue Bei: Zeng Bu Ben* [*Blood Memorials: New Edition*]. Hong Kong: Xue Bei Zeng Bu Ben Bianji Weiyuanhui, 1997.

Yong, C.F. and R.B. McKenna. *The Kuomintang Movement in British Malaya 1912–1949*. Singapore: Singapore University Press, 1990.

Yue-Him Tam. "To Bury the Unhappy Past: The Problem of Textbook Revision in Japan". *East Asian Library Journal* VII, 1 (Spring, 1994): 7–42.

Yule, Henry and A.C. Burnell. *Hobson-Jobson: The Anglo-Indian Dictionary*. Ware, Hertfordshire: Wordsworth Editions, 1996 (first published 1886).

Zhou Mei. *Elizabeth Choy: More Than a War Heroine*. Singapore: Landmark Books, 1995.

Newspapers

Asia Times online (http://www.atimes.com)
Berita Harian
British Malaya
China Press
Combatant's Friend
Chung Nan Daily
Daily Digest of the Chinese, Malay, & Tamil Press
Daily Mirror (London)
Eastern Sun
8 Days
Freedom News (see Ramakrishna, Kumar, under published works)
Indian Daily Mail
Japan Times
Kerala Bandu
Malay Mail
Malaya Tribune
Malaysiakini.com
Mirror of Opinion
Morning Tribune
Nan Chiao Jit Pau
Nanfang Evening Post
Nanyang Siang Pau
New Democracy

New Nation
New Straits Times
Sin Chew Jit Poh
Singapore Free Press
Singapore Herald
Singapore Standard
Star (http://thestaronline.com)
Straits Times (1941–2010)
Sun (Kuala Lumpur)
Sunday Times
Sunday Tribune
Syonan Sinbun
Tamil Murasu
The Statesman (Calcutta)
Times (London)
Utusan Malaysia
Utusan Melayu
Young India

School Textbooks

Malaysia

Sabihah Osman, Muzaffar Tate, and Ishak Ibrahim. *Sejarah Tingkatan 3: Kurikulum Bersepadu Sekolah Menengah* [*History for Form 3: Secondary School*]. Kuala Lumpur: Dewan Bahasa dan Pustaka, 1990.

Siti Zurainia Abdul Majid, Muhammad Yusoff Hashim, Abdullah Zakaria Ghazali, Lee Kam Hing, Ahmad Fawzi Basri, and Zainal Abdin Abdul Wahid. *Sejarah Tingkatan 5: Kurikulum Bersepadu Sekolah Menengah* [*History for Form 5: Secondary School*]. Kuala Lumpur: Dewan Bahasa dan Pustaka, 1992.

Ramlah binti Adam, Abdul Hakim bin Samuri and Muslimin bin Fadzil. *Sejarah Tingkatan 3: Kurikulum Bersepadu Sekolah Menengah* [*History for Form 3: Secondary School*]. Kuala Lumpur: Dewan Bahasa dan Pustaka, 2004.

Ramlah binti Adam, Abdul Hakim bin Samuri, Shakila Parween binti Yacob and Muslimin bin Fadzil. *Sejarah Tingkatan 5: Kurikulum Bersepadu Sekolah Menengah* [*History for Form 5: Secondary School*]. Kuala Lumpur: Dewan Bahasa dan Pustaka, 2004.

Singapore

Curriculum Development Institute of Singapore. *Social and Economic History of Modern Singapore*, Vol. 2. Singapore: Longman, 1985.

_____. *History of Modern Singapore*. Singapore: Longman, 1994.

_____. *Social Studies: Secondary 1*. Singapore: Longman, 1994.

_____. *History of Modern Singapore: Secondary 1*. Singapore: Longman, 1994.

Curriculum Planning and Development Division, Ministry of Education. *Understanding Our Past: Singapore From Colony to Nation*. Singapore: Federal Publications, 1999.

_____. *Social Studies: Discovering Our World: The Dark Years: Activity Book, 4B*. Singapore: Federal, 1999.

_____. *Social Studies: Discovering Our World: The Dark Years, 4B*. Singapore: Federal, 1999.

_____. *Understanding Our Past: Singapore from Colony to Nation*. Singapore: Federal, 1999.

Japanese School, Singapore, Ishiwata Nobuo, Masuo Keizo, eds. *Gaikoku no kyokasho no naka no Nihon to Nihonjin: Nihon no kokosei ga Shingaporu no chugaku kyokasho o hon'yakushite saihakkenshita Nihon kindaishi — Social and Economic History of Modern Singapore*. Singapore: Japanese School, 1988.

Oral Interviews and Talks

Bhupalan, Rasammah. Interview with Kevin Blackburn, Kuala Lumpur, 20 June 2005.

Choi Siew Hong: Interview with Kevin Blackburn in Kuala Lumpur, 16 December 2004.

Interview with Kevin Blackburn in Kuala Lumpur, 24 February 2009.

Das, K.R.: Interview with Kevin Blackburn at the Netaji Service Centre, 49 Leboh Ampang, Kuala Lumpur, 17 December 2004.

_____. Talk at the "Open Public Forum with Veterans and Members of the Wartime Generation", Singapore History Museum, 4 September 2005.

Grosse, Victor: Interview with Karl Hack at a veterans and families visit to Changi Prison, Singapore, 17 February 2002.

Ismail bin Zain: Interviewed by Tan Beng Luan on 5 September 1985, Accession Number A 000601/05, Reel 01, National Archives of Singapore.

Khoo, Henry Siaw Hua: Interview with Kevin Blackburn, Singapore, 2 October 1997.

Lee, Donald: Interview with Kevin Blackburn, Perth, Australia, 22 February 2005.

Lee Kip Lee: Interview with Kevin Blackburn, Singapore, 18 March 2005.

Lee Pamelia: Interview with Kevin Blackburn, 23 September 1997.

Mohd Anis bin Tairan: Interview with Kevin Blackburn at Kampong Siglap Mosque, Singapore, 15 February 2002.

Interview with Kevin Blackburn at Kampong Siglap Mosque, Singapore, 30 April 2004.

Interview in the three-disc DVD set, Discovery Channel, *The History of Singapore*. Singapore: Discovery Channel, 2006.

Interview with Kevin Blackburn at Kampong Siglap Mosque, Singapore, 19 February 2009.

Paglar, Eric: Interview with Kevin Blackburn, Singapore, 28 June 2005.

Tan Chong Tee: Singapore History Museum talk and interview afterwards, 14 February 2004.

Various "wartime generation": Interviewees in *Remembering Syonan-to*, documentary. Singapore, Channel News Asia, 10 September 2005, made using the veterans and contacts from the "Open Public Forum with Veterans and Members of the Wartime Generation", Singapore History Museum, 4 September 2005.

Wan Meng Hao, Executive Secretary of the Singapore Preservation of Monuments Board, 2006.

Television, Film and CD-ROMs

A War Diary. Singapore, MediaCorp, September 2001.

Between Empires, VHS. Singapore Broadcasting Corporation, 1992.

Desert Victory. British Ministry of Information, 1943 (reissued on VHS in 1999 by DD Video)

Embun. Kuala Lumpur: Golden Satellite, 2002, released as a VCD.

FINAS: Perbadanen Kemajuan Filem Nasional Malaysia (http://finas.gov.my/).

Hang Jebat. Singapore: Cathay, Cathay Keris, 1961 (reissued as a VCD in 2003).

Hang Tuah. Singapore, Shaw Brothers, Malay Film Productions, 1956, released as a VCD in 2003.

Heping De Dai Jia: The Price of Peace. Singapore, MediaCorp, 1997.

In Pursuit of Peace. Singapore, MediaCorp, 2001.

Leftenan Adnan. Kuala Lumpur, Golden Satellite, 2000, released as a VCD.

Matahari. Shaw Brothers, 1958, released in 2003 as a VCD.

Paloh. Kuala Lumpur, Speedy Video, 2003, released as a VCD.

Remembering Syonan-to. Singapore, MediaCorp, 2005.

Sarjan Hassan (*Sergeant Hassan*). Shaw Brothers, 1958, released in 2003 as a VCD.

CD-ROM: *Attacked!: The Japanese Occupation of Singapore 1942–1945*. Singapore, Daiichi Media and National Archives of Singapore, 1999.

Theses and Other Unpublished Material

Balakrishnan, Shahilla K. "Political Attitudes of Indians in Post-War Malaya 1945–1955". BA Honours thesis, National University of Singapore, 1991.

Chew Ju Ern, Daniel. "Reassessing the Overseas Chinese Legend of Dalforce at the Fall of Singapore". National Institute of Education, 2005.

Choi Siew Hong. Written statement from which he addressed the audience at the "Open Public Forum with Veterans and Members of the Wartime Generation", Singapore History Museum, 4 September 2005.

Halinah Bamadhaj. "The Impact of the Japanese Occupation of Malaya on Malay Society and Politics (1941–1945)". MA thesis, University of Auckland, 1975.

Hammond, Wally. "The Story of St. Luke's Chapel, Singapore and the Stanely Warren Murals: A Personal Viewpoint By Wally Hammond". Copy in authors' possession.

Hamzah Muzaini. "'Tense Pasts, Present Tensions': Postcolonial Memoryscapes and the Memorialisation of the Second World War in Perak". PhD Thesis, University of Durham, 2009. Available as an e-thesis from http://etheses. dur.ac.uk.

Malayan Union. Annual Report of Labour Department, 1946.

Mat Zin Mat Kib. "Persatuan Bekas Buruh Paksa dan Keluarga Buruh Jalan Keretapi Maut Siam-Burma 1942–46 Persekutuan Tanah Melayu 1958–1973: Satu Tinjauan Sejarah Perkembangannya [The All Malaya Association of Forced Labourers and Families of Forced Labourers of the Burma-Siam Death Railway, 1958–1973: A Survey of its Development]". BA thesis, School of Humanities, Universiti Sains Malaysia, 1988.

Mohd Anis bin Tairan. Written statement from which Mohd Anis bin Tairan addressed the audience at the "Open Public Forum with Veterans and Members of the Wartime Generation", Singapore History Museum, 4 September 2005.

Poh Guan Huat. "Lim Bo Seng: Nanyang Chinese Patriot". Unpublished diss., University of Singapore, 1972.

Ramachandra, G.P. "The Indian Independence Movement in Malaya, 1942–1975". MA thesis, University of Malaya, 1970.

Reynolds, E. Bruce. "The Thailand-Burma Railway: Reflections On a Regional Tragedy". In Symposium on the Japanese Occupation in Southeast Asia, 14–16 December 1995, National University of Singapore.

Shahriman bin Tunku Sulaiman, Tunku. "The Johore Military Forces". BA thesis, University of Malaya, 1958.

Subramanian, S. "Politics of the Indians in Malaya, 1945–1955". MA thesis, University of Malaya, 1973.

INDEX